Social Conflict

ESCALATION, STALEMATE, AND SETTLEMENT

McGraw-Hill Series in Social Psychology

This popular series of paperback titles is written by authors about their particular field of expertise and are meant to complement any social psychology course. The series includes:

Social Conflict

ESCALATION, STALEMATE, AND SETTLEMENT

THIRD EDITION

❖

Dean G. Pruitt

*Institute for Conflict Analysis and Resolution,
George Mason University*

Sung Hee Kim

University of Kentucky—Lexington

Boston   Burr Ridge, IL   Dubuque, IA   Madison, WI   New York
San Francisco   St. Louis   Bangkok   Bogotá   Caracas   Kuala Lumpur
Lisbon   London   Madrid   Mexico City   Milan   Montreal   New Delhi
Santiago   Seoul   Singapore   Sydney   Taipei   Toronto

Higher Education

SOCIAL CONFLICT
Escalation, Stalemate, and Settlement
Published by McGraw-Hill Higher Education, an imprint of The McGraw-Hill Companies, Inc., 1221 Avenue of the Americas, New York, NY 10020. Copyright © 2004 by The McGraw-Hill Companies. All rights reserved. No part of this publication may be reproduced or distributed in any form or by any means, or stored in a database or retrieval system, without the prior written consent of The McGraw-Hill Companies, Inc., including, but not limited to, in any network or other electronic storage or transmission, or broadcast for distance learning.

This book is printed on acid-free paper.

5 6 7 8 9 FGR/FGR 0 9 8 7

ISBN 978-0-07-285535-7
MHID 0-07-285535-5

Publisher: Steve Rutter
Sponsoring Editor: Rebecca Hope
Development Editors: Sienne Patch
Editorial Assistant: Katherine Russillo
Marketing Manager: Melissa Caughlin
Media Producer: Ginger Warner
Project Manager: Roger Geissler

Production Supervisor: Tandra Jorgensen
Designer: Jean Mailander
Photo Research: Brian Pecko
Art Editor: Cristin Yancey
Compositor: Thompson Type
Printer: Quebecor Fairfield

Permission is acknowledged to reprint the following material: *Page 91,* Reprinted from *Close Relationships* by Kelley et. al. Copyright © 1983 by W.H. Freeman and Company. Reprinted by permission; *176, 177,* Reprinted from *Thirteen Days: A Memoir of the Cuban Missile Crisis,* by Robert F. Kennedy, by permission of W.W. Norton & Company, Inc. Copyright © 1971, 1968 by W.W. Norton & Company, Inc. Copyright © 1968 by McCall Corporation; *201* From *Getting to Yes,* Second Edition, by Roger Fisher, William Ury, and Bruce Patton. Copyright © 1981, 1991 by Roger Fisher and William Ury. Reprinted by permission of Houghton Mifflin Co. All rights reserved; *241,* Reprinted with permission from *Negotiation Journal,* 1986, Vol. 2, p. 292; Certain materials in Chapter 3 appeared in a different form in D.C. Pruitt, "Strategic Choice in Negotiation," *American Behavioral Scientist,* 1983, Vol. 27, pp. 167-194. Copyright 1983 by Sage Publications, Inc. Reprinted by permission of Sage Publications, Inc. Reprinted by permission of Sage Publications, Inc.; Certain materials in Chapter 10 appeared in a different form in D.C. Pruitt, "Achieving Integrative Agreements," in M.H. Bazerman and R. Lewicki, eds., Negotiating in Organizations (Beverly Hills, Calif.: Sage, 1983), pp. 35-50. Copyright 1983 by Sage Publications, Inc. Reprinted by permission of Sage Publications, Inc. *Cover Photo* © Réunion des Musées Nationaux/Art Resource, NY. © L & M Services B.V. Amsterdam 20030414.

Library of Congress Cataloging-in-Publication Data

Pruitt, Dean G.
   Social conflict: escalation, stalemate, and settlement/Dean
 G. Pruitt, Sung Hee Kim.—3rd ed.
      p.   cm.
   Includes bibliographical references and index.
   ISBN 0-07-285535-5
     1. Social conflict.   2. Social conflict—Psychological aspects.
   3. Interpersonal conflict.   4. Problem solving.   I. Pruitt, Dean G.
   II. Kim, Sung Hee   III. Title
   HM291.P725   2004
   303.6—dc20

051872
CIP

www.mhhe.com

About the Authors

❖

DEAN PRUITT is SUNY Distinguished Professor Emeritus in the Department of Psychology at the University at Buffalo: State University of New York and Visiting Scholar at the Institute of Conflict Analysis and Resolution at George Mason University. He received his Ph.D. in psychology from Yale University and did postdoctoral work in psychology at the University of Michigan and in international relations at Northwestern University. His specialties are social conflict, negotiation, and mediation. He is a fellow of the American Psychological Association and the American Psychological Society and has received the Harold D. Lasswell Award for Distinguished Scientific Contribution to Political Psychology from the International Society of Political Psychology and the Lifetime Achievement Award from the International Association for Conflict Management.

SUNG HEE KIM is Associate Professor of Psychology at the University of Kentucky. She did graduate work at Seoul National University in South Korea and at the University of Illinois at Urbana-Champaign and received her Ph.D. in social psychology from Tufts University. She has received a Peace Scholar Fellowship from the United States Institute of Peace and the Chancellor's Outstanding Teaching Award from the University of Kentucky. Her research concerns social conflict, retributive justice, and group processes.

To the Memory of Jeffrey Z. Rubin

Contents

❖

Foreword

❖ ─────

Conflict has been a driving force in the development of social science in general and social psychology in particular. Indeed it could reasonably be argued that modern social psychology in the United States began from a broad thematic interest in the nature of human conflict in the era around World War II. Psychologists of that time were living in a cauldron of social conflict. It was a time of national fascism with its charismatic leaders and mass followers, power and dominance, war and violence, prejudice and discrimination; of tensions from changing work demands and new employment strategies; and of assimilation of immigrants from diverse backgrounds, as well as urban relocation of rural migrants. Some of those investigators analyzed the forces of change and resistance, as well as the conflict between the needs of a democratic society that requires consensus and conformity and the values of individual independence and autonomy. Other researchers recognized the role of persuasive rhetoric as central to democratic decision making, while allowing for a diverse audience to oppose some aspects of every message.

This generic involvement of social psychological researchers in conflict became ever more focused into the personal tension states it created within individuals. Kurt Lewin emphasized the motivational force of perceived discrepancies between the person's needs and goals and the norms of the group. His premier student, Leon Festinger, helped move social psychology toward a more cognitive orientation by recasting the tension-inducing nature of such discrepancy as taking place within a single person's cognitive system when private beliefs become dissonant with one's public actions. The cognitive dimension of human functioning now heavily influences contemporary social psychology. During the many decades that general psychology was held captive by the mindless, valueless doctrines of behaviorism, it was social psychology that remained rebellious, fighting the guerrilla wars of situationism, constructivism, Person X Stimulus interactionism, and cognitive involvement in human action. Social psychologists were also the ones who raised the banners of practical applications and socially responsible research. Social psychological researchers learned from their experimentalist brethren the tenets of rigorous, carefully controlled laboratory research, but added a new flair and ingenuity that infused the artificial setting with "mundane realism." But many social psychologists went beyond the confines of the laboratory testing of casual hypotheses; they got their notebooks dirty in the muck and mire of everyday life in the varied fields of humanity-at-work. They have brought their abiding curiosity for understanding the whys, whens, and hows of human experience and behavior into a seemingly endless array of vital venues—of education, health, law, politics, business, environment, and culture, to name but a few.

This innovative *McGraw-Hill Series in Social Psychology* has been designed as a celebration of the fundamental contributions being made by researchers, theorists, and practitioners of social psychology in improving our understanding of human nature and enriching the quality of our lives. It has become a showcase for presenting new theories, original syntheses, analyses, and current methodologies by distinguished scholars and promising young writer-researchers. Common to all of our authors is the commitment to sharing their vision with an audience that starts with their colleagues but extends out to graduate students, undergraduates, and all those with an interest in social psychology. Some of our titles convey ideas that are of sufficient general interest that their message needs to be carried out into the world of practical application to those who may translate some of them into public action and public policy. Although each text in our series is created to stand alone as the best representative of its area of scholarship, taken as a whole, they represent the core of social psychology. Teachers of social psychology may elect to use any of them as "in-depth" supplements to a general textbook, while others may choose to organize their course entirely around a set of these monographs. Experience shows that the current volume is also quite useful in courses in which social conflict is a core issue, across many disciplines dealing with this vital phenomenon.

All social conflict begins with one party wanting something that another party resists doing or giving. Those conflicts stretch from the daily, ordinary interactions of parents wanting reluctant children to clean their rooms or do homework, to challenges between legal adversaries in courts of law, to salespeople negotiating deals with customers, to political opponents compromising on line items in national or local budgets, to international peace conferences that can prevent war. Are there similar basic principles operating across such diverse settings? Does our understanding of how such conflicts between individuals (acting alone or as representatives of agencies) escalate, reach plateaus of stalemates, and become settled help us reduce the destructive aspects of such conflict by avoiding them or providing appropriate counsel to the conflicting parties? The authors of *Social Conflict* answer these questions in the affirmative, going on to illustrate exactly how each stage in a host of different conflict scenarios is best parsed, or perceptively analyzed, into underlying processes and paths that lead to desirable or undesired outcomes. Their wisdom guides the reader to see how effective problem solving strategies result in the most equitable resolution of human conflicts when they replace contentious strategies of domination or the unsatisfying strategies of yielding.

The success of the second edition of *Social Conflict* created a challenge for the authors and editor to enhance its strengths, correct some of its limitations, and extend its scope to encompass recent substantive areas and currently "hot" issues. They have succeeded admirably in meeting these goals. The dedicated scholarship, breadth of coverage, and currency of information shown in the third edition goes beyond what was admirable previously. The theoretical orientation has become more coherent and tightened, and more systematically applied throughout the presentation. New or augmented topics include identity-based conflict, the mobilization of conflict groups, blame direction and strategic choice, nonviolent resistance, forgiveness and reconciliation, conflict resolution training, and peacekeeping. Readers who enjoyed and learned from the earlier editions will be delighted by the range of updated examples of domestic conflict as well as source material on current national and international conflict. Among the most valuable additions to this popular text is the extended coverage of the impact of culture on conflict, which puts special emphasis on the role of collectivism vs. individualism. But this revised edition also adds to our understanding of the peace processes in Northern Ireland and South Africa, and of the diffculties with brokering peace in the Middle East. For good measure, we also learn much of value in the analyses of schoolyard killings in the United States, notoriously popularized by the Colombine High School shootings, as well as acquire valuable perspectives on the new terrorism that is transforming national and global priorities.

Finally, all readers will enjoy the smooth flow of the narrative style that makes for a delightful overall story even when the content is complex and sometimes unpleasant. I suspect that the enduring value of *Social Conflict* will lie in the many ways each of us become more savvy about dealing intelligently and sensitively with mundane conflicts in our own daily lives and more fully understanding the broad, emergent conflicts in the world around us.

Philip G. Zimbardo
Consulting Editor

Preface

———— ❖ ————

This is the third edition of a writing project that began in the early 1980's. Our intention then and now was to produce a readable and integrated synthesis of theory and research on social conflict and its resolution. We hoped that it would serve as an introductory text and a source of ideas and inspiration to researchers and practitioners. There are signs that we have been successful with both those goals. The earlier editions have been used in courses on social conflict in fields as diverse as psychology, sociology, business, political science, and international relations; our second edition was translated into Russian and received the Best Book Award in 1996 from the International Association for Conflict Management; and we have often seen our book cited in the theoretical and practical literature in this field.

Readers of the prior editions will find much that is familiar in this new version. We have retained the dramaturgic structure that starts with the nature and causes of conflict, moves on to the choice among strategies for dealing with conflict, thence to escalation, and finally to de-escalation, problem solving, and third party functions in conflict resolution. We have also retained our psychological focus. While we try to be true to the conflict literature as a whole, we use social psychological theory to integrate the field, leaning heavily on such concepts as social perception, attitude, emotion, and group dynamics.

Nevertheless, the book is extensively rewritten. Every part of the book contains new material that reflects progress in conflict studies or fills gaps in the prior volumes. Thus there are new or augmented sections on such topics as conflict group mobilization, culture and conflict behavior, narratives and metaphors, violence, nonviolent resistance, ripeness, de-escalatory spirals, conflict resolution training, peace keeping, peace building, forgiveness, and reconciliation. Furthermore, the illustrative material—the real-world examples that help the reader grasp the ideas—have been extensively updated. A lot of our prior examples were drawn from the Cold War, and we have kept the best of these. But our coverage now includes internal war, terrorism, schoolyard killings, recent peace processes, and (to add a little spice) the beanie baby craze.

Many people have helped us along the way to this revision. We are particularly grateful to Rebecca Hope and Kate Russillo of McGraw–Hill for their encouragement and editorial advice, and to Roger Geissler, who pushed this project to an on time completion. We would especially like to thank the following scholars who read our second edition and provided extensive and extremely helpful critiques: R. William Ayres, Camilo Azcarate, John Davies, Ronald Fisher, Terrence Lyons, Brian Polkinghorn, and Maurice Richter. Other critiques and bibliographic suggestions were provided by Leslie Ashburn-Nardo, Kevin Avruch, Nimet Beriker, Frank Blechman, Michele Gelfand, Monica Harris, Chistopher Mitchell, Oliver Moles, Richard Smith, Bert Spector, Catherine Tinsley, James Wall, and the students in several classes at George Mason University and American University. Paul Pruitt was very helpful with technical assistance in building the reference section. The Institute for Conflict Analysis and Resolution at George Mason University graciously provided an office for the first author where many parts of this book were written, and the Office of the President at the University at Buffalo: State University of New York provided funds for two trips for the first author to Lexington, Kentucky, in which we met to plan the project and to review the nearly finished manuscript. The Department of Psychology at the University of Kentucky granted the second author a sabbatical leave, which gave her much of the time she needed to work on the book. Finally, we could not have completed this project without the continued support and advice of our spouses, France Pruitt and Richard Smith.

Our book is dedicated to the memory of our colleague and mentor, Jeffrey Z. Rubin, with whom we wrote the prior editions. Jeff died tragically in a mountain climbing accident in 1995, but we often felt his presence as we were working on this new edition. Without Jeff, this project would never have begun and could not have been half as successful. He was responsible for much of the lucid theoretical analysis and graceful writing that characterized the prior editions. Admirers of Jeff's scholarship and writing style will be pleased to see his continued influence on the present volume.

Dean G. Pruitt
Sung Hee Kim

PART I

Conflict and Strategic Choice

1

Overview

———————— ❖ ————————

Toward a Theory of Conflict ♦ What Is Conflict? ♦ Some Good News and Some
Bad News about Conflict ♦ *The Good News* ♦ *And the Bad News* ♦ Summary and
Conclusions ♦ Plan of the Book

- Ben, age 18, has borrowed the family car, then forgotten to fill it up with gasoline. The next morning, Dad is late for work because he has to wait for gas in the middle of rush hour traffic. That night Dad lets his son know what inconvenience his forgetfulness has caused. Ben's apology is half-hearted, so Dad heats things up a bit. He complains about Ben's generally inconsiderate and irresponsible behavior on a number of fronts. Eventually Ben is provoked into yelling at his father, who, outraged by this uncalled-for behavior, demands the car keys back and announces that until further notice, Ben will no longer be allowed to use the family car. Around this time, Mom (with Sis looking on) intervenes in Ben's behalf, trying to persuade Dad that maybe he's being too hard on their son. When Dad tells Mom to mind her own business, Mom (as well as Ben and Sis) walks out the door, leaving Dad to wonder what went wrong.[1]
- Sales and Production are in the throes of an intense exchange regarding the delivery date for their company's new product. Sales argues that unless a delivery date can be scheduled no more than *three* months from now, potential new customers will be lost to the competition, visiting a minor disaster upon Sales and the company as a whole. Production argues in return that it

---

[1] This story is adapted from *When Families Fight* by Jeffrey Rubin & Carol Rubin (1989).

has a carefully organized and sequenced production schedule that must be maintained. Breaking that schedule, by making the new product available for distribution earlier than Production intends, would incur costs in time and money that would be detrimental to Production and the company. No, insists Production, the new product is scheduled for introduction *nine* months hence, and that's when it will appear! After days of acrimony, an agreement is reached in which each department settles for less than it originally wanted: a production schedule of *six* months.

- When U.S. President Jimmy Carter brought Egypt's President Anwar Sadat and Israel's Prime Minister Menachem Begin together at Camp David in October 1978, it seemed that Carter, the would-be mediator, had taken on an impossible task. The conflict over the Sinai Peninsula appeared entirely intractable, since Egypt demanded the immediate return of the entire Sinai; Israel, in turn, having occupied the Sinai since the 1967 Middle East war, refused to return a centimeter of this land. Carter's initial efforts to mediate a settlement, proposing a compromise in which each nation would retain half of the Sinai, proved completely unacceptable to both sides. President Carter and his staff persisted, eventually discovering that the seemingly irreconcilable positions of Israel and Egypt reflected underlying interests that were not incompatible at all. Israel's underlying interest was *security;* Israel wanted to be certain that its borders would be safe against land or air attack from Egypt. Egypt, in turn, was primarily interested in *sovereignty*—regaining rule over a piece of land that had been part of Egypt as far back as biblical times. After thirteen days of hard work, and twenty-three draft agreements developed by Assistant Secretary of State Harold Saunders, Carter's persistence as a mediator paid off. Israel agreed to return the Sinai in exchange for assurances of a demilitarized zone and new Israeli air bases. This agreement was put into effect in April 1982, and continues to the present day.[2]

- When Rodney King, an African American, was stopped after a high-speed police chase on March 3, 1991, then was subdued by the police after apparently resisting arrest, the incident seemed not particularly newsworthy. Thanks to a Los Angeles resident, however, who used his new video camera to record the arrest of King, the ordinary became extraordinary. The videotape clearly showed

---

[2] This analysis of mediation in the Camp David negotiations—particularly, the emphasis on the value of identifying underlying interests as a way of moving toward agreement—is adapted from Fisher, Ury, & Patton's *Getting to YES* (1991).

Rodney King being kicked and pummeled, hit with nightsticks forty times by some of the police officers, while others stood nearby, observing impassively. More than a year later, in late spring of 1992, a jury in Ventura, California, found the four patrolmen accused of the beating to be innocent of the charge of using undue force. Within hours, the city of Los Angeles erupted in riots. Buildings were burned to the ground as citizens, mostly African American residents, vented their rage at the police and at the government more generally. It took an appearance by President George Bush and the intervention of 2,000 National Guard troops to quell the three-day uprising.

TOWARD A THEORY OF CONFLICT

Though strikingly different in scale and significance, the four incidents just cited have a great deal in common. They all describe a conflict between two or more sides, a situation in which each party aspires to an outcome that the other is apparently unwilling to provide. The outcome may involve access to the family car, time, ease of scheduling, land, security, justice, tolerable living conditions—or any of myriad other possibilities. Note, moreover, that each example of conflict involves a distinctive set of moves, ways of pursuing the conflict in an effort to settle it. Are these moves similar? Not superficially. But they can be sorted into four main classes or strategies that reveal continuity from case to case. Indeed, one of the major objectives of this book is to describe in detail the different sorts of strategies used by parties experiencing conflict and to examine the causes and consequences of the use of these strategies.

One basic strategy is *contending*—trying to impose one's preferred solution on the other party. Dad presumably wanted an apology from his son, Ben, and tried to impose this by venting his anger and frustration. Sales and Production tried at first to argue each other into submission, as did Israel and Egypt in the early stages of the Camp David negotiations. In the dispute between Rodney King and the Los Angeles police, contending assumed a violent form, as did the response by angry Los Angeles residents to the jury verdict in the subsequent trial of the police officers.

A second strategy is *yielding*—lowering one's own aspirations and settling for less than one would have liked. This is the way Sales and Production resolved their dispute over timing. Each side settled for less than it aspired to and, in so doing, the parties managed to carve out a compromise agreement. Is the agreement a good one? That is, is it likely to be mutually satisfactory? We cannot be sure, but there is reason to wonder whether a "worst of both worlds" solution may have evolved. A delay of three months may have been sufficient to erode the profits that Sales hoped for, and moving up the production schedule by three months may have seriously disrupted the efficiency of Production's plan. Yielding created a solution, but not necessarily a solution of high quality.

A third fundamental strategy is *problem solving*—pursuing an alternative that satisfies the aspirations of both sides. Problem solving can occur during negotiation or with the assistance of an outside intervener, like President Carter at Camp David. With the mediation assistance of President Carter and his aides, Egypt and Israel engaged in just such a process when they moved toward an agreement to disengage in the Sinai Peninsula. In theory, Egypt and Israel could have engaged in problem solving without U.S. assistance; they could have identified their respective underlying interests and, on that basis, moved to satisfy them by developing a mutually acceptable solution. Because the two sides had a long history of intense conflict with each other, President Carter's intervention offered a perspective that perhaps made more likely both sides' satisfaction of their aspirations.

The fourth strategy is *avoiding*—not engaging in the conflict. This strategy can take two broad forms: inaction and withdrawal. *Inaction* involves doing nothing about the conflict. One remains inactive, often simply waiting for the other side to move. Though the Camp David negotiations ended in problem solving, inaction dominated much of the proceedings. This was not because the principals were slow-witted, fumbling decision makers, but by design. Each party waited endlessly for the other's next move. Indeed, in an effort to resolve the deadlock produced by this mutual inaction, President Carter finally imposed a deadline, beyond which he indicated he would withdraw from the negotiations. This galvanized the parties into action. *Withdrawal* involves abandoning the conflict. When Mom, Ben, and Sis walked out of the door, they were choosing this mode of avoiding.

It is well to note several things about these four strategies for dealing with conflict. First, most conflict situations—be they armed exchanges, labor strikes, international negotiations, family squabbles, or the tacit exchanges that occur when two drivers vie for position at an unmarked intersection—call forth a *combination*, and often a *sequence*, of the preceding strategies. Rarely is one strategy used to the exclusion of the others. Thus in the interchange with his Dad, Ben started with contending and ended with avoiding.

Second, two of these strategies, contending and problem solving, may be implemented through a wide variety of tactics. The terms *strategy* and *tactics* differ in scope. In our terminology, strategies are the four basic approaches that can be taken to any conflict. Tactics are the classes of moves by which these strategies can be enacted. For example, the strategy of contending can be enacted by means of the tactic of persuasion (as in the discussion between Production and Sales), the tactic of angry statements (as in the argument between Ben and Dad), the tactic of violent retribution (as when Rodney King was kicked and pummeled), or various other tactics. In this book we look primarily at strategic considerations, but we also keep a careful eye on the tactics that help transform strategic objectives into reality.

Third, contending, yielding, and problem solving are *active* strategies, in the sense that each involves a relatively consistent, coherent effort to settle a conflict: by trying to dominate, giving something up, or working jointly to solve the problem at hand. By contrast, avoiding is a *passive* strategy, in the sense that it involves no effort to settle conflict. The two broad forms of avoiding, inaction and withdrawal, are tactics of pause or abandonment.

Fourth, contending and yielding are mirror images of each other, in that contending entails efforts to win and yielding entails acceptance of at least partial defeat.

As the four opening examples illustrate, conflicts differ in their complexity and importance, in the strategies to which they give rise, and in the solutions to which they lead. Despite these differences, we believe that—regardless of the segment of society in which they occur—conflicts have much in common.[3] Conflicts at the interpersonal, intergroup, interorganizational, and international level are clearly not the same. Nevertheless, we believe it is possible to develop generalizations that cut across, and shed light on, most or all conflicts. Our aim in this book is to organize and report existing contributions to an emerging theory of social conflict and to add ideas of our own. Although we hope to improve the practice of dispute settlement, and therefore occasionally introduce prescriptive advice for doing so (particularly in Chapters 10 and 11), our aim is primarily *descriptive:* to account, as best we can, for the many interesting ways in which people go about addressing social conflict.

WHAT IS CONFLICT?

According to Webster (1983), the term *conflict* originally meant a "fight, battle, or struggle," that is, an overt confrontation between parties. But its meaning has grown to include a "sharp disagreement or opposition, as of interests, ideas, etc." The term now embraces the psychological underpinnings of overt confrontation as well as overt confrontation itself. In short, the term *conflict* has come to be so broadly applied that it is in danger of losing its status as a singular concept.

Our solution to this problem has been to adopt a restrictive meaning that builds on Webster's second definition. For us, conflict means *perceived*

---

[3] Harvard Law School Professor Roger Fisher gave a talk some years ago, entitled "Negotiating with the Russians and Negotiating with One's Spouse: Is There a Difference?" His answer, and ours as well: "Not as much as you might think."

divergence of interest, a belief that the parties' current aspirations are incompatible.[4] In other words, conflict is a belief that if one party gets what it wants, the other (or others) will not be able to do so. Examples would be Dad's belief that Ben's use of the car interferes with his work life and Ben's belief that Dad wants to block his use of the car.

Note that conflict, so defined, can produce overt confrontation (Webster's first definition) if the parties choose a contentious approach or engage in joint problem solving.[5] But it need not do so, because they may instead choose yielding, individual problem solving, or avoiding.

We have chosen this definition of "conflict" because it seems to be the best place to begin building theory. We are able to construct a simple yet powerful theory (presented in Chapters 2 and 3) by trying to explain the origins of perceived divergence of interest and the impact of this perception on strategic choice and outcome. Undoubtedly our decision in this matter was influenced by the fact that both of us are social psychologists and hence are accustomed to thinking in terms of the impact of mental status on social behavior. Nevertheless, we believe that this approach will be of value to scholars and practitioners from many other disciplines.[6]

Implicit in our definition of conflict is the deliberate exclusion of differences of opinion concerning facts and arguments over interpretation of objective reality. We are interested in seemingly incompatible aspirations—that is, incompatible goals and standards—rather than seemingly incompatible views.

In defining conflict in terms of perceived divergence of interest, we do not mean to slight overt confrontation (Webster's first definition). We will have a lot to say about this phenomenon, especially when we get to Chapters 5 to 8 on *escalation.* Escalation occurs when one or both parties adopt contentious tactics that are harsher than those previously used.

We are well aware that conflict often involves multiple parties, and we try to take such complexity into account at several points in our book. Still,

---

[4] Some authors (e.g., Hopmann, 1996) use the term "conflict of interest" rather than "divergence of interest."

[5] In *joint* problem solving, the parties work together in search of a mutually acceptable solution to their conflict; in *individual* problem solving, one (or both) of them seeks a mutually acceptable solution on its own. Joint problem solving almost always involves an initial airing of differences and, hence, a clash of aspirations. This means that it is a form of overt confrontation, though surely a mild form.

[6] By defining conflict as *perceived* rather than *true* divergence of interest, we depart from custom in the social sciences. We believe that this departure has merit because perceived divergence of interest is more useful in predicting what people actually will do. This is because perceptions ordinarily have an immediate impact on behavior (that is, in the case of conflict, on the choice among strategies), *whereas* reality works more slowly and with less certainty. We acknowledge that defining conflict in perceptual terms leaves open the possibility that one party will believe that there is a conflict of interest while the other does not. In such a case, one party must clearly be wrong, although each will probably act on its perceptions anyway.

the main thrust of our theory concerns dyadic conflict—conflict between two parties—for several reasons. First, most theory and research in this field focuses on the dyad. Second, as social psychologists we find ourselves best able to construct a plausible theory based on the unit of analysis we know most intimately: the interface between two individuals, two groups, or two organizations. Third, we find that conflict involving multiple parties often reduces to the dyadic case. Thus although the argument between Ben and Dad escalates to include Mom and Sis, the latter become allies of Ben, retaining the two-sided, "we versus they" structure of the conflict.

Because much of our analysis pivots around the dyad, we use a bit of jargon throughout the book. When our analysis is presented from the viewpoint of one side in a relationship, we refer to that person or group as *Party,* and we refer to the other person or group (the one toward whom Party's actions are directed) as *Other.* Because the parties to a conflict can be individuals or collectives, we use the pronoun "it" when referring to Party or Other.

SOME GOOD NEWS AND SOME BAD NEWS ABOUT CONFLICT

Although conflict is found in almost every realm of human interaction and although episodes of escalated conflict are among the most significant and newsworthy events of human life, it would be a mistake to assume that interaction necessarily involves conflict or that conflict usually takes a heavily escalated form. People manage to get along remarkably well with other individuals, groups, and organizations; they do so with consideration, helpfulness, and skill, and with little evidence of conflict along the way. When conflict *does* arise, more often than not it is settled, even resolved, with little acrimony and to the mutual satisfaction of the parties involved.

People have been interested in the study of conflict at least since biblical times. The nineteenth and early twentieth centuries provided a dramatic, energetic thrust whose impact is still felt today. Charles Darwin was interested in the struggle within species for "survival of the fittest." Sigmund Freud studied the internal combat of various psychodynamic forces for control over the ego. And Karl Marx developed a political and economic analysis based on the assumption that conflict is an inevitable part of society.

If we conclude, on the basis of the ideas of these three profound thinkers, that conflict is necessarily destructive, we miss the point of their work. For Darwin, the productive outcome of the struggle for survival was the emergence of inherited characteristics that foster survival; new species arise because of the genetic adjustments occasioned by the struggle to survive. Freud similarly envisioned individual growth and insight to result from the struggle to understand and address the conflicts within. And Marx, in his dialectical materialism, determined that conflict promotes social change, which moves inexorably in the direction of an improved human condition. All three men were keenly aware of the virtues and necessity of conflict; they all saw the beneficial as well as the costly consequences of conflict.

The point is that conflict can have both good and bad outcomes. We will mention a few of these in the next few sections, concentrating our attention on conflict that emerges into action, that is, overt confrontation.

The Good News

First, conflict, when it emerges into action, is the seedbed that nourishes social change. People who regard their situation as unjust or see current policies as foolish usually must do battle with the old order before they can be successful. Otherwise, old policies that may advance only a few people's interests will prevail. In Coser's (1956) words, "Conflict prevents the ossification of the social system by exerting pressure for innovation and creativity" (p. 197). Almost every new piece of legislation in the Congress of the United States is enacted after a period of debate and cross pressures from opposing interest groups. Where would we be if, in the interest of avoiding conflict, we routinely stifled reformers or they stifled themselves?

A second positive function of overt conflict is to discourage premature group decision making. A group that fears internal confrontation may adopt the first plausible suggestion in order to close off debate among its members.[7] Premature decisions are often poor decisions, in part because they reflect misunderstandings about where group members really stand. Research (Fry et al., 1983) suggests that such misunderstandings are sometimes found in courtship. Party is so afraid of antagonizing Other that it fails to push its viewpoint sufficiently for Other to understand it.

A third positive function is to facilitate the reconciliation of people's legitimate interests. Most conflicts do not end with one party winning and the other losing. Rather, some synthesis of the two positions—some integrative agreement—often emerges that fosters the mutual benefit of both parties, as well as the larger collectives of which they are members. If union and management, Egypt and Israel, Sales and Production, or two people arguing over an automobile can manage to reconcile their interests, they will

---

[7] It has been widely speculated that one reason the Wang Computer Company failed in the period after its founder's death has to do with an organizational culture that emphasized harmony and the avoidance of confrontation. Because of anxiety about conflict, managers were reluctant to make difficult decisions on their own. Rather than confront those with whom they disagreed, the managers waited for An Wang to intervene. As a result, the company had difficulty adjusting to Wang's death and a rapidly changing market.

contribute to their own individual outcomes and, indirectly, to the well-being of the larger organization, world community, or neighborhood of which they are members. If, in an effort to avoid friction, they are not allowed to make claims against one another, such deep-seated reconciliation will seldom be possible. In this sense, conflict can be considered a creative force.

A fourth positive effect is that by virtue of its first three functions, *within-group* conflict often fosters long-run group solidarity, that is, unity between the group members who have come into conflict. Without the capacity for social change or the reconciliation of individual interests, group solidarity is likely to decline and with it group effectiveness and enjoyment of the group experience (Coser, 1956). The eventual result can be group disintegration. Without conflict, groups are like the married couple in Ingmar Bergman's film *Couples,* who fail to recognize and confront the issues in their marriage and eventually split up because neither is getting anything out of their relationship.

A fifth positive function is that *between-group* conflict tends to produce solidarity within the groups that come into conflict. Waging the conflict becomes a unifying project within each group, bringing each group's members together in a common effort (Coser, 1956; Deutsch, 1958; Johnson, Johnson, & Maruyama, 1984). Thus America's solidarity, and the capacity of its citizens to work together, has increased in almost every international conflict from the Revolutionary War to the current struggle against terrorism. Research suggests that successful conflicts are more likely to have this effect than unsuccessful conflicts (Turner et al., 1984; Worchel et al., 1977), which may explain why the Vietnam War (which America lost) was the least unifying of all America's struggles.

And the Bad News

We have seen that much social exchange does not give rise to conflict. Moreover, when conflict does arise, it is often settled without pain and rancor while serving a number of positive functions. Nevertheless, conflict often has a downside. There is a limit to the amount of overt confrontation a society can tolerate, even when it ends up having productive consequences. Such conflict takes time and energy away from other pursuits. A group, organization, or country can become so embroiled in controversy that it is unable to cope with basic environmental demands. Furthermore, conflict that involves heavy contentious tactics is fully capable of wreaking havoc on whatever it touches—the parties to the conflict, third parties, and society in general.

People caught in severely contentious conflict are likely to suffer from a wide range of psychological and physical health problems including a weakened immune system (Kiecolt-Glaser et al., 1997), depression (Christian-Herman et al., 2001), alcoholism (O'Farrell & Murphy, 2002), and eating disorders (Van den Broucke et al., 1997). What is more, it is often the case that the conflicting parties are not the only ones who suffer. Overt marital conflict is linked to *children's* poor emotional and behavioral adjustment (Kline et al., 1991), problematic relationship with parents (Fauber et al., 1990), and aggressive behavior (Jouriles et al., 1991). Furthermore, marital conflict often casts its shadow onto the children's later marriages, increasing the likelihood that they will also be filled with conflict (Amato & Booth, 2001).[8]

Heavily escalated conflict, such as warfare, leaves a far-reaching residue on society in general. For example, nations experience postwar homicide waves regardless of whether they have won or lost the war or whether their postwar economies have improved or worsened (Archer & Gartner, 1984). During wartime, violent acts become socially accepted, legitimized, or even heralded as heroic. As a result, citizens' inhibitions against resorting to violence are diminished.

Perhaps the most compelling evidence for the toxic effects of conflict can be found in the pain and suffering of individuals who have been traumatized by heavy conflict. Although human beings can show remarkable resilience,[9] heavy conflict weakens this resilience and cripples people's coping mechanisms, often leaving deep, irreparable psychological scars. Individuals exposed to armed conflict tend to suffer from posttraumatic stress disorder (PTSD). Its symptoms include recurrent and intrusive recollections of the traumatic event, nightmares and flashbacks, emotional numbing, social withdrawal, and hypervigilance. One study finds that 90% of all survivors of the 1994 Rwanda genocide showed some or all of these symptoms (Carney, 1994).

In some cases, the horrors of conflict are so great that the human mind is simply unable to deal with them. An Afghan doctor succinctly summarizes the depth and magnitude of human sufferings caused by a prolonged armed conflict in that country: "I have been a doctor for 15 years, and we have been at war for 23. I don't think anyone outside Afghanistan can understand how that can empty a person of his sanity" (Healy, 2002).[10]

---

[8] See Gottman (2001) for advice about how parents in hostile marriages can buffer children from the toxic effects of marital conflict.

[9] Thomas Friedman's (1995) book, *From Beirut to Jerusalem,* provides some ingenious coping strategies that people used to deal with almost daily occurrences of bombings, kidnappings, and murders in Beirut during the early 1980s. One of the most widely used methods involved selective attention. That is, people would only focus on the things that they could control, while blocking out the things that they could not control. This gave them a sense of (although illusory) control over their fate, preventing them from plunging into helplessness. One resident explained this strategy well: "I am on my way to play tennis, and an Israeli F-15 suddenly flies overhead. Can I do anything about it? No. Is he coming to bomb me? I don't think so. So I continue on and play tennis" (p. 38).

[10] For a more detailed description of PTSD, see *American Psychiatric Association* (2000). See Shalev et al. (2000) for a comprehensive review of trauma-related topics.

Collective traumas, if they are left untreated, have a long shelf life and are often transmitted to following generations. According to Volkan (2001), an untreated wound of this kind becomes a "chosen trauma," which is a "shared mental representation of a massive trauma that the group's ancestors suffered at the hand of an enemy" (p. 79). Chosen traumas are core components of people's group identity. They are deposited deep into the collective memory bank of a group's grievances and periodically withdrawn to justify aggression against the adversary. Chosen traumas can keep hostility alive across many generations to come.

Events, such as terrorist attacks and the proliferation of nuclear weapons, acutely remind us that the Damoclean swords of nuclear and biochemical annihilation hang precariously over our heads. Given dangers such as these, it would be hard to deny that conflict remains the major problem of our times.

It may seem paradoxical that conflict can have both harmful and beneficial consequences, but this paradox is more apparent than real. What often happens is that the positive functions of conflict are swamped by the harmful consequences that derive from the use of heavy contentious tactics. Thus the struggle between Israelis and Palestinians may enhance solidarity within each group, but this positive effect is dwarfed by the pain and suffering produced by the struggle. In the throes of insult, threat, and physical assault, it is difficult to savor the positive functions of conflict.

Although conflict need not be destructive in its consequences, when it is bad it may well be horrid. And because destructive conflict—although far less prevalent than its more constructive cousin—is capable of doing so much damage to the people who are caught in its machinery, we will take a particularly close look in this book at the circumstances that lead conflict along a destructive, escalatory pathway.

SUMMARY AND CONCLUSIONS

The book focuses on dyadic conflict—conflict between two parties. These parties can be individuals, groups, organizations, or nations. Much of the theory of conflict applies to all four of these levels, though there are some differences between the levels. "Conflict" is defined as perceived divergence of interest—a perception by one of the parties ("Party") that its aspirations are incompatible with those of the other party ("Other"). Conflict poses a choice between four broad strategies: contending, yielding, problem solving, and avoiding. Two of these strategies—contending and problem solving—can be enacted in many different ways, which we call "tactics." When contending or joint problem solving is adopted by both parties, the result is overt confrontation, a behavioral form of conflict. Contrary to popular belief, overt confrontation can have many positive functions. However, if escalation occurs, these will often be overshadowed by negative functions.

PLAN OF THE BOOK

The book's organization reflects the set of guiding assumptions and interests that have characterized our introductory remarks. Chapter 2 elaborates on our definition of conflict, introduces a simple graphic analysis to clarify this definition, and summarizes the causes of conflict as well as the conditions that make conflict less likely to erupt. Chapter 3 deals with the topic of strategic choice. We first describe in more detail the four strategies for coping with conflict. We then turn to the set of considerations that lead Party to choose one strategy over another. Together, Chapters 2 and 3 comprise the theoretical heart of the book, presenting concepts that are used in most of the later chapters. Chapter 4 explores the set of contentious tactics that Party can use in an effort to prevail at Other's expense.

The next four chapters focus, in one way or another, on the important topic of escalation. Chapter 5 details the transformations that occur during escalation. It also examines two models that have been used to explain the escalation of conflict: the contender-defender and the conflict spiral models. Chapter 6 introduces a third escalation model, the structural change model, which deals with the psychological and group changes that often occur during escalation and that help explain why escalation tends to persist and recur. Chapter 7 examines the conditions that cause conflicts to escalate to high levels, and it contrasts these to conditions that keep escalation under control. Chapter 8 looks at the mechanisms that cause high levels of escalation to endure once they have been reached.

The last three chapters of the book concern de-escalation and conflict resolution. The focus of Chapter 9 is stalemate, the point at which Party and/or Other come to believe that it is no longer capable or willing to continue expending the effort necessary to sustain an escalating exchange. Stalemate represents the point of transition in a conflict-intensified exchange between the trajectory of escalation and the pathway of de-escalation and negotiation. Chapter 10 addresses the extremely important, constructive, and often creative strategy of problem solving. This chapter describes the several methods of moving toward an integrative solution that satisfies the aspirations of all concerned. The chapter ends with a discussion of reconciliation, which often must accompany problem solving for conflict settlements to last. The final chapter, Chapter 11, addresses the roles and functions of third parties in social conflict.

2

Nature and Sources of Conflict

❖

In Chapter 1 we defined *conflict* as perceived divergence of interest. In the present chapter, we elaborate on this definition by examining the several components that define conflict. In other words, we ask the question, How can we know when conflict exists? We also look at the processes by which conflict develops and the conditions that encourage conflict. The earlier part of the chapter concerns conflict as a whole, whether it takes place between individuals or groups. The latter part concerns those processes and conditions that are particularly relevant to intergroup conflict.

DEFINING COMPONENTS OF CONFLICT

By the term *interests* in our definition of conflict, we mean people's feelings about what is basically desirable. We use the term where others use *values* (Druckman et al., 1988) or *needs* (Burton, 1987). Interests tend to be central to people's thinking and action, forming the core of many of their attitudes, goals, and intentions.

There are several dimensions that can be used to describe interests. Some interests are tangible, such as water, money, territory; others are intangible, such as power, honor, recognition. Some interests are virtually universal, such as the basic human needs for physical well-being, security, identity, freedom, justice, respect, and clarity about the nature of one's world. Other interests are specific to certain actors, such as the Palestinians' desire for a homeland or Ben's wish to have access to the family car. Some interests are higher in priority (more important) than others, and such priorities differ from person to person. Some interests underlie other interests; for example, America's interest in security largely underlies its campaign against terrorism.

Before Party's interests can clash with those of Other, these interests must be translated into *aspirations,* mental representations of the things that Party strives for or believes it must achieve. Aspirations may take the form of *goals* that Party is striving for, such as an objective of earning $36,000 per year or of capturing Kandahar within a month. Or aspirations may be represented by certain minimal *standards* that Party aspires to meet or exceed, such as a rock-bottom salary requirement of $32,000 or of staying on good relations with one's allies. Aspirations have other sources in addition to interests, including Party's past achievement, the achievement of others with whom Party compares itself, accepted principles of fairness, and other social norms.

Conflict exists when Party sees its own and Other's aspirations as incompatible. This occurs when the available alternatives (options) seem incapable of satisfying both parties' aspirations.

A few graphs may help to clarify this concept. Figure 2.1 represents Party's conception of the joint outcome space for itself and Other.[1] The horizontal axis represents some dimension or combination of dimensions of value to Party, and the vertical axis represents a similar value dimension for Other. The dashed lines represent perceived aspirations. The line marked P represents Party's own aspirations; that marked O, Party's view of Other's aspirations. The points in the space represent various known alternatives. These alternatives can be a matter of Party's behavior, Other's behavior, or joint action by Party and Other. A and B can be thought of as partisan alternatives, providing value only to Party or Other, respectively; C is moderately favorable to both, a form of compromise; and D is highly favorable to both, an integrative solution.

Alternatives such as D in Figure 2.1 are called *integrative solutions* because they integrate—that is, reconcile—the two parties' interests. Anything that provides even a glimmer of hope of finding an integrative solution diminishes perceived conflict. For example, when Egyptian President

---

[1] This and subsequent diagrams have elements in common with those used by Thomas (1976).

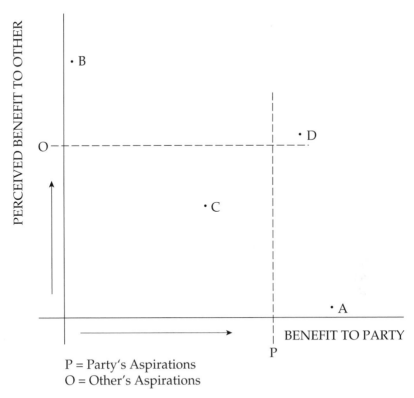

FIGURE 2.1

Party's conception of a joint outcome space with Other.

Anwar Sadat made his famous trip to Jerusalem in 1977, it began to seem possible that a solution could be found to the major differences between Egypt and Israel. As a result, the tension between Egypt and Israel diminished in the eyes of most people on both sides (Kelman, 1985).[2]

Figure 2.2 shows four possible patterns of perceived alternatives and aspirations. In Figure 2.2*a*, there is no perceived divergence of interest because a known alternative satisfies both parties' aspirations. (That alternative is represented by the point that lies above and to the right of the intersections of the two dashed lines.) Figures 2.2*b* through 2.2*d*, which can be contrasted with Figure 2.2*a*, depict various ways in which perceived divergence of interest can develop. In Figure 2.2*b*, Party's own aspirations have risen to a level where there is no viable alternative. In

---

[2] Sadat's trip to Jerusalem will be discussed more fully in the section on unilateral conciliatory initiatives in Chapter 9.

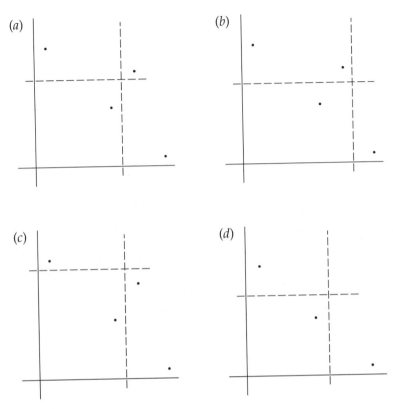

FIGURE 2.2

Four possible patterns of perceived alternatives and aspirations.

Figure 2.2*c*, Other's aspirations are perceived to have risen to such a level. In Figure 2.2*d*, the mutually acceptable (integrative) alternative that appeared in Figure 2.2*a* is no longer available, and the remaining alternatives have the character of a zero-sum game, where Party's advantage implies Other's disadvantage.[3]

---

[3] Though they provide an intuitive understanding of our ideas about conflict, graphs of the kind shown in Figures 2.1 and 2.2 have serious limitations in that they treat utility (an individual's level of benefit) as a single dimension. In reality, human needs in most situations are multidimensional. For example, people need both food and adequate housing, and they cannot readily trade more of one for less of the other, as implied by a simple utility concept. Rather than having a single level of aspiration, as implied by Figures 2.1 and 2.2, people are likely to have multiple aspirations, one for each realm of need involved in the controversy. Hence, a more sophisticated analysis would employ multidimensional graphs.

Conflict Size

Conflicts differ in *size* or magnitude—the apparent ease with which they can be resolved (Deutsch, 1991). One contributor to size is the apparent divergence of interest. Divergence of interest, and hence conflict, looks larger: (a) the higher are Party's own aspirations, (b) the higher are Other's apparent aspirations, and (c) the less promising are the known alternatives. (These three sources of size can be seen by comparing Figure 2.2*a* with Figures 2.2*b*, 2.2*c*, and 2.2*d*, respectively.) In addition (and this is not shown in Figure 2.2), conflicts are larger the more *rigid* are Party's and Other's apparent aspirations. Rigid aspirations are hard to change, making it difficult to resolve the conflict.

There are three conditions that make aspirations rigid and hence add to the size of conflict: (1) important interests underlie the aspirations, for example, basic human needs such as security, identity, and respect; (2) strongly felt principles underlie the aspirations, such as a belief that crime should not be rewarded; and (3) the available options are of an either-or variety (Party or Other either succeeds or it does not). Aspirations are rigid when there is an either-or issue because concession is tantamount to capitulation, requiring giving up one's interests altogether. An example would be a conflict about buying a car between a husband whose favorite color is red and a wife whose favorite color is green. Compromise (moving to a middle ground) is impossible in such a situation.

Aspirations are also quite rigid when either party regards its goals as legitimate or *just*, that is, as outcomes to which it is entitled. Legitimate aspirations are especially hard to give up and failure to achieve them is a source of special distress. For example, prior to the 1971 prison revolt at the Attica correctional facility in upstate New York, prisoners were led to believe (based on promises made by State Corrections Commissioner Russell Oswald) that they were entitled to numerous improvements in prison conditions. When, for a variety of reasons, these improvements were not forthcoming, the prisoners felt deeply disappointed. A long and extremely costly prison revolt was the result, in which nearly forty prisoners and corrections officers lost their lives (New York State Special Commission on Attica, 1972).

The Role of Relative Deprivation

Divergence of interest is often discovered as a result of harsh experience in which Party fails to achieve what it considers to be reasonable aspirations. Such an experience is called *relative deprivation*. Such deprivation is "relative" because Party feels deprived relative to a reasonable standard. An example of relative deprivation is the state of mind of the Attica prisoners just described. They failed to achieve what they thought they had been led to expect.

How do people decide what aspirations are reasonable? These decisions may be based on what others say they deserve, as in the Attica example. They may also be based on social norms that specify what anybody in their circumstances should get. Thus the rioters who protested the Rodney King beating described in Chapter 1 probably believed (correctly) that the norms of American society preclude being beaten by the police. Other sources of standards for comparing with one's outcomes include one's recent past experience and the outcomes achieved by other parties who are viewed as comparable to oneself (Brewer & Brown, 1998).

Relative deprivation has two effects: First, it alerts Party to the existence of incompatible interests. In searching for the source of the deprivation, Party learns whose interests are incompatible with its own. Second, the frustration and indignation associated with relative deprivation are a source of energy that increases the likelihood and vigor of efforts to cope with the deprivation. This energy is particularly high when the deprivation seems illegitimate. There is nothing quite as motivating as feeling that one has been deprived relative to a legitimate standard—that one has been treated unfairly or unjustly (d'Estree, 2003). If the assumed source of a deprivation is a person or group, this energy takes the form of anger, which inclines Party toward contentious action.

If relative deprivation continues, a sense of hopelessness may eventually develop. This usually causes aspirations to diminish, and hence, reduces conflict. Party adjusts its aspirations to fit reality, reducing the perceived divergence of interest. The broader point illustrated by this effect is that deprivation *per se* is not a cause of conflict. Rather it is deprivation *in comparison to* what Party expects or feels it should get, in other words, relative deprivation.

The role of relative deprivation is so common in the development of conflict that some theorists view it as a sine qua non for the emergence of conflict (Gurr, 1970; Kriesberg, 1998). We differ with this viewpoint, since we believe that Party can draw conclusions about divergence of interest from other evidence than that provided by relative deprivation, including Other's statements about its motives, and a lack of trust in Other.

CONDITIONS THAT ENCOURAGE CONFLICT

There are a number of conditions that encourage the development of conflict, that is, the development of perceived divergence of interest. When these conditions are not present, conflict is a good deal less likely to emerge. We have sorted these conditions into four categories: features of the situation, features of the parties, features of the relationship between the parties, and features of the broader community surrounding the parties.

Features of the Situation

Scarcity   Conflict often arises because parties pursue a limited resource. An example is two men vying for the affection of a single woman or Israelis and Palestinians arguing over who should control Jerusalem. Conflict arises because if one party gets a lot of the resource, the other necessarily gets little.

What is more, as the perception of scarcity increases, the desire for the limited resource *becomes stronger.* Whether it be territory, parking spaces, romantic partners, or the latest toy on the market, the less there is of any item, the more people will value it and seek its possession. This makes aspirations higher and more rigid, increasing the size of conflict. Why do people tend to place value on things they perceive to be scarce? This is partly because scarce items tend to have greater value, so people learn to associate scarcity with value. It is also because people find any restriction on their freedom unpleasant. If an item's scarcity suggests they may not be able to obtain it, people react by seeking that item so as to re-gain their lost sense of freedom (Cialdini, 2001).

Competition over a scarce item also makes it seem even more valu-able, increasing the likelihood of conflict. Anyone who has gone through the beanie baby frenzy (or the Pokémon card frenzy) would readily agree to this point. (Beanie babies are cloth animals filled with beans.) When-ever a new shipment of beanie babies arrived at a toy store, people darted to the store to grab those "few" available items, while elbowing off, push-ing away, and even knocking down, other competitors. Even fistfights often broke out! At the height of the frenzy, some people were willing to spend hundreds of dollars for a small toy whose real value was less than ten dollars. The scarcity of an item (in this case deliberately created by the Tyco company), combined with other people's vying for it, excites desire that can approach a panic state.

Besides making an item seem more valuable, the presence of a com-petitor tends to produce time pressure. There is no time to think of broader issues, such as whether the beanie baby is really worth fighting for. This makes panic behavior even more likely.

Rapidly Expanding Achievement   People become more hopeful as things get better, causing their aspirations to rise. In periods of rapidly expand-ing achievement, such rising aspirations can sometimes outstrip reality. A case in point is the period of growing African American awareness, self-confidence, and agitation during the 1960s, after two centuries of subjuga-tion. Enforcement of civil rights had improved markedly in the prior decade, especially with the landmark Supreme Court decision outlawing school segregation; and the pace of this advance was accelerated in the 1960s, which saw the passage of much new legislation and widespread changes in the attitudes of whites. Paradoxically, this period also saw more discontent and agitation among African Americans than any other time before or after. What may well have happened is that the progress made in civil rights encouraged expectations of rapid further change, producing unrealistic aspirations. We do not contend that these aspirations were illegitimate, only that they were inconsistent with the aspirations of others and therefore produced conflict.

Conflict is especially likely to occur after a period of expanding achievement if there is a slowdown or reversal in this achievement. Davies (1962) presents evidence that revolutions occur when a period of expanding "economic and social development is followed by a short period of sharp reversal" (p. 5). Cialdini (2001) sums it up well: "It is not the traditionally most downtrodden people—those who have come to see their deprivation as part of the natural order of things—who are especially likely to revolt. Instead, revolutionaries are more likely to be those who have been given at least some taste of a better life" (p. 219).

Features of the Parties

Zero-Sum Thinking   The belief that the other's gain is one's own loss, and vice versa, is zero-sum thinking (also known as the "fixed-pie" assumption). This belief encourages conflict because there seems to be no way both sides can achieve their aspirations. To be sure, it is often the case that issues really are zero-sum in nature, as when there are scarce resources. Only one beanie baby is left, and both parties want it. At least as often, however, conflict is encouraged not because issues are truly zero-sum in nature[4] but because the parties treat them this way. In this case, zero-sum thinking is a *faulty* belief. In actuality, the parties do have compatible interests, but they are blind to this fact.[5] Such a faulty belief is found to be a main culprit for encouraging conflict (Thompson & Hrebec, 1996).

Features of the Relationship between the Parties

Ambiguity about Relative Power   Conflict is especially likely when ambiguity exists about the nature of power such that each party can conclude—

---

[4] Indeed, even when issues are zero-sum, it is often possible to transform them into non-zero-sum equivalents. Some of these ways to do this are described in Chapters 9 through 11.
[5] A story with which one of the authors (SHK) grew up may illustrate this point. It is about the key difference between "heaven" and "hell." As the story goes, there are virtually no differences between the two places. Consider mealtime. Both places serve the identical kind and amount of food in identical-looking cafeterias with identical-looking utensils. The food served is a heap of thin, but large and round, pancakes that are placed in the middle of a long dining room table. Each person is given a pair of very long chopsticks (or a fork with a

through a process of wishful thinking—that it is stronger than the other. This state of affairs tends to produce incompatible aspirations, leading to conflict. The Vietnam War offers a good example. Because of differing military technologies, both the United States and North Vietnam believed that they would win and kept their aspirations high. Many years of war were required to discover which of these parties had drawn the right conclusion (it was North Vietnam).

Invidious Comparisons   Conflict is also encouraged when Party develops an awareness that Other is of no greater merit than Party, yet Other is afforded greater wealth or privilege. This leads to an invidious comparison, in which aspirations rise for either realistic reasons (because it is believed that Party *can* do as well as Other if Party tries) or idealistic reasons (because it is believed that Party's outcomes *should* be as good as Other's).

The importance of a comparison figure in the development of conflict is illustrated by the events in Henrik Ibsen's classic play *A Doll's House.* The heroine, Nora, is a traditional housewife who is dominated by her husband. She becomes acquainted with Christine, a more liberated woman, and the contrast between their two conditions causes Nora to aspire to greater freedom and privilege. This brings her into conflict with her husband, whom she eventually leaves.[6]

Invidious comparisons may in part explain the behavior of Nabil Halabiyeh, a suicide bomber who tried to kill as many Israelis as possible. Before this suicide attack, he was known for his passion for sports not politics. But things apparently began to change for this young man when he started working in Israel. His cousin explains, "Seeing the luxurious life they [Israelis] live there, and probably he started asking questions: Why are they leading a better life than us?" (Hockstader, 2001). Many of the Palestinian suicide bombers have been impelled by other motives

---

very long handle, if you prefer). There are only two rules that everyone must obey. One is that people must use the chopsticks to eat the pancakes; the other is that if they drop a pancake, nobody is allowed to eat it. Despite the identical conditions, people in heaven seem always well fed and happy while those in hell seem always hungry and angry. How could that be? In hell, people are not very nice or very trusting. Hence, they hurry to pick up a pancake because they think that the more pancakes there are for others, the less there will be for themselves. But because of the unwieldy chopsticks, they frequently drop the pancake, which by rule is lost to the entire group of diners. Many pancakes are dropped; few are left on the table. People get into frequent squabbles and fights over those few left, only causing more droppings. By contrast, the heaven dwellers pick up a pancake with the chopsticks—and feed it *to the person sitting across the table.* The long chopsticks hinder them from feeding the pancake to themselves, but enable them to feed it to their fellow heaven dwellers. In short, zero-sum thinking prevails in hell, while win-win thinking prevails in heaven.

[6] Equity theorists (Adams, 1965; Walster et al., 1978) argue that invidious comparisons are especially likely to be made when people whose outcomes are better than our own seem similar to us in basic merit (the technical term for merit is contributions) or when people whose outcomes are equal to our own appear to have lower merit than we do.

(e.g., pressing for improved conditions for their group, revenge), but Mr. Halabiyeh seems to have been heavily affected by invidious comparisons.

There are also several studies showing that U.S. communities with greater disparities between rich and poor show a higher murder rate (Berkowitz, 1993). Invidious comparisons may help to account for these findings. The richer the wealthy are and the poorer the poverty stricken are, the more resentful the latter are likely to be.

How can invidious comparisons be prevented, thus discouraging conflict? The fairest approach is to work for greater equality in the distribution of resources and privileges. Two other approaches are commonly used. One is to develop a firm set of norms that link rewards to a single, easily measured criterion, such as seniority or educational attainment. This is the method used to minimize invidious comparisons in the United States civil service system. The other, which is commonly used in organizations, is to conceal information about employee rewards. Salary information is particularly easy to conceal, and many organizations do so in an effort to avert conflict.

Status Inconsistency   Invidious comparisons are particularly likely when there is status inconsistency (Kriesberg, 1998). Status inconsistency (also called *rank disequilibrium*) exists when there are multiple criteria for assessing people's merit or contributions, and some people are higher on one criterion and lower on another criterion than others. In our society, for example, both experience and education are sources of on-the-job status. People with experience tend to believe that experience makes the most relevant contribution, whereas people with education tend to believe the opposite. When these two kinds of people have to work together, each is likely to feel more deserving of rewards than the other, and conflict is especially likely to develop.

In contrast, when there are unambiguous status systems, so that the same people are top dog on all criteria, people are not so likely to compare themselves with others of different status. Hence, conflict is diminished. Such systems are most effective when backed up by myths that picture the more advantaged segments of society as more deserving. For his ideal state, the republic, Plato recommended the establishment of such a myth: the rulers should be viewed as containing gold in their makeup, the auxiliaries silver, and the farmers and other workers iron and bronze. Myths about racial and sexual inferiority serve a similar purpose. In our society, African Americans and women have traditionally been viewed as intellectually and emotionally deficient and hence less deserving of reward. Quite often they have subscribed to these myths themselves. Such myths encourage the belief that the more advantaged segments of a community are the more deserving, thereby discouraging the "upward comparison" that often produces feelings of relative deprivation (Wood,

1989). Hence, they reduce the likelihood of conflict, though often at the expense of social justice.

Distrust   Distrust is a belief that Other is hostile or indifferent to Party's welfare. Distrust operates to arouse a perception of threat in ambiguous circumstances, and this can lead to conflict (Pruitt, 1965). An example is given by Zinnes et al. (1961) in their analysis of the events leading up to World War I. In 1914, there were two antagonistic coalitions in Europe, one consisting mainly of Germany and Austria, the other of England, France, and Russia. These coalitions were highly distrustful of each other. When a citizen of Serbia assassinated Austrian Archduke Ferdinand, Austria declared war on that country. In an effort to deter an Austrian attack on Serbia, Russia mobilized its troops. Fearing that it was about to be attacked by Russia and its allies, Germany then attacked France through Belgium, beginning the war. The German Kaiser's high level of distrust had apparently caused him to misinterpret the Russian mobilization and assume that it was a prelude to a massive attack on his country. He tried to head off this attack by grasping the military initiative.

Trust, the opposite of distrust, implies a belief that Other is positively concerned about Party's interests. The concern need not be genuine, in the sense of being based on positive feelings toward Party. It is quite possible for Party to trust Other because it believes that Other is dependent on Party, and for this reason unlikely to risk Party's anger. Trust, so defined, discourages conflict by causing Party to believe that Other will accommodate Party's interests in areas of special importance to Party.[7]

Features of the Community

We use the term "community" to refer to the larger set of parties of which potential disputants are a subset. Thus for a married couple, the community would be their family or the town in which they live. For two neighboring towns, the community would be the county, state, or province within which they are situated. For two nations, the community would be the other nations in their region or the "community of nations" as a whole. Two parties may share membership in more than one community. Community characteristics often affect the likelihood of conflict between members of the community.

The Security Dilemma   In 1914, the distrust between the two rival European coalitions was partly due to what Snyder and Diesing (1977) call a

---

[7] We shall have more to say about trust and distrust in Chapters 3 and 6.

security dilemma. In well-functioning communities, there is little reason to distrust one's neighbors because powerful third parties—police and courts—protect citizens from each other. But powerful third parties who are willing to intervene are usually not found in international relations, which means that nations or coalitions of nations must defend themselves. Another way of putting this is that the international community is perpetually in a state of anarchy (Mearsheimer, 2001). This tends to produce insecurity and distrust, of the kind that developed in the years before 1914, producing preparations for war. Such preparations further heighten the insecurity and distrust in the system, producing still more preparations (e.g., an arms race) and still more distrust. This kind of situation involves a *dilemma* because it is rational for each nation to arm for fear of attack, but the world would be better off if they trusted each other and none of them did. Unfortunately, the state of anarchy does not permit that. The security dilemma is a version of the famous non-zero–sum game, the prisoner's dilemma (Pruitt, 1997; Rapoport & Chammah, 1965). In this game, individual rationality encourages noncooperative behavior, but both sides would be better off if they could cooperate with each other.

Security dilemmas and the problems of distrust they create are found in other settings that lack effective third-party protection. Examples would be lightly populated frontier regions (consider the Western part of the United States during its settlement), poorly policed center cities, and some prisons.

Lack of Normative Consensus   Communities and the groups within them are constantly developing *norms* (i.e., rules) to govern the behavior of their members. These norms include goals people are supposed to pursue, role definitions, procedures for decision making, and guidelines concerning which community members are higher and lower in status and authority. A major function of such norms is to dovetail the aspirations of potential opponents and hence reduce the likelihood of conflict (Thibaut & Kelley, 1959). An example is the norm against stealing. If this norm did not exist, conflict would be so pervasive and severe that society would be virtually unworkable. A less earthshaking example is the minimum wage law. By specifying a single wage level for routine jobs, this law limits the aspirations of both workers and employers and thus reduces the likelihood of conflict between them. A similar function is played by the norm, subscribed to in many families, that one spouse cooks and the other does the dishes.

When communities lack normative consensus, some community members will have aspirations that are incompatible with those of others and conflict will be common. The present troubled period in relations between husbands and wives is a case in point. Society today provides much less clarity than in earlier times about what kinds of behavior spouses can reasonably expect from one another (Rubin & Rubin, 1989).

Low-conflict communities have particularly clear norms governing those interpersonal relationships that are most prone to conflict, such as authority and status relationships. For example, employers and workers have plenty of opportunity for conflict because their activities and wishes are so intimately linked. But most people go into the job situation with a fairly clear idea of their appropriate roles. Workers expect to do more or less as they are told and to try to make a good impression; employers expect to provide clear direction and both positive and negative reinforcement. Considering the potential for conflict, the workplace is amazingly conflict free.

When a set of norms has broad support among the more powerful segments of a community, disadvantaged groups—even if they are sizable—are relatively unlikely to develop aspirations that threaten these norms. Most people learn to fit in and make the most of what may be a constricted set of options. Their aspirations fit social reality.

This does not mean that everybody is happy in such a community. The least advantaged—be they African Americans, women, students, or slaves—may be quite unhappy. But most of them are sufficiently discouraged (by the fact that everyone else seems to support the norms) or frightened (by the techniques used to enforce the norms) that they aspire to no better than they have. Of course, there are always people in such settings who are restless about their rights and benefits. Conflict is avoided if these people can readily escape, as many Americans did by moving to the western frontier from nineteenth-century New England.

SOURCES OF INTERGROUP CONFLICT

The first part of this chapter dealt with processes and conditions that affect the likelihood of conflict as a whole, whether the parties are individuals or groups. We now turn to an additional set of conditions that only affect the likelihood of conflict between groups. A "group" can be defined as two or more people who have a common identity and a capacity for coordinated action. We use this term to refer to all kinds of collectives, whether they be couples, workgroups, organizations, political factions, or nation–states. There are, of course, differences between these types of groups, and we will try to point them out when we come to them. But there are many general principles that apply to groups at all levels, and these will be highlighted in this section.

The Robbers Cave Experiment

In the summer of 1954, an isolated, spacious state park in the Sans Bois mountains of Oklahoma, known as Robbers Cave, was the setting for one of the best-known field studies on intergroup conflict. The principal investigators, Muzafer Sherif and his colleagues (Sherif et al., 1961; Sherif & Sherif, 1969) carefully selected twelve-year-old boys who were similar in virtually all ways. They were divided into two groups of twelve each and brought separately to the campsite, so that for several days they were unaware of the presence of another group. The boys did typical summer camp activities—canoeing, swimming, making meals, setting up tents, playing baseball at a nearby baseball field, and the like. As expected, group bonding—"we" feelings—emerged quickly. Both groups adopted a group name: the "Rattlers" and the "Eagles."

After several days, the groups discovered one another's presence and were eager to compete with each other in team sports. Even before actual contact took place, competitive, often hostile emotions erupted. And both groups were confident that they would crush the other in competition.

When the first day of the competitions arrived, the researchers displayed the tournament prizes in the cafeteria—a shiny trophy, splendid-looking medals, and four-bladed knives—prizes that would be given *only* to the winning team. As expected, these prizes heightened competitive and hostile feelings even further.

As soon as the competitions began, so did the name-calling. Although both groups initially tried hard to be good sports, this soon ceased and insults became the norm ("bunch of cussers," "bums," "sissies," "little babies"). Hostile actions rapidly escalated. Both groups engaged in tit-for-tat attacks and counterattacks. They tore down each other's flags, trashed one another's cabins, and so on. Also, they secretly amassed weapons—bats, sticks, socks filled with rocks. By the end of the tournament period, the groups were sworn enemies.

Fortunately, there was a happy ending to the camp experience. The investigators were able to successfully transform this hostile group relationship into a cooperative one. We will come back to how this was achieved in Chapter 9. But, for now, we will focus on what gives rise to intergroup conflict. Why was it so easy for the Rattlers and the Eagles to become hostile to each other?

Realistic Conflict vs. Social Identity

The development of conflict in the Robbers Cave experiment has been explained in two ways. Sherif attributed the conflict to the competitive situation he imposed on the boys. He felt that the tournament produced a divergence of interest between the groups to which they reacted with contentious tactics, producing an escalation. This explanation is based on what Campbell (1965) calls *realistic conflict theory*, which assumes that conflict can always be explained by some tangible (like territory, money, prizes) or intangible (like power, prestige, honor) resource that is desired by both groups and is in short supply. Such an explanation surely has a good deal of value, but there is a problem with it in the case of the Rattlers and the Eagles. Their hostility toward each other started *before* they got into the competitive situation—indeed it began the day they learned of each other's existence.

To remedy this problem, Tajfel and Turner (1979, 1986) developed *social identity theory.* This holds that "the mere awareness of the presence of an out-group is sufficient to provoke intergroup competitive or discriminatory responses on the part of the ingroup" (Tajfel & Turner, 1979, p. 38). The reason for this is that the groups to which one belongs are part of one's self-concept, one's *identity.* Hence, one seeks to view these groups positively, so as to gain self-respect. This produces an ingroup bias, in which one thinks more highly of and discriminates in favor of the ingroup in comparison to outgroups (Brewer & Brown, 1998). This need not lead to conflict, but it is likely to do so if people are disdainful of or insulting to outgroups or take resources for an ingroup that are needed by an outgroup.

Social identity theory is supported by many studies of the "minimal group" or "social categorization" effect (Tajfel, 1970). In these studies, two temporary "groups" of people are created on the basis of a trivial and arbitrary criterion. For example, after being given a fake test of artistic preference, one set of people might be told that they prefer artworks by Klee in contrast to another set of people who prefer Kandinsky. There is no interaction with fellow group members or members of the opposite group. Nevertheless, people like better, think more highly of, and discriminate in favor of members of their own group as opposed to members of the other group (Gaertner & Dovidio, 2000). These findings help to explain why ethnocentrism—favoring one's own group over other groups—is so universal a human phenomenon (Sumner, 1906).[8]

There are also many historical examples of conflict that resemble the minimal group effect and can be explained by social identity theory. One that stands out is the horrific battle between the "greens" and the "blues" in Constantinople during the sixth century A.D. (Ridley, 1996). Chariot races were a favorite sport among the citizens of that city. One group of drivers wore blue outfits, while the other wore green, so that they would

---

[8] As an example of ethnocentrism, Rubin (Rubin et al., 1994) reports the experience he had at the YMCA pool at which he swam each morning at 6 A.M., of discovering how quickly bonds formed among the swimmers who happened to frequent the pool at that hour. Indeed, the sense of "groupness" was so compelling that newcomers to the pool were typically treated with hostility and contempt simply because they were *new.* They had to earn their way into the group's good graces.

be easily distinguished. This seemly insignificant means of identification soon divided the whole city into two factions, green supporters and blue supporters. The animosity between these two groups, quickly infused with religion and politics, produced a riot on a massive scale—the greens massacred over 3000 blues and the blues killed over 30,000 greens. Much of the city was burned to the ground. Although recent "soccer wars" in Europe do not reach this level of violence, we can readily see similarities. And, it seems that the categorization process, creating a we-versus-they mentality, is a key culprit in producing these conflicts.

Group Aspirations and Their Frustration

Groups usually have aspirations—group goals and standards—that are shared by most group members. This means that groups can come into conflict with each other. A trivial example would be the conflict between a married couple and a car dealership over the price of a new car. A profound example would be the conflict between Israelis and Palestinians over the existence and shape of a Palestinian state.

Group aspirations can often be traced back to powerful underlying needs that group members feel for their group (Fisher, 2000). Thus, many Israeli positions can be traced to a deep concern about national *security*—not surprising in light of the many enemies surrounding them. Underlying needs for the Palestinians include *recognition, self-determination,* and *fair treatment*—again not surprising for a group of people that has been controlled by outsiders for hundreds of years. Both groups are concerned about the free *exercise of cultural traditions,* which at least partly accounts for their disagreement about who should control Jerusalem.

The wells of passion attached to the needs of one's group are often deeper than those attached to one's individual needs. This helps explain the suicide attacks on New York and Washington, D.C., that occurred on September 11, 2001. Though woefully misguided, the actions of the men who flew hijacked airliners into the World Trade Centers and the Pentagon appear to have been the expression of a deep desire to defend their ethnic and religious groups.

Relative deprivation can occur at the collective as well as at the individual level. Conflict often ensues when people see their group as deprived in comparison to other groups or to reasonable standards. This is called *fraternalistic deprivation,* in contrast to *egoistic deprivation,* which is relative deprivation at the individual level (Runciman, 1966). Consider the experience of the African American residents of Los Angeles in the aftermath of the Rodney King beating discussed at the beginning of Chapter 1. Many people expected that the police officers responsible for this savage beating would be brought to trial, convicted, and punished. When the officers were found innocent, this outcome inflamed the passions of a great many people, who saw this as an injustice to African Americans *as a group*. The riots that ensued were the product of this fraternalistic deprivation. Several studies have shown that fraternalistic, rather than egoistic deprivation is a major source of intergroup prejudice and political violence (Brewer & Brown, 1998).

Social identity theory helps explain why people often become upset when they experience fraternalistic deprivation. Attacks on their group are viewed as assaults on their own self-worth.

Group Identity

For people to work hard for group goals and feel acute fraternalistic deprivation, they must be highly *identified* with their group—they must see themselves first and foremost as a Muslim, or an African American, or a citizen of Detroit, or a member of the high school band, and so on. It follows that groups with strong group identity (whose members are highly identified with the group) will be involved in conflict more often and more deeply than those without. Thus African American causes should produce more sparks than Italian American causes, as they do.[9]

When there is strong group identity, people feel deeply the suffering of any and all group members. Thus Muslims as far from the Middle East as Indonesia may take to the streets to protest harsh treatment of the Palestinians.

Even the most superficial and ephemeral groups develop some group identity. This is shown by studies of the minimal group effect that were discussed earlier. These studies demonstrate that even a brief encounter between people who have a superficial similarity to each other, in comparison to another group, can give them a sense of group identity. Think of how much stronger group identity should be among people who have historical ethnic or religious ties and perceive that they are being illegitimately deprived in areas that touch on their core values or basic human needs. In the next section, we discuss the processes of conflict group mobilization by

---

[9] Group identity must be distinguished from group identity *needs*. Group identity is the average degree to which a group's members identify with their group (regard that group as central to their self-image). Group identity needs include concern about the survival of the group and its distinctive culture; desire to use cultural vehicles including distinctive "language, history, dress, schooling, rituals and territory" (Leatherman et al., 1999); and need for recognition and respect from other groups. The frustration of *group identity needs* often produces intergroup conflict (Stein, 1996). Such conflict is likely to be more intense, the greater the *group identity* on the two sides.

which strong group identities develop, along with high group aspirations that produce intergroup conflict.

Conflict Group Mobilization

The theory of conflict group mobilization (Azar, 1990; Coleman, 1957; Dahrendorf, 1959; Gurr, 1996) examines the processes and conditions that cause a loosely knit, politically inactive set of people to develop into a well-organized *conflict group* that is capable of challenging the status quo. The theory is mainly designed to understand how low power groups develop the capacity for protest, revolt, and revolution. The theory helps to understand the rise of public protest against a plan to fluoridate the water in Northampton, Massachusetts; the development of the black movement in South Africa; the unification of the people in the thirteen North American colonies that led to the Revolutionary War; and even possibly the mobilization of Al Qaeda, the Islamist organization that attacked the World Trade Center and the Pentagon.

The theory starts with what Dahrendorf (1959) calls a *quasi-group* with *latent interests*, that is, a set of people who have interests in common but are not fully aware of them. The road to group mobilization often starts with a *trigger event* (or series of events) that alarms or otherwise arouses people in the quasi-group (Azar, 1990). An example would be the Sharpsville Massacre in South Africa in which unarmed black protestors were shot by the white authorities. Another would be the British tax on tea that alarmed many colonists in eighteenth-century North America, leading to the "Boston Tea Party," in which this tax was protested by throwing a cargo of tea into the harbor. Communication about such incidents among members of the quasi-group heightens their sense of fraternalistic deprivation.[10] Furthermore—and this is crucial—leaders emerge who articulate people's concerns, strengthen their group identity and sense of frustration, identify the adversary, and organize action to redress the group's grievances. A conflict group is thus formed, consisting of people who feel strongly about a shared identity, who have a common set of grievances against a commonly agreed target, who have aspirations to redress these grievances, and who are in communication with each other either directly or through their leadership.

---

[10] Research on the *group polarization effect* shows that communication among like-minded group members tends to strengthen psychological states such as attitudes, judgments, and plans for action (Isenberg, 1986). This happens for two reasons: (1) group members are further swayed in the direction they favor when they hear new arguments in support of that direction; and (2) many people learn that there are other group members who are more extreme than they are in the direction they favor. This allows them to shift further in that direction because they gain the courage of their convictions or wish to be in the vanguard of those who share their views.

If a number of local groups with similar interests come into existence, a further stage may be found involving "the formation of a single movement led by charismatic organizers who seek to unite the disparate groups and force the attention of the government to the grievances" (Zartman, 1995, pp. 13–14). Examples of such charismatic organizers are Nelson Mandela in South Africa, George Washington in North America, and Osama bin Laden in the Islamist world.[11]

The leader of such a revolutionary group (for example, bin Laden) can be thought of as the center of an onion. The next layer around the leader is his or her immediate organization, which is busy waging the conflict (Al Qaeda, which means "base"). That organization is surrounded by a larger group of people—the aroused conflict group—who support them actively, providing recruits, money, and political protection (the radical Islamist community). Beyond that, in the outer layer of the onion, one often finds an even larger group of people who sympathize with some or all of the aims of the leader and his or her organization but are unwilling to provide support for the tactics employed by this organization (large parts of the Islamic world).

Conditions that Encourage Conflict Group Mobilization   Dahrendorf (1959) has specified three conditions that allow the mobilization of conflict groups and thereby encourage intergroup conflict. One is the capacity for communication among the people in question. Communication strengthens common group identity, encourages the development of group goals, and heightens the sense of fraternalistic deprivation. At times, ruling groups have been able to suppress communication among members of dissatisfied quasi-groups—for example, by limiting the right of assembly, separating prison buddies, or contriving controversies between subgroups who would otherwise unite. Such tactics—which attempt to produce either physical or psychological separation—may prevent conflict groups from coalescing or developing a program. However, efforts to produce physical separation are becoming increasingly difficult with the advent of e-mail and web communication. Indeed these innovations facilitated the kind of world-wide communication that allowed Al Qaeda to flourish and made it possible for that organization to launch the September 11 attacks.

The second and most important condition is the availability of leadership to organize the conflict group and formulate a program for group action. In William Golding's (1954) novel *Lord of the Flies*, two leaders

---

[11] *Islamists* must be distinguished from *Islamic* people. The former are highly orthodox in their religion and highly militant in their politics. The latter have neither of these characteristics but may sympathize with some of the Islamist's goals. Lumping Osama bin Laden with Nelson Mandela and George Washington does not imply a moral equivalence but rather an equivalence in the roles they played within their groups.

rapidly emerge when a band of children is shipwrecked on an isolated island. One of them, Ralph, is inclined to lead by orienting the small children to the circumstances that will facilitate their escape and rescue. In contrast, the other one, Jack, seems motivated to turn the band of fearful children on the island into a conflict group prepared to combat all forms of authority except Jack's own. Jack prevails, at least for a while.

Again, ruling groups often try to eliminate emergent leaders. They may imprison, exile, or kill such leaders, but actions like that are often self-defeating, hardening the conflict group's resolve. Alternatively, they may try to "co-opt" such leaders by bringing them into closer association with the ruling group. This tactic was formerly used by the South Korean government, which gave dissident leaders important positions in the government. For example, a university president attracted much support from radical students because of his criticism of the government's plans for educational reform. The government then appointed him the secretary of education. Once he assumed that position, he withdrew his initial complaints and began to support the government's stand. Cooptation can easily nip conflict in the bud.

Dahrendorf's third condition is group legitimacy in the eyes of the broader community—or at least the absence of effective community suppression of the group. Thus, it is easier to organize groups of dissenters in democracies than in dictatorships, though the latter is by no means impossible. Conflict groups are also much less likely to become revolutionary in democracies because their governments tend to change in response to their protest.

Two other conditions that encourage the mobilization of conflict groups are implied by an extension of social identity theory (Tajfel & Turner, 1979) and supported by research evidence (Brewer & Brown, 1998). One is that there be little or no opportunity for *social mobility*, that is, individual movement from the low status to the high status group. A case in point is the relationship between the dominant Tutsi and the subordinate Hutu in Rwanda. For five centuries, mixing between these groups was the rule. As Gourevitch (1998) indicates, "Hutus and Tutsis spoke the same language, followed the same religion, intermarried, lived intermingled without territorial distinctions on the same hills, sharing the same social and political culture in small chiefdoms" (pp. 47–48). But, during the colonial period, ethnic lines were reinvented, sharpened, and made impermeable. This produced what Jowitt (2001) calls "barricaded identities," which persisted into the post-colonial period, severely restricting intergroup contact and mixing. These barricade identities help explain the 1994 massacres, in which over 800,000 Tutsis and moderate Hutus were killed in just 100 days.

If social mobility is possible, it tends to dampen group mobilization "and instead encourages individuals to dissociate themselves from the group and try to gain acceptance for themselves and their immediate family in the dominant group. The belief in social mobility is enshrined in Western democratic political systems" (Hogg, 1995, p. 558) and protects these systems from severe intergroup conflict. This belief implies that if Party's outcomes are lower than Other's, it is because of Party's inferior ability. Accordingly, Party has no legitimate claim to greater reward, and no legitimate basis for making invidious comparisons.

The other condition is that the high status group seems weak or illegitimate, and hence easily challenged. If this is not the case—if the high status group seems strong and legitimate—members of low status groups are likely to engage in *social creativity* rather than mobilize for an assault on the system. Social creativity means persuading themselves that they are superior to the high status group, by pointing to dimensions in which they excel (African Americans have "soul") or by comparing themselves with even lower status groups (African Americans are superior to "white trash").

SUMMARY AND CONCLUSIONS

Conflict, defined as perceived divergence of interest, occurs when no alternative seems to exist that will satisfy the aspirations of both parties. This can occur because the parties have high aspirations or because integrative alternatives appear to be in short supply. Conflict is particularly sizable if the parties have rigid aspirations that they regard as legitimate, because this blocks a solution by yielding. Divergence of interest is often discovered as a result of relative deprivation; and the frustration engendered by relative deprivation adds vigor to the pursuit of conflict objectives.

Conditions that encourage conflict, at both the interpersonal and intergroup levels, include scarcity of resources; rapidly expanding achievement, especially if followed by a slowdown; zero-sum thinking; ambiguity about relative power; invidious comparisons; status inconsistency; distrust; and lack of normative consensus. A tendency toward intergroup conflict is produced by the mere presence of another group, because favorable intergroup comparisons are a source of self-esteem. Intergroup conflict is even more likely if group aspirations are frustrated, producing a sense of fraternalistic deprivation. (The term "group" applies to small groups, political entities, organizations, and nations and any other set of people with a common identity and a capacity for coordinated action.)

Group mobilization must take place before sets of people with common interests can become involved in conflict. Group mobilization involves developing a common group identity, producing a leadership structure, and adopting group goals in pursuit of the common interests. Group mobilization is encouraged by the capacity for intragroup communication, the availability of leadership, group legitimacy in the eyes of the broader community, perceived weakness or illegitimacy of outgroups that are seen as blocking group achievement, and the absence of social mobility. Group mobilization is hard to reverse once it has taken place. The genie is out of the bottle.

Rulers can employ three kinds of tactics to prevent the mobilization of groups that challenge their authority: interfering with intragroup communication, getting rid of potential leaders, and co-opting these leaders. Other tactics that can be used to suppress conflict are implied by the many principles discussed in this chapter. Such tactics contribute to the stability of society and hence may seem superficially attractive. But their use can easily be counterproductive. They tend to consign society to a state of affairs that is static, sometimes unjust, and often unworkable in the long run.

We turn now to strategic choice. Chapter 3 deals with the conditions that determine how Party chooses among the four strategies for coping with conflict: contending, yielding, problem solving, and avoiding.

3

Strategic Choice

--- ❖ ---

P eter Colger has to make a decision. For months he has been looking forward
to taking his two weeks of vacation at a quiet mountain lodge where he can
hunt, fish, and hike to lofty scenic overlooks. Now his wife Mary has rudely
challenged this dream. She has told him that she finds the mountains boring and
wants to go to Ocean City, Maryland, a busy seaside resort that Peter dislikes intensely. Peter must decide what strategy to employ in this controversy.

As we saw in Chapter 1, four basic strategies are available to Peter. Three of
these are active strategies, aimed at settling the conflict. He can engage in *contentious behavior* and try to lower Mary's aspirations. He can take a *problem-solving
approach* and try to find a way to go to both places or to a vacation spot that satisfies both sets of interests. Or he can *yield* to Mary's demands and agree to go to
the seashore. The fourth is a more passive approach: he can *avoid* the conflict altogether, by being inactive or withdrawing from the controversy.

This chapter examines the conditions that determine how Peter—and, more generally, anyone facing a conflict—decides among these basic strategies.

NATURE OF THE STRATEGIES

Contending refers to any effort to resolve a conflict on Party's terms without regard to Other's interests. When Party employs this strategy, it maintains its own aspirations and tries to persuade or force Other to yield. Various tactics are available to Party when it chooses this strategy. These include arguing for one's own position, making threats (in our example, perhaps to take a separate vacation if Mary does not agree to go to the mountains), and imposing penalties with the understanding that they will be withdrawn if Other concedes (for example, being cold to Mary until she agrees to his proposal). If Party is trying to reach a negotiated settlement of the controversy, contending may also involve presenting persuasive arguments, making demands that far exceed what is actually acceptable, committing itself to an "unalterable" position, or imposing a deadline. A detailed discussion of contentious tactics will be found in Chapter 4.

In contrast, *problem solving* entails an effort to identify the issues dividing the parties and to develop and move toward a solution that appeals to both sides. When Party employs this strategy, it maintains its own aspirations and tries to find a way of reconciling them with Other's aspirations. Problem solving can be joint, in which the parties discuss the issues with each other, or individual, in which one of the parties tackles the issues on its own. Various tactics are available to implement the strategy of problem solving. These include risky moves, such as conceding with the expectation of receiving a return concession, mentioning possible compromises as talking points, and revealing Party's underlying interests. They also include cautious moves, such as hinting at possible compromises, sending disavowable intermediaries to discuss the issues, communicating through back channels, and communicating through a mediator. Problem-solving tactics will be taken up in Chapter 10.

Yielding, which involves lowering Party's aspirations, need not imply total capitulation. It may also imply a partial concession. For example, Peter Colger might decide to give up his secondary goal of hiking to mountain overlooks in order to make it easier to find a mutually acceptable agreement. He could then engage in problem solving, seeking a quiet resort that permits hunting and fishing where his wife can also accomplish her major goals of spending time at a busy seaside resort.

The fourth strategy, *avoiding,* entails not engaging in the conflict. This strategy can take two broad forms, inaction and withdrawal. Party is *inactive* if it remains in contact with Other but fails to address the conflict. Thus

Peter Colger might simply say nothing about the conflict, hoping that the issue will blow over. Or, if his wife insists on talking about the vacation, he could employ evasive tactics, such as "speaking about (the) issue in abstruse terms, making distracting or procedural remarks, or asking unfocused and conflict-irrelevant questions" (Van de Vliert, 1997, p. 33). While inaction permits future reopening of a discussion or fight, withdrawal terminates it. Thus Peter Colger could withdraw from the conflict by saying that he does not want to talk any more and arranging to go on his own vacation or to take no vacation at all.[1]

CHOOSING A STRATEGY

There are trade-offs among the four basic strategies, in the sense that choosing one of them makes choosing the others less likely. Avoiding is totally incompatible with the other three strategies, since the other three involve one or another kind of effort to resolve the conflict. Though sometimes found in combination with each other (Van de Vliert, 1997), contending, yielding, and problem solving are partially incompatible with each other, for three reasons. First, these strategies are alternative means of moving toward the same end, settling the conflict. If one of them is ruled out by the circumstances, Party is more likely to employ the others. Second, these strategies require different psychological orientations; for example, it does not seem quite right to try to push Other around while also yielding to or working with Other. Third, these strategies tend to send out contradictory signals to Other. Yielding often implies weakness, which is incompatible with putting effective pressure on Other. Contending may undermine Other's trust, reducing the likelihood of effective problem solving.

Most of the rest of this chapter is devoted to four sets of theoretical notions about the conditions that affect choice among the basic strategies. The first, which is summarized in a *dual concern model,* traces strategic choice to the relative strength of concern about Party's and Other's outcomes. The second, which we call the *perceived feasibility perspective,* attributes this choice to the perceived likelihood of success and the cost or risk of enacting the various strategies. The third concerns the impact of

---

[1] Avoiding is not a pure strategy, because it favors the status quo. Hence, it is tantamount to yielding in the hands of a party who is challenging the status quo and to contending in the hands of a party who is favored by the status quo. For example, suppose I am trying to persuade you to lend me a book. If I become inactive or withdraw, this is usually a sign that I have given up, that is, yielded. If you become inactive or withdraw, this is tantamount to a contentious tactic that will deny me the book. Given all this, it should be no surprise that avoiding is found to be much more popular in the eyes of those favored by the status quo than those opposing it (Peirce et al., 1993).

blame direction, and the fourth the impact of culture on strategic choice. These theoretical notions are complementary in the sense that each deals with issues ignored by the others.

A good deal of evidence will be cited in support of these theoretical notions, much of it derived from laboratory experiments on simulated negotiation. *Negotiation*, a form of conflict behavior, occurs when two or more parties try to resolve a divergence of interest by means of conversation. Laboratory studies of negotiation typically place experimental participants (often college students) in a simulated negotiation setting and manipulate variables that are thought to be relevant. Careful measurements of reactions to these variables are taken.[2]

THE DUAL CONCERN MODEL

The dual concern model appears in Figure 3.1. It postulates two types of concerns: *concern about Party's own outcomes (also called "self-concern")*, which is shown on the horizontal axis, and *concern about Other's outcomes (also called "other-concern")*, which is shown on the vertical axis. These concerns are portrayed as ranging from indifference (at the zero point where the two axes come together) to high concern.[3]

The two concerns in this model are defined as follows: Self-concern means that Party places importance on its own interests in the realm under dispute. When Party is strongly self-concerned, its aspirations tend to be rigid and high and it is quite resistant to yielding.[4] Other-concern implies placing importance on Other's interests—feeling responsible for the quality of Other's outcomes. This concern is sometimes *genuine*— Party has an intrinsic interest in Other's welfare. But it is more often *instrumental* (strategic): Party helps Other in order to advance its own interests. For example, Party may be helpful in order to ingratiate itself with a powerful Other.

The dual concern model makes the following predictions about the antecedents of strategic choice: Problem solving is encouraged when Party has a strong concern about both its own and Other's outcomes. Yielding is

---

[2] Detailed discussion of this kind of research can be found in Pruitt (1981), Pruitt & Carnevale (1993), and Rubin & Brown (1975).

[3] Although not shown in Figure 3.1, it is theoretically possible for Party to have negative concern about Other's outcomes and even about its own outcomes. In other words, we might have extended the coordinates in the figure downward and to the left. A few points about negative concerns will be made in this chapter, and we will have more to say about them when we discuss escalation in Chapters 5 to 8. See McClintock (1988) for a discussion of negative concerns about Party's and Other's outcomes.

[4] See Kelley et al. (1967) for a sophisticated discussion of the concept of resistance to yielding.

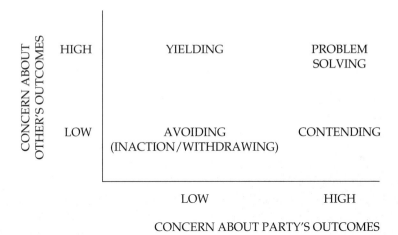

FIGURE 3.1
The dual concern model.

encouraged when Party has a strong concern only about Other's outcomes. Contending is encouraged when Party has a strong concern only about its own outcomes. Avoiding—and inaction, in particular—is encouraged when Party has a weak concern about both its own and Other's outcomes.

Some versions of the dual concern model (Blake & Mouton, 1964; Rahim, 1983; Thomas, 1976) include a fifth strategy, "compromising," which involves an effort to find a middle ground between the two parties' demands—a fifty-fifty solution. This is located at the center of diagrams like Figure 3.1, equidistant from the other four strategies. In our view, this is not a distinct strategy but a kind of "lazy" problem solving, involving a half-hearted attempt to find a solution serving both parties' interests.[5]

Thomas (1976) notes that the two concerns in the dual concern model are often erroneously reduced to a single dimension, with selfishness (self-concern) on one end and cooperativeness (other-concern) on the other. This is an incorrect simplification, because it is clear that both concerns can be strong at the same time. Party can be both selfish and cooperative (leading it to engage in problem solving). By postulating dual

---

[5] The dual concern model is sometimes presented with the axes rotated 90 degrees. An "integrative" axis runs from avoiding to problem solving, and a "distributive" axis runs from yielding to contending. As Van de Vliert (1997) points out, this provides a useful descriptive vocabulary but does not help explain why people choose one strategy over another, as does the dual concern model shown in Figure 3.1.

concerns, we are forced to distinguish between two ways of cooperating with Other, yielding and problem solving. These were not sufficiently separated in a prior theory of strategic choice (Deutsch, 1973), which proposed only a single motivational dimension ranging from competition to cooperation. Postulating dual concerns also forces us to distinguish between two ways of advancing Party's own interests, contending and problem solving.

The Dual Concern Model as a Theory of Conflict Style

The dual concern model was originally developed as a theory of individual differences in conflict style (Blake & Mouton, 1964; Filley, 1975; Rahim, 1983, 1986; Thomas, 1976). Conflict style is the way a person most commonly deals with conflict (Pruitt & Carnevale, 1993). The dual concern model implies that conflict style is determined by the strength of two independent individual difference variables: self-concern and other-concern.

If conflict styles exist, people should show some consistency in the strategies they employ across various conflict situations, and that has been found in two studies (Sternberg & Dobson, 1987; Sternberg & Soriano, 1984). A number of questionnaires have been designed to measure these consistencies (Kilmann & Thomas, 1977; Lawrence & Lorsch, 1967; Rahim & Magner, 1995), allowing us to determine, to some degree, whether a person generally favors problem solving, contending, yielding, avoiding, or compromising.

Other studies have performed a multidimensional scaling analysis on people's self-report about the methods they use in dealing with conflict (Van de Vliert, 1990; Van de Vliert & Prein, 1989). The findings of these studies are largely consistent with the predictions of the dual concern model: a two-dimensional solution is found, with the largest distances between contending and yielding, and between problem solving and avoiding. The only discrepancy from the dual concern model, as shown in Figure 3.1, is that yielding and avoiding are closer to each other than problem solving and contending.[6]

The Dual Concern Model as a Theory of the Impact of Conditions

The dual concern model also serves as a theory about the impact of various conditions on strategic choice. This theory assumes that an individual will find all of the strategies attractive at one time or another, depending

---

[6] To see this, look at Pruitt & Carnevale, 1993, p. 106.

on the circumstances. Thus Peter Colger would adopt a contentious approach if he was very anxious to hunt and fish (high self-concern) and considered his wife's doubts about the mountains "silly" (low other-concern). He would engage in problem solving if he was very anxious to hunt and fish (high self-concern) but was also determined to please his wife (high other-concern), either because he loved her or because she would make his life miserable if he did not. He would yield to his wife's preferences if his main concern was to please his wife (low self-concern and high other-concern). He would take an avoiding approach if he lost his desire for a vacation and was not concerned about pleasing his wife (low self-concern and low other-concern).

The notion that conditions often influence strategic preference is not incompatible with the notion that there are individual differences in preferred conflict style. Peter Colger may prefer a contentious approach for dealing with people in general (style) but may adopt a problem solving stance with his wife because of her negative reactions when he tries to push her around (conditions).

Some of the conditions that affect strength of self-concern and other-concern will now be discussed.

Conditions Affecting Self-Concern   High self-concern inclines parties toward contending and problem solving and away from yielding and avoiding. The strength of self-concern can be traced to a number of determinants. One is the importance of the interests at stake (Druckman, 1994; Druckman et al., 1988). As noted in Chapter 2, important interests produce high, rigid aspirations, which is the same thing as having strong self-concern. For example, suppose that employee A has an extremely taxing job and hence needs a lot of rest and relaxation during vacation and employee B does not. If management proposes to both employees that they scrap their vacation plans, A is likely to defend his or her plans by means of contentious or problem-solving activities, whereas B may yield or avoid the conflict. In addition, when deeply felt principles of right and wrong underlie Party's preferences, self-concern is likely to be particularly strong and yielding or avoiding particularly unlikely (Pruitt, 1995).

Another determinant of Party's self-concern in any one realm is the importance of outcomes in other realms. Party does not have an infinite amount of time or energy, so it cannot pursue all of its interests with equal intensity. Hence, a strong concern about one issue can easily lead to a weak concern about others. For example, an employee may be indifferent about getting a vacation because of being wrapped up in job-related issues, a political campaign, or some other absorbing activity.

Party's concern about its own outcomes is also affected by the way these outcomes are framed. When Party focuses on its potential gains in a conflict, it employs a positive frame; when it focuses on its potential losses, it employs a negative frame.[7] It has been found that negotiators with a positive frame make more concessions than those with a negative frame (Neale & Bazerman, 1985; Schweitzer & DeChurch, 2001; Thompson, 1990a). Seeing outcomes as various degrees of *gain* makes it easy to yield ground, but seeing them as various degrees of *loss* highlights the potential costs of doing so. This suggests that negative framing produces more self-concern than positive framing.

Fear of confrontation causes self-concern to diminish. This is because contending and joint problem solving entail confrontation. This fear is a personality predisposition for some people and a product of conditions for others. An example of the latter is when Party is attracted to (or dependent on) Other but is uncertain about Other's feelings, a circumstance that is especially common at the beginning of a relationship when people are getting to know each other. Party is likely to avoid confrontation with Other, and Other may well reciprocate.[8] Research on newly formed romantic couples suggests that such sentiments tend to block all forms of assertiveness, including both contentious and problem-solving behavior (Fry et al., 1983).

Self-concern in Groups   Self-concern is also found in intergroup conflict, where it takes the form of concern about a group's outcomes. Especially strong concern about group outcomes is found in cohesive groups whose members are highly identified with one another because they share a similar life situation and discuss their common fate with one another. This is particularly likely when the members of such groups regard themselves as part of a broader social movement, making common cause with similar groups in other locations (Kriesberg, 1982).

When the parties are groups or organizations, the actual conflict behavior is usually carried out by representatives (e.g., in a labor-management dispute). Druckman (1994) finds that negotiators who are representatives tend to be more reluctant to yield than are individuals negotiating on their own behalf. This is because they are trying to please their constituents and typically view the latter as nonconciliatory. The effect disappears in those infrequent cases where the constituent is known to have a conciliatory bias (Benton & Druckman, 1974; Tjosvold, 1977).

Other studies show that representatives are especially reluctant to yield when they are anxious to please their constituents, such as when

---

[7] For example, suppose the workers demand $16 per hour, while management insists on $12 per hour in a labor dispute. One option would be "splitting the difference," that is, agreement on $14. If the workers see this as a $2 loss (since $14 is $2 less than their original demand), they are employing a negative frame. In contrast, if they see the option of $14 as a $2 gain (since $14 is $2 more than management's initial offer), they are employing a positive frame.

[8] Situations such as this are said to involve "false cohesiveness" (Longley & Pruitt, 1980).

they have low status in their groups (Kogan et al., 1972), are distrusted by their constituents (Wall, 1975), value continued association with the group (Klimoski, 1972), or have female as opposed to male constituents (Pruitt et al., 1986). All of these conditions can be viewed as increasing representatives' concern about the outcomes of their group.

Accountability to constituents has much the same effect. Representatives are accountable to the extent that they must report the results of a negotiation to powerful constituents. Accountable representatives are especially reluctant to yield (Druckman, 1994), suggesting high concern about own-group outcomes. As a result, they are particularly likely to adopt a contentious or problem-solving approach (Ben-Yoav & Pruitt, 1984b; Neale, 1984).

Conditions Affecting Other-Concern   High other-concern inclines parties toward yielding and problem solving and away from contending and avoiding. As mentioned earlier, other-concern takes two basic forms: genuine concern, based on an intrinsic interest in Other's welfare, and instrumental concern, aimed at advancing Party's own interests. There is an important difference between the two. Because instrumental concern has the aim of impressing Other, it is stronger when Other is more concerned about its own outcomes. By contrast, genuine concern aims at serving Other, regardless of Other's degree of self-interest.

Genuine other-concern is fostered by various kinds of *interpersonal bonds,* including friendship or love (Clark & Mills, 1979; Zubek et al., 1992), perceived similarity (Hornstein, 1976), and kinship or common group identity (Brewer & Kramer, 1986; Fisher, 1990). This is probably because interpersonal bonds induce *empathy* with the other party, a state of mind that produces helping behavior (Batson, 1998). Other sources of empathy include actively putting oneself into Other's shoes and hearing sympathetic, humanizing information about Other. Genuine other-concern is also fostered by having a *positive mood*, which may result from succeeding in an important task, getting a small gift, eating good food, hearing a humorous remark, and so on. A positive mood has been found to encourage cooperation (Baron, 1990; Carnevale & Isen, 1986) and helping behavior (Isen & Levin, 1972; Salovey et al., 1991).[9]

Instrumental other-concern is common whenever Party sees itself as dependent on Other—when Other is seen as able to provide rewards and penalties. An example is the expectation of future interaction, which has been shown to encourage concession making (Gruder, 1971) and problem

---

[9] Paradoxically, some kinds of negative moods such as guilt have also been shown to enhance helping behavior (Carlson & Miller, 1987; Cialdini & Kenrick, 1976). One explanation for this is that helping someone is instrumental to ridding Party of its bad mood (Carlson & Miller, 1987).

solving (Ben-Yoav & Pruitt, 1984a, b). Dependence leads Party to conclude that it must build or maintain a relationship with Other.[10]

It is useful to distinguish between *positive* dependence, where Other is able to provide rewards, and *negative* dependence, where other can only provide penalties. There is evidence that people are more cooperative when they are positively dependent on Other than when they are negatively dependent (Pruitt, 1967, 1970; Van de Vliert, 1997). This is probably because negative dependence encourages fear and resentment and can lead to hard feelings if Other imposes its penalties. These emotions tend to neutralize other-concern.

Dependence is by no means a one-way street. *Mutual* dependence is quite common and can encourage either mutual yielding or mutual problem solving.

For Party to be aware of its dependence on Other, it must think about the future, to experience what Axelrod (1984) calls the "shadow of the future." This point is important for understanding conflict because people embroiled in escalating conflicts often lose awareness of the future. They concentrate so hard on winning in the present that they lose track of the importance of maintaining good relations with Other. In such situations, future perspective can be regained in a number of ways. One is to take time out—to become disengaged from the controversy for a while so that one can regain perspective on it.

Although bonds and dependencies usually foster other-concern, under certain conditions they can produce exactly the opposite reaction: antagonism toward Other and the use of contentious tactics. This reaction is especially likely when people to whom we are bonded—friends, relatives, people we admire—fail to fulfill their minimum obligations or severely frustrate us (Bersheid, 1983; Fitness, 2001). We feel that these people owe us preferential treatment; hence, we become especially angry and aggressive. A similar reaction occurs when people on whom we are dependent are unresponsive to our needs (Gruder, 1971; Tjosvold, 1977). The ordinary reaction to dependence is concern about Other's outcomes. But if Other is perceived as taking advantage of our concern, it often seems necessary to reverse gears and retaliate.

Research Support for the Dual Concern Model

Many laboratory experiments on negotiation have been done to test the dual concern model as a theory of the impact of conditions. A meta-analysis that took an overview of seventeen of these studies found strong support

---

[10] Rusbult and her associates (Drigotas & Rusbult, 1992; Rusbult et al., 1991) call the desire to build or maintain a relationship "commitment" and have shown that it is central to accommodation in marital conflict.

for the model (De Dreu et al., 2000). In study after study, high self-concern coupled with high other-concern led to problem solving. And high self-concern coupled with low other-concern led to contending, as predicted by the model.

One study in this meta-analysis is particularly interesting because it shows the practical value of the dual concern model (Ben-Yoav & Pruitt, 1984b). The setting for the study was a simulated wholesale market in which representatives of two companies negotiated over the prices of several products. Managers oversaw their activities. The results showed that the representatives were most likely to employ problem solving and to reap high benefits for their companies when they were highly accountable to their managers (high self-concern) and also expected to continue dealing with the other negotiator in the future (high other-concern). By contrast they were most likely to employ contentious tactics and reap low benefits when they were highly accountable to their managers (high self-concern) and *did not* expect to have further contact with the other negotiator (low other-concern). The broader implications of this finding are that the best way to organize negotiation is to make negotiators highly accountable, by requiring them to report back to powerful supervisors, but also to encourage them to develop lasting relationships with their counterparts on the other side. Note that we are talking here about high accountability not close supervision; the study shows that negotiators should be required to report back the *results* of their negotiations not the detailed *methods* they used to achieve these results. The problem with close supervision is that it can erode innovation and thus block the discovery of integrative solutions that provide benefit to both sides.

The strong support that has been found for the dual concern model does not mean that this model provides a full explanation of strategic choice but only that it helps understand a fair number of decisions about what strategy to employ. Multiple causation is the name of the game in social science, and most theories embody only a few of the variables that impact a phenomenon to be explained. We will now consider three other perspectives that further cast light on strategic choice: the perceived feasibility perspective and the perspectives of blame direction and cultural differences.

THE PERCEIVED FEASIBILITY PERSPECTIVE

Choice among the three active strategies is also a matter of *perceived feasibility*—the extent to which a strategy seems capable of achieving Party's goals at an acceptable cost and risk. Considerations of feasibility supplement those specified by the dual concern model. The dual concern model indicates the strategy that is *preferred* in a particular circumstance. But for a strategy actually to be *adopted*, it must also be seen as minimally feasible.

If not, another strategy will be chosen, even if it is less consistent with the current combination of concerns.

For example, consider a Party that is mainly concerned about its own outcomes. Contending is Party's preferred strategy because this strategy holds the promise of getting something for nothing. But problem solving is a close second if the contentious approach appears unworkable or too costly. This is because problem solving also serves self-interest, though at a cost in helping Other that Party would otherwise prefer not to pay.

This line of reasoning helps explain a two-step sequence of strategies that is often found in negotiation (Pruitt, 1981). The parties start by advancing proposals that are favorable to their own interests and defending these proposals by persuasive arguments and other contentious tactics. But if an agreement is not reached, they will often shift to problem solving and try to find an option that satisfies both of their interests. Problem solving is adopted when it becomes clear that contentious behavior is unworkable.

The next three sections deal with the perceived feasibility of the three active strategies: problem solving, contending, and yielding.

Perceived Feasibility of Problem Solving

Perceived Common Ground   Problem solving seems more feasible the greater the *perceived common ground (PCG)*. PCG is Party's assessment of the likelihood of finding an alternative that satisfies the aspirations of Party and Other. The more likely it seems that such an alternative can be found, the more feasible problem solving appears to be. PCG is greater (1) the lower Party's own aspirations, (2) the lower Other's aspirations as perceived by Party, and (3) the more integrative solutions (alternatives favorable to both parties) that are available or can probably be devised.[11]

PCG is the mirror image of conflict as defined earlier. As PCG goes up, conflict, in the sense of perceived divergence of interest, goes down.

The graphs in Figure 3.2 further explain PCG. The horizontal axis in these graphs maps Party's own benefits; the vertical axis, Party's perception of Other's benefits. The large dots refer to known alternatives, the medium-sized dots to alternatives that seem potentially discoverable, and the smallest dots to long shots. As before, the location of a point in the space shows the perceived value of that alternative to the two parties.

---

[11] The reader may be surprised to learn that lower aspirations make problem solving seem more feasible. Superficially, this seems inconsistent with the point made earlier that low self-concern (which produces low aspirations) reduces the likelihood of problem solving. However, these points are not contradictory. We are talking about two countervailing forces that are simultaneously activated when self-concern declines. The one makes problem solving seem more *feasible*, and the other (by permitting the strategy of yielding) makes problem solving seem less *necessary*.

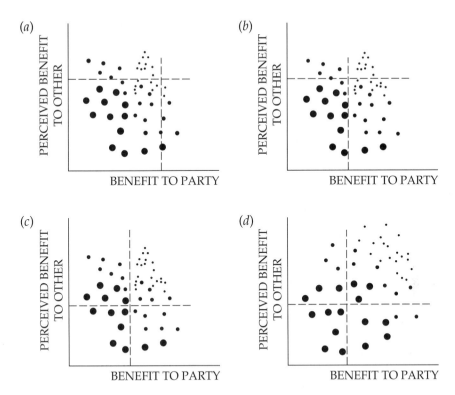

FIGURE 3.2

Four levels of perceived common ground (PCG), ranging from none in *a* to high in *d*.

The vertical dashed lines refer to Party's own aspirations and the horizontal dashed lines to the aspirations Party perceives Other to hold.

PCG is greater the more points there are to the northeast (above and to the right) of the intersection of the aspiration lines and the darker these points are. In Figure 3.2, PCG is greater in graph *b* than in graph *a* because Party's own aspirations are lower. It is greater in *c* than in *b* because Other's perceived aspirations are also lower. It is greater in *d* than in *c* because there appears to be a richer set of available alternatives—that is, integrative solutions seem easier to find (as shown by the fact that the darker points are farther from the origin in the northeast direction).

A number of conditions produce greater PCG and hence contribute to Party's choice of problem solving:

- *Faith in own problem-solving ability.* Party may be a good communicator and/or may understand how to devise mutually beneficial alternatives. This will lead it to see considerable integrative potential in almost any situation and to favor problem solving. Less capable parties will tend to view conflict as more intractable and to adopt strategies of yielding or contending rather than problem solving.

- *Positive-Sum Thinking.* Positive-sum thinking is the view that the two parties' interests are not totally opposed and hence that problem solving is feasible. This is the opposite of zero-sum thinking, which was discussed in Chapter 2.
- *Momentum.* Momentum refers to prior success at reaching agreement in the current controversy. The more frequent and recent such successes have been, the greater will be Party's faith that success can happen again and hence that problem solving is feasible. Huber et al. (1986) have shown that scheduling easier issues earlier in a negotiation can encourage momentum, making it easier to solve the difficult later issues.
- *Availability of a third party.* Third parties often serve as communication links between the parties, coordinating movement toward compromise or helping to develop integrative solutions. Their availability should make problem solving seem more feasible.
- *Other's perceived readiness for problem solving.* It is risky to engage in unilateral problem solving, because Other may regard it as a sign of weakness and adopt a more contentious approach. Hence problem solving seems more feasible to the extent that Other seems ready to participate in it.

Trust   For Party to embark on problem solving requires a belief that there is some flexibility in Other's position, that Other may be ready to accept a reasonable solution. Otherwise, there is no point in adopting this strategy; the strategy seems infeasible. One source of this belief is trust, the perception that Other is concerned about Party's interests.

Although trust allows Party to adopt a problem-solving strategy, it is no guarantee that this strategy will be adopted. Indeed, trust can sometimes have quite the opposite effect, encouraging high, rigid aspirations defended by contentious behavior. This happens when Party has no intrinsic interest in Other's welfare and comes to regard Other as a pushover. Trust then amounts to a perception of weakness.

To avoid such a perception, Other must appear to be *firm* as well as trustworthy—ready to cooperate, *but only if Party is cooperative.* Evidence for this comes from several negotiation studies that examined Party's response to helpful actions by Other, which presumably generated trust. Party was only willing to reciprocate these actions if Other also showed signs of firmness, that is, (a) had been unwilling to make unilateral concessions in the past (Komorita & Esser, 1975; McGillicuddy et al., 1984), (b) had been unyielding or competitive in the past (Harford & Solomon,

1967; Hilty & Carnevale, 1993), (c) had high threat capacity (Michener et al., 1975; Tjosvold & Okun, 1976), or (d) had tough constituents (Wall, 1977).

Trust develops in a number of ways. It is encouraged by a perception that Other has a positive attitude toward Party, is similar to Party, or is dependent on Party. As an example of the latter point, Solomon (1960) has shown that trust is greater when Party sees itself as having a capacity to punish Other for failing to cooperate. Trust is also likely to develop when Other is a member of Party's own group (Kramer & Brewer, 1984; Yamagishi & Sato, 1986) or when Party expects that third parties will punish Other for being uncooperative (Yamagishi, 1986). Another source of trust is Other's helpful or cooperative behavior, especially if it has occurred recently (Kelley & Stahelski, 1970). Furthermore, trust tends to develop when *Party* has been helpful toward *Other* (Loomis, 1959), since people often assume that others will reciprocate their helpful behavior.

Perceived Risk of Engaging in Problem Solving   Even if PCG and trust exist, Party may fail to adopt a problem-solving strategy. This is because problem-solving behavior poses three possible risks: image loss, position loss, and information loss (Pruitt, 1981). The first of these, *image loss*, is a perception that Party is weak in capability or determination, and thus ready to make extensive concessions. This perception, a possible result of Party's conciliatory behavior, encourages Other to employ a contentious strategy in an effort to pressure Party to make those concessions.[12] The second risk, *position loss*, is a perception that Party has conceded from a previous position. Other may develop such a perception if Party makes tentative suggestions of possible changes in position, a common tactic in problem solving. The third risk, *information loss*, occurs when Party reveals its underlying interests or lower limit. Other can use this information to gain an advantage.

Perceived Feasibility of Contending

The feasibility of contending is a function of Party's apparent capabilities and Other's apparent weaknesses. Does Party have good arguments? Does Other have good counterarguments? Is Party adept at arguing its case? How effective is Other as a debater? Can Party punish Other? How good are Other's defenses against such tactics?

Capabilities such as these are sometimes lumped together under the familiar concepts of *power* and *counterpower*. These concepts have some merit in that they allow us to make a few broad generalizations. For example, it is usually the case that more powerful parties have higher aspirations and

---

[12] To counteract image loss, Party must appear firm as well as conciliatory.

make greater use of contentious tactics, regardless of the source of their power. But there is a tendency to overuse these concepts in social science theory, making facile generalizations with little real meaning. The problem is that there are many kinds of power, each with a different set of properties (French & Raven, 1959; Raven & Rubin, 1983).

Contending also seems more feasible when Other appears to lack determination, to have low self-concern or resistance to yielding. If Other's aspirations seem relatively easy to dislodge, contentious behavior gets a boost. By contrast, it is useless to put pressure on an opponent who has extremely strong feelings, has powerful and resolute constituents, or has already yielded as much as possible. Moreover, there is no point in pressuring an opponent who has a more attractive alternative away from the negotiation table.[13] Other tactics, such as yielding and problem solving, are likely to seem more feasible.

The points just made imply that contentious behavior is often self-liquidating, a victim of both failure and success. If contentious behavior fails, this indicates that Other's resistance is greater than originally thought, so Party will abandon the tactic. If it succeeds and Other yields, Other's resistance to further yielding is likely to grow because Other will come closer and closer to its limit. Again, Party must eventually abandon the tactic.

Research suggests that contending is more likely the greater the size of the conflict (Deutsch, 1973). The higher and more rigid are the parties' aspirations and the less promising are the available alternatives, the more likely is Party to elect this approach. This is because sizable conflicts make yielding and problem solving seem infeasible. With the parties so far apart, there is no way these strategies can yield an acceptable agreement. This leaves contending as the only feasible active strategy. Conflict size also enhances the frustration Party is likely to feel about its inability to achieve its goals, further strengthening the push toward contending.

Perceived Risk of Engaging in Contentious Behavior   Contentious behavior, particularly in its more severe forms, runs the risk of alienating Other and starting a conflict spiral. There is also some danger of third party censure. Such considerations may deter contentious behavior, particularly when Party is dependent on Other or on third parties that are concerned about Other's welfare. Party must also be careful about not developing a reputation for being overly contentious in its dealings with others. Research shows that parties with such reputations can hurt themselves because others will tend to avoid them or to engage in strictly contentious behavior when dealing with them (Tinsley et al., 2001).

---

[13] This is the concept of BATNA (best alternative to negotiated agreement), as described by Fisher et al. (1991). If Other has a strong BATNA, contending may drive Other to take that best alternative.

Perceived Feasibility of Yielding

The success of problem solving and of contending are sometimes in doubt because they depend on Other's responses, which are not under Party's control. In contrast, it is much easier for Party to yield, because this strategy relies primarily on Party's own behavior. This does not mean that yielding is always a feasible or effective strategy.

Time pressure has been found to encourage yielding (Pruitt & Drews, 1969; Smith et al., 1982). This is probably because yielding is the fastest way to move toward agreement. There are two sources of time pressure: cost per unit time of engaging in the controversy and closeness to a deadline. In negotiation, time pressure may be due to any cost of continued negotiation, including time lost from other pursuits, the expense of maintaining negotiators in the field, or rapid deterioration of the object under dispute (such as fruits and vegetables). Deadlines are points in the future at which significant costs are likely to be experienced if the controversy has not been resolved. At a strike deadline, the union pulls workers out of the factory; at a hiring deadline, the job offer is withdrawn. The closer Party is to a deadline and the larger the penalty for passing that deadline without agreement, the greater the time pressure and hence the more likely Party is to yield.

Perceived Risk of Yielding   Because it can be seen as a sign of weakness, yielding may result in image loss to Party. This may be costly as it encourages Other to use a contentious strategy; Other may jack up the pressure in an effort to lower Party's aspirations. Furthermore, the image of being weak also invites exploitation from future adversaries, who come to view Party as a "pushover." Fear of image loss discourages yielding.[14]

BLAME DIRECTION AND STRATEGIC CHOICE

When people experience a negative event, they usually want to know why it has occurred (Shaver, 1985). Conflict is no exception. People ask attributional questions such as, "Who is responsible for this conflict?" and "Who is to blame?" (Orvis et al., 1976; Shaver, 1985). The answer to these questions can direct the finger of blame in one of three directions: the other party (other-blame), themselves (self-blame), or both parties (mutual-blame).

---

[14] Party's early yielding can sometimes be costly to *Other* as well as to Party. One reason for this is that early yielding can lead to premature settlement, before the parties have had a chance to search for mutually beneficial (integrative) solutions. Another reason is that Party's early yielding can make Other so contentious that integrative solutions are not found or agreement is not reached (Pruitt & Carnevale, 1993).

Using the conflict between Peter and Mary Colger described earlier, we will examine how the direction of blame impacts strategic choice.

Other-Blame

A prevailing, self-serving tendency in conflict is to blame the other side for the conflict (Finkel, 2001; Morris et al., 1999; Sillars et al., 2000). When this happens, strategic choice is likely to go in the direction of contending. Consider what would happen if Peter felt that Mary was being selfish, if he thought: "I've been going through some stressful times at work and need a quiet place to relax. But, does she care about me? No! She always forces me to do what she wants to do." This would probably lead him to press for his own ideas and not be concerned about hers, in other words, to act contentiously.

There are three main reasons why other-blame inclines Party toward contending. One is that blame is likely to cause Party to adopt a zero-sum perspective—to think that "either she wins or I win" (Gelfand et al., 2001; Pinkley, 1990; Sillars, 1981). Such a perspective is found to encourage contending (Thompson & Hrebec, 1996). Another reason is that other-blame often generates a sense that one has been unfairly treated at the hands of Other (Finkel, 2001). Such feelings offer a handy rationalization for taking contentious actions (Miller, 2001). Finally, other-blame produces anger (Lazarus, 1991), which encourages contending of a particularly harsh kind (Averill, 1983; Berkowitz, 1993). In Deutsch's (2000b) words, "Blaming tends to be inflaming" (p. 52).[15]

Self-Blame

Though blame for the conflict tends to be laid at the door of the other party, self-blame is not uncommon. Peter may fault himself for creating the unpleasant confrontation with Mary. Rather than asking her about her preferences, he simply announced that they should go to a mountain lodge for their long-awaited vacation. Hence he blames the conflict on his own selfish, uncaring behavior.

Research suggests that self-blame is often motivated by a desire to maintain a sense of control over events (Andrews & Brewin, 1990; Bulman & Wortman, 1977). Blaming oneself rather than others makes one feel less vulnerable to negative events over which one has little control.

Self-blame inclines people toward yielding. This is at least in part because self-blame tends to evoke guilt (Lazarus, 1991) and a sense that one

---

[15] Note that the causal link between the perception of injustice and anger is bidirectional in that the perception of injustice can lead to anger and that anger can lead to the perception of injustice. See Miller (2001) for a thorough coverage of this issue.

must atone for one's misdeeds (Freedman et al., 1967; Konoske et al., 1979). Thus Peter may agree to Mary's proposal, in order to unburden himself from guilty feelings.[16]

Though Party may blame itself when conflict is mild, research suggests that blame almost always falls on Other when conflict is intense (Sillars, 1981). There are two main reasons for this (Brehm, 1992): One is ego-defensive, a product of the self-serving attributional bias. The larger the conflict, the more blame must be allocated. Since it is painful for Party to blame itself, it becomes increasingly hard to do so as conflict intensifies. The other reason is perceptual, a product of differences in perspective between actors and observers (Fiske & Taylor, 1991). In a conflict spiral, Party is more likely to perceive that it is reacting to Other's provocative behavior than that Other is reacting to Party's. This is because Party is well situated to see the sources of its own behavior but not so well situated to see the sources of Other's behavior. It is hard to peer into Other's head. Hence, as escalation develops and conflict becomes more intense, Party finds more and more evidence that this is through no fault of its own.

Mutual-Blame

When the parties feel that both of them stand liable for the conflict, they are likely to take a problem-solving approach. One explanation for this is that mutual-blame encourages a win-win perspective, rather than a win-lose (zero-sum) perspective (Gelfand et al., 2001; Pinkley, 1990).[17] People with a win-win perspective tend to recognize a compatibility of interests. They perceive common ground between themselves and their opponent, which as noted earlier, increases the likelihood of problem solving. Another reason is that compared to other-blame and self-blame, mutual-blame is less likely to generate a sense of unfairness, anger, guilt, or shame, all of which encourage strategies other than problem solving.[18]

---

[16] In some cases, self-blame may evoke shame rather than guilt and cause Party to adopt the strategy of avoiding. According to Lazarus (1991), when feeling guilty, people are likely to make amends for the harm that they have done (e.g., by yielding). But, when feeling shame, they are likely to "hide, to avoid having [their] personal failure observed by anyone, especially someone who is personally important" (p. 244). This implies an avoidance strategy.

[17] Pinkley (1990) and Gelfand et al. (2001) use the term "compromise" for a win-win perspective and the term "win" for a win-lose perspective.

[18] A fourth possibility is blaming someone or something external to both parties. Peter may blame the conflict on his company's stingy vacation policy. If his company would allow its employees to take a longer paid vacation, he and Mary could go to both the mountains and the shore. Though there is no evidence on this matter, it seems reasonable to assume that such a perception will lead to problem-solving behavior, since both parties can be seen as having a common enemy.

CULTURE AND STRATEGIC CHOICE: INDIVIDUALISM VS. COLLECTIVISM

Broadly defined, culture is the set of shared and enduring meanings, values, and beliefs that characterize national, ethnic, or other groups (Faure & Rubin, 1993). It is an important determinant of people's attitudes, self-construal, and behavior, and hence their strategic choice.[19]

Culture varies from society to society. One dimension along which it varies is individualism vs. collectivism (Hofstede, 1980; Triandis, 1995). Members of individualist cultures tend to view themselves as independent of each other, and their personal goals and interests take precedence over group goals and interests. Members of collectivist cultures tend to view themselves as interdependent with others, and group goals and interests take precedence over personal goals and interests (Markus & Kitayama, 1991). Individualist cultures, such as found in North America, place great value on independence, personal achievement, rights, freedom, and equity, whereas collectivist cultures, such as found in East Asia, place great value on interdependence, group welfare, group harmony, and equality.

The rest of this section concerns the impact of collectivism and individualism on strategic choice. We lean heavily on studies that compared citizens of the United States and Canada to people from the three largest collectivist societies in East Asia: China (including Hong Kong), Japan, and Korea.

Confrontation vs. Indirection

A marked difference between these two types of cultures is that individualists strongly prefer confronting conflict rather than avoiding it (Ohbuchi et al., 1999). Their initial approach to conflict tends to be one of contending, assertively arguing for the merits of their position and challenging the other side's claims (Keating et al., 1994). If that does not work, they are likely to turn to joint problem solving, asking directly for information about the other side's interests and proposing new ideas that may be jointly acceptable.[20]

---

[19] For the broader impact of culture on conflict processes, see Avruch (1998), Cohen (1991), and Faure & Rubin (1993).

[20] Individualists' inclination toward these vigorous, open forms of problem solving may explain the research finding that they are more likely to reach integrative solutions than are collectivists. For example, Tinsley & Brett (2001) have found that compared to Hong Kong Chinese, Americans resolved a greater number of issues and came up with more integrative solutions. However, research findings are not uniform on this cultural difference. Tjosvold and his colleagues (Tjosvold et al., 2000, 2001) have shown that collectivists can and will also adopt vigorous, open, joint forms of problem solving and reach integrative solutions when they feel that their overt discussions and demands will not jeopardize harmony. These inconsistent findings indicate the need for further research and for meta-analytic syntheses of research, as Tinsley & Pillutla (1998) have suggested.

By contrast, collectivists tend to avoid dealing with conflict if they can, and have an aversion to confrontation, especially of a contentious kind. Indeed, Japanese students have been found to avoid confrontation even when they consider confrontative strategies to be more effective in handling their conflicts (Ohbuchi & Takahashi, 1994). These preferences do not mean that they are free of conflict. Conflict often arises and requires their attention, just as in other societies. However, collectivists differ from individualists in the ways that they go about addressing conflict.

While avoiding open (joint) problem solving, collectivists do engage in indirect, covert problem solving (Gelfand et al., 2001), such as working through intermediaries.[21] They are quite likely to ask third parties to handle their conflicts, particularly high status third parties. Thus, Tse et al. (1994) found that Chinese managers (collectivists) were more likely to consult with their superiors in a conflict than were Canadian managers (individualists). Similarly, Tinsley and her colleagues (Tinsley, 1997; Tinsley & Brett, 2001; Tinsley & Pillutla, 1998) found that, in conflicts with their peers, Hong Kong Chinese preferred asking superiors to resolve the conflict, whereas Americans preferred direct problem solving with the other party. Keating et al. (1994) found that American college students almost never seek third-party intervention (mediation, arbitration, intermediation) into their everyday disputes, though they often approach third parties for other reasons such as comfort, approval, or advice.

Another form of indirection, which is very common among collectivists, is to engage in high-context communication (Hall, 1976), meaning that they rely less on spoken than on unspoken messages. Thus, they embed key information in emotional expressions, level of voice, or eye contact. Collectivists pay more attention to *how* something is said than to *what* is said, and silence is highly valued.[22] By contrast, individualists, engaging in low-context communication, rely heavily on what is said. They value specificity and clarity of communication (Triandis, 1994),[23] and silence is not valued. To individualists, "yes" clearly means "I agree with you." To collectivists, "yes" means many things including "I'm listening to you." Individualists often say "no," but collectivists are much more

---

[21] We will discuss covert problem solving in detail in Chapter 10.

[22] One essential social skill for Koreans is "nunch'i," which translates roughly as "eye measure." It is the ability to silently discern and detect other people's state of mind and mood. People heavily rely on each other's nunch'i to resolve conflict. Steers (1999, p. 209) notes: "If a Hyundai employee asked for a favor that his supervisor either could not or would not grant, the supervisor would likely use nunch'i to signal his negative response, thereby avoiding a loss of face to either party by formally—and publicly—declining the request." Koreans without nunch'i are doomed to be social failures.

[23] A Korean journalist who is fluent in English says: "Korean is not a good language to argue in because there are so many shades of meaning. It is so easy to be misunderstood. English is a language for clarity and logic. It's a beautiful language to argue with. My wife and I switch to English when we argue" (Breen, 1998, p. 35).

hesitant about this word, fearing loss of face for both parties (Cohen, 1991; Fang, 1999).

A scene in the movie, *The Joy Luck Club*, illustrates some differences between high-context and low-context communication cultures. A young Chinese woman invites her American boyfriend to meet her family. After having brought out various, delicious-looking Chinese dishes to the dining room table, this woman's mother carefully carries out the last dish, the one of which she is proudest. She says humbly, "This dish isn't salty enough. No flavor. It's too bad to eat! But, please." All Chinese family members show a clear anticipation for the dish, which they fully expect to enjoy—except the American boyfriend. When he tastes the dish, he exclaims, "All it needs is some soy sauce!" and then douses the dish with this salty fluid, ruining its delicate flavor. One can see a "collective" shock on the faces of the Chinese family members. When mother says, "It's too bad to eat," she is in fact claiming that it is her best dish. Far from expecting criticism, she is readying herself for lavish praise. Of course, the American boyfriend accepts what she has said at face value.

Sources of the Differences

What explains these differences in response to conflict? They stem in part from different views of conflict. For individualists, who put personal rights over group harmony, conflict is a natural by-product of social life and is not inherently negative. They believe that people are entitled to their own views and interests, which may differ from those of others. Hence, occasional clashes are inevitable and may be beneficial if properly handled (Ting-Toomey, 1994).

Collectivists, on the other hand, view conflict as dangerous because of their concern for group harmony (Chen, 2002; Ohbuchi & Takahashi, 1994; Ting-Toomey, 1994). A Chinese saying reflects this view: "When a family is united, everything prospers; when a family argues, everything fails." Hence, confrontational conflict should be avoided and covert communication should be employed when conflict arises.

In collectivist cultures, direct approaches to conflict risk losing "face," that is, social reputation, because of the danger of disturbing harmony (Blackman, 1997; Fang, 1999). In the view of individualists, overt displays of differences and demands are a sign of honesty—not a sign of hostility.

A related point has to do with differences in the legitimacy of asserting personal rights and interests. In individualist cultures, "pursuit of one's own interests is legitimate and even admired; hence actions that are aversive to others may be justified" (Tedeschi & Bond, 2001, p. 268). To individualists, "A squeaky wheel gets the grease." In collectivist societies, group harmony trumps self-concern. Asserting personal rights and interests is viewed as dangerous to group unity, and such public displays are likely to bring out strong social sanctions. To collectivists, "A nail that stands out gets pounded down."

Three other cultural differences provide further understanding of the individualist's attraction to contending and the collectivist's special aversion to this strategy. One has to do with the assignment of blame. Ohbuchi and Takahashi (1994) found that Japanese who became involved in conflict felt that they had contributed to the disturbance of social harmony even though they were not objectively responsible for the conflict. Thus, they considered themselves partly to blame for the conflict. Similarly, Gelfand et al. (2001) found that for the identical conflicts, Japanese thought that both parties were to blame, whereas Americans blamed the other side. As discussed earlier, other-blame tends to encourage contending, which is the first-choice strategy for most Americans.

A second difference is that individualists tend to pay less attention to the other side's interests and thus fail to realize that they have shared interests with the other party. This also encourages contending (Thompson & Hastie, 1990). For example, Gelfand and Christakopoulou (1999) found that compared to collectivists (Greeks), individualists (Americans) were more likely to commit the "fixed pie" error. This error is a judgment that a conflict is zero-sum even though common interests in fact exist between the parties.[24] Not surprisingly, Americans engaged in contentious tactics—such as threats, warnings, and put-downs—more frequently than did Greeks.

A third difference is that individualists are more likely to exhibit an egocentric fairness bias, that is, to view their own behavior as fairer than Other's behavior. Research evidence shows that this self-serving bias encourages contending (Morris & Gelfand, in press).

Asking superiors to resolve conflict also reflects the fact that human relationships in collectivist cultures tend to be vertically ordered (Tinsley, 1998, 2001; Triandis, 1995), and this is especially so in East Asia. As Confucian teaching emphasizes, each person has a different social standing, and people are expected to be aware of each other's rank. Those with lower status are expected to pay respect to those with higher status, who are in turn expected to treat the former with benevolence (Steers, 1999). By contrast, in individualist cultures, most human relationships tend to be horizontal, and people accept equality as a given (Triandis, 2000).

Culture and the Treatment of Ingroup vs. Outgroup Members

Compared to individualists, collectivists are much more affected by whether they share a common group identity with the opponent in a

---

[24] Interestingly though, the Americans believed erroneously that they had gained a better understanding of their counterparts' interests than did the Greeks.

conflict. They are more likely to distrust outgroup members (Fukuyama, 1995), to have a weak sense of universal principles of fairness (Yamagishi & Yamagishi, 1994), to employ deceptive tactics in negotiation with out-group members (Triandis et al., 2001), and to sue a stranger (Leung, 1988). In distributing resources, collectivists tend to use the equality rule (to di-vide equally) or the generosity rule (to give a larger share to others) with ingroup members but to use the equity rule (to divide according to each party's contribution) with outgroup members. Individualists tend to use the equity rule regardless of group membership (Leung & Bond, 1984). What is more, collectivists tend to adopt much harsher contentious tactics against outgroup members (Leung, 1988). Summing up these differences, Triandis (1990) asserts that, "collectivists are extremely hospitable, coop-erative, and helpful toward their ingroups but can be rude, exploitative, and even hostile toward their outgroups" (p. 42).

According to Bond and Wang (1983), Confucianism offers extensive guidelines about how to maintain harmony with ingroup members but few guidelines about how to deal with outgroup members. To collectivists, outgroup members become "nonpersons" or "unfamiliar faces" against whom violence can easily be justified. Outgroup members are excluded from one's moral community and thus lack the protection accorded to in-group members.

This means that when outgroup members appear to threaten ingroup welfare, collective violence tends to be employed, often of an excessive and extreme kind (Parish & Whyte, 1978). For example, in traditional China, collective physical punishment was used against criminals. A thief was brutally beaten by a large group of his or her villagers (Smith 1900/1972). In modern times, the Chinese and North Korean communist governments have relied on this collective form of violence to punish out-group members. Coming to a village where there was no prior hostility between landowners and peasants, the communist party members would first brand landowners as "the people's enemies" who exploited peasants, thus turning them into an outgroup (Bond & Wang, 1983). Afterwards, the party members would hold a public meeting where several peasants were asked to speak out about their "mistreatment and suffering" in the hands of these enemies. Soon, a large band of villagers would become so enraged by what the landowners were accused of doing that they beat them to death (Hinton, 1966). After the Cultural Revolution, "children in kinder-gartens were throwing balls at targets pasted with pictures of the dis-graced Gang of Four as part of their sports practice. *In China one is in, or unequivocally out*" (Blackman, 1997, p. 13, italics added).

SUMMARY AND CONCLUSIONS

The strategies for handling conflict—contending, problem solving, yield-ing, and avoiding—are somewhat incompatible with each other. Hence, conditions that encourage the use of one of them make the others less likely to be chosen. There are four main approaches to understanding the conditions that favor one or another of these strategies: the dual concern model, the perceived feasibility perspective, blame direction analysis, and analysis of the impact of culture. All of these approaches have merit.

The dual concern model postulates two kinds of motive: concern for own outcomes (self-concern) and concern for Other's outcomes (other-concern). The model makes the following predictions: (a) A combination of high self-concern and high other-concern encourages problem solving. (b) High self-concern and low other-concern encourages contending. (c) Low self-concern and high other-concern encourages yielding. (d) Low self-concern and low other-concern encourages avoiding. This model, which has received support from many laboratory studies of strategic choice, has been useful in understanding conflict style and the conditions that favor specific strategies.

Conditions favoring high self-concern, and hence the use of contending and problem solving, include high importance of the issues, the involvement of principles of right and wrong, and negative framing of the issues. Concern about the outcomes of one's group (a form of self-concern) is high for cohesive groups with strong group identity. Group representatives show special concern about their group's outcomes when they have low status in their group and when they are highly accountable to or distrusted by other group members.

Other-concern can be genuine or instrumental. Genuine other-concern is fostered by positive mood and by bonds of friendship, kinship, and common group identity. Instrumental other-concern arises from dependence on Other.

The perceived feasibility perspective holds that choice among the strategies depends on an assessment of their effectiveness and the risks they pose. These considerations supplement the forces specified in the dual concern model. For example, high concern about own and Other's outcomes may cause Party to favor problem solving. But this strategy will only be adopted if it there is some possibility of success at a reasonable cost. The perceived feasibility of problem solving is a function of perceived common ground—the belief that it is possible to find an alternative that satisfies both parties' aspirations. Problem solving is also encouraged by trust, but only if Other is seen as firm about not letting itself be exploited. Contending seems more feasible the greater one's power and the less resolute the other appears to be. Time pressure has been found to encourage yielding, probably because this strategy is the easiest way to reach a fast agreement. The greater the conflict size, the less feasible are yielding and problem solving and hence the more likely is Party to opt for contending.

Blaming Other for a conflict favors a contentious strategy; blaming oneself, a yielding strategy; and blaming both parties, a problem-solving strategy.

The individualism-collectivism dimension of culture has a big impact on strategic choice. Collectivists tend to avoid conflict if possible, and they make less use of confrontational strategies—contending and joint problem solving—than do individualists. When collectivists seek to resolve a conflict, they usually employ indirect, covert approaches—putting the conflict into the hands of an intermediary, asking a high status group member to solve it, or employing high context communication. This is because of their concern for ingroup harmony and their belief that harmony is disrupted by the bold assertion of personal rights and interests. Collectivists' concern for harmony often stops at the outer edge of the ingroup, and they tend to use harsher tactics in conflicts with outgroup members than do individualists.

While presenting an in-depth discussion of the forces that influence strategic choice, we have not said a lot about the nature and impact of the four basic strategies. In Chapter 4, we turn to a detailed consideration of one of them, contending.

4

Contentious Tactics

❖

Ingratiation ✦ Promises ✦ *Determinants of the Success of Promises* ✦ *Some Advantages of Promises* ✦ *Some Problems with Promises* ✦ Persuasive Argumentation ✦ Shaming ✦ Tit-for-Tat ✦ Threats ✦ *Determinants of the Success of Threats* ✦ *Some Advantages of Threats* ✦ *Some Problems with Threats* ✦ Coercive Commitments ✦ *Determinants of the Success of Coercive Commitments* ✦ *Some Advantages of Coercive Commitments* ✦ *Some Problems with Coercive Commitments* ✦ Violence ✦ Nonviolent Resistance ✦ Summary and Conclusions

The aim of contending is quite straightforward: Party seeks to impose its preferred solution on Other. This usually involves persuading or forcing Other to yield. Occasionally it entails what is called *fait accompli*, taking advantage of Other—grab Other's tricycle and ride off, take the money and run. There are a wide variety of contentious *tactics*—the moves and countermoves, the gestures and ploys, the things that Party does to dominate Other.

The tactics to be explored here are an assortment of odd bedfellows ranging from ingratiation, promises, and persuasive argumentation, to shaming, tit-for-tat, and threats, to coercive commitments and various forms of violence. Our analysis of these tactics is guided by the following premises:

First, there is nothing inherently destructive or baleful about contentious tactics other than violence. Rather, it is the end to which these tactics are used that can render them harmful. For example, although threats are most easily conceived of as instruments of destruction or malevolence, they may also be used to signal Party's unwillingness or inability to bend beyond some critical point in a generally

63

collaborative arrangement. Similarly, coercive commitments can be used not only in the service of imposing Party's will on Other but to signal Party's determination to keep the relationship together, under even the most difficult circumstances. In short, most contentious tactics can be used to advance the interest of collaboration as well as to defeat Other.

Second, we assume that contentious tactics differ along a dimension of lightness-heaviness. We define *light tactics* as those whose consequences for Other are favorable or neutral. By contrast, *heavy tactics* impose, or threaten to impose, unfavorable or costly consequences on Other. For example, promises are lighter than threats, and threats are lighter than violence.

Third, we assume that contentious tactics are more often than not deployed in an escalative sequence, moving from light to progressively heavier.[1] One reason for this sequence is that lighter tactics are typically less costly for Party than heavier ones. Such a sequence serves notice on Other, and on any bystanders who may happen to be observing, that Party is a "reasonable" person, someone who is moved to use heavy tactics only as a last resort. The transition from light to heavy implies that Party has tried to prevail by utilizing carrots and has been dragged only reluctantly into the use of sticks as a result of Other's intransigence. The light-to-heavy shift thus permits Party to blame its own contentious behavior on Other.

In keeping with the preceding points, the order of presentation of contentious tactics in this chapter conforms roughly to the light-to-heavy sequence. We will first look at the tactics of ingratiation and promises, both of which constitute relatively lightweight maneuvers designed to make subsequent moves more effective. Then we will look briefly at persuasive argumentation and shaming before turning to such heavier contentious tactics as threats and coercive commitments. Our penultimate topic is violence. The light-to-heavy sequence breaks down at the very end of the chapter, where we take up nonviolent resistance—a specialized set of coercive tactics that have been developed for parties that are unable or unwilling to employ violence to challenge authority. We save this topic for last, because these tactics need to be contrasted with violence.[2]

---

[1] Escalative sequences will be discussed in much greater detail in Chapters 5 to 8.

[2] While we believe that the contentious tactics explored here are among the more interesting and important, there are many other contentious tactics. These include gamesmanship (Potter, 1948); guilt trips (Rubin et al., 1994); fait accompli (Falbo, 1977; Falbo & Peplau, 1980); angry statements (which Averill [1982] has shown to help more often than to hurt relationships); and more indirect approaches, such as hinting (Falbo & Peplau, 1980).

INGRATIATION

Ingratiation is a type of tactic in which Party tries to make itself more attractive to Other in an effort to prepare Other for subsequent exploitation.[3] The effectiveness of this tactic stems from Other's very ignorance of Party's ultimate designs. To the extent that Other is able to "see through" Party or discern Party's true intentions, this tactic is likely to prove ineffectual and may even backfire.

How do ingratiators go about their business? Jones and Wortman (1973) make a number of suggestions. First, they argue for the importance of flattery or "complimentary other-enhancement," a class of tactics that exaggerates Other's admirable qualities while soft-pedaling Other's weaknesses. This technique relies for its effectiveness on the assumption that people find it hard to dislike those who say kind things about them, as when a woman is told by her date that she is a "beautiful and sensitive person" or a subordinate heaps praise on a boss.

The second class of ingratiation tactics involves what Jones and Wortman describe as "opinion conformity." By expressing agreement with Other's opinions, Party attempts to create the impression of having attitudes that are similar to Other's—a state that social psychologists have found generally induces interpersonal attraction (Byrne, 1971). A third set of ingratiation tactics involves the giving of favors, on the grounds that people tend to like those who do nice things for them (Cialdini, 2001; Regan, 1971).

Finally, Jones and Wortman describe several tactics of "self-presentation" that may be adopted by the successful ingratiator. The idea is for Party to present its own virtues in such a way that Other finds them attractive. Self-presentation is tricky business. Too forthright a description of one's virtues may lead Other to conclude that Party is conceited or has manipulative intentions; too subtle a description of Party's virtues may dilute the intended effect to the vanishing point (Jones & Gordon, 1972). Jones and Wortman advise ingratiators to address this dilemma by using indirect but clear-cut methods of "tooting their own horn," such as doing rather than merely saying self-aggrandizing things. "Rather than telling the target person that (one) is a good cook," they write, "an ingratiator can invite the target person to a gourmet dinner" (p. 23).

When used in a contentious exchange, ingratiation tactics soften Other up for later concessions, not through coercion, assertion, or aggression but through charm and guile. How much easier and less costly it is

---

[3] See Gordon (1996), Jones (1990), and Stengel (2000) for fuller treatments of ingratiation. For writings on the use of ingratiation by employees in organizational settings, see Eastman (1994), Harrell-Cook et al. (1999), Vonk (1998, 1999), and Wortman & Linsenmeier (1977).

to charm Other into surrendering something of value rather than extracting it through the imposition of will.

As mentioned earlier, it is important for successful ingratiation that Other not attribute Party's behavior to ulterior motives. Paradoxically, the greater Party's power relative to that of Other, the more effective Party's ingratiation tactics are apt to be (because Other is less likely to attribute Party's behavior to ulterior motives)—but the less necessary such tactics are in the first place. Conversely, it is when Party is in a position of relatively low power vis-à-vis Other that Party is most dependent on ingratiation tactics—and these tactics are least likely to be effective. The more Party needs Other, the more suspicious Other is likely to be of Party's attempts to make a good impression.

PROMISES

Promises are messages from Party announcing its intention to reward Other if Other complies with Party's wishes. Thus a parent might promise to take a child to the movies if the child cleans up his or her room.

Determinants of the Success of Promises

For a promise to be effective, the reward that is promised must be better for Other than what is lost through compliance (Tedeschi et al., 1973). Effective promises also need to be credible, that is, believable. There are three parts to credibility, all in Other's eyes. Other must believe that Party is *capable* of providing the reward promised, *intends* to provide the reward if Other complies and to withhold it if Other fails to comply, and has enough *surveillance* over Other's behavior to tell whether Other has complied.

Credibility of surveillance is fairly easy to achieve, since Other is motivated to provide evidence of compliance in order to get the reward; but it is necessary for Party to be able to tell when Other is falsifying this evidence. Research has shown that credibility of intent is enhanced if Party has been consistent about honoring past promises (Schlenker et al., 1973) and has been accommodative in the past (Tedeschi et al., 1973).

Some Advantages of Promises

Promises have much to recommend them in a contentious encounter, for three main reasons. First, unlike their "hard" counterpart, threats, most promises are relatively "nice" (light) tactics. They offer something that is presumed to be attractive to Other in exchange for Other's compliance. Promises don't just take, they give in return. As a result, they cause little negative residuals after being delivered—unlike threats. In keeping with these observations, it is no surprise that promises are generally rated as more attractive than threats and that the promisers themselves are seen as friendlier (Rubin & Lewicki, 1973). It should also be no surprise that promises beget promises in return.

Second, promises are quite effective at eliciting compliance—without much resistance and resentment—provided that the promiser has a track record of honoring his or her commitments (Lindskold & Tedeschi, 1971). Imagine how difficult it would be for parents, without relying on promises, to persuade their children to eat broccoli, clean their room, put away their dirty clothes, lower the volume of their music, etc.

A third virtue of many promises is that they often create a sense of indebtedness in the mind of the Other. Not all promises have this characteristic; payment for merchandise or for services rendered does not typically engender indebtedness, nor would ice cream in exchange for eating broccoli. On the other hand, there are a great many situations where the making and fulfillment of a promise imply that Party is in some way doing Other a favor, which Other has an obligation to return. Like the apparently benevolent acts of the Godfather, promises often have long strings attached that, at least in principle, give Party future leverage over Other.

Some Problems with Promises

Given these several virtues of promises, one might expect them to be used with greater frequency and success in contentious encounters than in fact turns out to be the case. There are several problems with promises that are not at first apparent.

First, and of paramount importance, an effective promise costs Party whatever reward was promised. By contrast, a threat that works as intended costs Party nothing. Hence, successful promises are more expensive than threats.

A second problem is that the fulfillment of a promise may, paradoxically, make it less likely to work in the future. Other may become tired of the favors Party has available to dole out in exchange for compliance. Ice cream in exchange for eating broccoli works only so long as Other is not tired of ice cream. Having sampled the best that Party has to offer, Other may be tempted either not to comply in the future or to try to extract increased rewards in exchange for such compliance.

A third problem is that the repeated tender and fulfillment of promises may create the problem not of satiation but of undue dependence. Other may come to expect Party to deliver continued benefits in the future, which may prove quite costly for Party in the long run.

Because of the problems just described, it might appear sensible for Party to make promises but not to keep them. Unfortunately, this creates a fourth problem: Promises are often costly to break. Consider the political cost to President George Bush (senior) when he broke his campaign promise not to raise taxes ("Read my lips! No new taxes."). To renege on a promise is to create a situation in which Party is almost certain to be disliked and distrusted and in which Other may feel duty-bound to respond punitively. Moreover, Party is not likely to be believed if and when it makes promises in the future.

A fifth problem with promises is that it is often difficult to decide how much to promise. For Party to offer Other too paltry or measly a reward is to run the risk of failing to elicit the desired behavior and even of antagonizing Other with an insulting offer. For this reason, Party would be well advised to offer large rewards in exchange for Other's compliance. However, rewards that are too attractive may be regarded by Other as a bribe. Other may come to view Party as having far more to gain from Other's compliance than it is willing to reveal. Under these circumstances, Other may be tempted either to avoid compliance, in an effort to discover what has motivated Party to make so lavish a promise, or to blackmail Party, arguing, in effect, that if compliance is important enough to Party to justify so lavish a reward, then perhaps Party should pay even more in order to have his or her way.

PERSUASIVE ARGUMENTATION

Ingratiation and promises are preparatory tactics in the sense that they erode Other's resistance to lowering aspirations rather than acting on these aspirations directly. In contrast, a number of contentious tactics are applied in a direct effort to induce Other to reduce aspirations. The lightest of these tactics is *persuasive argumentation,* a technique whereby Party induces Other to lower its aspirations through a series of logical appeals.

The skill required for successful persuasive argumentation should not be underestimated. Party must convince Other to surrender something that it holds dear and that Party covets—not through coercion or the lure of reward, but through persuasion. This is a tall order in a contentious encounter.[4] Social psychological theory and research in the area of persuasion has received much attention over the years.[5] Rather than dwell on this broad literature, we shall simply describe two general types of appeals that can be useful when there is conflict of interest.

First, Party may try to persuade Other that Party has a legitimate right to a favorable outcome in the controversy. If I can persuade you that

---

[4] A movie, *12 Angry Men,* offers a splendid example of the power of persuasion. It is about a jury whose task is to decide whether or not a teenaged boy accused of killing his father is guilty. Except for one mild-mannered man (played by Henry Fonda), the rest of the jurors think that the boy is definitely guilty. But, Henry Fonda gradually persuades them to change their hasty conviction of the boy.

[5] See, for example, Chaiken et al. (2000).

it is "your money or *my* life"—that is, I am in considerable jeopardy unless you grant my wish—I may be able to persuade you to lower your aspirations. Such is the case when negotiators argue that they are in danger of being fired, demoted, or replaced unless they can return a particularly favorable division of resources to their constituents. Israel has often employed such arguments in asking the United States for money to help them resist attacks from their neighbors.

A second major form of persuasive argumentation requires Party to convince Other that lower aspirations are in the latter's interest. This is really quite an extraordinary maneuver: I am persuading you that it is in your interest to permit me to prevail. Consider a failing business whose management persuades labor negotiators that unless workers accept pay cuts and layoffs, the business will go down with all hands aboard. Sounds farfetched? If so, recall the recent successful effort by USAirways to persuade its pilots to accept deep pay cuts in order to increase the chances of corporate survival. In this and similar cases, Party convinced Other to embrace lower aspirations by pointing to a credible alternative that appeared to be even less attractive.

SHAMING

Shaming is the act of causing Other to feel the emotion of shame, the painful feeling characterized by a global condemnation of oneself (Smith et al., 2002). Shaming is usually achieved by publicizing Other's defects or transgressions.

Shaming is a highly potent way to elicit compliance.[6] Indeed, it has long been the most powerful tool of social control (Braithwaite, 1989). The classic novel, *The Scarlet Letter,* provides a literary example of this phenomenon. Hester Pryne was forced to parade herself before the people of Salem with the letter "A" for adultery on her dress. She had to endure "the heavy weight of a thousand unrelenting eyes, all fastened upon her, and concentrated at her bosom." The pain of shame became so intense that Hester wanted to "shriek out with the full power of her lungs, and cast herself from the scaffold down upon the ground, or else go mad at once" (Hawthorne, 1850/1962, p. 45).

Puritan forms of shaming no longer exist—at least in America. But, other forms have taken their place as compliance inducers in homes (Dutton, 1999), workplaces (Graham, 2000), legal settings (Braithwaite, 1989), and international arenas (Scheff, 1994). These forms of shaming can be as subtle as a frown or as direct as the verbal admonition, "Shame on you!" They can be promulgated in a group as small as a family of three, as when parents

---

[6] A woman convicted of welfare fraud wanted to serve time in jail rather than wear a sign: "I stole food from poor people" (Etzioni, 2001).

criticize a child for not saying "please," or broadcast widely via the mass media, as in the printing of deadbeat parents' names (Braithwaite, 1989).

The downside of shaming is that it can easily backfire on Party if Other sees the shaming as unjustified humiliation. In Braithwaite's term, this is "stigmatization," a type of shaming that produces many unfortunate side effects. One is that Other reacts with anger and aggression. Another is that this type of shaming can disintegrate a social bond between the parties. Other may break off from Party—and even from the community of which they are members—joining others who are similarly stigmatized. Thus, a teenager who has been a target of shaming by his schoolmates may join a gang that offers a value system opposed to that of the school (Cohen, 1955). Being sent to a principal's office for his or her misbehavior now becomes a badge of honor rather than a source of shame, and shaming has lost its power to shape behavior.

To avoid these side effects, Party should employ what Braithwaite calls "reintegrative shaming." Shaming should be followed by gestures of reaffirmation of the social bond between the parties. These gestures may range from a smile to a formal ceremony designed to publicize reconciliation.

TIT-FOR-TAT

Another tactic for manipulating Other involves matching Other's behavior—rewarding Other when it cooperates and punishing Other's noncooperation. This is called *tit-for-tat*. Thus a parent who is trying to get a boy to stop teasing his sister can praise him when he doesn't annoy her and send him to his room when he does. Research on the prisoner's dilemma shows that tit-for-tat is quite effective as a way to get Other to cooperate (Axelrod, 1984; Kim & Webster, 2001). This tactic works in at least two ways. It amounts to simple reinforcement of behavior, producing learning of the kind that is found in most animals. And it produces an image of Party as firm but ready to cooperate if Other is also ready (Komorita & Esser, 1975).

Two problems arise when using tit-for-tat. One results from the fact that immediate retaliation is required from Party, even if Other has made a momentary mistake. If Other is also employing tit-for-tat, as is often the case, doing so may start an unnecessary conflict spiral in an otherwise good relationship. Other fails to cooperate once, so Party punishes Other; Other then retaliates, causing Party to further retaliate, etc. This may hurt the parties' relationship and endanger their well-being. In addition, if Other's failure to cooperate came at the beginning of their interaction, Other may never learn that good behavior pays off. Instead, Other may develop an incorrect view of Party as a nasty creature who never cooperates and should be avoided or disciplined.

This problem can be avoided if Party gives Other a grace period, continuing to behave positively for a while in response to Other's unpleasant or self-serving behavior. Including a warning during this grace period is often effective. New difficulties may arise if Other begins to exploit the grace period, again and again annoying Party until close to Party's breaking point, and then quickly "reforming" to get back into Party's good graces. Research shows that Party can protect itself from this by also being slow to forgive once it has retaliated (Bixenstine & Gaebelein, 1971).

Another solution to this problem is for Party to explain tit-for-tat in words, "I can be nice if you work with me instead of against me" (Deutsch, 1973). This can be combined with shifting occasionally to unilateral cooperation to test whether Other is ready for an improvement in the relationship.

The second problem with tit-for-tat is that its effectiveness is often limited to the period in which it is employed. Other's cooperative behavior is likely to taper off if Party stops using the tactic. Learning theorists have found that the effect of tit-for-tat lasts longer after the tactic is discontinued if Other has been rewarded for cooperation intermittently rather than every time (Kazdin, 1975).

THREATS

A *threat* is a message from Party announcing the intention to hurt Other if Other fails to comply with Party's wishes.[7] Threats differ in their degree of explicitness. Some are clear statements of precisely what will happen if Other fails to behave in a specific way. Thus a parent might say, "If you take your sister's toys from her once more, you will go to your room." Others are vague with regard to the action or the penalty; and still others involve subtle and often ambiguous communication, such as a well-timed frown or cough. Many threats are totally implicit in the situation, such as the threat of a police citation for running a red light. If the concept is broadened to include the subtle and the implicit, it is clear that our lives are surrounded by threats. Threats are a reality of social life and are seldom a problem unless they get out of hand.

Threats need to be distinguished from *warnings*. A warning is a prediction that Other will get hurt if it fails to act in a particular way. The critical difference from a threat is that, in a warning, Party (the source of the warning) does not control whether Other gets hurt (Tedeschi et al., 1973). Somebody or something else will be the source of the predicted hurt, or Party will be forced to act. Thus a mother might say, "If you annoy your sister once more, your *dad* will send you to your room" or "If you annoy your sister once more, I *will be forced* to send you to your

---

[7] The term "threat" sometimes has another meaning, as danger that hangs over one's head and is difficult or impossible to control, such as the threat of illness or of nuclear war (Milburn & Watman, 1981). We call such a danger *noncontingent* threat. This contrasts with *contingent* threat, the topic of this section, where Party controls whether Other suffers.

room." The latter kind of warning is admittedly in a gray area between threats and warnings.

We begin our analysis with a review of conditions that affect the likelihood that threats will be successful. Then we consider the potential advantages of using threats, and finally, the potential drawbacks of using them.

Determinants of the Success of Threats

For a threat to be effective, the harm that is threatened must be worse for Other than what can be gained from noncompliance (Tedeschi et al., 1973). This means that up to a point, threats will be more effective the larger the penalty threatened (Horai & Tedeschi, 1969). We say "up to a point" because threats that are out of line with the behavior requested are unlikely to be believed (Schelling, 1960, 1966). In most families, a threat to deny food for a week to a boy who annoyed his sister would not be believed and hence would fail.

This gets us into a second requirement: like promises, threats must be *credible* to be effective. Other must believe that Party is capable of hurting Other in the threatened way, intends to hurt Other if Other fails to comply *and* to withhold this punishment if Other complies, and has enough surveillance over Other's behavior to tell whether Other has complied. Thus in the example used above, the boy may fail to comply because he doesn't think his parent is able to send him to his room, doesn't think his parent actually intends to send him to his room, thinks his parent will send him to his room regardless of what he does, or doesn't think his parent can tell when he is misbehaving.

Researchers have paid most attention to the conditions that produce credibility of intent, that make Other think Party intends to carry out its threat. Credibility of intent is partly a matter of Party's reputation for truthfulness. Thus *past consistency* makes Party more believable. Party's threats will seem hollow if past threats have not been enforced (Horai & Tedeschi, 1969) or past promises have not been honored (Schlenker et al., 1973). Having high status or a reputation for being *tough or unpleasant* can also contribute to threat credibility. Threats are more believable when they come from high ranking individuals (Faley & Tedeschi, 1971) or people who are viewed negatively (Schlenker et al., 1970).

Threats lose credibility to the extent that they are *costly to enforce*. There are almost always some costs to following through on a threat. Even mildly disciplining a child can be wearing if the child protests. The point here is that as costs increase, Party becomes less likely to enforce a threat. Knowing this, Other will see the threat as less credible and be less likely to comply with it (Mogy & Pruitt, 1974).

Seriousness of intent can also be signaled by making preparations to carry out the threat. Thus a parent might back up a threat by taking the child's schoolbooks to his room, saying "I've put your books in your room so you'll have something to do while you're grounded."

Successful threateners often find ways to *commit* themselves to carrying out a threat. The aim is to leave themselves no choice if Other fails to comply, in other words, to turn a threat into a warning. One means of commitment is for Party to make a *public statement* of the threat, so that Party will be embarrassed if it fails to follow through. For example, the parent might speak to the boy in front of the rest of the family. A second approach is to attach the commitment to a hallowed principle or rule that Party is duty bound to uphold. Thus the parent might tell the boy that he is breaking the basic societal rule of the sanctity of private property, which the parent is trying to teach him. A third method of commitment is to turn over enforcement of the threat to a third party who is duty bound to carry through. This is the function of legal contracts and injunctions.

Some Advantages of Threats

Threats may not be as nice as promises, but they are more tempting to use as a means of eliciting compliance. This is so for several reasons:

First, the threat that works costs Party nothing; there is no reward to be doled out *and* no punishment to be imposed. Threats work because of the leverage provided by Other's desire to avoid a cost—rather than the cost itself. As Schelling (1966) observes, where brute force often fails because it increases Other's resistance and pluck, the *threat* of such force may succeed.

Second, threats are often highly effective; their value has been demonstrated repeatedly and consistently (for example, Bonoma & Tedeschi, 1973; Mogy & Pruitt, 1974). Indeed in some situations, threats are more effective at motivating Other to comply than are promises. This is in part because threateners usually seem more powerful and controlling than promisers. It is also because threats have been found experimentally to *be very credible* forms of influence, often more so than promises (Pruitt & Carnevale, 1993; Rubin & Brown, 1975). And it is also because people are ordinarily more highly motivated to avoid a possible loss than to obtain a possible reward (Taylor, 1991). Hence, they are more likely to yield when confronted with a threat.

A third potential "virtue" of threats is that threateners can benefit even when they renege on a threat. If Party elects not to enforce a threat when Other fails to comply, this choice may be regarded by Other not as weak or foolish but as humane. Whereas a reneging promiser is almost certain to be seen by Other as a person who cannot be trusted to do what he or she says, a reneging threatener may be regarded as powerful but compassionate—the sort of person (like a kindly parent) who understands the wisdom of forbearance. To be sure, reneging on a threat runs the risk of reduced credibility in the eyes of Other. But the potential cost for Party associated with reneging on a threat may be offset, at least in part, by the possibility of a charitable interpretation of Party's actions.

A fourth virtue of threats, causing them to be used with considerable frequency by people in conflict, is that they are consistent with the sense of justice and rectitude that often accompanies such interactions. People in contentious encounters often believe, or act as though they believe, that they have God and Right on their side. Under these circumstances, what better way of exerting influence than by means of a threat? If Other does what Party demands, this is only right and proper and deserves no special reward. But if Other fails to do what Party requests, then punishment is the appropriate response to this wrong. ("If Johnny doesn't have the good sense and respect to stop bothering his sister, then he deserves his punishment. He knew what was coming to him.")

Some Problems with Threats

The most serious problem associated with the use of threats is that they tend to be resented by Other (Smith & Anderson, 1975). This is partly because Party is signaling an intention to hurt Other. It is also because Party is asking for compliance without giving anything in return. This means an uncompensated loss of freedom for Other and implies that Party thinks it is superior to Other and has the right to make further demands.[8] The resentment produced by these perceptions often leads Other to counterthreaten rather than comply. This can defeat the purpose of the threat and encourage a negative spiral of intensifying hostility of the kind discussed in Chapters 5 and 6 (Deutsch & Krauss, 1960; Youngs, 1986).

Threats can also erode the relationship between Party and Other, producing distrust that makes it difficult for the parties to engage in effective problem solving. Still another problem with threats is that they can be expensive if Other fails to comply. Punishing a defiant Other is often difficult and time consuming and can lead to even greater resentment and retaliation from Other.[9]

There are three ways to diminish these problems. One is to combine threats with promises—to employ both "the carrot and the stick." This approach is akin to tit-for-tat. It offers Other a meaningful reward for swallowing its pride and complying. A second approach is to employ threats that are legitimate—such as a judge's threat to impose a fine if a defendant

---

[8] In a study by Heilman (1974), participants who were threatened felt that they were being treated like a child. Most adults would deeply resent such treatment.

[9] For empirical evidence about the negative effects of threats in organizational settings, see Freedman (1981).

is caught speeding again. Legitimate threats evoke less resentment than illegitimate threats (Milburn & Watman, 1981). A third approach is to employ deterrent, as opposed to compellent, threats (Schelling, 1966). Deterrent threats request that Other *not take* a particular action while compellent threats request that Other *take* a particular action. The latter involve pushing Other around and hence are more likely to be resented and less likely to work than the former.

COERCIVE COMMITMENTS

Threats are "if-then" assertions by Party in the following form: "If you don't conform to my wishes, I will punish you." By contrast, coercive commitments take the following form: "I have started doing something that punishes you and will continue doing it until you conform to my wishes." Continued punishment of Other is usually costly or risky to Party. Hence, what coercive commitments do is put the locus of control over both parties' welfare into Other's own hands, giving Other the last clear chance to avoid harm to both parties. Let us consider two rather different examples, the first drawn from the fabled game of chicken, the second from international relations.

As it was played in old James Dean and Marlon Brando movies, chicken involves two participants who are driving their cars at breakneck speed on a direct collision course. The loser in this game (the "chicken") is the first person to turn aside in order to avert a head-on collision and almost certain death for both players. More generally, the game of chicken can be observed whenever two or more parties lock into a contest of wills in which neither side is willing to concede first and both stand to lose a great deal through joint intransigence. A divorcing couple in the throes of a nasty child custody dispute and labor and management in a costly industrial strike are also good candidates for a chicken analysis.

President John F. Kennedy's choice of tactics in the Cuban missile crisis of 1962 is a dramatically different illustration of coercive commitment. Several months before the crisis, the Soviet Union (under Premier Nikita Khrushchev) had begun sending shipments of medium-range missiles and nuclear warheads to the island of Cuba, with the unmistakable intention of targeting these weapons, once assembled, at the major urban centers of the eastern United States. The crisis began when incontrovertible photographic evidence of this activity was brought to the attention of President Kennedy. The President responded by committing the United States to a naval blockade of all Soviet shipments to Cuba. He made it clear that this blockade would continue unless and until the Russians stopped all further shipments and destroyed those weapons and sites already on the island. American warships were sent to the region and began stopping Soviet vessels. As we shall see in Chapter 9, this tactic was successful and the Soviets removed their missiles.

Determinants of the Success of Coercive Commitments

Like promises and threats, coercive commitments must be credible to be effective. Other must believe that Party is capable of continuing to punish Other, intends to do so if Other fails to comply *and* will lift the punishment if Other complies, and has enough surveillance over Other's behavior to tell whether Other has complied.

Since punishing Other is usually costly or risky to Party, the main issue is credibility of *intent*, whether Other believes that Party will continue delivering the punishment until Other gives in. For instance, in the game of chicken example, Party could fling its steering wheel out the window in full view of Other (Schelling, 1960). The message conveyed through such action is that now only Other has control over what will happen. Party has irrevocably committed itself to a potentially disastrous course of action that can only be stopped if Other yields. In the Cuban missile crisis, Kennedy's firm verbal commitment to impose a blockade was supplemented by visible movements of military personnel, the arrival of warships in the region, and actual interference with Soviet shipping. It is hard to imagine a more credible commitment than this one. The locus of control over the outcome of the exchange was shifted from American shoulders to those of the Soviet Union, which became the only country capable of preventing mutual catastrophe.

There are several things Party can do to bolster its credibility of intent. First, Party may wish to employ the services of some third person who has been given instructions that are virtually impossible to change, such as a courier sent to deliver a message by a person who cannot subsequently be contacted or influenced. Schelling (1960) gives an example, "At many universities the faculty is protected by a rule that denies instructors the power to change a course grade once it has been recorded" (p. 38). This places the registrar in the position of a messenger conveying information that Party is now unable to change.

A second way to enhance credibility of intent is to pledge commitment in public rather than in private, thereby laying on the line Party's reputation for consistency in word and deed. Writing in the context of negotiation, where parties are often trying to commit themselves not to make any concessions, Schelling says, "If national representatives can arrange to be charged with appeasement for every small concession, they place concession visibly beyond their own reach" (p. 29).

A third method of enhancing credibility of intent is to demonstrate that Party has a constituency looking on that will hold it responsible for any deviation from the commitment. In effect, Party attempts to argue that its neck is in a noose that is about to be drawn tight by intransigent constituents who are watching every move that is made.

A fourth technique to increase credibility of intent involves confronting Other with evidence of Party's resolve. There is nothing like an eyeball-to-eyeball exchange for letting Other know the depth and intensity of Party's commitment. In the absence of such direct interpersonal confrontation, Party's forcefulness cannot truly be grasped, and this tactic is less likely to work as intended.

In addition to lack of credibility, coercive commitments can fail if Other has a way of overcoming Party's punishing behavior. Thus, in 1948, at the beginning of the Cold War, the Soviet Union tried to force the United States and its allies out of West Berlin by instituting a land blockade of the city. A great airlift of supplies was instituted, which kept the city going. With their coercive commitment a failure, the Soviets lifted the blockade in 1949.

Some Advantages of Coercive Commitments

If used successfully, coercive commitments force Other to do the work of bringing about agreement. They put the ball in Other's court, and hence have the capacity to elicit concessions from Other. If you and I are approaching an intersection in our respective automobiles, and you believe (because I am staring straight ahead of me) that I am unaware of your presence, the responsibility for what happens to the two of us is not mine but yours; it is you who must do the work of jamming on your brakes to prevent a collision. Many a Boston driver has put this very tactic to good use in an effort to slip through a busy intersection (Rubin et al., 1974).

A second virtue of coercive commitments is that they do not require Party to hold power that is equal to or greater than that of Other. All that is required is for Party to present itself as being in a position, even temporarily, of doling out costs that matter to Other. Thus a lowly garbage man who did not get a Christmas tip from a powerful patron can drop eggshells on his patron's lawn from December 26 onward until the tip is forthcoming. Indeed Schelling (1960) has observed that the weaker party is often, paradoxically, in the stronger bargaining position with this tactic. This is because its very weakness can enhance the credibility of its commitment. The garbage man's poverty and hence his desperate need for money make it all the more credible that he will keep on using this tactic. A cornered animal and a man with his back to a wall are surely in a weak position, but they can be counted on to fight. Their weakness makes their commitment to punishing the adversary more credible than it otherwise would be.

A third virtue of coercive commitments is that they often work without Party or Other ever witnessing the commitment's ultimate consequences.

The United States did not have to blockade Cuba for long. When Party has a history of "honoring" commitments of various kinds, this history may be sufficient for Party to prevail without carrying through to the bitter end.

Some Problems with Coercive Commitments

Precisely because of their irreversibility or apparent irreversibility, coercive commitments often entail considerable risk. Party's fate is placed in the hands of an Other who may not be ready to make the concessions necessary to avoid disaster. If Other is not ready to make these concessions, the disaster often will be mutual; both chicken players are killed, or the Soviet Union strikes back, producing a nuclear interchange. Coercive commitment is a risky tactic indeed.

There are at least four reasons why Other may fail to make the concessions this tactic is designed to evoke. First, Other may not understand the consequences of the commitment that has been made. If you cannot see me behind the wheel of my car and therefore do not know that I am unaware that we are both approaching the same intersection, the two of us have a serious problem. Second, Other may want to comply with Party's wishes but be unable to do so—as when the other driver in the chicken game has lost control of the brakes and is therefore unable to stop in time, or when a kidnap victim has no access to ransom money.

Third, Party may think it is committed to take the stated action, but Other may doubt that commitment. Other may reason that coercive commitments are so risky that Party is not really committed. Such a misunderstanding has the makings of tragedy.

Fourth, and most important, Party may misjudge the relative value to Other of the options it is forcing Other to choose between. Party may believe Other will prefer capitulation to disaster, but Other may actually prefer disaster. In launching the blockade on Cuba, Kennedy had to assume that Khrushchev would prefer an embarrassing withdrawal to fighting a naval battle or threatening nuclear retaliation. To minimize the danger of misjudgment, it is important for Party to have a thorough knowledge of Other's perceptions and values. For a newcomer to a relationship, making a coercive commitment can be playing with fire.[10]

Because of these four risks, it is desirable for Party's coercive commitments to be reversible if necessary. Party would be well advised—before flinging its steering wheel out the window in a game of chicken—to engineer a second steering mechanism, unseen by Other, that can be used to

---

[10] This may help explain Kelley's (1966) experimental finding that commitments not to concede further tend to be made late in negotiations, and that this is especially true for experienced negotiators.

avert a last-minute disaster in the event that the tactic fails to work. Under most circumstances it is better to be seen as a fool or a trickster than to die. The most effective unilateral commitment may be one that Other believes to be irreversible but that can be modified if absolutely necessary.

In addition to their riskiness, another problem with coercive commitments stems from the fact that they must be used preemptively. It is the first party to strip itself of control in the game of chicken who is likely to prevail. For Party to throw its steering wheel out the window at the same moment as, or immediately after, Other does the same thing is to be both terribly brave and terribly foolhardy. It makes sense to surrender control over events only if Party can count on Other's retention of control.

We have seen that coercive commitments carry with them potential problems of credibility and risk. The most serious problem, however, stems from the contribution to escalation often made by such commitments unless they are strictly nonviolent (see below). These tactics tend to beget responses in kind that, instead of bringing an end to the contentious exchange, are likely to cause each side to dig in its heels, to take positions from which it feels it cannot budge without losing face, and thereby to exacerbate an already difficult situation.

VIOLENCE

We define "violence" as behavior that is intended to physically injure another person or an object valued by another person. The term is often stretched well beyond that definition. For example, Opotow (2000) includes in her definition "structural violence," which means denying to some members of society the "basic resources needed for human well-being and dignity" (p. 404). While structural violence is well worth examining and seeking to remedy, it has different origins and effects than physical violence, which is the phenomenon of interest here.

It is useful to distinguish between instrumental and emotional violence (Berkowitz, 1993). *Instrumental violence* is a means to an end. Its aim is to advance Party's cause in a conflict with Other. Several of the tactics described earlier may, but need not necessarily, involve instrumental violence. Thus tit-for-tat and threat enforcement may take violent (spanking a boy when he teases his sister) or nonviolent (sending him to his room) forms. Coercive commitment can involve violence (torturing prisoners until they name their confederates) or nonviolence (keeping prisoners in the interrogation room until they name their confederates). Party can also use instrumental violence to overpower Other or in self-defense.

In *emotional violence*, harming Other is an end in itself rather than a means to an end. The emotions involved in this kind of violence—such as anger, hostility, or the desire for revenge—are directed toward Other. Such emotions may derive from perceived annoyance by Other; that is, they may reflect an insult, pain, or relative deprivation to oneself or one's group that is blamed on Other. Or they may originate in some other setting and be *displaced* onto Other. For example, a parent who has had a bad day at work may come home and strike a child for some minor offense.

Most instances of violence have both instrumental and emotional roots, in greater or lesser measure. Thus the torturer is mainly motivated by an instrumental goal of getting information from the prisoner but may also be expressing anger at the world that is due to being abused as a child. The frustrated parent is mainly impelled by anger at his boss but may also have the instrumental goal of persuading the child not to make noise, talk back, or whatever the child did that elicited the parent's rage.

Violence by groups is usually much more damaging than violence by individuals. Group violence takes different forms depending on the group's strength and level of authority. Governments and other powerful groups usually operate openly through police or military forces. Smaller and less powerful groups usually operate by stealth, acting as *guerrillas* or *terrorists* against the more powerful groups they are challenging. They send individuals or small teams, in secret, to destroy bridges or buildings and kill people on the other side. Their reason for using terrorist tactics is straightforward. If these groups operate openly, their members will usually be arrested before they accomplish their mission.

Terrorist actions, such as Al Qaeda's attack on the World Trade Center, usually have at least four goals. One, an emotional goal, is to express real or imagined ingroup grievances by retaliating against the more powerful enemy. The other three are instrumental goals: (a) to annoy the adversary enough that it makes concessions in an effort to stop the violence, (b) to weaken the adversary and thus protect the ingroup, and (c) to show that the adversary is vulnerable—a "paper tiger"—and thus recruit other ingroup members to the struggle.[11]

NONVIOLENT RESISTANCE

Nonviolent resistance is a set of tactics that can be used by low power groups to challenge the status quo without employing violence.[12] It can be viewed as a substitute for guerrilla action and terrorism that puts real pressure on the powerful but avoids the drawbacks associated with violence. These drawbacks include suffering on both sides (reactions to terrorism

---

[11] For information about terrorism, see Laquer (1999), Lifton (1999), Rubenstein (1987), and White (1998).

[12] Discussions of the tactics of nonviolent resistance will be found in Ackerman & Kruegler (1994), Erikson (1969), Gandhi (1967), King (1963), Sharp (1970), and Steger & Lind (1999).

often involve violence against the group the terrorists claim to represent), destroying the relationship with the adversary, and alienating third parties who might otherwise put pressure on the adversary.

Examples of nonviolent resistance include such events as Mohandas K. Gandhi's fasts in order to secure concessions from the British forces that occupied India, the boycotts and sit-down strikes by courageous African Americans in the South of the 1950s and early 1960s, and refusal to register for the draft or to move out of the way of approaching tanks as a means of protesting a national war effort. Although many of us admire the courage, determination, and moral conviction that characterize such actions, we must not lose sight of the essentially contentious tactics at work, which are designed to prevail in an intensely conflictive exchange. As Gandhi (1949) wrote, "Non-violence . . . does not mean meek submission to the will of the evildoer, but it means putting one's whole soul against the will of the tyrant" (p. 4). Indeed, nonviolence requires great bravery, because the authorities may respond with violence, and great discipline, because the protestor must remain nonviolent in the face of a violent response from the adversary.

As with guerrilla action and terrorism, nonviolent resistance works by annoying or weakening the adversary and recruiting further adherents to the cause. A further virtue, which is not shared with guerrilla action and terrorism, is that nonviolent resistance will often produce *outside sympathy* with the resistor's cause. Thus Gandhi's nonviolent stance made him quite popular around the world (including some segments of British society!). When he began his fasts, there was worldwide concern and mounting pressure on Britain to make the concessions he sought so as to avoid his death. Outside sympathy can be particularly strong if the authorities use violence against nonviolent protestors, because the response seems vastly disproportionate to the challenge. Thus the 1960 Sharpsville massacre, in which white South African police killed 67 nonviolent African protestors, helped to mobilize world public opinion against the South African government. This eventually led to worldwide economic sanctions against that country that contributed to its replacement by a popularly elected, black–African dominated government in 1993.

Nonviolent resistance is probably best thought of as a set of tactics rather than a monolithic entity. Sharp (1970, p. 32) has distinguished three classes of nonviolence: *nonviolent protest,* which includes "marches . . . picketing . . . 'haunting' officials . . . distributing protest literature," and which "produces an awareness of the existence of dissent" and of the arguments endorsed by the dissenters; *nonviolent noncooperation,* such as "economic boycotts . . . strikes . . . civil disobedience, and mutiny," which "present the opponent with difficulties in maintaining the normal efficiency and operation of the system;" and *nonviolent intervention,* including "sit-ins, fasts, nonviolent obstructions, nonviolent invasion, and parallel government," which actively harass the adversary.

Within the terms of this chapter, Sharp's second and third classes of nonviolence are forms of coercive commitment. Thus economic boycotts, strikes, sit-ins, and fasts are aimed at communicating an irrevocable commitment to a set of demands and a nonviolent course of action that, in one way or another, is punishing to Other (the more powerful party). If effectively conveyed to Other, such a commitment shifts the locus of responsibility for what happens squarely onto Other's shoulders; the ball is in Other's court. In announcing his intention to begin fasting in protest of British policies in India, Gandhi served notice on the British that they now had exclusive responsibility for determining the outcome of the crisis. Nothing would budge Gandhi from this stance other than British surrender to his wishes, and it fell entirely to the British to decide whether to accede to Gandhi's demands or let him die. Gandhi was taking a risk, but on virtually every occasion in which nonviolence was tried in India—both by Gandhi alone and as a form of mass, collective action—the tactic worked as intended.

As is often true of coercive commitments, parties using nonviolence are successful, not because of their greater pool of resources but because they are able to commit themselves in ways that are costly to Other and that appear irreversible. Gandhi's power to compel the British to modify their policies in India stemmed not from superior physical resources but from his very weakness. Commitment of his frail body to a fast that it could not endure for very long was a powerful lever to force the mighty British to yield. Weakness can thus be a source of strength, provided that the coercive commitment is highly credible.

SUMMARY AND CONCLUSIONS

In this chapter we have tried to outline several of the more important contentious tactics that Party uses in an effort to prevail in conflict. Most of the tactics—ingratiation, promises, persuasive argumentation, shaming, tit-for-tat, threats, coercive commitments, and violence—were presented in an order that moved from lighter contentious tactics to their heavier counterparts. This light-to-heavy sequence is often seen as conflict unfolds (though not all the tactics in our list are found in every conflict), reflecting the common tendency for conflict to escalate. The final tactic, nonviolent resistance, is not part of the light-to-heavy sequence, but was presented at the end of the chapter as a contrast to violence.

A few of the more important points in our presentation will be summarized here. Ingratiation—which can take the form of flattery, opinion conformity, or positive self-presentation—can be a powerful tool if Other does not see that it is being manipulated. Shaming is seldom discussed in our society, but it is a common and powerful technique around the world.

The greatest danger with shaming is that it will drive Other away from the group, weakening the group's future influence on Other. The solution to this problem is reintegrative shaming, which combines shaming with gestures that reaffirm Other's bonds with the group.

Tit-for-tat—rewarding Other for cooperation and punishing Other for noncooperation—may well be the most common of all the contentious tactics. Its main drawback is that it can create a conflict spiral—a vicious circle of action and reaction—which leaves Other without a clear understanding that it can do business with Party. This problem can be mitigated by giving Other a grace period before administering a punishment, by explaining the tit-for-tat procedure in words, and by occasionally shifting to cooperation during a conflict spiral with the hope that Other will reciprocate.

Promises, threats, and coercive commitments all must be credible to be effective. This means that Other must see Party as having the *capability* and *intent* to take the action that has been mentioned and having enough *surveillance* over Other's behavior to tell whether Other has complied. Credibility of intent is always a two-edged sword. On the one hand, Party must demonstrate that *if Other complies,* it will receive the reward promised or not get hurt. On the other hand, Party must also demonstrate that *if Other fails to comply,* it will not receive the reward promised or will get hurt. Many an actor has failed to influence his or her target by deploying only one side of this sword, only emphasizing what will happen if Other complies or what will happen if Other fails to comply.

Violence—by which we mean physical harm to person or property—can have emotional as well as instrumental (strategic) sources, and its use often reflects both kinds of sources working together. Instrumental violence is frequently coupled with one of the tactics mentioned above: tit-for-tat, threat, or coercive commitment. Terrorist violence is a tactic of weak groups, aimed at eroding the power or determination of strong groups that are viewed as dominating or otherwise frustrating them.

Nonviolent resistance, like terrorism, is a tool of the weak that puts pressure for change on the strong. But unlike terrorism it does not produce runaway escalation and hence leaves few harmful results. Most nonviolent campaigns take the form of coercive commitments, such as Gandhi's fasts to the death or sit-ins in government buildings. As a weapon, nonviolent resistance has two strengths that are not shared with terrorism, both resulting from the disproportion between the mild (though persistent) tactics employed by the resisters and the heavy, punitive response these tactics often produce. One is that this disproportion can elicit third party sympathy for the protestors and resulting outside pressure on the target. The other is that it can provoke guilt among some members of the target group, which may hasten a change in that group's policies.

Throughout this chapter, we have portrayed Party as the initiator of contentious moves and Other as their recipient and reactor. This portrayal is sometimes accurate, but it is often a distortion. The interactions of antagonists are often more like a minuet in which the steps of *each* side are matched quite precisely by corresponding moves on the part of the other. Each side takes, in turn, the stance of the initiator and that of the recipient, and escalation is as much (or more) the product of a conflict spiral or vicious circle as of a sequence of tactical initiatives on the part of only one side. Both kinds of patterns will be closely examined in the next four chapters, which concern the processes and conditions that produce escalation and that cause so many escalated conflicts to persist.

PART II

Escalation

5

Escalation and Its Development

❖

Development of the Cold War ◆ Transformations That Occur During
Escalation ◆ A Domestic Escalation ◆ Escalation Models ◆ *The Contender-Defender
Model* ◆ *The Conflict Spiral Model* ◆ *Relationship Between the Contender-Defender
and Conflict Spiral Models* ◆ Summary and Conclusions

*T*he term *escalation* brings the realm of international relations most prominently to mind. Hence, we start with an example from this realm, the development of the Cold War. However, escalation is not limited to this realm
and can occur at all levels of society. Accordingly, we will present examples from
several other realms as well.

DEVELOPMENT OF THE COLD WAR

The Cold War was a vast political conflict between the United States and the Soviet
Union, which began to develop immediately after 1945 and persisted until the late
1980s. In its time, this harsh, often frightening conflict was the dominant feature on
the international landscape, and it affected the lives of a tremendous number of
people around the globe. It never led to a full-scale war between the superpowers,
though war came close at the time of the Cuban Missile Crisis (to be described in
Chapter 9). However, most of the wars in this period were outgrowths of the Cold

War, including the Korean and Vietnam Wars and the Soviet military action in Afghanistan. Today the Soviet Union is gone, and the rivalry between these regions of the world has largely disappeared. But the Cold War has left a continuing legacy in many of our institutions and much of our literature. Here is the story of how the Cold War developed.

The United States and the Soviet Union were allies during the Second World War, which ended in 1945 with high hopes for continued cooperation. But the Soviets emerged from the war with deep suspicion of the West. This led them to seek control of the nations adjoining their territory, making it difficult to maintain East-West cooperation. The Soviets built a communist satellite system in Eastern Europe, supported communist guerrillas in Greece, and applied political pressure to Turkey. In 1947 the United States responded to these actions in three ways: It gave military aid to Greece and Turkey. It created the Marshall Plan, designed to revitalize the economy of Western Europe and weaken Communist parties in Western European countries. And (in conjunction with Britain and later with France) it began the slow process of unifying West Germany and rebuilding its economy, as a further bulwark against Soviet expansion.

The latter move was viewed with considerable alarm by the Soviet Union, which had been at war with Germany twice in the preceding thirty years. The Soviets responded at first with protests. Then, in 1948, they tried sporadically interrupting communications between Berlin (which was under joint control but was an enclave surrounded by the Russian controlled portion of Germany) and West Germany. Finally, after the West introduced a unified currency in West Germany, the Soviets installed a full blockade of Berlin, claiming that they were repairing the routes to the city. The United States and its allies responded by launching a successful airlift between Berlin and West Germany. They also began negotiations that led to the formation of the North Atlantic Treaty Organization (NATO), a military alliance involving the United States and most of the Western European nations. This latter development led eventually to the rearmament of West Germany, which caused considerable further alarm in the Soviet Union.

The Cold War continued until the late 1980s, but we interrupt the story at this point because we have said enough to give a dramatic example of conflict escalation.

TRANSFORMATIONS THAT OCCUR DURING ESCALATION

There are two related meanings of the term *escalation*. It may mean that one of the participants in conflict is using heavier tactics than before—is putting greater pressure on the other participant. Or it may mean that there is an increase in the intensity of a conflict *as a whole*. These meanings are related, since escalation by one participant usually leads to escalation by the other and hence an intensification of the conflict as a whole. We use the term in both senses in this book, but mainly in the latter sense.

As conflicts escalate, they go through certain incremental transformations. Although these transformations occur separately on each side, they affect the conflict as a whole because they are usually mirrored by the other side. As a result of these transformations, the conflict is intensified in ways that are sometimes exceedingly difficult to undo. The aim of this chapter and the next is to understand the nature of these transformations and some of the processes by which they take place.

At least five types of transformations commonly occur during escalation. All may not be found in a single conflict, but all are very common. The five transformations are as follows:

1. *Light→heavy.* As we observed in Chapter 4, Party's efforts to get its way in a contentious exchange typically begin with light influence attempts: ingratiation overtures or persuasive arguments. In many cases, these gentle tactics are supplanted by their heavier counterparts: threats, coercive commitments, and so on. Eventually even violence may erupt. The events of 1948 illustrate this kind of transformation. The Soviet Union moved from protest to disrupting communication and eventually to blockading a city. The United States and its allies also moved decisively from strengthening a new ally to the formation of a full military alliance.

2. *Small→large.* As conflict escalates, there is a tendency for issues to proliferate (McEwen & Milburn, 1993). There is also a tendency for the parties to become increasingly absorbed in the struggle and to commit additional resources to it in an effort to prevail. Both tendencies may be seen in the Cold War crisis. On the Soviet side, the initial general suspicion of the West mushroomed into a large number of specific complaints: the program to weaken Communist parties, the rebuilding of West Germany, the introduction of a separate West German currency, and finally the formation of a hostile military alliance. From the viewpoint of the United States, new issues appeared at every turn: the introduction of a communist dictatorship in Czechoslovakia, the support of guerrillas in Greece, the Berlin blockade. Both sides rapidly increased the resources allocated to the conflict, and the conflict developed into a national obsession on both sides.

3. *Specific→general.* In escalating conflict, specific issues tend to give way to general issues (Coleman, 1957), and the overall relationship between the parties deteriorates. Over the painful history of an escalating exchange, small, concrete concerns tend to be supplanted by grandiose and all-encompassing positions and by a general intolerance of the other side.

These changes were very clear in the United States during the development of the Cold War. The concern about specific incidents that was seen in 1945 and 1946 changed rapidly into a general indictment of the Soviet Union and of communism as a whole. The Soviets were seen as new incarnations of Hitlerite Germany, a totally untrustworthy "evil empire" bent on conquering the world. This led to such excesses in the United States as McCarthyism, a refusal for many years to recognize the People's Republic of China, and participation in the Vietnam War. The relationship between the United States and the Soviet Union deteriorated so badly that at times there was practically no communication at all.

4.   *Doing well→winning→hurting Other.* In the early stages of many conflicts, Party is simply out to do as well as it can for itself, without regard for how well or how poorly Other is doing. This outlook has been described by Deutsch (1958) as an "individualistic orientation," an outlook characterized by self-interest that is quite independent of Other's fate. As conflict escalates, however, Party's simple interest in doing well is supplanted by a clearly competitive objective. Now doing well means outdoing Other. Finally, as escalation continues and Party's costs begin to mount, its goals tend to shift again. The objective now is to hurt Other and, if Party is experiencing cost, to hurt Other more than Party is hurting (Glasl, 1982). For every drop of blood that Party has shed, a far more terrible bloodletting must be forced on Other. This is competition in the extreme.[1]

Accompanying these motivational changes are changes in Party's feelings toward Other. Positive feelings quickly dissipate as conflict escalates, while mild negative feelings—such as irritation—take their place. As escalation continues, these mild feelings turn into much stronger ones—such as anger, hostility, and eventually intense hatred. Feelings like this support, and are supported by, the changes in objectives just described.

Such transformations were apparent in Soviet-American relations after 1945. What began as a desire to reverse specific policies was transmogrified into a broad competition, in which each party had strong negative feelings about the other and sought to defeat the other in every corner of the globe. The importance of this competition in the United States was reflected in the widespread and politically explosive view that China had been "lost" as a result of

---

[1] Fisher & Keashly (1990) add a fourth stage in which the parties aim to destroy each other. Translated into the terms of the dual concern model encountered in Chapter 3, this progression of goals produces a *negative* other-concern, which is not shown in Figure 3.1.

its 1949 revolution. In the thinking of many on both sides, the logical solution to the problem was to weaken the other side or even, for a few people, to destroy it.

5. *Few→many.* Conflicts that begin with the agitation of a small number of participants often grow, in the face of continued conflict, into collective efforts. An illustration of this is the development, during the Cold War, of two large military alliances: NATO and its Eastern counterpart, the Warsaw Pact. This transformation may be due, in part, to tactical thinking by Party. If Other won't do as Party wants—and if Party is unable to get its way by threatening, promising, or in some other way manipulating Other—then it is in Party's best interest to find others who are willing to band together with it. What Party cannot accomplish on its own it may well be able to achieve with the increased support and muscle of its associates. This transformation may also be due to changes in the thinking of formerly neutral third parties. Alarmed by the demands Other has placed on Party or the tactics Other has used, some of these of these third parties may throw their support to Party; while other third parties, equally alarmed by Party's demands and tactics may gravitate into Other's camp. The result is community polarization, a condition that will be discussed more fully in Chapters 6 and 8.

A DOMESTIC ESCALATION

The transformations just described are not limited to the international arena. Indeed, they are found just as often in domestic settings. Consider this example (Peterson, 1983) involving a young married couple, as recounted by the wife:

> We were in the car on the way to visit my parents. We had had a tough time getting ready for the trip and were both tired. Paul was in the back of the station wagon reading. I was driving. We were on the Turnpike, and I asked him to move to the side. I wanted to pass and I couldn't see through him. He told me to look out the side mirror or turn around and look. I'm accustomed to using the rear view mirror and I didn't feel I should have to change my driving habits when he could move to the side a little so I could see. A little later I said, "Will you move?" . . . He just sat and glared. Twice more I asked him to move and finally he blew up and told me to pull over so he could drive. Then he told me he'd show me how he could pass without looking in either mirror by looking around. Paul kept on with some more nasty remarks. (p. 360)

This escalation ended a few minutes later with an apology from the husband, in reply to his wife's suggestion that he had overreacted. Thus, it was brief and by no means momentous. Nevertheless, three of the transformations we mentioned earlier occurred. The conflict went from *light to heavy,* with the husband first glaring, then showing anger, and finally becoming insulting. It went from *small to large,* with the wife reiterating her demands to the point that they overwhelmed the husband, and both of them become fixated on the quarrel. It went from *doing well to hurting Other,* with the husband first simply declining to move and eventually shifting to efforts to make his wife suffer. We are not told the nature of the husband's "nasty" remarks, but if they were a general indictment of his wife's driving skills, it would mean that a transformation from *specific to general* had also occurred.[2]

ESCALATION MODELS

To understand escalation, we must know what processes occur within and between Party and Other as their conflict intensifies. There are three broad models[3] of escalation (Pruitt & Gahagan, 1974): the *contender-defender* model, the *conflict spiral* model, and the *structural change* model. These models provide three accounts of what is happening when escalation takes place. All three have some value, accurately describing the developments in some kinds of escalation. None can be discarded in favor of another. We deal with the contender-defender and the conflict spiral models in this chapter, then turn to the structural change model in Chapter 6, which also deals with deteriorating relationships.

---

[2] For another domestic illustration of escalation, recall the Chapter 1 story of Ben and his father. There, light tactics were supplanted by heavier ones, the number of issues proliferated (starting with the car, then moving on to various other concerns), motivation shifted, and the number of parties to the conflict increased to the point of including the entire family. While the anecdote does not provide information about precisely what was said in the escalating exchange, one can imagine Dad shifting from a focus on the car to a focus on his son's traits of laziness and selfishness—in which case the shift in focus from specific to general issues would be present as well.

[3] A model is an abstract pattern of thought from which explanations or predictions of particular events can be derived. It is quite common for alternative models to be available for explaining or predicting the same event, and more than one of these models may be correct. For instance, suppose we are trying to explain how a child has learned that 7 times 7 equals 49. If we derive an explanation from the reinforcement model of learning, we might conclude that the child acquired this knowledge because he or she was praised for correctly stating "Seven times seven is forty-nine." If we use instead a social learning model, we might conclude that the knowledge was formed because the child imitated people he or she respected, who were saying "Seven times seven is forty-nine." People often try to choose *between* two explanations of this kind, but it is frequently the case that *both* explanations are correct. The equation could first be acquired by imitation and then become a permanent part of memory by rewarded repetition.

The Contender-Defender Model[4]

The contender-defender model draws a distinction between Party (the contender) and Other (the defender). Party is viewed as having a *goal of creating change* that places it in conflict with Other. Party's goal may be to take something from Other, to alter reality at Other's expense, or to stop Other's annoying behavior. Party ordinarily starts with mild contentious tactics, because this is the least risky approach. But if these do not work, Party moves on to heavier tactics, continuing to escalate until Other gives in or the cost of continued escalation is greater than the value of the goal sought. Other may be passive in such a sequence or may escalate in response to Party's escalation. But if Other escalates, its reasons for doing so are strictly defensive, whereas Party's are not.

Many past campaigns of conquest have involved escalation of this kind, including the efforts by Cortez and Pisarro (contenders) to defeat the Aztecs and Incas (defenders) so as to steal their gold, and Napoleon's campaign against Russia. This model also helps understand one of the stages in the development of the Cold War. This is the point at which the Soviet Union adopted the goal of blocking the unification of West Germany, a severe source of annoyance to them. At first the Soviets (the contender) employed the mild tactic of protest. When this did not work, they moved to a heavier tactic of sporadically interrupting communications between Berlin and West Germany. When this was unsuccessful, and the West (the defender) introduced a unified West German currency, the Soviets employed an extremely heavy tactic, a full blockade of Berlin.[5]

Our driving (domestic escalation) story also describes a contender-defender sequence. The husband is the contender. Annoyed by persistent demands from his wife, he moves from mild persuasive arguments, to angry nonverbal displays, to insulting remarks. However, we must be careful about how we characterize this incident as it is the wife who is telling the story, which may be incomplete (see below).

The contender-defender model also fits the results of an experiment on individual and group response to persistent annoyance (Mikolic et al., 1997). Persistent annoyance was produced by Other (a confederate of the researchers) withholding supplies that Party (the participant) needed for the task it was doing. Party was allowed to call Other at any time, and seven contentious tactics were identified in a content analysis of these calls. The participants (the contenders) used these tactics in a standard, escalatory sequence. First they requested the supplies, then demanded them, then complained about Other's behavior, then got angry with Other, then

---

[4] The contender-defender model was called the "aggressor-defender model" in earlier editions.
[5] While this series of incidents involved unilateral escalation by the Soviet Union, the overall process that produced the Cold War was circular in nature and better fits the conflict spiral model. This point will be elaborated below.

threatened Other, then repeatedly harassed Other, and finally insulted Other. Few participants went all the way to the top of this sequence, but most went part way up in the order just listed. Interestingly, groups, on the whole, escalated considerably further than did individuals.

School Shootings   The contender-defender model helps us understand the school shootings that have plagued the United States in recent years. A common pattern found in many shootings is that the shooters had been subjected to persistent annoyance, in the form of taunting and bullying by some of their fellow students. Ultimately, the taunted individuals (the contenders) resorted to lethal violence against their adversaries and often against other schoolmates and teachers, an extreme form of escalation. Nothing can justify this violence, but understanding that it is usually a matter of revenge may help to prevent future tragedies of this kind.[6]

Consider fourteen-year-old Michael Carneal of Paducah, Kentucky. He was reported to have been teased and picked on by his schoolmates because of his small size. On December 1, 1997, he burst into a morning prayer group meeting at his school, killing three students and wounding five. Similarly, Evan Ramsey, 16, of Bethel, Alaska, was said to have been harassed throughout his school years for his slight frame and shy manner. He was called "Screech," after a nerdy character in the TV program, *Saved by the Bell*. On February 19, 1997, he went into a crowded gathering area of his school and opened fire, eventually killing one student and the principal and wounding two other students.[7]

The escalation in these and other similar cases differs from others we have discussed (e.g., the behavior of the husband in the driving story) in that it moves suddenly to an extreme reaction rather than through gradations of hostile behavior. The future killers probably avoided more moderate tactics because they had discovered that these produced even more teasing and bullying. Instead they suppressed their desire to retaliate until it became an overwhelming force in their lives. At that point, they had a sense of "I can't take it anymore; enough is enough."

What psychological forces are at work in such cases? The taunting and bullying experienced by the future killers almost always occurred in the full view of other people. Such public humiliation is a threat to Party's

---

[6] The most frequent motive behind school shootings is revenge for past annoyance, according to a study conducted by the U.S. Secret Service that examined the cases of 41 youths involved in 37 school shootings, from 1974 to 2000 (Vossekuil et al., 2000).

[7] The demeaning experiences of these future killers appear to be the outgrowth of a prevailing sense in many American schools that it is right for dominant groups to tease and taunt deviants. Thus after the Columbine shootings, a Columbine football player was reported to say, "Columbine is a good clean place except for those rejects. . . . Sure we teased them. But what do you expect with kids who come to school with weird hairdos and horns on their hats? . . . If you want to get rid of someone, usually you tease 'em" (Aronson, 2000, pp. 71–72).

image, in its own and other people's eyes, and can evoke an overwhelming sense of *shame*. Research shows that feelings of shame often produce a desire for revenge (Scheff, 1994). James Gilligan (1996), a psychiatrist who has worked with many violent criminals, asserts: "I have yet to see a serious act of violence that was not provoked by the both parties' experience of feeling shamed and humiliated, disrespected and ridiculed, and that did not represent the attempt to prevent or undo this 'loss of face'—no matter how severe the punishment, even if it includes death" (p. 110).

Furthermore, there may have been an element of *ego depletion* in these cases, a reduction in the capacity for self-control resulting from too much prior suppression of the desire to retaliate. In a study of this process (Finkel & Campbell, 2001), participants watched emotionally charged film clips. While doing so, they were asked to either suppress their emotional reactions to the clips (high ego depletion) or not (low ego depletion). Afterwards, they were asked to indicate how they would react to offensive behavior from their romantic partner. As predicted, those who had suppressed their emotional reactions indicated that they would react more punitively than those who had not. Prior emotional suppression had led to a reduction in self-control.[8]

Of course, taunting and bullying are common in schools (Nansel et al., 2001), and violent revenge is a rare occurrence. What sets these killers apart from the ordinary victims of public humiliation? Here theory is weak and we cannot begin to give a definitive answer, but two points can be made. One is that the killers either operated as groups or had social support from other rejected students, and we know from the experiment mentioned earlier (Mikolic et al., 1997) that groups escalate further than individuals. Most of the individual killers shared their shooting plan with other humiliated peers (Vossekuil et al., 2000) and got encouragement and sometimes help from them. Some friends even urged an escalation of the plan. Again, take the case of Evan Ramsey. He told two of his friends that he wanted to bring a gun to school so that he could scare his tormentors by brandishing it. His friends urged him to shoot so as to be sure to get people's attention. Ramsey put three people on his hit list, but these friends suggested eleven others. Ramsey claimed that he did not plan to shoot the principal, but he did so at the urging of one of his friends who disliked the principal (Dedman, 2000). The other point is that all these killers had access to guns, a weapon that was vastly more lethal than any other available in their environment.

---

[8] We do not mean to imply that the school killers acted impulsively in a spur-of-the-moment explosion of anger. Most of them made a plan for revenge and carefully selected their weapons and initial targets (Vossekuil et al., 2000). Rather, the point is that ego depletion removed the moral and future-oriented controls that would otherwise have moderated their plans. The concept of ego depletion was developed by Baumeister and his colleagues (see Baumeister et al., 1999).

Perspective on the Contender-Defender Model   Though the contender-defender model fits some cases of escalation like the school shootings, it is given too much weight in everyday thinking. Indeed, this is the only model that most people use in trying to understand escalation. The problem with this model is that it postulates a *unidirectional* causal sequence, with one party always taking the lead in escalation, whereas most cases of escalation involve a *circular* process. Party reacts to Other's contentious behavior, followed by Other reacting to Party's contentious behavior, followed by Party reacting to Other's contentious behavior, and so on. To understand such sequences, we need the conflict spiral model.

The popularity of the contender-defender model is probably due to the fact that it satisfies the natural urge to look for somebody to blame for unpleasant events. One side (which is usually labeled the "aggressor") is viewed as taking the lead in heating up the conflict, while the other (which is labeled the "defender") is viewed as legitimately trying to counter the first side's outrageous behavior. For example, in the Cold War most Americans viewed the Soviet Union as the ultimate source of the escalation and hence as the "aggressor." In reality, both sides were contributing about equally to the conflict, and the conflict spiral model was a better fit.[9]

The Conflict Spiral Model

The conflict spiral model holds that escalation results from a vicious circle of action and reaction. Party's contentious tactics encourage a contentious retaliatory or defensive reaction from Other, which provokes further contentious behavior from Party, completing the circle and starting it on its next iteration. The conflict spiral model is a bilateral reaction model, because each party is reacting to the other party's prior actions.[10]

In a conflict spiral, the motivation on both sides is partly a matter of revenge—to punish Other for the suffering it has produced. This motivation

---

[9] Parties involved in conflict usually view the other side as the "aggressor," because this makes them feel better about themselves or their group. Thus, most Soviet citizens had a mirror image of the United States as unilaterally responsible for the conflict (Bronfenbrenner, 1961; Frank, 1982; White, 1984). Today, Israelis blame the Palestinians and Palestinians blame the Israelis for destructive actions that are mainly part of a conflict spiral.

[10] The conflict spiral model is found in the writings of many theorists, including North et al. (1964), Osgood (1962, 1966), and Richardson (1967). The distinction between the conflict spiral model and the contender-defender model is hardest to grasp in the case of escalation in response to persistent annoyance. In this case, Party (the contender) is reacting to Other's behavior and Other may escalate in response to Party's escalation. What makes this a case of contender-defender rather than conflict spiral is that Party does not escalate in response to Other's escalation but only in response to the persistent annoyance from Other. Hence there is no spiral of action, reaction, and *further* reaction.

is also partly a matter of defense or deterrence—to protect against Other's preparations, teach Other a lesson, and make Other suffer enough that it will stop its annoying behavior.

Conflict spirals are often hard to stop once they get started because each side feels that failing to retaliate will be seen as a sign of weakness, inviting further annoying behavior from the other side. Each side feels that its reputation for resolute self-defense is on the line. In addition, neither side is willing to make conciliatory moves that might break the cycle. One reason for this is that Other is not trusted to reciprocate such moves; requitement is not expected from a party that has gone as far as Other has gone. A second reason is the fear that making a conciliatory move will reward Other and hence encourage more annoying behavior. A third reason is that Other is typically seen as the "aggressor" and hence blamed for the conflict spiral. This implies that Other (rather than Party) has the responsibility to make the first conciliatory move.

Tactics move from light to heavy in most conflict spirals, because (up to a point) each reaction is more severe and intense than the action that provoked it. Why should this be? There are three main reasons. One is that conflict spirals produce the transformation from small to large mentioned earlier. Each retaliatory or defensive reaction in the spiral provides a new issue for the target of this action. Hence, each party's list of the other's transgressions grows longer and longer as the spiral continues, provoking a heavier and heavier reaction. The second reason is that each side's own losses in a conflict usually look larger than the other side's losses (Baumeister et al., 1990). Hence, what looks to each side like a measured response to the other's provocation looks to the other like undue escalation, deserving a response in kind. The third reason is that people often overlook the fact that they are in a conflict spiral and view themselves as responding to persistent annoyance from Other. They start with mild contentious tactics because these involve the least risk. But if these tactics are unsuccessful, they adopt heavier tactics in what they view as a rational effort to find a level of pressure that will persuade Other to desist. The irony of this is that Other is reacting in the same way to *their* level of escalation. Hence, they would be better off *de*-escalating rather than escalating.

The conflict spiral model provides insight into the broader Cold War escalation, which involved a vicious circle.[11] In response to Soviet moves in Eastern Europe and in Greece and Turkey, the United States and its allies began to establish a West German state. In response to this action, the Soviet Union instituted a blockade of Berlin. In response to that blockade, the United States and its allies formed NATO and began to arm West Germany. And so on.

---

[11] The events that were mentioned earlier in which the Soviet Union adopted increasingly heavy tactics in an effort to block the unification of West Germany can be thought of as a contender-defender episode within this larger conflict spiral.

In our driving story *as told by the wife*, only the husband escalated. But this may well be a self-serving distortion of what really happened. It is possible that her "will you move" was said in an angry tone, followed by something like "D**n it, I can't see through you." If so, her husband may have been reacting to her escalations as she was to his, and the process may have actually been a conflict spiral.

A third example of a conflict spiral can be seen in the violent struggle between Israel and the Palestinians that erupted in 2000 and continuously escalated through the point at which this chapter was written (April 2002). Every week, there were new violent actions from each side that provoked increasingly more violent retribution from the other. After trying milder tactics, the Palestinians began to send suicide bombers in ever increasing numbers, while the Israelis resorted to progressively more repressive military actions. Each side viewed itself as engaged in unilateral "defensive" escalation against an implacable "aggressor," with its own illegitimate agenda. Hence for each side, the only reasonable course of action was to escalate still further so as to "knock some sense into the other" and cow the other into stopping its aggression. The result was a tragedy of epic proportions.[12]

The conflict spiral between Israel and the Palestinians was exacerbated by a strong belief on both sides that they had winning weapons: suicide bombers on the part of the Palestinians and conventional military force on the part of Israel. It was hard, at that time, to tell objectively which of these weapons was stronger, hence, the optimism on both sides.

In addition to explaining the development of escalation, the conflict spiral model helps understand the *perpetuation* of high levels of escalation—that is, the fact that heavy tactics, once used, often continue to be employed. Consider a standard fistfight. If I hit you, you may well hit me back, which leads me to hit you again, and so on. At first, the blows become heavier and heavier and the conflict escalates. Then, because of limitations in human strength, the blows reach an asymptote beyond which they cannot grow heavier. Each of us is retaliating at about the level of provocation received. A conflict spiral is still going on, but it is now producing a highly escalated steady state rather than further escalation. The perpetuation of escalation will be discussed in much greater detail in Chapter 8.

---

[12] The word "tragedy" is used here in the sense of a classical Greek tragedy in which an individual takes actions, for what appear to be good and sufficient reasons, that produce tragic consequences for that individual. In escalating conflict spirals, both parties are in that same self-destructive boat.

Relationship between the Contender-Defender and Conflict Spiral Models

Combinations of contender-defender dynamics and conflict spiral dynamics are often found in escalating conflict. For example, contender-defender sequences are often part of larger conflict spirals, as in the Soviet Union's reaction to the plan to unify West Germany (see footnote 11). In such cases, the goal that impels the contender is persistent annoyance from the defender.

A further example of this phenomenon is the Nazi German effort to conquer Europe in the late 1930s and 1940s, a unilateral escalatory action by any definition of the term. Most people do not realize that this effort was in large part a reaction to the humiliation of Germany after the First World War—the reparations Germany had to pay, the resulting inflation. Hence, the contender-defender sequence of the Second World War can be viewed as embedded in a larger conflict spiral that began before the First World War.

Another kind of combination is where a conflict spiral is embedded in a larger contender-defender episode, in which Party is employing escalating tactics in an effort to influence Other. An example of this is the violent escalation between Israel and the Palestinians discussed earlier, which originated (in the year 2000) in an effort by Palestinian youth groups and militants (the Second Intifada) to persuade Israel to give up its West Bank and Gaza settlements and remove the Israeli army that guards these settlements. At first they threw rocks at Israeli soldiers and then began to shoot at Israeli soldiers and settlers.[13] Take away the conflict spiral, and you would still have had some serious assaults from the Palestinian side because of their resentment of the Israeli occupation—though by no means as many.

SUMMARY AND CONCLUSIONS

Escalation—the use of progressively heavier contentious tactics—is by no means an inevitable outcome of conflict, but it is an important one because of the great human cost it often produces. Escalation is commonly accompanied by several other transformations: issues proliferate, parties become increasingly committed to the struggle, specific issues give way

---

[13] Some would say that the escalation began with the Israeli occupation of the West Bank or with Ariel Sharon's walk on Jerusalem's Temple Mount (Haram ash-Sharif) rather than with the Palestinian rock throwing. However, we mark this as the beginning of the round of violence that began in the year 2000, defining violence as efforts to physically harm people on the other side.

to general ones, the desire to succeed turns into a desire to win, which turns into a desire to hurt Other, positive feelings give way to negative feelings, and both sides grow by recruiting formerly neutral individuals and groups.

Two models of escalation are discussed in this chapter: the contender-defender model traces escalation to Party's (the contender's) effort to take something from Other (the defender), alter reality at Other's expense, or stop Other's annoying behavior. If milder tactics fail, Party moves to heavier ones in an effort to prevail. In response to this offensive, Other may remain passive or escalate defensively. The conflict spiral model traces escalation to a vicious circle of action and reaction—the two sides escalate in response to each other. Escalation is often best explained by invoking both models, viewing the progressively heavier tactics as either a contender-defender episode embedded in a broader conflict spiral or a conflict spiral that is part of a larger contender-defender dynamic.

In Chapter 6, we turn to a third and more complicated escalation model, the structural change model.

6

The Structural Change Model

❖

Psychological Changes ✦ *Emotional Changes* ✦ *Hostile Attitudes, Perceptions, and Goals* ✦ Changes in Groups ✦ *The Crisis at UB* ✦ *Nature, Source, and Impact of Group Changes* ✦ Changes in Communities ✦ Summary and Conclusions

The structural change model,[1] to which we turn in this chapter, provides further insight into the development of escalation. This model describes changes (i.e., processes) that occur when escalation takes place and that push the escalation forward. These changes can also cause escalation to persist and recur. Some of these changes are *psychological states* (e.g., hostile attitudes) that develop within individual disputants or group decision makers. Others are changes in the *way groups function* (e.g., the development of militant leadership). Still others are changes in the *communities* surrounding the disputing parties (e.g., community polarization). All are called "structural" changes because they are changes in one or another feature of the situation affecting the parties' choice of tactics.

Two versions of the structural change model can be constructed, one building on the contender-defender model and the other on the conflict spiral model. The two versions are similar in the sorts of changes they describe, so only the latter

---

[1] This model is implied by the writings of Burton (1962), Coleman (1957), Pruitt & Olczak (1995), and Schumpeter (1955, first published in 1919), among others.

will be presented here.[2] This version is shown schematically in Figure 6.1. Here a conflict spiral is seen, in which heavy tactics used by Party produce structural changes in Other (segment A), which encourage a harsh reaction from Other (segment B), producing structural changes in Party (segment C), which encourage further heavy tactics from Party (segment D), and so on around and around. We call the process seen in this figure a *cycle of escalation.*

This version of the structural change model embodies Deutsch's "crude law" of conflict development (Deutsch, 2000a). In the terms used in our book, the crude law says that processes that produce heavy contentious tactics are also produced by those tactics.[3] These processes include all of the structural changes discussed in this chapter. For example, if we insert "hostile attitudes" in the boxes marked "structural changes" in Figure 6.1, we see that hostile attitudes both produce and are produced by heavy contentious tactics.

The value of the structural change model is that it helps us derive hypotheses about the conditions under which conflicts will escalate and under which escalation will persist and recur. This is because we know a lot about the conditions that allow and encourage the changes described in the model, in other words, the conditions that strengthen the causal sequences shown in segments A and C of Figure 6.1. We also know something about the conditions that encourage expression of these changes—that strengthen the causal sequences shown in segments B and D. By the logic of Figure 6.1, all of these conditions should make conflict spirals more likely to go forward and persist, and hence should encourage conflicts to escalate and stay escalated. Most of the discussion of these conditions will be presented in the two chapters following this one.

PSYCHOLOGICAL CHANGES

Emotional Changes

Some psychological changes involve emotions or emotionally related perceptions. Emotions can have a powerful effect on behavior. They can build up to the point where they overcome caution and produce heavily escalated behavior. Nevertheless, they are usually temporary states, re-

---

[2] After reading this chapter, the reader may want to work out the details of a contender-defender version of the structural change model.

[3] The original statement of this law was considerably broader. Deutsch (2000a) states his "crude law of social relations" as follows, "The characteristic processes and effects elicited by a given type of social relationship also tend to elicit that type of social relationship" (p. 29).

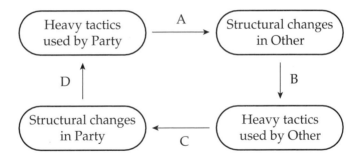

FIGURE 6.1

Structural change model. The circle of arrows represents a cycle of escalation.

lated to the events of the moment and persisting only so long as the conflict spiral persists. Once the conflict spiral abates, emotions tend to disappear. We will discuss four such states here: blame, anger, fear, and image threats.

Blame and Anger   Blaming Other was mentioned as an antecedent of contentious behavior in Chapter 3. Here we are treating blame as a *variable* and saying that greater blame leads to more heavily escalated actions. Blame encourages escalation for two reasons: One is that blame encourages anger (Averill, 1983), which produces a desire to hurt Other. The second is that blame makes it seem necessary to punish Other with the hope of teaching it a lesson.

There are a number of perceptions that encourage blame when Other takes actions that harm Party's interests. Blame will be greater if it appears that Other could foresee that its actions would be harmful (Dyck & Rule, 1978). This makes the harm seem voluntary rather than accidental. Also, actions that seem freely taken are likely to evoke more blame than those that result from heavy environmental pressures (Geen, 1990). Even the latter actions may evoke some blame if Other is supposed to be responsible for resisting such pressures. Actions that break social norms (Mallick & McCandless, 1966) or are atypical of the way other parties behave are also viewed as especially blameworthy (Ferguson & Rule, 1983). Other must have a compelling excuse to avoid blame in such circumstances.

The implication of these points is that conflict is especially likely to escalate when Party sees Other's contentious behavior as illegitimate and not attributable to chance or extenuating circumstances. Under these conditions, Party is particularly likely to become angry at or see a need to discipline Other, producing punitive behavior that will provoke Other in turn and hence start or continue a conflict spiral.

Fear   Sometimes Other's harsh actions seem threatening and evoke *fear* instead of, or in addition to, blame and anger. Fear produces a different kind of conflict spiral than that produced by blame and anger. Blame and anger are prominent in *retaliatory spirals,* where each party punishes the other for actions it finds aversive. Examples are shouting matches, fist-fights, and the like. Fear, on the other hand, is prominent in *defensive spirals,* in which each party is trying to protect itself from a threat it finds in the other's self-protective actions. An example is an arms race, in which two nations steadily increase their stockpile of arms, each doing so in response to an increase in the other nation's arms (Richardson, 1967). Escalation is often a combination of both retaliatory and defensive spirals, the Cold War and the story of Ben and Dad (in Chapter 1) being cases in point.

Image Threats   Threats to Party's image—the way Party appears to self or others—are an important source of escalation. Escalation is particularly likely when there are threats to Party's image of adequacy—of having power, status, forcefulness, autonomy, or integrity (Coleman, 1997; Felson, 1982). Such threats produce both anger and fear.[4]

Toch (1970) gives an example of a conflict spiral that appears to have involved threats to both parties' images of strength, status, and forcefulness. The incident took place in a state prison.

> We were watching these cats play cards, and we were standing behind this dude. He was one of these big iron lifters, you know. About ninety feet wide, you know, he was one of those. And he turned around and told us, "Don't stand behind me, punk, when I'm playing," you know. And I just looked at my partner and he looked at me, you know, . . . and he turned around again and said, you know, "I told you not to stand behind me." And he said you know, "Bless you, man." And the dude got up, man, so I hit him on one side and the other dude hit him, and we were both on him, man. And we beat him to a pulp. . . . And after that I felt like a king, man. I felt like, you know, I'm the man; you're not going to mess with me. (pp. 164–165)

Image threats of this kind are as important to nations as to individuals. Nations are often immensely concerned about their reputation for having power and being ready to use it. Many wars have been fought to produce such an image, an example being American involvement in the Vietnam War. Vietnam had no strategic importance to the United States,

---

[4] Such image threats were mentioned earlier as contributing to many of the school killings. Fear of image loss, discussed earlier, is a related concept.

but American officials were concerned about the challenge to their country's image posed by the communist guerilla movement there. They feared that the United States would be seen as weak-willed if it did not fight this movement, inviting communist aggression in other parts of the globe. This was part of a broader belief in interlocking commitments summarized in the statement, "If we aren't willing to fight them anywhere, we will have to fight them everywhere."

It is easy to belittle image-related concerns, to view them as senseless or even childish. But these concerns are a rational (though often shortsighted) reaction to being in an unregulated "jungle," such as the international arena, the "Wild West" during American expansion into that region, center city ghettos, and many state prisons. Environments of this kind lack adequate third party enforcement of norms against exploitation and assault. Hence, people feel they must defend themselves by developing an image of toughness—a reputation for strength and readiness to fight. There are other, less violent ways to avoid physical threats and attacks, but most people do not know or trust them. The usual motto, in Leo Durocher's words, is "Nice guys finish last."

The problem with this motto and with image-related concerns is that they often get people into serious trouble. In trying to look tough, people enrage or frighten others into a comparable reaction, starting a conflict spiral.[5] Paradoxically, people often end up as targets of the very assault they are trying to deter (Glasl, 1982). This is the security dilemma that was mentioned in Chapter 2.

Hostile Attitudes, Perceptions, and Goals

We turn now to another class of psychological states: hostile attitudes, perceptions, and goals, and two particularly potent kinds of perception: dehumanization and deindividuation. Like blame, anger, fear, and image threat, these states encourage the use of heavy contentious tactics. Hence, they can also be placed in the boxes marked "Structural changes" in Figure 6.1. But they have a quality of persistence that is absent in emotional states. They tend to outlast the conflict in which they were developed and affect the *relationship* between the parties, either (a) encouraging new escalation when another conflict arises or (b) causing the parties to perceive new conflicts where none exist.

It is common for hostile attitudes and perceptions to develop in conflict. Other comes to be distrusted, in the sense of being seen as indifferent or even opposed to Party's welfare. Party tends to attribute uncomplimentary traits to Other, such as being self-centered, morally unfit, or (in

---

[5] In the resulting conflict spirals, power-related image concerns become stronger and stronger, a phenomenon described by Winter (1987).

extreme cases) a diabolical enemy. This causes a phenomenon noted in Chapter 5, a transformation of issues from specific to general; instead of dealing with a particular threat from Other, Party must now deal with the general issue of how to resist an immoral enemy. It becomes hard to empathize with Other because of dehumanization or deindividuation. And there is a tendency to break off contact—to be unwilling to communicate. Zero-sum thinking often develops—it's *either* victory for Other *or* victory for Party. These changes typically occur on both sides of the dispute, because of the dynamics of the conflict spiral.

Such psychological changes help to account for the escalation that led to the Cold War, and for the flinty persistence of this escalation. Profound distrust, enemy images, and an inability to empathize took root in the United States during the early period of the Cold War and persisted until the early 1990s. Zero-sum thinking was extremely common, producing an inordinate fear of any communist advance. This fear gripped every American president from Truman onward; none wanted to be in office when another country fell to communism. Most Americans became unable to empathize with the genuine Soviet security needs that underlay a large proportion of their actions. Most communication with the Soviet Union was broken off in the late 1940s and early 1950s, and it remained at a low level until the period of de-escalation under President Gorbachev.

What are Attitudes and Perceptions?   An *attitude* is a positive or negative feeling toward or evaluation of some person or object. A *perception* is a belief about, or way of viewing, some person or object. Attitudes and perceptions tend to be consistent in valence. In other words, if Party has negative (positive) attitudes toward Other, Party also tends to have predominantly negative (positive) perceptions of Other.[6]

The following kinds of perceptions are particularly characteristic of escalated conflict: Other tends to be seen as deficient in moral virtue—as dishonest, unfriendly, or warlike. Other tends to be seen as different from Party in basic values, and most particularly to be selfish and inhumane (Struch & Schwartz, 1989). Other also tends to be distrusted; Party believes Other to be hostile to Party's welfare, and sometimes as having unlimited goals of defeating or even destroying Party. In addition, Other may be seen as lacking in ability or achievement (Blake & Mouton, 1962), though this kind of perceptual distortion is less likely because of the greater availability of sound evidence about these characteristics (Brewer, 1979). In contrast, Party usually sees itself as more moral than Other and often as a victim of Other's aggression (Hampson, 1997; White, 1984).

---

[6] There is an extensive social psychological literature on attitudes and perceptions. See Bar-Tal (2000), Erwin (2001), and Petty & Cacioppo (1996).

When groups are in conflict, these perceptions sometimes take the form of stereotypes coloring Party's perceptions of all members of the other group. Alternatively, Party may entertain what White (1984) has called the "evil-ruler enemy image." This is the perception that ordinary members of the other group feel neutral or even positive toward us, but their leaders are hideous monsters. If there is hostility on the other side, it is because ordinary people are being misled by their leaders. During the Cold War, American views of the Soviet Union and Soviet views of America reflected such images. The evil-ruler enemy image permits a decidedly negative view of Other while realistically acknowledging that not all members of any group can be evil.

Because they are part of a cycle of escalation, attitudes, and the perceptions that accompany them, tend to be similar on both sides of a controversy. This is known as the "mirror image" phenomenon (Bronfenbrenner, 1961; Frank, 1982; White, 1984). For example, the profound distrust felt by most Americans toward the Soviet Union had its counterpart in a somewhat less intense Soviet image of the United States. There is a similar mirror image in Israeli-Palestinian relations today; both sides view the other side as an implacable enemy. Unfortunately, the existence of a mirror image often goes unrecognized. Party tends to distrust Other without realizing that Other also distrusts Party.

Effects of Hostile Attitudes and Perceptions   Hostile attitudes and perceptions of Other encourage escalation and discourage the settlement of conflict in at least seven ways.

First, hostile attitudes and perceptions make it easier to blame Other for Party's unpleasant experiences. Because people look for culprits to explain such experiences and because the evidence about whom to hold responsible is often ambiguous, a disliked and distrusted Other tends to be blamed—while a liked Other is given the benefit of the doubt. Since blame often leads to the adoption of harsh, contentious tactics, this implies that hostile attitudes tend to encourage escalation.

A finding by Blumenthal et al. (1972) illustrates the impact of attitudes on blame. During a period of political turmoil in the United States, in the summer of 1969, people were found to blame the conflict on groups whose views they did not like. Liberals blamed the police, whereas conservatives blamed the demonstrators. Both tended to use the term "violence" to describe the behavior of groups they disliked and the term "justified force" to describe the behavior of groups whose views they favored. People were also more sympathetic to the use of force against the groups they blamed.

A second, related way in which hostile attitudes and perceptions lead to escalation is when Other is distrusted and its ambiguous actions are seen as *threatening* (Pruitt, 1965). Other is given little benefit of the doubt or credit for good intentions. This encourages fear and defensive escalation. The tendency to misinterpret Other's behavior is one reason why escalation is so difficult to escape. Other, growing tired of escalation, often tries to escape it by making goodwill gestures.[7] If Other is distrusted, as is likely to be the case after heavy escalation, such gestures will often be misinterpreted, and the escalation will grind on.

A third way hostile views of Other encourage escalation is by diminishing *inhibitions against retaliation* when Party has been provoked. Party is reluctant to aggress against an Other who is liked and respected, even when Other can clearly be blamed for unpleasant experiences. But Party is quite willing to aggress against an Other who is not liked or respected. The finding that southern white students (many of whom can be assumed to have been prejudiced) retaliated more vigorously when insulted by an African American than by a white (Rogers & Prentice-Dunn, 1981) supports these generalizations.

A fourth way in which hostile attitudes encourage escalation is by *blocking association* and *interfering with communication.* People tend to avoid those toward whom they are hostile. The point is well put by Coleman (1957): "As controversy develops, associations . . . wither between persons on opposing sides" (p. 11). This contributes to misunderstandings and hence to the proliferation of conflictful issues. It also makes it difficult to reach a peaceful settlement of the controversy. This occurred during the Cold War in the period before the Cuban Missile Crisis and also characterized relations between Israel and the Palestinian Liberation Organization (PLO) before the secret Oslo negotiations in 1992. In the latter case, communication with the PLO was actually illegal in Israel (Pruitt et al., 1997).

It is not altogether clear why this happens. Why stop meeting and talking when Party becomes hostile toward Other? A possible reason is that Party is afraid that associating with Other will be falsely interpreted as accepting Other's position or tactics. This phenomenon may also have deeper emotional roots. According to balance theory (Heider, 1958), hostile attitudes toward any object psychologically imply a hostile relationship with that object and, hence, a desire to put psychological distance between oneself and that object.

A fifth mechanism is that hostile attitudes and perceptions tend to reduce *empathy* with Other (White, 1984). Other seems so different from Party that it is hard for Party to put itself in Other's shoes. Furthermore, there is an easy explanation that makes empathy seem unnecessary: Other's actions stem from evil motives. Absence of empathy is like distrust and the absence of communication, in that it fosters misunderstandings. It also encourages escalation by blocking insight into the conflict spiral. Awareness that Other's hostile behavior is a reaction to Party's

---

[7] Such gestures, technically called *unilateral initiatives,* are discussed in Chapter 9.

own hostile behavior often causes Party to limit its escalation. But if Party lacks empathy into Other's motives, Party is unaware of its own role in encouraging Other to aggress and is likely to escalate unthinkingly.

Sixth, hostile attitudes and perceptions foster *zero-sum thinking,* which tends to make problem solving seem like an unworkable alternative. Positions become rigid, and creativity tends to disappear. This makes conflicts hard to resolve and encourages a sense that contentious behavior is the only way to succeed. Escalation is likely to be the result.

Seventh, and finally, when hostile perceptions grow really severe, Other comes to be viewed as a *diabolical enemy* (White, 1984) and the conflict is seen as a war between light and darkness. We are the chosen people; they are the "evil empire" (to quote President Ronald Reagan's Cold War description of the Soviet Union) or the "axis of evil" (which was used by President George W. Bush to describe Iraq, Iran, and North Korea). In such circumstances, Party is ready to blame Other for all that goes wrong and to believe the wildest stories about Other's perfidy.[8] Communication often takes a nosedive, empathy is especially weak, and problem solving is extraordinarily hard to sustain. Heavily escalated tactics tend to become the rule; and new controversies regularly develop, confirming Party's view of Other.

Hostile Goals   As a result of the changes just described, hostile and competitive goals often emerge—to look better than, punish, discredit, defeat, or even destroy Other. This is the transformation from doing well to hurting Other mentioned in Chapter 5. This escalation of goals leads to an escalation of tactics. Hostile goals, like hostile attitudes and perceptions, often have a lasting quality that cause them to persist after the conflict in which they were generated is over.

The desire for revenge, a hostile goal, is frequently implicated in the escalation of conflict (Kim & Smith, 1993; Morrill & Thomas, 1992). A conflict even over minor matters, when infused with vengeful feelings and desire, can escalate quickly and violently, as seen in many feuds. Take the notorious case of the feud between the Hatfields and the McCoys, two rural American families who lived along the border between Kentucky and West Virginia. Although the precise trigger for this feud, which lasted for twelve years, from 1878 to 1890, remains in dispute (Evans, 2001), it appears that it started when Randolph McCoy realized that one of his pigs was missing. He became outraged and immediately suspected the Hatfields. Soon, he confronted Floyd Hatfield about his suspicions, and

---

[8] Charles Lane (1992), Berlin bureau chief of *Newsweek,* reported the following observation from Belgrade, in former Yugoslavia: "My favorite outrageous Belgrade T.V. report concerned the Serb babies whom Muslims fed to the lions at the Sarajevo Zoo. I was amused, until I heard the story repeated verbatim by a 55-year-old woman standing in line outside the Yugoskandic bank. 'That's why the Serbs had to kill the animals,' she explained."

this confrontation quickly escalated into a cycle of reciprocal killings. The question of what happened to the pig was forgotten, and each side concentrated on the goal of destroying the other (Rice, 1982).

Several features of revenge encourage escalation. First, revenge tends to breed revenge, which means that conflict spirals are often impelled by this motive. Such spirals can take place on the world stage as well as in rural America. For example, suicide bombings by Palestinian militants provoke retaliatory actions from the Israelis, which in turn bring about another round of suicide bombings. Each side tries to avenge its sufferings at the hands of the other side, and these vengeful actions only harden the other side's resolve to press forward with counter-revenge. Thus, the cycle of bloodletting continues, deepening mutual hatred.[9]

A second feature of revenge that fuels escalation is that the urge for revenge is usually intense and powerful—so much so that it can outweigh almost any other concern (Marongiu & Newman, 1987). Milovan Djilas, a founder of the Yugoslav communist party, writes in his autobiography, "Revenge is an overpowering and consuming fire. It flares up and burns away every other thought and emotion. . . . Vengeance . . . was the glow in our eyes, the flame in our cheeks, the pounding in our temples, the word that had turned to stone in our throats on our hearing that our blood had been shed" (cited in Elster, 1990, p. 871). This intensity means that people who are motivated by vengeance often resort to extreme forms of contentious tactics, as can be seen in many school shootings (Vossekuil et al., 2000), feuds (Kuschel, 1988), terrorist attacks (Mylroie, 2000), sabotage (Greenberg, 1996), workplace violence (Folger & Skarlicki, 1998), and genocide (Scheff, 1994).

The intensity of vengeful urges also explains why certain conflict episodes seem to defy common sense. Weaker parties usually avoid aggressing against stronger parties for fear of getting hurt. But in the grip of a vengeful impulse, they may take retaliatory action regardless of its consequences and suffer grievous harm or even death as a result (Kim et al., 1998). Such is the fate of the suicide bomber.

Third, revenge tends to be excessive; it often returns greater harm than that received (Fellman, 1998).[10] Consider the story of a man who sought revenge against his estranged wife. Had he wanted to directly harm her, there was ample opportunity to do so. But, his goal was to inflict on her the greatest pain a mother can experience—by taking the lives

---

[9] Note that the *fear* of revenge can discourage escalation by making potential harm-doers think twice before they act. Thus Bies et al. (1997) have found that this fear serves as an informal social control device that prevents many organizational conflicts from escalating. However, once revenge has occurred, it is often followed by counter-revenge, which pushes parties in the opposite direction.

[10] In this regard, the well-known maxim "an eye for an eye, a tooth for a tooth" can be considered not as an endorsement of revenge but as a prescription that has been evolved to restrain its propensity to excess (Jacoby, 1983).

of four of her children (three from her first marriage and one from her marriage with him). While she was out for a morning walk, he quietly slipped into her house, systematically killing all four children and also himself (Boxall, 2002). This real-life revenge story is a carbon copy of the ancient play, *Medea,* by Euripides. The tragic heroine, Medea, murders her own children to exact revenge on Jason, her husband, who has left her for a younger woman.

Why is revenge prone to excess? One reason is that people who are provoked tend to feel that they are victims, which produces a powerful sense of injustice. This provides a rationalization for taking harsh action against the party who is annoying them (Miller, 2001). Another reason is that people tend to magnify their own suffering while minimizing the suffering of those against whom they retaliate (Baumeister et al., 1990).[11] As a result, they see themselves as retaliating in a just and equitable manner, while in fact they are overreacting.

A fourth feature of vengeance that feeds escalation involves the persistent nature of memories of past victimization and the motives they generate (Frijda, 1993). Even when vengeful actions are suppressed, the urges underlying them can continue to fester. Indeed, vengeful urges can grow even stronger over time. Consider the case of Curtis Thompson. In 2002, he broke into Janet and James Geisenhagen's home and shot them to death allegedly in retaliation for a lawsuit brought by Janet Geisenhagen *fifteen years earlier,* which Thompson had actually won (Hughes, 2002).

At a group level, there are also many examples that illustrate the long duration of vengefulness. For example, the Bosnian Serbs still remember the humiliation that their ancestors suffered at the hands of the army of the Turkish Sultan during the Battle of Kosovo 600 years ago. Although the desire for vengeance was not a direct cause of the 1992–1995 armed conflict in Bosnia-Herzegovina, it certainly contributed to Serbian violence against the Bosnian Muslims.

Dehumanization and Deindividuation   *Dehumanization*—the perception that Other is less than human—has been shown to make it easier to aggress against Other (Bandura, 1990; Kelman & Hamilton, 1989; Struch & Schwartz, 1989). This is probably because dehumanization reduces empathy with Other and puts Other outside one's moral community and hence not protected by the social norms against aggression (Opotow, 2000).

Research suggests that Other is dehumanized when it is seen as rejecting values that are important to Party (Schwartz & Struch, 1989). Calling people names ("nigger," "idiot") also has a dehumanizing effect. Name-calling strengthens the impression that Other is morally inadequate and dissimilar to Party. Some names—such as the epithet "pig,"

---

[11] An Angolan proverb captures the magnitude of this perceptual gap: "The one who throws the stone forgets; the one who is hit remembers forever."

which was hurled at the police during the riots that followed in the wake of the Rodney King beating—make Other seem particularly subhuman and thus particularly easy to assault.

People are *deindividuated* when they are perceived as members of a category or group rather than as individuals. This perception erodes inhibitions against acting aggressively in much the same way as dehumanization, by reducing empathy and diminishing the strength of norms against aggression. Deindividuation was probably at work in an experiment by Milgram (1992). Participants in the role of "teacher" gave more painful shocks to others in the role of "learner" when the latter were at a distance or out of sight than when they were close at hand. Deindividuation of the enemy may be what makes it easier for fliers to drop bombs on unseen targets than for foot soldiers to shoot an enemy they can see.

Deindividuation is countered by receipt of information that makes Other seem unique. For example, guards in Nazi prison camps are said to have treated prisoners more leniently when they knew their names (Zimbardo, 1970).[12] Another way to discover that outgroup members are individuals is to have friendly relations with them over a period of time. It follows that residential settings that foster interracial friendships should diminish white prejudice against African Americans, an effect that has been demonstrated in two survey studies (Deutsch & Collins, 1951; Hamilton & Bishop, 1976). Before he led a protest demonstration, Gandhi would sometimes ask for hospitality from the local English governor and thus make friends with him. This was a way of individuating himself and his movement in the eyes of the authorities, thereby reducing the aggressiveness of the tactics used by the government.

Similar reasoning suggests that aggressive or discriminatory impulses should lead Party to deindividuate Other, by a process akin to rationalization. In this way, Party will feel more comfortable about its own hostile behavior. Evidence favoring this prediction emerges from a study by Worchel and Andreoli (1978). It was found that subjects who were angry with, or were expected to shock, another person were especially likely to forget individuating information about that person (such as his or her name) and to remember deindividuating information (such as his or her race).

This finding implies that deindividuation is another way station in the circle of conflict escalation. Party deindividuates Other in order to rationalize its own initial contentious moves. This then makes it easier to take more severe measures against Other, contributing to escalation.

In addition to viewing Other as deindividuated, it is possible for Party to see *itself* in this way—in other words, to lose awareness of its own dis-

---

[12] During the Spanish Civil War, George Orwell was unable to shoot an enemy soldier who was running away while holding up his trousers with both hands. "I had come here to shoot at 'Fascists'; but a man who is holding up his trousers isn't a 'Fascist,' he is visibly a fellow creature, similar to yourself, and you don't feel like shooting at him" (1968, p. 254, cited in Brehm & Kassin, 1993).

tinct identity. This also facilitates aggression. Among the sources of self-deindividuation are acting in concert with others, [13] wearing nondistinctive clothing, emotional arousal, and lack of sleep. In a study of the effect of clothing on aggression, Zimbardo (1970) found that college women playing the role of punitive teachers were especially likely to give shocks when they were wearing a hood. Such apparel reduces Party's distinctiveness and inhibitions. Military and police uniforms probably have a similar effect.

CHANGES IN GROUPS

Psychological changes occur in all escalated conflicts, whether the actors are individuals or groups. But when groups (e.g., families, departments, organizations, nations) are involved, structural changes may also occur *in the group.* Hostile attitudes, perceptions and goals are accentuated by group discussion and tend to become group norms. Group goals of defeating the enemy tend to develop, and subgroups are established to implement these goals. Increased cohesiveness, resulting from having an outside enemy, contributes to the force of these norms and to the dedication of group members to the newly found goals and the means of implementing them. New, more militant leadership often emerges, contributing further to the group's orientation toward struggle. Doves are replaced by hawks. If one of the parties is an unorganized set of individuals, conflict sometimes encourages the development of a new group—precipitated out of the mix of strong individual emotions—which then takes up the cudgel against the adversary. As mentioned in Chapter 2, we call such a new group a *conflict group* and the process by which it develops, *group mobilization.*[14]

All of these changes can result from escalation as well as contribute to it. Hence, any of these changes can be placed in the boxes marked

---

[13] Research indicates that the bigger the group Party is a member of, the more Party is likely to lose self-awareness and engage in aggressive behavior. The phenomenon of deindividuation may partly explain the beating of Rodney King by Los Angeles police offers. It is reported that many other officers, besides the four who were actually involved in hitting Rodney King, watched the beating as it took place.

[14] New conflict groups do not necessarily become involved in heavy escalation. Their activities are often limited to decorous tactics such as petition and efforts to influence elections. But escalation is also possible, with the aggrieved group becoming militant and taking heavier and heavier actions, accompanied by stronger feelings, more extreme demands, increasing cohesiveness, more pressure for uniformity, and increasingly militant leadership.

At the end of an escalated controversy, militant conflict groups often go on to assume a legitimate place in the community. To do so, their leaders (whether the old ones or a new set) must take the role of advocates of their group's interest in a peaceful political process. Thus in South Africa, the militant African National Congress (ANC) became a political party that put up candidates for election. The American labor movement, violent and revolutionary at first, eventually became a staid part of the political establishment. Indeed, Lyons (2002) has argued, in the context of internal war, that escalated intergroup conflicts cannot be permanently solved unless such a transition takes place.

"Structural changes" in Figure 6.1. Like changes in attitudes, perceptions and goals, group changes of this kind tend to persist and affect the relationship between the parties.

Group changes were important in the escalation of the Cold War. In the United States, hostile norms became so strong that people who had a good word for the Soviet Union were made to feel uncomfortable and were sometimes hauled up before congressional committees. The country even flirted for a time in the 1950s with highly militant leadership, in the person of Senator Joseph McCarthy, a virulent anticommunist with a large political following. Fortunately for the nation, some of these collective excesses were overcome by the 1960s.

The Crisis at UB

Before embarking on a detailed discussion of these group changes, we will describe a conflict that occurred at the State University of New York at Buffalo (or UB as it is known locally), where one of the authors (DGP) formerly taught. This narrative (based on a chronology provided by Pruitt & Gahagan, 1974), offers a striking illustration of a conflict spiral involving all three kinds of structural changes—particularly changes in groups.

The years from 1964 to 1969 saw the growth of a national student movement, aroused about such issues as racial discrimination and U.S. involvement in the Vietnam War and greatly distrustful of the adult world. This movement touched many campuses, including UB. As it began the 1969–1970 school year, UB had a large number of students who were concerned about such issues and a sizable contingent of campus radicals who were ready to provide any emerging student action with the necessary leadership.

The crisis began on a cold winter night in late February with the appearance of city police on campus at the time of a demonstration by African American athletes against the physical education department (the African American athletes played no further part in the demonstrations after this incident). The next night, forty to fifty white students, including many of the campus radicals, proceeded to the acting president's office to demand an explanation for the police appearance. The acting president, who was in a meeting about the African American athletes, refused to talk with the students, whereupon some of them threw rocks at his windows. The campus police arrived in riot gear, and the acting president instructed them to arrest the window breakers. Moving to the student union, the police apprehended two of the radicals, beating one of them in front of an excited crowd of student onlookers. Some members of this crowd then chased the police officers across the campus, and one officer was badly injured when a metal trash barrel was thrown at him. Someone called for city police reinforcements, who confronted a crowd of about 500 enraged students and arrested several dozen of them.

During the next two days, the student government and the radical student leadership organized rallies to decide upon a student response to these incidents. The thousands of students who attended these rallies clearly rejected the student government proposal for communication with the administration and endorsed a plan developed by the radical leadership to organize a strike against class attendance. A set of nine demands was endorsed, including the barring of city police from campus, the resignation of the acting president, and the abolition of ROTC and of research supported by the Defense Department. During the first night, enraged students firebombed the library. By the end of the second evening, it had become clear that the student government was no longer respected by the bulk of the politically active students. As a result, this government collapsed and was replaced by a radically led Strike Committee, which even took over the student government office suite.

The Strike Committee, consisting of about 400 active members, put together a well-organized campaign to discourage students from going to class. The strike was only partly successful, with class attendance being curtailed by about 30 to 40 percent. The Strike Committee then moved to heavier tactics, occupying the administration building and turning on its fire hoses. In an effort to defend itself, the administration suspended a group of radical leaders and eventually summoned the Buffalo police back onto the campus. Early on a Sunday morning, eleven days into the crisis, 400 Buffalo police officers quietly moved into position. The student response was initially a series of symbolic events, such as a mock funeral for the university. Eventually an ultimatum was issued to the administration, and a "war council" was held to decide on appropriate action. The night of the war council, a large group of students began taunting and throwing objects at the police, who were massed in front of the administration building, presumably to defend it. The police finally broke ranks and charged into the crowd with clubs swinging, injuring and arresting a number of students.

The next day, forty-five faculty members held a sit-in at the acting president's office. The police removed them from the building and arrested them. No more student demonstrations were held after this time; but, angered by the arrest of their fellows, the faculty senate passed a motion of no confidence in the administration.

The rest of the semester witnessed a moderately successful effort to reunite the campus. As part of this effort, a committee made up of student, faculty, and administration representatives was organized to discuss the demands made by the Strike Committee and related matters. This committee made a number of recommendations that were adopted as campus policy, including the abolition of ROTC.[15]

---

[15] The reader can no doubt detect in the UB conflict a set of relatively predictable moves and countermoves by the students and faculty, on the one hand, and the administration and police, on the other. Those who want to understand the pattern of this pas de deux should read *The Rhetoric of Agitation and Control* by Bowers & Ochs (1971).

Nature, Source, and Impact of Group Changes

When small groups, organizations, or nations become involved in contentious conflict, these collectives (groups, as we call them) tend to change in at least six ways that contribute to the cycle of escalation.

First, *group polarization* takes place. The average group member on each side becomes increasingly hostile toward the other side. This is partly because extremists on each side do battle with each other, producing egregious incidents that inflame more moderate group members and lead them to join the extremists. The crisis at UB illustrates this process. The initial battle was between campus radicals and a campus police force in riot gear. This confrontation alarmed people on both sides, who joined in the fray creating more incidents and more recruitment to the extremes. Eventually the campus became polarized into two hostile camps: most of the students and faculty on one side and most of the administration on the other.

Group polarization also occurs because of ordinary group discussion. Research shows that when group members share any view (any attitude or perception) and discuss it with one another, that view becomes stronger (Moscovici & Zavalloni, 1969; Pruitt, 1971). Two main mechanisms account for this phenomenon (Isenberg, 1986). One is that group members hear one another's views and the arguments underlying them. Finding that others agree with them, they feel that their views are validated, and they also learn new arguments favoring them. The other is that a sort of competition develops among the group members, in which each person strives to hold an opinion that is at least as extreme in the direction favored by the group as that advocated by the average group member. As a result of both mechanisms, many members shift their opinions further in the direction initially favored by the group. If there is conflict going on, this means discussions among group members make them progressively more hostile toward the other side and increasingly more motivated to take action.

The development of *contentious group goals* is a second common outcome of conflict. Examples are Party's ambition to defeat or even destroy Other. Such goals arise from the experience of conflict and further fan the flames. In addition, groups are capable of pursuing their goals in ways that are not available to individuals, because the activities of a number of individuals can be coordinated. A division of labor among group members adds to this capability, permitting highly complicated contentious routines such as the recruitment and training of an army. Hence, groups are particularly effective at conflict escalation if their members are so inclined. One group goal that resulted in a significant escalation during the UB crisis was the decision by the Strike Committee to try to close down all classes.

A third kind of change is the development of *runaway norms* supporting a contentious approach to the controversy (Raven & Rubin, 1983). A norm is any attitude, perception, goal, or behavior pattern that is seen as "right thinking" by most members of the group. Norms are taught to new group members and imposed on old members who appear to question them. Most of the psychological changes mentioned earlier in this chapter—including negative attitudes, distrust, zero-sum thinking, and a reluctance to communicate with Other—can become the subject of norms. When this happens, they gain strength and stability. They become group traditions rather than the property of separate individuals. Hence, they are more likely to contribute to escalation. This happened in the United States in the early stages of the Cold War. The aforementioned pressures on Americans to join the anti-communist crusade during the Cold War are a case in point.

A fourth kind of change that can contribute to escalation is the development of *group identity and group cohesiveness* (solidarity). Groups are cohesive to the extent that their members find them attractive.

Cohesiveness affects group behavior in three important ways. It encourages conformity to group norms (Festinger et al., 1950). This conformity is due to enhanced communication within the group (Back, 1951); member fear of being ostracized (Festinger, 1950); and social pressure, which is especially strong in cohesive groups (Schachter, 1951). Cohesive groups are also capable of especially vigorous action in pursuit of their goals. And there is reason to believe that members of cohesive groups are particularly convinced of the rightness of their cause and the effectiveness of their intended actions (Janis, 1972; Kriesberg, 1998). The UB Strike Committee was a highly cohesive group that exhibited all of these characteristics.

For all these reasons, we can expect group cohesiveness to augment or multiply the effect of the psychological states discussed earlier in this chapter. If the attitudes toward an outgroup are generally negative, they should be particularly strong in a cohesive group. If the other group is distrusted or is seen as a threat, cohesiveness should strengthen these perceptions. If the goal of defeating Other is adopted and contentious tactics for achieving this goal are developed, a cohesive group will mount a particularly vigorous campaign in this direction.

Contentious conflict has been repeatedly shown to enhance group cohesiveness (Dion, 1979; Ryen & Kahn, 1975; Worchel & Norvell, 1980). It follows that enhanced cohesiveness is still another mechanism in the cycle of escalation, resulting from prior escalation and contributing to its continuation. In making this point, we do not intend to say that cohesiveness per se encourages antagonism or escalation. Research evidence (Dion, 1973) does not support such a position. The point is rather that contentious conflict encourages cohesiveness, and cohesive groups are particularly militant when involved in contentious conflict.

A fifth type of change that often occurs in groups engaged in heavy conflict is that *militant leaders* take over (Sherif et al., 1961). Most groups have leaders. Some are formally designated as such; others are highly influential people without titles. Leaders usually gain their positions because they resonate with the dominant sentiments of group members and are good at the activities to which the group is dedicated (Hollander, 1978). This is as true of groups in conflict as of groups engaged in any other kind of activity. If conflict involves negotiation, people with bargaining skills are likely to come to the fore. But if it involves heavy contentious activity, leadership is more likely to fall into the hands of militants, who can mirror the anger of the membership and build a fighting force. Such individuals have particularly strong negative attitudes and perceptions of the adversary and are especially rigid in the demands they make. Accordingly, once they take over, they tend to reinforce and augment the group's commitment to extreme tactics.

Leadership changes of this kind occurred on both sides in the UB crisis. The controversy began to heat up when the campus police clubbed several demonstrators in the student union. At first, officers of the student government tried to exercise leadership over the campus, promising to negotiate with the university administration. But the students were so angry at the administration that they shunted these officers aside in favor of a group of radicals who had not previously exerted much influence. Similar changes occurred in the university administration. A vice president who wanted to mediate the controversy was excluded from decision making, while other officers who advocated sterner measures became very influential.

In addition to devising tactics for dealing with the opponent, leaders of groups that are in conflict often try to strengthen their members' dedication to the struggle by tarnishing the image of the adversary (Bowers & Ochs, 1971). An example is President George Bush's comparison of Saddam Hussein with Hitler during the Persian Gulf crisis.

The sixth type of collective change that occurs in escalating conflict is the development of *militant subgroups*. Such a subgroup is sometimes part of a well-established organization, for example, a new department to deal with the emerging conflict. At other times, it is an entirely new outfit, as seen in the development of the Strike Committee at UB.

CHANGES IN COMMUNITIES

When two individuals or groups come into heavy conflict with each other, it is often hard for other community members to remain neutral. They tend to support or join one side or the other, a phenomenon called *community polarization*. Community polarization is another participant in the cycle of escalation—it is produced by earlier escalation and contributes to later escalation.

Community polarization is produced by escalation in two ways. First, neutral community members are recruited by participants in the controversy, who demand that nonparticipants decide whether they are "with us or against us." Second, the use of escalated tactics is often annoying or frightening to the broader community. It is hard to remain indifferent when people are yelling at each other, damaging each other's property, or hurting each other. There is a tendency to cast blame in such circumstances and to support the side to which one is closer or the side that seems less blameworthy.

Community polarization contributes to further escalation for two reasons. One is that new supporters and recruits give added strength to the individuals or groups on either side. They provide manpower, materials, and money, and they enhance the group's confidence in the validity of its position and its likelihood of winning, making it easier to justify the use of heavy contentious tactics. The other reason is that polarization divides a community into two opposing camps. The bonds within each camp become stronger while those between camps deteriorate (Coleman, 1957). This causes a destruction of crosscutting group memberships[16] and a disappearance of neutral third parties who would otherwise urge moderation and mediate the controversy.

Community polarization underlies the transformation from few to many. It occurred during the Cold War in that most nations felt forced to choose sides between the United States and the Soviet Union. It also occurred in the UB crisis, with many members of the wider Buffalo community choosing sides between the students and the administration (most of them embraced the side of the administration). In 2001, the entire world became polarized, with most governments supporting the United States in its war against the Taliban government of Afghanistan and many people in the Arab world supporting the Taliban. It is notable that one of the combatants, the United States, began its campaign with President George W. Bush announcing that the world would have to choose up sides: "You are either with us or against us."

SUMMARY AND CONCLUSIONS

This chapter has introduced a third conflict model, the structural change model, which builds on the conflict spiral model. We have described a set of changes in the individuals and groups involved in conflict and the communities to which they belong. These changes are way stations in the cycle of escalation: they result from prior escalation *and* contribute to further escalation. A cycle of escalation might, for example, start with Party's receipt of what it considers to be an insult from Other. If this makes Party angry and fearful about its image of adequacy, these emotional changes

---

[16] Crosscutting group memberships are discussed in Chapter 7.

could produce a return insult from Party. This might then produce similar emotional changes in Other, encouraging still another insult. The cycle would then be complete, but it could be followed by further cycles, causing the conflict to become increasingly escalated.

Psychological changes take place in individuals, but they can also affect the behavior of groups when they are widespread among group members. In addition to emotional changes (blame, anger, fear, and perceived threat to one's image), psychological changes include dehumanization, deindividuation, and the development of hostile attitudes, perceptions and goals. Dehumanization and deindividuation are similar in that they erode inhibitions that would otherwise prevent aggression. Party can become deindividuated in its own eyes, which also erodes inhibitions. Development of a goal of seeking revenge is a particularly potent structural change, which can produce heavily escalated behavior long after an annoyance has been experienced.

Structural changes can also occur in groups. Group changes include the development of hostile group goals, the emergence of runaway norms, enhanced group identity and cohesiveness, and the emergence of militant subgroups and leaders. Groups can also polarize, with their members moved from moderation to militancy, as can the communities surrounding the conflicting parties. All of these changes result from prior escalation and contribute to further escalation.

Emotional changes are products of the moments and tend to disappear quickly once a conflict episode is over. But the other kinds of structural changes tend to persist as residues that injure the relationship between the parties. These residues make it hard for escalation to dissipate once it gets started and tend to encourage renewed conflict and escalation at a later time.

Having laid out the mechanisms that produce escalation, in this chapter and the one before it, we turn, in Chapter 7, to the conditions that allow conflict to escalate and those that stabilize the situation so that the parties draw back from escalation and the structural changes producing it.

7

Conditions That Encourage and Discourage Escalation

❖

A Light Escalation ✦ A Heavy Escalation ✦ Basic Antecedents of Escalation ✦ *Conflict Size* ✦ *Instability* ✦ Features of the Situation ✦ Features of the Parties ✦ *Personality Differences and Childhood Experiences* ✦ *Age and Gender Differences* ✦ *Conflict Models Employed by the Parties* ✦ *Cultural Differences* ✦ *Features of Groups* ✦ *Prior Escalation and Structural Change* ✦ Features of the Relationships Between Parties ✦ *Social Bonds* ✦ Features of the Broader Community ✦ *Outside Support* ✦ *Conflict-Limiting Norms* ✦ *Conflict-Limiting Institutions* ✦ *Community Structure: Crosscutting vs. Overlapping Bonds* ✦ Stability Through Threats ✦ *Balance of Power Theory* ✦ *The Balance of Terror* ✦ *Problems with Basing Stability on Threats* ✦ Summary and Conclusions

In Chapter 1, we defined conflict as perceived divergence of interest, involving two or more parties who believe that their aspirations are incompatible—that if one of them succeeds, the other must fail. We pointed out that mild conflict is often benign, encouraging the parties to develop new ways of meshing their interests and producing needed social change. But heavy conflict can be destructive, and this is where escalation comes in. Escalation is what gives conflict its bad name. Though a little escalation may be part of a constructive process, heavy escalation is usually a problem for the parties involved and for the surrounding community.

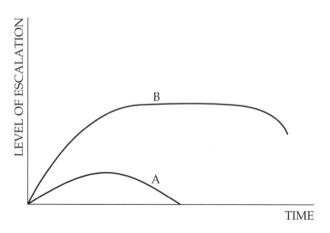

FIGURE 7.1

Course of escalation in two contrasting conflicts. Curve A represents a case of light escalation, and Curve B a case of heavy escalation.

To understand the difference between light and heavy escalation, compare the curves in Figure 7.1, which trace the course of escalation over time in two contrasting conflicts. Curve A represents a case of light escalation. Tactics and the feelings associated with them become harsher for a period of time. But they are limited in intensity and duration, and the situation quickly returns to normal. A good example of such a conflict is the husband-wife spat about driving the car, described in Chapter 5. The two parties argued briefly and then resolved their quarrel.

Curve B represents a case of heavy escalation. Tactics and feelings rapidly become more intense, moving to a higher level and lasting longer. The Cold War and the UB crisis fit the pattern shown in curve B.

This chapter and the next concern the processes and conditions that determine whether a conflict will escalate in accordance with curve A or curve B. Note that these curves differ in two ways: One is that conflict escalates *more rapidly to a higher level* in B than in A. That is the topic of the present chapter, which concerns the determinants of whether light or heavy escalation takes place. The other is that conflict *remains* escalated for a longer period of time in B than in A. That is the topic of the next chapter, which concerns the persistence of escalation.

A LIGHT ESCALATION

Another escalation that fits curve A can be seen in a story told by a college student about his brief confrontation with a friend (Kim, 2002):

I was studying for a chemistry exam with a group of people in my room. It was about 11:00 P.M., and we needed a break. We started goofing off by playing music and telling jokes. At this time one of my friends left my room for a while, and when he returned, he found the door locked. As a group we started laughing at him, telling him that we were not going to let him in. All of a sudden, he started kicking the door from the outside—until the door was broken down. The lock and the door had been destroyed. And I was starting to get pissed off. I ran up to his room and proceeded to kick his door down. He followed me up to his room and didn't do anything, but watched me kicking his door. After a few good kicks, I stopped because I realized I was being foolish. But it felt good to release my tensions. He started laughing and said if I kicked his door in, both of us would have had to pay for damaged locks. He said "sorry," and that was that. Afterwards, we acted as if nothing ever happened.

A HEAVY ESCALATION

Curve B is illustrated by an event, dubbed the "Rink Rage" case, in which the father of a young hockey player killed the father of another player. What started as a minor quarrel quickly escalated into a shouting match, then a shoving match, and finally a deadly fistfight. In the end, one man was dead, another was convicted of involuntary manslaughter, children were traumatized by witnessing the beating, and the lives of two families were shattered.

According to newspaper accounts (Daniel, 2002), Michael Costin of Lynnfield, Massachusetts, was supervising a noncontact hockey game involving his three sons and two of their friends. Costin asked Thomas Junta's son, then 10½, and some of his friends, all from Reading, Massachusetts, to join the game. The game turned rough, resulting in children fighting. Noticing that Costin was doing nothing to stop the fight, Junta allegedly yelled at Costin to control the situation. Costin reportedly replied, "That's hockey!" and they exchanged some words. Junta claimed that as his son was getting off the ice, one of the Lynnfield players elbowed him in the side of the face. He took his son and his friends to the locker room, urging them to get ready to leave the place. Then Costin appeared, and the two men resumed arguing, swearing, and screaming. Soon, they scuffled, but some adults pulled them apart. An employee of the ice rink asked Junta to leave the facility. Junta did so but returned a few minutes later. He allegedly came back because he was concerned about his son's safety. There were conflicting witness testimonies about who first threw a punch. Some said that it was Costin who threw it and that Junta reacted to it with three punches. Others testified that the 270-pound Junta marched back to the rink and pinned the 150-pound Costin on the floor with his knee, repeatedly punching him, while horrified children were looking on. Junta claimed he did so in self-defense. Costin never regained consciousness and died a day later of massive head injuries.

BASIC ANTECEDENTS OF ESCALATION

Unlike the dormitory door case, the rink rage case went through several iterations of a conflict spiral, getting more and more severe until a tragedy happened. Such a runaway escalation has two kinds of antecedents: large conflict size and instability.

Conflict Size

As indicated in Chapter 2, conflicts look large when there are lofty, rigid aspirations on both sides and alternatives that provide little benefit to the parties. In such circumstances, yielding is unthinkable and problem solving seems hopeless. Hence, contending looks like the only way to succeed. It seems necessary to put pressure on Other; and the larger the perceived size of the conflict, the heavier the contentious tactics that seem to be needed. If contentious action is in fact taken, it will often provoke a similar response from Other, starting a conflict spiral.

Conflict size was part of the problem in the rink rage case. The two men had different views about how hockey should be played, and their positions were so rigid that a seemingly unbridgeable gap developed between them. Part of this rigidity probably resulted from image threats of the kind discussed in Chapter 6. Neither man could back down because it would be an acknowledgment of weakness. Concerns about image threats are common in conflicts between men, especially when they are observed by a masculine audience (Felson, 1982), as in this case.

However, none of this seems sufficient to explain the extreme violence that occurred in this incident. Men often get into scrapes with each other, yet few of them are killed as a result. It follows that we must look to sources of *instability* for a full explanation of what happened.

Instability

Most of this chapter will focus on instability, those aspects of the situation that encourage Party to act harshly when it perceives a divergence of interest or is confronted with contentious behavior from Other. Situations are said to be highly unstable if minimal divergence of interest or provocation can push one or both parties into heavily escalated action. The opposite of instability is *stability*, which describes situations in which conflict does not easily escalate—where the pattern usually looks like curve A in Figure 7.1. Stability is a relative matter. Even the most stable of situations will escalate if conflict or provocation is large enough; and in extremely unstable situations, a whisker of conflict is enough to set escalation going.

There are three basic types of instability. One is *a tendency to overreact to annoyance or threat*. For example, people who are in an aroused or tense state of mind are especially likely to get angry in the face of provocation. Perhaps one (or both) of the men in the rink rage case was in such a state at the time of their encounter—due to a difficult work situation or domestic problems—making him overreact to the other's contentious actions. This tendency to overreact is often due to a party being prone to one or another of the structural changes discussed in Chapter 6.

A second basic type of instability is *reduced inhibitions against aggressive behavior*.[1] We know, for example, that bonds of common group membership, friendship, or interdependence between Party and Other tend to inhibit—that is, restrain Party from—the use of heavy contentious tactics. Such bonds are sources of stability, as they probably were in the dormitory door case, which involved two friends. But if such bonds are absent or diminished, Party may use harsh tactics when conflict arises. In the rink rage case, there is no reason to believe that the two men knew each other, so there were no bonds between them.

A third basic type of instability is *reduced capacity for conflict management*. Situations tend to be stable when the parties are willing and able to talk about their differences, or third parties are available to keep order. In the rink rage case, the two men were so angry at each other that rational discussion was impossible. At one point in the conflict, third parties exerted control by pulling the men apart and asking Junta to leave. But adequate third party intervention was not available in the final episode when Costin was killed.

All three of these basic types of instability encourage harsh reactions to provocation. Such reactions are the building blocks of the conflict spiral (cycle of escalation) shown in Figure 6.1 (the reader should turn back to this figure). If the conditions encourage Party to respond harshly to provocation from Other (by energizing path C and/or D in this figure), the cycle of escalation will turn more rapidly and generate faster and more extensive escalation. If the conditions also encourage Other to respond harshly to Party's provocations (by energizing path A and/or B), the cycle will become a veritable flywheel. Party will react harshly to provocations *from* Other, producing provocations *for* Other, which will start the cycle around again. Such escalation may become almost boundless if harsh responses are directed not only at Other but also at those identified with Other—family, associates, or ethnic group members—as exemplified by escalation of the conflict between Israelis and Palestinians over the last few years.

This chapter will examine a set of conditions that encourage stability or instability, under four headings—those pertaining to the *situation*, the *parties*, their *relationship*, and the *community* that surrounds them. All of these conditions operate by activating or deactivating one or more of the

---

[1] Inhibitions are cognitive constraints against certain kinds of actions.

basic types of escalation just discussed. At the end of the chapter, there will also be a special section on stability through threats.

FEATURES OF THE SITUATION

Research on aggression (see Berkowitz, 1993; Geen, 1990) has helped understand those aspects of the situation that encourage harsh reactions to provocation from Other. Two kinds of conditions can be distinguished: those that affect the extent to which *anger develops* in response to Other's provocation, and those that affect the extent to which this *anger is expressed* in behavior.[2] Looking back at Figure 6.1, the first kind of condition can be viewed as influencing path C (or its counterpart, path A); the second kind, as influencing path D (or its counterpart, path B).

Autonomic arousal promotes a tendency to overreact. People get angrier when they are provoked, provided that they attribute this arousal to the provocation. This implies that conflict is more likely to escalate when Party has exercised recently, although not so recently as to be aware of the source of the arousal (Zillmann et al., 1974). Folklore to the contrary, a fast game of basketball is more likely to exacerbate conflict than to cure it. Escalation is also more likely when Party is in a sexually excited state (Zillmann, 1971), or when there is considerable noise (Geen, 1978) or atmospheric pollution (Rotton & Frey, 1985).

The effect of autonomic arousal on anger tends to persist well after the arousal is gone (Bryant & Zillmann, 1979). For example, if Party exercises just before Other provokes it, Party's likelihood of aggressing against Other several months later will be strengthened. What probably happens is that the original anger, augmented by exercise, becomes translated into some form of negative attitude or goal that persists as a residue.

An overreaction to provocation is also more likely when Party has been *recently angered in some other situation*. Pent-up anger can turn Party into a coiled spring, poised to displace its anger onto Other. For example, Berkowitz, Cochran, and Embree (1981) found that participants who were forced to hold their hand in very cold water were more aggressive toward fellow participants than those who held their hand in moderately cold water.

Pleasurable experiences, in contrast, tend to block an aggressive response to provocation. Humor (Baron, 1978), mildly erotic stimuli (Baron & Bell, 1977), and soft, sweet music (Konecni, 1975) tend to diminish aggressive expression, presumably by putting Party in a good mood. It is

---

[2] We embrace the common-sense view that anger is one source of aggression. This view is accepted by some theorists (e.g., Allred, 1999; Zillmann, 1979) but not by others (Berkowitz, 1993).

not altogether clear whether such experiences interfere with the development of anger or with the expression of anger in the form of an aggressive response.[3]

Drinking alcohol is probably the best-known antecedent of escalation. Barroom brawls are legendary, and alcohol is believed to have contributed to 64 percent of the homicide cases in Philadelphia between 1948 and 1953 (Wolfgang & Strohm, 1956). The effect of alcohol is to concentrate attention on the most salient stimuli in the situation (i.e., the provocation), making Party oblivious to the wider social context and the future impact of its actions (Steele & Josephs, 1990; Taylor & Leonard, 1983). This presumably produces an escalative effect in two ways: (1) by making the provocation seem larger; and (2) by reducing social and cognitive inhibitions, thus increasing the likelihood that Party's anger will be released.

Time pressure—the necessity of a quick response—also tends to produce an overly aggressive reaction to provocation and thus encourages escalation (Ohbuchi, 1995; Yovetitch & Rusbult, 1994). The probable reason for this is similar to that for the impact of alcohol. When faced with provocation, people first pay attention to the provocation itself and only later to broader issues that are likely to inhibit aggressive responding, such as the importance of the relationship with the provoker or the opinions of third parties who frown on overreaction (Pruitt, 1997). If there is time pressure, people will often not get to the second stage of this process.

Another anger-releasing experience is exposure to an *aggressive model*, somebody engaging in aggression (Baron & Kepner, 1970; Wheeler & Caggiula, 1966). Seeing aggressive behavior on television has a similar effect, especially if the portrayal is realistic (Geen, 1975) and the model is engaged in retaliatory aggression (Geen & Stonner, 1973). A possible explanation for these effects is that the expression of anger is ordinarily under strong normative control. People have learned that society frowns on aggression. Hence, they tend to feel guilty or afraid of criticism about aggression and normally hold their anger in. But when an aggressive model appears, it places a temporary seal of social approval on aggression. The old norm—and the inhibitions it produces—suddenly seems less binding. If the model can do it, why not I? This allows the pent-up anger to be expressed.

Aggression is also sometimes inhibited by *competing activities*. For example, moderate heat provokes aggression; but severe heat provokes flight if the situation allows it, a response that is incompatible with aggression

---

[3] A case can be made for either of these interpretations. However, the fact that humor and small gifts also reduce contentious behavior in negotiation (Carnevale & Isen, 1986; O'Quin & Aronoff, 1981) suggests the latter interpretation—that the effect is on the response production side. Anger is not usually prominent in negotiation; hence, the effect of pleasurable experience on negotiation behavior is not likely to be mediated by anger.

(Bell & Baron, 1976). Similarly, a favorite way to stop children from angry crying is to divert them with a pleasurable competing activity.

We can summarize the points made in this section by examining their practical implications. For example, suppose you were traveling with a male companion who constantly got into arguments and fights along the way. What could you do to prevent further outbreaks and escalation? You could try to remove him from any situation in which conflict was brewing. In addition, you could try to keep his arousal level low by avoiding noise, pollution, or heavy physical exertion. You could avoid provoking him yourself to make him less of a coiled spring with others. You could keep him out of bars and away from violent movies and television shows. You could also take a nonviolent, problem-solving approach to the situation yourself, so as to provide him with a model of conciliatory behavior. Finally, you could try to keep him busy with all manner of pleasurable activities, so as to put him in a good mood and encourage responses incompatible with escalation.

The preferred target for Party's expression of anger is the Other who is blamed for the aversive experience. However, it is not always possible to indulge this preference. The source of annoyance may be well protected, there may be extenuating circumstances that reduce its culpability, or it may be impossible to identify the source. Under these circumstances, Party's desire to punish is sometimes *displaced* onto another offending target. If one cannot hit an enraging boss, one overreacts to trivial frustration and yells at the spouse or kicks the cat.

Evidence of displacement may be seen in a study by Hovland and Sears (1940), who found an inverse correlation between the price of cotton in the South and the number of African Americans lynched over a 49-year period. The lower the price of cotton, the greater the number of lynchings. What presumably happened is that white farmers were frustrated by the decline in the cotton market but could not legitimately aggress against the cotton merchants who were paying them less. They took it out on a handy displacement object, an African American who had stepped out of line in some way. Other evidence of displacement can be seen in the finding that people who have been abused as children tend to become aggressive as adults (McCord, 1986). The abuse makes them angry inside and they take it out on people they encounter in later life.[4]

FEATURES OF THE PARTIES

When individuals are involved in conflict, differences in personality, age, or gender may be important. The behavior of individual participants may

---

[4] See Marcus et al. (2000) for a meta-analytical review on displaced aggression.

also be affected by the conflict models[5] they use for analyzing their dispute. Culture also produces differences in the way people handle conflict. Such variables are also important for understanding intergroup conflict provided the groups are homogeneous in the types of people involved. In addition, there are stable intergroup differences that affect the way conflict is handled by groups.

Personality Differences and Childhood Experiences

Research on aggression suggests that conflict spirals are particularly likely to occur when certain kinds of personalities are involved. There is evidence of consistent individual differences in aggressive response to provocation (Geen, 1990). Some people are particularly *irritable*, reacting with anger to minor provocation (Berkowitz, 1993). Among these are the hard-driving, success-oriented "Type A" individuals, who tend to overreact when others get in their way (Carver & Glass, 1978). Other people are especially *impulsive*, reacting too fast for inhibitions to take hold and easily expressing their anger when aroused (Hynan & Grush, 1986). Still others are extremely vigilant for *threats to their image* of strength or adequacy (Toch, 1969). For example, people who tend to have high but unstable self-esteem are easily provoked and often respond aggressively in an effort to repair their image (Baumeister et al., 1996). All three types of people are especially likely to get into escalative sequences, and they often end up hurting themselves and others.

Other personality traits contribute to stability in interpersonal relations. For example, people who are high *in need for social approval* or feel *guilty about aggression* tend to underreact when provoked (Dengerink, 1976). These findings suggest that aggressive responding, and hence the likelihood of escalation, is reduced in those who are highly motivated to adhere to social norms. In addition, there is evidence that *empathy* with others produces inhibitions against retaliating when provoked (Rusbult et al., 1991). Empathic people are sensitive to the needs of others, leading them to think twice about harming others' interests even when it seems justified. Hence, they are probably less likely to get involved in escalation.

The personality traits just discussed are due, at least in part, to childhood experiences. Rewarding children for aggressive responding can make them more likely to become involved in conflict spirals as adults (Berkowitz, 1993). Rejection and harsh treatment by adults can also have this effect. This may be due to displacement; the abuse makes children feel angry inside and they take it out on people they encounter in later

---

[5] The term "model" in this context refers to a pattern of thought used in developing explanations rather than to a human being who is taking a particular kind of action.

life. Rejection is especially likely to produce an aggressive child when it is accompanied by inadequate monitoring and inconsistent discipline (McCord, 1986). In addition, children who are brought up by parents who fight each other tend to become aggressive (McCord, 1986).

Could personality help understand the rink rage tragedy? There is some evidence on this issue. Both Costin and Junta had a troubled past ("A just verdict," 2002), including some history of assaulting other people. This suggests that they had built-in tendencies to overreact to challenges from others or lacked normal inhibitions against aggressive responding.

Age and Gender Differences

In the United States, young men (between the ages of 20 and 30) are especially likely to become involved in murder, both as perpetrators and victims (Berkowitz, 1993). This suggests that they are especially prone to severe escalation. Buss (1999) interprets similar data as implying that "the proportion of young males in a population may be the best, or one of the best, predictors of violent aggression" (p. 293). This helps understand the September 11 attack on the United States. The Arab world from which the terrorists came "is going through a massive youth bulge, with more than half of most countries' populations under the age of 25" (Zakaria, 2001, p. 32).

Other research supports the gender aspect of Buss's conclusion. Men, on the whole, are more physically and verbally aggressive than women (Eagly & Steffen, 1986; Felson, 1982; Ohbuchi & Tedeschi, 1997). However, these conclusions apparently do not apply to reactions to persistent, illegitimate annoyance, where women have been found to protest more vigorously than men (Da Gloria & De Ridder, 1979; Mikolic et al., 1997).

Escalation Models Employed by the Parties

In Chapters 5 and 6, we presented three escalation models—contender-defender, conflict spiral, and structural change—as aids to a scholarly analysis of conflict. But they can also be seen as models of participant thought—concepts that help parties interpret what is happening in a conflict. Each model has implications with respect to the extent to which conflict will escalate.

A firm belief in the *contender-defender* interpretation often serves to exacerbate a conflict spiral. Party acknowledges that it is escalating but fails to see that this is a reaction to Other's escalation, which is a reaction to its own prior escalation. Instead, it views its behavior as a legitimate response to Other's persistent annoyance and redoubles its efforts to get Other to stop what it is doing. Other is the basic source of the problem and Party is only reacting. If Other also interprets the conflict by means of the contender-defender model, it is likely to redouble its efforts as well, spawning a new round of contentious activity.

A belief that Party is in, or is in danger of entering, a *conflict spiral* can have the opposite effect of dampening or preventing that spiral in order to avoid escalation (Richardson, 1967). This kind of analysis is likely to lead Party to tone down its reactions to Other's aggressive actions, and to be conciliatory in the hope that Other will reciprocate (Tetlock, 1983). Party will behave like a dove, in contrast to the hawks, who make a contender-defender analysis.

Neither doves nor hawks have a monopoly over the truth. If the doves are right that they are in a conflict spiral, they can escape the conflict by de-escalating. For example, in 1977 President Sadat of Egypt, concluding that his country was involved in a conflict spiral with Israel, made a gesture of goodwill in the form of a personal journey to Jerusalem. This started a de-escalative spiral in relations between these countries that resulted in the eventual resumption of diplomatic relations.

But if the hawks are right, a soft, conciliatory stance may encourage the adversary to redouble its efforts to force Party to yield. For example, after surrounding Indian outposts in 1961, Chinese forces withdrew in an effort to signal a desire to be conciliatory. Unfortunately, Indian leaders "interpreted the Chinese withdrawal as a sign of timidity [and] became even bolder in their efforts to occupy as much of the disputed territory, east and west, as was possible" (Lebow et al., 1984).

Because both hawks and doves may have the right answer at times, it is wise for groups (including organizations and nations) to cultivate both kinds of bird among their members and to allow them to engage in what is usually an endless debate. However, it should be borne in mind that the hawkish analysis is the more common one, strengthened by a self-serving tendency for Party to think that Other must be the "aggressor" because Party's side cannot possibly be in the wrong. Hence, cultivating doves is often the more elusive and challenging enterprise.

A structural change analysis of the conflict Party is experiencing implies a third set of tactics. For example, Party may try to avoid structural changes in its own constituency that will contribute to further escalation. Thus a leader who fears that a permanent defense establishment will become a strong advocate for hawkish policies may insist that a temporary establishment be formed to meet a current threat. A structural change analysis also implies the importance of *timing* in reversing or repudiating actions that are taken by Party and resented by Other (Pruitt & Gahagan, 1974). For example, it seems reasonable to assume that the UB campus crisis would have dissipated quickly if the administration had publicly apologized for the initial violence by the campus police, made restitution to the students who were assaulted, and arranged to drop the charges against those who were initially arrested. Such actions would probably have prevented the formation of the Strike Committee. Timing was important because once the Strike Committee had developed, and numerous students had taken leadership positions in it, the campus was consigned to an extended period of heavy conflict.

Cultural Differences

In *Culture of Honor: The Psychology of Violence in the South,* Nisbett and Cohen (1996) assert that cultures that emphasize honor—a concern for the public image of status and toughness—encourage harsh reaction to provocation. These authors have demonstrated that the culture of honor largely accounts for the far higher homicide rates among southern white males than those among their northern counterparts in the United States. This regional difference occurs only for homicides stemming from an argument or quarrel, where honor is at great stake, not for those stemming from, for example, robbery or burglary. Also, although southerners differ little from northerners with regard to their support for violence in general, they express more support than northerners do for the use of violence in honor-related matters, such as protecting oneself or one's family from affronts. What is more, when insulted, southerners show more anger, experience more hormonal changes indicative of stress (increase in their cortisol level) and of aggressive readiness (increase in their testosterone level), and act more aggressively against another person than do northerners.

Why has the culture of honor emerged more in the South than in the North? According to Nisbett and Cohen, it has to do with a security dilemma arising from the herding of cattle, which was the original economy of this region. Cattle are a highly portable form of property that is an easy target for thievery. Since law enforcement was weak at first, individuals needed to cultivate a reputation for being ready to retaliate violently when threatened in any way. To this end, even trivial slights could not go unanswered, because tolerating them might invite further affronts and lead eventually to the loss of the herd. The dilemma inheres in the fact that rational individual efforts to burnish the image of toughness in self-defense lead to an irrational outcome for society as a whole. With everybody on a hair trigger, many fatal fights will occur that could otherwise be avoided. One kind of evidence for this theory is that the culture of honor is universally present in herding societies (Nisbett & Cohen, 1996).

Although the conditions that produced the culture of honor—herding and weak law enforcement—no longer exist in the South, this culture has a staying power in that region. People are expected to avenge slights to their honor even if doing so no longer gains economic benefits.

Similar cultures of honor exist in many impoverished, inner-city black communities. There, violence is a main means of handling conflict, particularly conflict involving affronts. Young men's fights often begin with an incident in which one of them perceives he has been "dissed" (disrespected). Anderson (1999) calls this culture "the code of the streets."

This inner-city culture also derives, in part, from the security dilemma. Crime is rampant in these neighborhoods, and police are not very effective. Hence, people must defend themselves by developing a reputation for toughness. In addition, there are few means available to gain status and regard except through building such a reputation. People, particularly young men (and increasingly young women as well), earn respect by responding to even the slightest affront to their honor (for example, maintaining eye contact too long) with harsh, sometimes lethal violence. Being respected is the core value in this street culture; hence, many young men aspire to be "the baddest dude on the street."

Features of Groups

Conflict between groups is more likely to escalate than conflict between individuals. The mere existence of an ingroup and an outgroup leads the outgroup to become the object of negative perceptions and discrimination (Crocker et al., 1987; Tajfel, 1970) and produces more vigorous competition for scarce resources (Komorita & Lapworth, 1982). Furthermore groups, when annoyed, have been found to protest more adamantly and retaliate more harshly than individuals (Jaffe & Yinon, 1983; Mikolic et al., 1997; Rabbie & Lodewijkx, 1995). Groups also behave less cooperatively in the prisoner's dilemma (Schopler & Insko, 1992). There are a number of explanations for these effects, most prominently, *social identity theory*, which was mentioned in Chapter 2. This theory holds that groups are more contentious than individuals because the self-respect of their members is tied to believing that their own group is better than other groups (Tajfel & Turner, 1979, 1986).

In Chapter 6, we discussed a number of structural changes that occur in groups during escalation and tend to encourage further escalation. The most important of these are the establishment of subgroups that are dedicated to the struggle, the ascendancy of militant leaders, and the development of contentious group norms and goals. Escalation is more likely when there are conditions that allow these changes to take place, such as the capacity for communication among group members and the availability of militant leadership.

Prior Escalation and Structural Change

Most of the structural changes discussed in Chapter 6, once they are in place, tend to persist. These include hostile attitudes and perceptions, hostile individual and group goals, militant subgroups and leaders, and community polarization. Severe conflicts usually eventually taper off, with issues at least partially solved or forgotten and heavy tactics diminished or in abeyance. But if structural changes have taken place, these make the situation more vulnerable to a new conflict if it arises (Coleman, 1957). Hostile attitudes and perceptions—distrust, dehumanization, hatred, and the like—once established, make it easier for Party to misinterpret or overreact to a new challenge from Other. Militant leaders, once in place, can easily spring into action when a new issue arises. And a community, once polarized, has difficulty resolving new conflicts along its fault lines.

What this means is that prior escalation, and the structural changes it produces, can be a source of future instability. When new conflicts arise, these changes tend to make escalation more likely and more severe.

FEATURES OF THE RELATIONSHIP BETWEEN THE PARTIES

Social Bonds

As mentioned in Chapter 3, social bonds tend to encourage yielding and problem solving. They also reduce the use of contentious tactics, especially those of the harsher variety. Hence, social bonds are a source of stability in relationships—they reduce the likelihood of escalation. The bonds in question include positive attitudes, respect, trust, friendship, kinship, perceived similarity, common group membership, common ethnic and cultural identity, and future dependence. As an example of the inhibiting effect of friendship on social conflict, Ransford (1968) found that African Americans who had socialized with whites were less willing to endorse the use of violence in pursuit of racial justice than were those who had not. The impact of kinship is demonstrated by the finding that close kin seldom murder each other (Daly & Wilson, 1998).[6] Evidence that common group membership protects parties from escalation comes from (a) an experiment by Kramer and Brewer (1984) in which two groups were less likely to compete for common resources when their members saw themselves as coming from the same geographical community rather than two different communities, and (b) a qualitative study of community conflict by Coleman (1957), which suggested that identification with one's community tends to moderate the tactics used for pursuing disagreements with other community members.

The opposite side of this coin is that the absence of bonds is a source of instability. This is particularly true for perceived dissimilarity, membership in different groups, ideological disparity, and cultural divergence, since

---

[6] This finding holds up throughout the animal kingdom; closer relatives tend to receive more help and are less often targets of aggression (Buss, 1999; Pfennig & Sherman, 1995).

people who are different from oneself are often viewed with suspicion and sometimes with alarm. Thus Struch and Schwartz (1989) have found that aggression is more likely between Israeli groups whose members look or act very different and therefore cannot easily move from one group to the other. Huntington (1996) has argued, on the basis of a great deal of case material, that escalation is particularly likely between groups that differ in culture and religion. He uses the term "fault lines" to describe regions of the world where such groups come into contact and argues that conflicts will be particularly severe and long-lasting in such regions. One example is the Middle East, where Israelis (mainly westernized Jews) and Arabs (mainly Muslim) have fought each other for generations.

The stabilizing impact of bonding is often masked by the fact that people who are more securely bonded to each other usually interact more and feel less constrained by the canons of politeness. Hence, they are likely to experience more episodes of conflict and to argue more vigorously, at least for a while. Still, if conflict persists, they are more likely to engage in problem solving and less likely to employ harsh contentious tactics. This paradox was observed in a laboratory study of cohesiveness (solidarity) in dyads (Back, 1951). When a difference of opinion arose, more cohesive dyads argued more vigorously but also eventually reached fuller agreement. This is a pattern that is often found in successful marriages.

Dependence   Dependence is the most complicated source of bonding and hence deserves separate discussion. Party is dependent on Other to the extent that Other has control over certain of Party's outcomes and can reward Party for desired behavior and/or punish Party for undesired behavior. Dependence, unlike most other kinds of bonds, is often unidirectional. Party can be dependent on Other without Other being dependent on Party.

As mentioned in Chapter 3, dependence usually encourages yielding and problem solving and discourages the use of heavy contentious tactics (Ben-Yoav & Pruitt, 1984a, b; Heide & Miner, 1992). The more Other can help or harm Party, the more careful Party must be not to annoy Other by pressing petty claims or employing harsh tactics. Hence, dependence ordinarily contributes to stability, especially if it is positive and bilateral (each can reward the other). An example is the high level of cooperation and absence of escalated conflict in relations between the United States and the Soviet Union during the Second World War, when they were dependent on each other for support in the common battle against Germany and her allies. This relationship deteriorated drastically as soon as the common battle was over, producing the Cold War.

Dependence is a two-edged sword, because it can produce escalation rather than stability if Other fails to cooperate. For example, if Party depends on Other for rides to work and it is costly for Other to provide them, their interests are divergent. If Other is haphazard in providing this service and Party cannot find another source of rides, Party is likely to employ contentious tactics in an effort to improve Other's performance. The more dependent Party is on Other, the harsher the tactics Party will employ in order to teach Other an enduring lesson. This is why friends and family members so often get into escalated conflict, despite their bonds of affection and common group membership. Such people are highly interdependent and have a lot of potential divergence of interest.

The Destruction of Bonds   When conflict escalates, bonds tend to disintegrate. Relationships are severed; love turns to hate, and people shift their dependencies to other, less difficult partners. Structural changes of this kind are often long-lasting. As a result, conflict spirals persist and new conflicts between the parties are more likely to escalate. In short, prior escalation destroys interparty bonds, enhancing the likelihood of further escalation.

Evidence of this comes from studies of conflict management in marriage. Distressed marriages, where the partners have hostile attitudes and negative perceptions of each other, are prone to *negative reciprocity*—responding to the partner's criticism with return criticism (Bradbury & Fincham, 1992; Rusbult et al., 1991). This means that each new conflict, however trivial, is likely to escalate into a heavy, new argument.

FEATURES OF THE BROADER COMMUNITY

The stability or instability of a relationship between two parties is very much a function of the broader community of which they are a part. Some features of communities (e.g., outside support to the disputants) contribute to instability and underlie the development of escalation. Others (e.g., conflict-limiting norms and crosscutting) contribute to stability and tend to diminish or prevent escalation.

Outside Support

Conflict tends to be waged more vigorously, and in a more escalated fashion, when the parties have outside support, that is, supporters in the community. For example, a conflict between two neighboring families was exacerbated by outside support. It started as a simple argument over use of a common driveway. Then friends on each side urged an uncompromising stance, and an escalation ensued. Finally, a teenage boy from one family threw a firecracker at children from the other family, who had the boy arrested and sent to jail. The conflict was resolved in a community mediation session, during which both families vowed to ignore their friends' opinions about the conflict.[7]

Outside support sometimes takes the form of *audiences*—people who are observing a dispute taking place. Audiences are usually unhappy about conflict and try to stop it, as in the rink rage example. But this is not always the case. Some audiences are amused by conflict and urge the participants to escalate, even to the point of threatening their images by calling them cowards if they do not fight. Such encouragement, which is most often found when men observe a conflict between other men, may have been present during the fight in the state prison described in Chapter 6. Heavy escalation is a frequent result of such encouragement (Brown, 1968).

Outside support can also contribute to escalation in intergroup and international conflict. For example, the heavily escalated conflict between Palestinians and Israelis that started in 2000 can be attributed in part to moral and material support, from the Arab world on the one hand and the United States on the other.

A related phenomenon is the impact of broad social movements on local community dissent. A case in point is the radical student movement of the late 1960s, which arose on campuses around the globe and inspired the campus radicals who started the crisis at UB that was described in Chapter 6. Some people thought that off-campus student leaders were pulling the strings at UB, but this was not the case. Rather, the international student movement provided moral support and examples that could be imitated. Indeed, the student demonstrations that spread rapidly between 1968 and 1970 often seemed to contain an element of "keeping up with the Joneses." The news that students had started a demonstration in one location encouraged the belief that it was possible and desirable elsewhere. Pride in one's own local movement depended in part on having a demonstration comparable to those on other campuses.

It follows that communities are less stable when there exists a national or international movement consisting of dissident groups in other communities (Coleman, 1957). Once such a movement gets started, it is hard to put the genie back in the bottle. Each militant action serves as an example to other communities, which then serve as examples to still others in a chain reaction. An example is the overthrow of one communist regime after another in Eastern Europe in 1990.

Conflict-Limiting Norms

Community norms often contribute to stability, prohibiting the use of harsh contentious tactics and prescribing problem solving or adjudication

---

[7] Community mediation will be discussed as part of a larger section on mediation in Chapter 11.

as the proper approach to conflict between group members. "Don't let the sun set on your anger" and "Love thy neighbor as thyself" are but a few examples of maxims that may serve as guiding norms in the regulation of conflict.[8]

Like all norms, conflict-limiting norms are especially effective with parties who are well socialized and those who feel that the community has their interests at heart. They are effective with other types of parties to the extent that the community has the capacity for enforcement—that is, for learning about and punishing norm violation. Escalation is more likely when societies lack these elements, a point that is further developed in the next section.

Conflict-Limiting Institutions

Most communities also provide forums and third party services for helping their *members resolve* conflict peacefully. Such institutions contribute to stability by giving people a nonviolent and face-saving way to resolve their disputes (Glasl, 1982). Examples include legislative bodies, courts, and services that provide mediation and arbitration.

Stability—that is, lack of escalation—within communities depends on the availability and effectiveness of these institutions. For these institutions to be effective, they must be seen as fair and powerful. If they are absent or seem unfair or weak, vigilante action is likely to develop. People will "take the law into their own hands," employing harsh contentious tactics in an effort to settle conflicts in their own favor, thereby escalating these conflicts. The Hatfield-McCoy conflict, which was described in Chapter 6, involved vigilante actions that produced severe escalation. These two families lived in a mountainous area at a distance from an effective police force; hence they saw the need for direct action against each other, producing a deadly feud that lasted for twelve years. The Rodney King riots, which were described at the beginning of Chapter 1, can also be seen as vigilante action, resulting from perceived unfairness on the part of the police, who were seen as opponents rather than protectors.

The most important source of perceived fairness is *voice*—having a say in the decision process. Thus people see trials, police actions, and job performance reviews as fair to the extent that the authority seems to have heard and given consideration to their perspective. The relationship of voice to escalation is seen in interviews with African American residents of Los Angeles after the Watts riots of 1965. Those who felt that it was not possible for the average citizen to influence government decisions were

---

[8] Norms such as these must be distinguished from substantive norms and norms about who makes what decisions. As mentioned in Chapter 2, the latter two types of norms tend to diminish the likelihood of conflict arising at all rather than the likelihood of escalation.

especially likely to endorse the use of violence in pursuit of racial justice (Ransford, 1968). Other sources of perceived fairness are a belief that the authority is unbiased, consistent, and careful in its decision making (Lind & Tyler, 1988; Tyler, 1990).

When communities are severely divided, the perceived fairness of their institutions often rests on whether the various groups within the community are represented in running them. Hence, power-sharing arrangements can be a route to stability (Hampson, 1996; Zartman, 1995).

In addition to being seen as fair, conflict-limiting institutions must have enough power—enough of a monopoly on force—that they can enforce decisions on those who are reluctant to follow them. Otherwise, conflicts are likely to escalate. In recent years, the world has witnessed many examples of escalated ethnic conflicts that have arisen when central governments become weak or discredited. For example, the internal wars in Serbia, Bosnia, and Croatia were partly due to the discrediting of the Communist Party and the breakdown of the central government in the former Yugoslavia (Bloomfield, 1997).

Community Structure: Crosscutting vs. Overlapping Bonds

By "community structure" is meant the distribution of bonds across the members of a community. Bonds of friendship, kinship, ethnic identity, type of work, and so on, link some community members and divide others.

The stability of a community depends on the extent to which the bonds between its members are crosscutting, as opposed to overlapping (Coleman, 1957). In a community with a heavily *overlapping* structure, most kinds of bonds link the same people together. In other words, there are two or more groups that differ from each other in almost every respect. Catholics may be mainly recent emigrants from Italy, holding laboring jobs, and living in a particular geographical region; while Protestants may be mainly old Americans, holding white-collar jobs, and living in another region.[9] If (as is probable) these groups also have no kinship and few friendship or business relations with each other, we are dealing with a severely overlapping and *highly unstable* structure. If conflict develops across the fault lines between these unrelated groups, the community is likely to polarize, producing heavy escalation.

In a community with a heavily *crosscutting* structure, almost everybody is linked with almost everybody else by at least one kind of bond. Thus some of each religious group are management and some are workers.

---

[9] The term "overlapping" may not be altogether clear. In the example just given, religious, ethnic, social class, and geographical differences all overlap. This means that all of these dimensions sort the community members into the same two groups.

Some of both these groups are newcomers to the community and some are old guard. And friendships and business relationships have little to do with demographic characteristics. This is a *highly stable* structure, because a conflict between any two (or more) individuals or groups will be held in check by the bonds they have with each other, or their friends and associates have with each other.

Figure 7.2 shows schematic drawings of a heavily overlapping structure (Case 1) and a partially crosscutting structure (Case 2). We make the simplifying assumption that there are only two kinds of bonds: religion: Catholics (A) vs. Protestants (B), and social class: unionized workers (C) vs. managers who belong to trade and professional associations (D). In Case 1, these dimensions overlap and the community consists of two groups with no bonds between them: Catholic workers (A,C) and Protestant managers (B,D). In Case 2, social class crosscuts religion. Some Catholics are workers (A,C) while others are managers (A,D); and some Protestants are workers (B,C) while others are managers (B,D). Our theory assumes that Case 2 is more stable than Case 1.

Crosscutting provides stability in both dimensions of Case 2. Religious conflicts are held in check by crosscutting memberships in union and management, and labor conflicts are held in check by crosscutting memberships in religious organizations.

Crosscutting reduces the severity of community conflict for at least three reasons. One is that bonds between some community members cause them to exercise restraint—to refrain from polarization and escalation when divergence of interest arises or they annoy each other (Vanbeselaere, 1991). Thus if there is a Catholic-Protestant squabble, Catholic workers are inhibited from using heavy tactics against Protestant workers and Catholic managers against Protestant managers; and Protestant workers and managers will adopt a similar stance. A second reason is that members of crosscutting groups will try to exercise control over their fellow group members who do not belong to crosscutting groups. Thus on both sides of the religious divide, workers and managers will try to restrain shopkeepers and high school students (who are not part of crosscutting groups) from assaulting members of the opposing religious group. A third reason is that members of crosscutting groups can act as mediators to resolve the community's problems. Thus Catholic and Protestant union members can discuss the religious conflict because they are part of the same organization, as can Catholic and Protestant members of professional associations. Hence, crosscutting memberships provide a capacity for conflict management.

Varshney (2002) has studied crosscutting in Indian cities and found that cities with ethnically integrated organizations—trade unions, professional associations, political parties, business groups—were less likely to have heavy Hindu-Muslim rioting than those without such organizations. He found that when religious conflicts loomed, members of these organizations

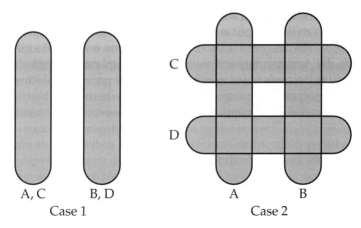

FIGURE 7.2

Case 1 represents a community with overlapping bonds; Case 2, a community with crosscutting bonds.

moved to try to manage them. For example, they worked to quell unfounded rumors of atrocities by one religious group against the other.

Gluckman (1955) gives two anthropological examples of crosscutting. He found that when a Nuer man moves away from his hometown, he becomes a mediator in quarrels between his relatives and residents of his new location. He probably has two motives for doing so. One is the fear of retribution from his new neighbors, causing him to urge caution on his kin. The other is that "he is likely to urge his kin to offer compensation, since he has many interests in the place where he resides" (p. 12). Gluckman also points out that marriage produces stability in those African societies in which the wife must move to her husband's village. Thereafter, she exerts a calming influence whenever there is conflict between her original village and that to which she has moved. Both examples illustrate crosscutting because the person who has moved becomes a member of both groups.

Closer to home, the United States today can be regarded as a heavily crosscutting system. For example, the rivalry between North and South, which once spawned a civil war, is now held in check by the fact that there are thousands of strong nationwide organizations, such as the Republican Party and the Roman Catholic Church. There is also heavy crosscutting between social classes and between most other societal divisions. In such a system, few subsets of people can form an unambivalent alliance against any other subset.

An historical exception to this description was the division between African Americans and whites in our society, because there were relatively few bonds between these groups. The theory presented here would view the civil rights movement, with its effort to introduce African Americans into every institution of our society, as a massive program to develop crosscutting bonds and the stability that goes with them, whether or not this was intended by activists in that movement.

The Impact of Mild Conflict in Crosscutting Systems   There is one other wrinkle to the theory of crosscutting group memberships—a paradoxical one. In a crosscutting situation, mild conflict between social groups can actually contribute to the overall stability of the community, making severe conflict less likely (Coleman, 1957). Imagine a community of Yankees and Italians in which some people from each ethnic group are managers (and belong to management associations and clubs) and others are laborers (and belong to unions). A little conflict between management and labor should make it more difficult for Yankee-Italian antagonisms to escalate, because Yankees and Italians have served together on both sides of the industrial battle line and recognize that they may need to do so again. Likewise, a little conflict between Yankees and Italians should diminish the intensity of future conflict between labor and management. Hence—and this is the crucial point—if there has been a little conflict in both sets of groupings, severe escalation is likely to be avoided in both. Almost everybody in the community recognizes almost everybody else as a past or potential future ally.[10]

An example of this can be seen in the United States Congress. Coalitions change from issue to issue in this body, so antagonisms usually do not run very deep. Members maintain decorous relations with one another and observe many informal conflict-limiting norms in order to be able to work together in future coalitions. Today it may be the farm states against the manufacturing states, tomorrow North against South, the next day those who want to maintain social programs against those who want to cut them. One never knows whose help may be needed in a future conflict, so it is foolish to let current differences get out of hand.[11]

Crosscutting systems like those just described are highly resistant to escalation. But no system is completely escalation-proof. A really severe

---

[10] In addition, mild controversy sometimes contributes to the development of institutions (such as representative committees and mediation services) that stand ready to resolve more serious future controversies. We will revisit such institutions in the discussion of conflict management systems in Chapter 11.

[11] Although crosscutting memberships reduce the likelihood of heavy contentious behavior between groups, they are not always beneficial to society as a whole. Society needs active competition between certain groups. For example, society must resist the development of interlocking directorates among corporations that produce the same kind of product, because of the need for competition between these corporations (Schoorman et al., 1981).

conflict of interest between two groups can break through any bonds, however secure, producing a runaway escalation and a set of antagonisms that may take years to repair.

Combating Polarization in Divided Communities   There are four methods for combating polarization in divided communities like that in Case 1. One is to try to strengthen loyalty to the broader community. Flags and national anthems serve this function in the nation-state. The second is to install or strengthen a central authority that can threaten or use force to prevent escalation. The third is to foster antagonism with an outside enemy. An example is the Argentine occupation of the Falkland/Malvinas Islands in 1982, which appears to have been designed to unite a divided domestic polity around a patriotic issue.

The fourth and best way to combat polarization in a divided community is to encourage the development of bonds between individuals on both sides of the divide, thus moving in the direction of crosscutting. This method is used whenever ruling groups incorporate (co-opt) members of agitating factions into their decision making. Likert (1961) recommends the use of co–optation in organizations, urging that interdepartmental committees be formed involving representatives of conflicting departments. Membership in such committees will give these representatives a common group identity, and committee meetings will allow them to engage in problem solving about matters of common concern. Such representatives are called "linking pins." Royal families used a similar method in the past when they arranged for their sons and daughters to marry foreign princesses and princes in an effort to achieve peaceful relations with other countries.

Such procedures produce a cadre of people in each group who oppose the use of heavy contentious tactics and are ready to serve as mediators when conflict arises between the groups. If one linking pin on each side can contribute to community stability, two should be better and two hundred even better.

STABILITY THROUGH THREATS

The safeguards discussed so far—conflict-limiting norms and institutions, fear of escalation, social bonds, crosscutting group memberships—have tremendous force, accounting for the quiet way in which most conflicts are pursued and the high rate of peaceful conflict resolution ordinarily found in human affairs. However, these safeguards are not always present or strong enough to avert escalation.

Under such circumstances, parties often use *threats and punitive actions* to dissuade others from employing harsh tactics. Dramatic forms of threat and punishment can be seen in the apprehension and incarceration of violent criminals or in the military preparations that are so common in the international arena.

Less obvious, but nevertheless of vast social significance, are the subtle threats and small penalties that all human interactions exhibit. All people have means of imposing costs on those around them. Children cry, workers move slowly, wives get angry, and husbands come home late. Most people are also adept at subtly signaling their discontent: the slow response to a statement, the lapse of attention, the lifted eyebrow, the frown, the sigh. These signals are tantamount to stating a full-blown threat, in that the recipients realize that punitive action will be forthcoming if they are not careful. In short, threats and penalties that are aimed at deterring others from taking bothersome actions are omnipresent in social relationships.[12]

Balance of Power Theory

Several theories of threat-induced stability have been developed for international affairs, where other sources of stability are often at their weakest. The oldest and most famous of these theories *is balance of power.* This theory can be adapted so that it is broadly applicable to the use of threats in all social situations.

In one interpretation of this theory, a balance of power exists when all nations in a system are deterred for military reasons from attacking all others. Assuming conventional (non-nuclear) weapons, deterrence is a function of the existence of natural and artificial barriers to attack, the military capability of the target of a potential attack, and the assistance it can recruit from other nations. These are effective deterrents either by making it impossible for aggression to succeed or by imposing unacceptable costs on an aggressor.

There are several mechanisms by which a balance of power can be achieved. Collective security, in which all other nations come to the rescue of a nation under attack, is often regarded as the ideal mechanism. Such a mechanism was built into the charter of the United Nations and was realized, to some extent, in the campaign against Iraq during the Gulf War. But collective security has been difficult to activate in most controversies, because some nations sympathize with one side and some with the other.

Barring effective collective security, nations that are faced with a strong opponent try to maintain or restore the balance of power by arming themselves and seeking allies. Some analysts argue that the most stable situation

---

[12] Threats were extensively discussed in Chapter 4.

is one in which all potential opponents are equal in military strength; others argue that the least aggressive nations must have a preponderance of military strength (Pruitt & Snyder, 1969). The existence of a balancer nation contributes to both kinds of stability. Balancers are nations that change alliances from time to time in order to side with the underdog. In earlier times, England played the role of balancer in the European system of nations.

Balance-of-power theory can be translated into other arenas of human interaction. For example, small groups, such as interdepartmental committees or families, usually try to deter overly aggressive members who attack others or try to dominate discussions. Collective security is common in such situations, with most other group members forming a temporary coalition against the aggressor.[13] Barring this, smaller coalitions of like-minded individuals may form, and the members of each coalition support one another so that none can be overwhelmed. The situation will also be stable if a few people act as balancers, forever shifting to the defense of the underdog. The group leader frequently plays the role of balancer.

There are at least two problems with balance-of-power theory. One is that it is often difficult to identify and measure power; hence it is hard to know how much of what is needed to deter the adversary. Indeed "power" is one of the most difficult concepts to define and measure in the social sciences. This problem is particularly acute when different sorts of weapons are used on the two sides of a conflict, for example, conventional armaments on one side and guerrilla or terrorist forces on the other. Such conflicts often become highly escalated because both sides believe that they are winning for a long period of time. This is part of what prolonged the Vietnam War and has made the Israeli-Palestinian conflict so severe and difficult to resolve.

The other problem is that balance of power is ineffective if the military advantage lies heavily with whichever country attacks the other first. The greater the apparent advantage of striking first, the more likely is escalation, regardless of the distribution of military force. Such situations are unstable for two reasons: (1) because of the temptation to strike first; and (2) because of fear that another nation is about to strike first, which can motivate a preemptive first strike.

A highly unstable situation of this kind existed in 1914, when it was believed that the first European nation to mobilize could gain a major advantage over its neighbor by loading its troops onto trains and rushing them to the border for a massive assault. The result of this instability was the First World War. This war began when Russia, attempting to deter an Austrian attack on Serbia, mobilized troops along its southern border. Germany, perceiving that this mobilization put it at a military disadvantage,

---

[13] Recall that Mom and Sis took sides with Ben in the Chapter 1 story.

launched a preemptive attack against Russia's ally, France, striking through Belgium.

The Balance of Terror

The development of nuclear weapons has forced some changes in thinking about the balance of power in international affairs. These weapons are fantastically destructive and there is (so far) no real defense against them. The only way to protect oneself militarily is to threaten to retaliate in the hope of deterring the other side from using these weapons. Such retaliation is called a *second strike*. It follows that a critical issue for stability is second-strike credibility: how believable it is that an aggressor will be destroyed. When second-strike capability exists on both sides, we have a situation that is known as "mutually assured destruction."

According to *deterrence theory*, efforts to establish credibility must take somewhat different forms depending on whether the nation attacked has nuclear weapons or is the ally of a nuclear nation (Kahn, 1960). It is ordinarily assumed that nuclear nations under nuclear attack will retaliate in kind if they can. Hence, only second-strike *capability* is considered to be at issue—that is, whether the nation can retaliate after suffering a nuclear first strike. In contrast, in the deterrence of attack against a non-nuclear ally, *intentions* are the main issue. Will the nuclear nation run the risk of a devastating counterattack from the aggressor by actually retaliating? Willingness to come to the defense of an ally has always been an issue, even in strictly conventional contests; but it is more difficult to establish the credibility of intent in the age of nuclear weapons, because the cost of retaliation is so much greater.[14]

Second-strike capability is believed to depend on the security of the carriers (missiles and planes) of nuclear weapons and on their capacity to penetrate the adversary's defenses. The security of weapons carriers can be achieved in a variety of ways, including increasing their numbers, dispersing them, moving them frequently, concealing them, and shielding them. For example, several countries have nuclear weapons constantly on the move in submarines that are virtually impossible to locate and destroy.

Provided that its second-strike capability is secure, a nation can afford to have dramatically less nuclear capability than its adversary(ies) and still be secure. During the Cold War, the United States was way "ahead" of Russia in destructive capacity, but there is little evidence that the Russians

---

[14] It can be argued that the credibility of Party's willingness to protect allies depends heavily on the strength of its bonds to these allies. Hence, trade, travel, and statements of friendship with allies may help to deter attacks against them.

were worried about an attack. Despite the military inequality (and, hence, the absence of a balance of power), mutually assured destruction existed and there was a stable "balance of terror."

Problems with Basing Stability on Threats

There are many problems with efforts to base security on threats, and hence with reliance on the balance of power or the balance of terror. Such approaches assume that it is possible to clearly communicate Party's resolve to a potential aggressor. Yet history reveals many failures in this regard (Lebow et al., 1984). They also assume that a would-be aggressor will be rational, able to predict accurately, and ready to avoid taking action if the risks are high or the probability of success is low.

It follows that threat-based deterrents are likely to fail and escalation to materialize in international relations, when the responsible decision makers: (1) are mentally or emotionally incapacitated, and so unable to use the information available to them; (2) regard the military future as so bleak or the military balance as changing so fast against them that they feel they have little to lose by aggressing; or (3) are impelled by foreign or domestic political interests of such gravity that they are willing to take large risks in a military adventure. Lebow, Jervis, and Stein (1984) cite the Japanese attack on Pearl Harbor and two Egyptian attacks on Israel as examples of the latter condition. What happened is that under the pressure of compelling political considerations, national leaders engaged in wishful thinking about the likelihood of winning a war.

The instability of threat-based systems can also be seen in domestic settings. Consider, for example, the impoverished section of Los Angeles portrayed in John Singleton's brilliant film, *Boyz n the Hood*. Intent on impressing local audiences and with little thought for the future, two young men get into a shoving and shouting match. The quarrel is continued by their friends and relatives—most prominently, by a man whose life and future are so empty that he seems unafraid of the consequences of violence. The local authorities are worse than useless, confining their activities to noisemaking and random assaults that keep everyone in a high state of autonomic arousal. Eventually a series of shootings takes place, eliminating most of the main characters in the movie.

Another problem with the use of threat-based deterrents is that they can actually encourage escalation. They involve "fighting fire with fire"; hence, they run the risk of contributing to a conflict spiral. This means that threat-based deterrents are capable of producing the very problem they are designed to avoid. There are three reasons for this. One is that Party's threats tend to challenge Other's image of independence and strength, producing resentment. This problem is particularly acute when there is a moderate (as opposed to a large) difference in power between Party and Other, because the more powerful party often feels free to employ threats while the less powerful one refuses to acknowledge its inferiority and becomes resistant or belligerent (Pruitt & Carnevale, 1993). The problem is less acute when the threats are consistent with social norms and therefore at least moderately legitimate, as in the case of most threats of retaliation. Yet threats of this kind may still produce some resentment.

A second reason for escalation is that deterrent threats are often misinterpreted by Other (Jervis, 1976). An army mobilized to resist invasion may be misconstrued as an instrument of potential aggression. Missiles designed only for a second strike may be seen as a first-strike capability. A boys' gang organized to protect its members may seem to threaten another gang's "turf." Such perceptions produce defensive counter-reactions that tend to start (or continue) a conflict spiral.

The third reason for escalation is that even if it is clear that Party's preparations have defensive motives, Other may still be cautious lest Party *later* adopt aggressive motives. Hence, Other may feel the need to attack in order to diminish Party's capacity to do harm at a later time.

What can be done to avoid such interpretations and misinterpretations of defensive preparations? Party can carefully explain its behavior, trying to tie it, action by action, to Other's behavior so that Party is seen as essentially reactive. Furthermore, preparations that are clearly defensive and cannot be converted to offensive use should be favored, for example, building a wall or wearing a bulletproof vest. It may also be possible for Party to couple a carrot with the stick, offering a reward for cooperation as well as a punishment for aggression. This works because the carrot provides Other a nonaggressive avenue for goal achievement and makes it harder for Other to believe that Party is preparing for aggression. Efforts to diminish tensions in other realms are also advisable, so as to reduce the likelihood that Other will view Party's military efforts through the prism of anger and indignation (White, 1984).

Such procedures are sometimes effective, but threats are so often problematic that it seems preferable to avoid them altogether and to substitute other forms of conflict management, such as positive bonds, the building of social norms, and efforts to find solutions to the issues in dispute.

SUMMARY AND CONCLUSIONS

Events as dramatic as the Cold War, the UB crisis, and the travail of the rink rage fight are unusual. But moderate escalation is not uncommon; almost any conflict can become intensified. The likelihood that a conflict will escalate is partly a function of conflict size—the extent of perceived divergence of interest and the rigidity of the parties' aspirations. It is also a function of what we call "instability." Situations are highly unstable if even a small conflict can launch a massive escalation; they are highly stable if only a very large conflict can have this impact.

Instability (and hence escalation) results if one or both of the parties is prone to overreact to annoyance, or has weak inhibitions against aggressive responding. At the individual level, conditions that encourage overreaction include autonomic arousal, being angry because of a prior incident (especially if has not been possible to identify or punish the source of this incident), belonging to a culture of honor, and having supporters or audiences that favor harsh reacting. People with irritable personalities also tend to overreact. Conditions that erode inhibitions against aggressive responding include exposure to aggressive models and impulsivity. Drinking alcohol and time pressure have both of these effects—encouraging overreaction and reducing inhibitions.

Stability is encouraged if both parties have strong inhibitions against aggressive responding or the situation encourages conflict management. Inhibitions against aggressive responding result from an understanding of the conflict spiral, empathy toward Other, having bonds (of friendship, kinship, common group membership, etc.) with Other, dependence on Other (if Other is generally accommodating), the existence of conflict limiting norms, being in the presence of peace-loving third parties, pressure from allies who are negatively affected by the conflict, and being a person who needs social approval. Conflict management is encouraged by bonds with Other that allow meaningful conversation, an understanding of the structural change model, and the easy availability of conflict limiting institutions such as police, courts, mediators, and the like.

Several of the conditions just listed also produce stability in intergroup relations. These include bonds and dependencies, pressure from allies, and the availability of conflict limiting norms and institutions. In addition, the likelihood of intergroup escalation is reduced by loyalty to the broader community and the existence of crosscutting bonds—friendships and organizational memberships that cut across two groups in conflict. As an example of the latter, escalated conflict between Indian Hindus and Moslems is less likely in a community that contains ethnically integrated trade unions, professional associations, political parties, and the like. This is because people in these crosscutting associations are inhibited from escalation and because they engage in conflict management so as to preserve their associations.

Prior escalation is a major source of instability, because the structural changes that are produced by escalation tend to erode many of the safeguards against future escalation, at both the individual and group levels.

In the absence of constraints and conditions that encourage conflict management, conflicting parties tend to fall back on threats and threat enforcement in an effort to protect themselves. Stability is achieved in such anarchic situations if the circumstances make it unwise or impossible for any party to mount or sustain an attack on any other. In international relations, a balance of military capability or mutual assured destruction may have this impact. However, major problems can easily arise for parties and communities that rely on threat alone.

In Chapter 8, we continue our discussion of escalation by taking up a number of confirmatory mechanisms that cause structural changes to endure once established. These mechanisms underlie the tendency for escalation to persist and recur once established, and they help understand the deterioration of human relationships.

8

The Persistence of Escalation

❖

The Tail of Cerberus ♦ Overview of Theory ♦ The Persistence of Psychological Changes ♦ *The Self-fulfilling Prophecy* ♦ *Rationalization of Behavior* ♦ *Selective Information Processing* ♦ *Autistic Hostility* ♦ *The Persistence of Hostile Goals* ♦ The Persistence of Changes in Groups ♦ The Persistence of Community Polarization ♦ Overcommitment and Entrapment ♦ *An Aside on the Dollar Auction* ♦ *Characteristics of Entrapment* ♦ *Combating Entrapment* ♦ Summary and Conclusions

Escalation occurs when Party's contentious tactics become heavier, putting more pressure on Other and often inflicting greater suffering. Escalation is accompanied by a series of incremental transformations, discussed in Chapter 5, where we also described two conflict models that show how escalation develops: the contender-defender model and the conflict spiral model. In Chapter 6, we introduced a third conflict model: the structural change model. This model assumes a cycle of escalation: Party's heavy tactics produce structural changes that encourage reciprocal tactics from Other, provoking changes that encourage Party to employ further heavy tactics. We described the nature of these changes, as these occur in individuals, groups, and communities. Chapter 7 continued the story with a discussion of conditions under which conflict is likely to go into heavy escalation and conditions under which this outcome is unlikely.

151

Chapter 8 completes the discussion by examining why heavy escalation so often persists—as shown in the long right-hand tail of Figure 7.1B[1]—and why it sometimes recurs when new conflicts arise between the same parties.

THE TAIL OF CERBERUS

According to Greek mythology, there stands near the entrance to Hades a three-headed dog named Cerberus. Cerberus has a scaly, spiked, powerful tail that allows the souls of the dead to pass into Hades with ease. Once a soul has passed the tail of Cerberus, however, the tail's spines and scales make it impossible to return. Many animal traps have similar properties, allowing the quarry to pass unimpeded into the trap, perhaps in search of bait, only to find that it is not possible to retreat. The treadles in parking garages, which allow cars to pass smoothly in but damage the tires of any car that tries to drive out, operate on the same principle.

So it is with heavy escalation. Once established, it is exceedingly difficult to eliminate. In this sense, escalation is like a rubber band. Up to a point, a rubber band may be stretched and, when released, still return to its original form and shape. Beyond that point, however, further stretching either breaks the rubber band or produces a change in its elasticity that prevents it from resuming its original dimensions. Like a rubber band stretched beyond its physical limits of tolerance, the relationship between individuals in an intensifying conflict may pass a psychological or collective threshold—a point of no return—that transforms the relationship into a new, conflict-intensified state.[2] Consider this simple example of the crossing of a threshold. Party and Other are having an argument one day, and the exchange begins to heat up rather precipitously. Party is assailing and yelling at Other, and vice versa. At some point during the angry exchange of words, Party announces that it has never really respected or valued Other. Eventually the argument subsides, as most arguments do, but the relationship is likely to have changed—and not for the better. The words Party has uttered, perhaps primarily to goad Other and not out of deep-seated conviction, may have changed Other's attitude toward Party in ways that do not easily permit recovery.

---

[1] The tail in Figure 7.1B stays elevated for most of its length but declines somewhat toward its end. The reason for showing it this way is that escalated conflicts eventually end, at some point, by one or another of the processes discussed in Chapter 9.

[2] A geometric model that makes predictions about the location of points of no return is found in Pruitt (1969).

OVERVIEW OF THEORY

Broadly speaking, the answer to why escalation persists lies in three kinds of process. One is the cycle of escalation already discussed (see Figure 6.1). This constitutes a vicious circle, which comes back around to reinforce itself (Allred, 1999). In the early stages of escalation, if the parties hit harder than they are hit, this cycle will heat things up. But at some point contentious behavior reaches an asymptote, and it can stay there—at least for a while—because of the cycle of escalation.

While it improves our understanding, the cycle of escalation is by no means a full explanation for the persistence of escalation. People usually tire of conflict after a while, gain insight into vicious circles, and find ways of escaping them if that is all there is.

Unfortunately, there are many other mechanisms—and more potent ones at that—which keep escalation going. This is the second kind of process. These mechanisms cause structural changes, once formed, to endure. They make it hard for disputants to climb down the escalation ladder once they have climbed up. They are the main mechanisms that produce what Azar (1990) calls "protracted conflicts" and Goertz and Diehl (1995) call "enduring rivalries." And they are what will mainly concern us in this chapter. We will present these mechanisms under three headings: the persistence of psychological changes, the persistence of changes in groups, and the persistence of community polarization. The chapter ends with a discussion of a third kind of process, entrapment in an escalating course of action.

THE PERSISTENCE OF PSYCHOLOGICAL CHANGES

Some psychological changes—the development of emotions like anger and fear—are of a temporary nature and hence do not explain the persistence of escalation. But attitudes, perceptions, and goals are notoriously long-lived, for reasons that will now be explained. Most of our attention in this section will be focused on attitudes and perceptions. There will be a short discussion of the persistence of goals at the end of this section.

Hostile attitudes and perceptions tend to endure once established because they support each other. Negative beliefs validate negative feelings, and negative feelings make negative beliefs seem right (Pruitt & Olczak, 1995). In addition, there are six kinds of confirmatory mechanisms involving *self-reinforcement*. When these mechanisms are at work, negative views of Other have consequences that ultimately reinforce the views that gave rise to them. These mechanisms involve the self-fulfilling prophecy, rationalization of behavior, three kinds of selective information processing, and

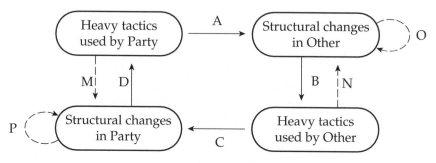

FIGURE 8.1

Augmented structural change model. The figure shows a cycle of escalation with some additional confirmatory pathways.

autistic hostility. Their impact is shown diagrammatically in Figure 8.1, which traces a cycle of escalation like that shown in Figure 6.1, with the addition of some confirmatory pathways. The elements of this figure will be explained as we go along.

The Self-fulfilling Prophecy

One mechanism of self-reinforcement involves the *self-fulfilling prophecy*, a phenomenon in which Party's beliefs and attitudes about Other make Party behave in ways that elicit behavior from Other that reinforces these beliefs. Consider the case of Ben and the family car, first mentioned in Chapter 1. Dad clearly perceives Ben as careless and inconsiderate, and presumably lets him know this from time to time. Dad's criticism, in turn, contributes to Ben behaving in ways that confirm Dad's perceptions, as when Ben spitefully fails to gas up the car.

The self-fulfilling prophecy is implicit in the cycle of escalation shown by the solid arrows in Figure 8.1. Starting at the lower left, if structural changes in Party involve the development of negative perceptions of Other, these encourage Party to behave in ways that are resented by Other (pathway D), evoking negative perceptions in Other (pathway A), which produce behavior (pathway B) that confirms Party's original views (pathway C). A similar circular process can confirm Other's negative views of Party.

Since the self-fulfilling prophecy is implicit in the cycle of escalation, it is not really different from the explanation of persistence that was given at the beginning of this chapter, concerning the vicious circle that comes back around to reinforce itself. However, it puts a different slant on this explanation and hence deserves separate attention.

The self-fulfilling prophecy is more than a hypothesis. It has been demonstrated experimentally, in both laboratory and natural settings (see

Jussim & Eccles, 1995; Olson et al., 1996). For example, in a classical study by Rosenthal and Jacobson (1968), the researchers told elementary school teachers that some students in their classes were expected to be "late bloomers" intellectually during the school year. In reality, the researchers randomly drew the names of these students from the class lists. Thus, there was little difference in intellectual abilities between these students and their classmates—except the fact that their teachers now held positive expectations for the former. At the end of the school year, these "late bloomers" indeed achieved more intellectual gains than their counterparts did. Although the teachers appeared unaware of it, they had treated the students they believed were more capable in ways that fulfilled this expectation.

Rationalization of Behavior

A second mechanism that encourages the persistence of hostile attitudes and perceptions involves rationalization. Party's negative views lead to hostile actions against Other, which Party then rationalizes by reaffirming the views that gave rise to the actions. This causal sequence, shown by the dashed lines M and N in Figure 8.1, is more common than it sounds. Consider the case of Ben again. Suppose that Ben's negative attitude toward Dad causes him to fail to get gasoline. The reasons for his behavior are likely to be at a fairly unconscious level, so that he must ask himself, "Why am I not getting gas?" He will then have to construct a rationalization. For example, he may come to believe that Dad is hostile to his interests. This will further reinforce Ben's negative attitude. A real-life example of behavior that plausibly reinforces beliefs and attitudes is the Protestant marches that take place in Northern Ireland every summer during the "marching season." These commemorate earlier triumphs over the Catholics (Sandole, 2002). Those who march presumably strengthen their negative views of Catholics or their desire to dominate the Catholic community, thereby contributing to the continued conflict in that province.

What psychological processes operate in the rationalization effect? One involves self-perception. Self-perception theory (Bem, 1972) suggests that people infer their attitudes from their actions. Thus they end up developing hostile attitudes toward those they hurt (Glass, 1964).

Another process involves dissonance reduction. Cognitive dissonance theory (Festinger, 1957) posits that inconsistencies between people's behavior and attitudes create an unpleasant arousal state known as dissonance. And this uncomfortable state motivates people to find ways to reduce it—for example, by making their attitudes consistent with their behavior.

Dissonance is especially strong when one's behavior compromises one's view of oneself (Cooper, 2001; Steele, 1988). Party is likely to see itself as a decent and reasonable person or group that would not harm innocent people. This view of the self is inconsistent with its hostile actions against Other, causing acute dissonance. Hence, Party is highly motivated to reduce the dissonance by adopting the rationalization that it is compelled to act in hostile ways because of Other's unsavory qualities. Dissonance is thus reduced by maintaining or even strengthening the hostile views of Other that gave rise to Party's original behavior.

Selective Information Processing

Once Party has formed a negative impression of Other—once the image of Other as an undesirable, unsavory, untrustworthy, unpleasant character has been shaped—selective information processing leads Party to pay attention to, search for, interpret, retain, and recall information in ways that confirm the initial negative impression (Hopmann, 1996). Instead of gathering and evaluating data in scientific fashion, Party tends to locate information that supports these preconceptions. As a result, these preconceptions are reinforced or become even stronger. An adversary who was first seen as rigid may now be regarded as stubborn, and eventually as hopelessly intransigent.

Note that the structural changes supported by selective information processing are self-reinforcing in a way that is quite independent of anything Other may say or do. Selective information processing feeds on itself entirely, as represented by the circular loops O and P in Figure 8.1.

Although the term *selective information processing* has a negative ring (implying that Party develops a biased view of reality), the process is actually a hallmark of effective psychological functioning. The world is an immensely complex place, flooding everyone with far more social and nonsocial information than we can possibly hope to process. In response to this tendency toward "information overload," it is necessary to find ways to process information selectively, thereby reducing this input to manageable proportions.

Offsetting this virtue is the liability that stems from fitting impressions into a Procrustean bed—stripping away Other's rich individuality in the service of developing a manageable stereotype. Moreover, in the midst of escalating conflict, selective information processing is particularly dangerous. It can confirm and further strengthen Party's unfavorable views of Other. These negative views, with the aid of selective information processing, color Other's actions in the worst possible light. If Other moves its troops, Party assume that it is about to be attacked. If Other makes conciliatory overtures, Party fails to notice them or regards them as devious ploys (Hopmann, 1996). Selective information processing in escalating conflict sustains the existing level of escalation or may cause it to edge upward.

A paper by Cooper and Fazio (1979) helps understand the way in which selective information processing operates to maintain escalation.

These authors discuss three interrelated forms that selective information processing can take: self-serving evaluation of behavior, the "discovery" of evidence that supports Party's expectations, and attributional distortion. Let us consider each in turn.

Self-serving Evaluation of Behavior   When there are strong views, an identical event can be judged quite differently depending on whether the source of the event is seen as a "good guy" or a "bad guy" (White, 1984). In an interesting study of student reactions to a Princeton-Dartmouth football game won by Princeton, Hastorf and Cantril (1954) found that the events of the game were judged very differently as a function of the viewer's allegiance. Princeton and Dartmouth students saw a film of the game and were asked to note all infractions. The Princeton students thought that the Dartmouth Indians had committed twice as many infractions as the Princeton Tigers, whereas the Dartmouth students saw no difference in the number of violations. In conflict it appears, reality is too often in the eye of the beholder.

Similarly powerful results have been obtained in other social psychology experiments. For example, during the Cold War, Oskamp (1965) presented American college students with two parallel lists of conciliatory and belligerent acts that had been undertaken by both the United States and the Soviet Union. The same acts (for example, "The government has provided military training and assistance to smaller nations") that were rated favorably when performed by the United States (the good guys) were rated extremely unfavorably when attributed to the Soviet Union (the bad guys). The tendency to evaluate behavior in self-serving ways is particularly pronounced when people evaluate their own conflict behavior. People consider their own conflict behaviors as more constructive and benign than those of the other side (De Dreu et al., 1995). This self-serving evaluation contributes to escalation by creating frustration and impairing problem-solving ability.

Evidence of selective evaluation is not confined to the experimental laboratory. Most Palestinians view suicide bombings as selfless acts of heroism, while most Israelis view them as outrageous and immoral.

The "Discovery" of Confirming Evidence   It is one thing for Party to attend selectively to those aspects of Other's manner or behavior that conform to Party's own preconceptions. It is quite another matter to "stack the deck" by gathering information in a way that encourages Other to behave in accordance with these preconceptions.

Mark Snyder and his colleagues have conducted several experiments that, although not directly related to the dynamics of escalation, nevertheless shed light on the "discovery" of confirmatory evidence. In one of these studies, Snyder and Swann (1978) provided participants with hypotheses about other people and then allowed them to seek information about these people. Some participants were given the personality profile of an introvert while others were given a description of what an extrovert is like. All participants were then asked to choose twelve questions to be posed to the targets in an effort to test whether they had that personality profile.

Snyder and Swann found that people who were testing an "introvert" hypothesis (even though this hypothesis did not specifically apply to the target, about whom nothing was yet known) chose to pose interview questions that seemed to assume that the target was *already known* to be an introvert: "In what situations do you wish you could be more outgoing?" "What things do you dislike about loud parties?" Those who were testing an "extrovert" hypothesis instead listed questions that presumed the target to be an extrovert: "What would you do if you wanted to liven up a party?" "In what situations are you most talkative?" When, in a subsequent session, the participants were actually permitted to pose the respective questions they had formulated, the response of their targets was such that the interviewers concluded that the targets matched the profile they had been given at the outset. It is clear from this that people selectively arrange for evidence to be available that confirms their hypotheses.

If this phenomenon is powerful in the world of everyday interaction, as Snyder and his colleagues have shown, we can expect it to be all the more powerful in heavy conflict where emotions run high, distrust and suspicion mount, and the desire to harm the other grows strong. In such situations, people tend to process information superficially or heuristically (Thompson & Nadler, 2000). As a result, they are unlikely, or unmotivated, to notice disconfirming evidence, which requires careful, systematic processing. Rather, they increase their reliance on evidence consistent with their hypotheses.

What happens if people are forced to attend to disconfirming evidence? Usually, they are quite capable of explaining it away. A young American school teacher (Wood, 1934) describes this process:

> In my first contact with Greek students, a few happy cases of cheating in examinations occurred, and without my realizing what was happening, my attitude toward the Greeks as a people became biased by this. . . . A conflict existed, however, between the new attitude that I was forming toward the Greeks and my deep admiration for the ancient Greek culture. It was difficult to reconcile the two, but I found a way out. I looked up all the evidence that I could find to substantiate the claim that the modern Greeks are not the lineal descendants of the Greeks of the Classical Period and hence have no rightful pride in that glorious tradition. (p. 268)

Fortunately for humanity, there are ways of escaping the tendency to gather evidence that confirms one's views. This tendency diminishes when people are strongly motivated to develop accurate impressions (Neuberg, 1989) and when they are forewarned about the pitfalls of this phenomenon (Swann, 1987).

Attributional Distortion   One of the basic tasks in social interaction is to make *attributions*—causal inferences—about why other people behave as they do. These attributions have a profound impact on subsequent emotional reactions to, and behavior toward, these people (Allred, 2000).

Errors often arise in attribution formation. One of these is *attributional* distortion, a phenomenon that has been demonstrated in a number of experimental studies (Hayden & Mischel, 1976; Regan et al., 1974) and in studies of troubled married couples (Bradbury & Fincham, 1990; Holtzworth-Munroe & Jacobson, 1985). Information about Other that supports Party's private hypotheses about Other tends to be attributed to *dispositional* causes, whereas information that is discrepant with Party's hypotheses tends to be attributed to *situational* causes. That is, information in keeping with Party's expectations is seen as reflecting Other's enduring and stable characteristics, whereas information that violates Party's expectations is attributed to temporary environmental pressures on Other.

The net effect of attributional distortion in escalating conflict is that there is virtually nothing that Other can do to dispel Party's negative expectations. If Other behaves in a nasty way, this is taken as a true indicator of Other's hostile intentions, or belligerent disposition. If Other turns the other cheek and displays friendly behavior, this is explained as a temporary fluke. An example is the thinking of John Foster Dulles, who was the American Secretary of State at the beginning of the Cold War and regarded the Soviet Union as an implacable enemy. When the Soviets behaved contentiously, Dulles saw this as evidence of their depravity; whereas when they adopted a conciliatory strategy, he concluded that they were weakening (Holsti, 1967). Either way, his attributions supported American escalation of the conflict.

Given these three forms of selective information processing—self-serving evaluation of behavior, the "discovery" of confirming evidence, and attributional distortion—it is small wonder that conflicts can more easily escalate than move back down the ladder. Once that genie emerges from the bottle, these three processes combine to make it exceedingly difficult to lure it back. As represented by the loops (O and P) of Figure 8.1, these are self-reinforcing processes. They feed on themselves in ways that lead escalation to persist.[3]

---

[3] The same cognitive processes that operate in the service of conflict escalation sometimes also serve more positive ends. Two people who are wildly in love, for example, may be expected to see one another "through rose-colored glasses"—to continually find support for the hypothesis that the other is the most wonderful person in the world; to bias the explanations for their beloved's behavior in ways that discount negative information ("He was very grumpy this morning—must be the damp weather"); and to overstate the stability of positive information ("She just cracked another joke. What a wit she is!"). In other words, these processes are capable of reinforcing positive as well as negative impressions. Murray & Holmes (1997) have found support for this hypothesis in studies of romantic relationships.

Autistic Hostility

As we mentioned in Chapter 6, there is a tendency to stop interacting and communicating with people we do not like or respect. An extreme example is the perhaps apocryphal case of two brothers who ran a store. One accused the other of stealing $1 from the cash register; the other denied it, where-upon the first brother stopped talking to the other. Thirty silent years later a stranger walked in, confessed to the theft (which had been preying on his conscience), and made restitution. Communication between the brothers was restored.

The problem with an interruption of communication is that it makes it impossible to resolve the issue that fostered the initial breach. The par-ties are consigned to maintain their prior views of each other, including the ones that brought communication to a screeching halt. In effect, these views have initiated a process that perpetuates itself. This is called the phenomenon of autistic hostility (Newcomb, 1947). It is another self-reinforcing process, again represented by the two semicircular loops, O and P, in Figure 8.1.

A communication vacuum often provides a greenhouse in which ru-mors flourish. Facts are embellished or distorted, and personal attacks can be the rule, moving conflict along an escalatory path. Consider the confrontation between African Americans and Hasidic Jews in the Crown Heights section of New York City during the summer months of 1991. It was ignited by an incident in which a Hasidic Jewish driver hit two African American children, killing one and critically injuring the other. Following the accident, unsubstantiated rumors circulated widely in the community. One was that a Hatzolah ("rescue" in Hebrew) ambulance arrived before a city ambulance and drove the Hasidic driver away, aban-doning the two critically wounded children at the scene. This rumor, found to be untrue according to police records and eyewitness testimony, triggered the violent murder of a Jewish man by a group of young African Americans.

The development of rumors in the absence of communication be-tween groups is also illustrated by a study mentioned in Chapter 7. Varshney (2002) found that rumors triggered violence between Hindus and Muslims in Indian cities that did not have organizations (trade unions, political parties) linking these two communities.

The Persistence of Hostile Goals

Mitchell (2000) has hypothesized that people who suffer for their goals tend to perpetuate them. This phenomenon can be derived from cogni-tive dissonance theory and has been demonstrated in several psychologi-cal experiments (Smith & Mackie, 2000). It can be used to explain the persistence of many kinds of goals including the hostile ones that often underlie escalation.

One kind of hostile goal, the *desire for vengeance*, is notoriously persistent. Indeed, it often becomes "one's life instead of being a part of one's life" (Murphy & Hampton, 1988, p. 105). What can account for that? One explanation rests on the assumption that unfulfilled vengeance often leads to *hatred*, which is a combination of anger and a belief that Other possesses evil traits—is inherently bad (Elster, 1999). Anger is ordinarily a transient emotion, but in combination with such a belief, it tends to persist as hatred.[4]

Another explanation for the persistence of vengeful desires is that people often engage in *dysphoric rumination* or brooding (Berkowitz, 1993). They rehearse, over and over in their mind, the details of an insult or deprivation suffered by themselves or their group. Rumination usually strengthens people's sense that they have been treated unjustly and that punishment should therefore result (Bushman, 2002). Rumination is usually involuntary, an uncontrolled intrusive stream of thoughts; but some people actively court it as a way of maintaining and bolstering their resolve for taking revenge when the opportunity arises (McCullough et al., 2001).

THE PERSISTENCE OF CHANGES IN GROUPS

Most of the processes that cause changes to persist at the individual level have the same impact at the group level. An example is the self-fulfilling prophecy, which is modeled by the cycle of escalation represented by the progression of solid arrows in Figure 8.1. Negative views of another group are likely to produce group behavior that encourages actions by the other group that make these views seem justified. For example, the newsman Dilip Hero (2002) has hypothesized that U.S. President George W. Bush's labeling of Iran as part of an "axis of evil" pushed that country into improving its relations with Iraq, another country also so labeled.

Dysphoric rumination, which was mentioned just above, can also occur at the group level. Through various means including songs, stories, novels and poems, and movies, group members engage in collective rumination on the wrongs and injustices suffered by their group at the hands of outgroup members. For example, Serbian schoolchildren were required to memorize a poem, "The Pit," that described atrocities committed by

---

[4] See Ben-Ze'ev (2000) and Elster (1999) for more detailed discussions of hatred, particularly in its comparison to anger. See Naimark (2001) and Kaufman (2001) for the role of hatred in ethnic cleansing and Horowitz (2001) for the role of hatred in ethnic riots.

Croatian Ustasha (Neuffer, 2001): "I'm lying on the corpse: pile of cold meat/. . ./Flashes in my consciousness, when a woman screams./ I turned around in a fever, towards the scream/ I reached out: felt a slippery wound" (p. 19). Of course, collective rumination is heavily focused on one's own group's suffering, not on the other group's suffering inflicted by one's own group. As a result, it contributes to the persistence of escalation.[5]

In Chapter 6 we described six kinds of group changes that result from and contribute to the escalation of conflict: group polarization, runaway norms, contentious group goals, cohesiveness, militant leadership, and militant subgroups. There are confirmatory mechanisms that encourage several of these changes to persist. As was true of the psychological changes, these mechanisms involve self-reinforcement or self-perpetuation. In other words, group changes often encourage new developments that confirm or strengthen these changes.

Norms of all types tend to be self-perpetuating, including those that encourage competitive goals and aggressive behavior toward the outgroup. They often outlive the reasonable purpose for which they were first developed. This usually occurs because of *social pressure*, real and imagined. People who challenge a norm tend to be punished by the group. Others who doubt the validity of a norm remain silent for fear of being labeled deviates or, in the case of intergroup conflict, traitors. Still other group members then follow the norm because they do not realize that it is controversial. Processes like this may have perpetuated the culture of honor in America's South well beyond the time at which it was a rational response to the prospect of losing one's herd (see Chapter 7).

Contentious group goals also tend to be lasting. This is partly because they are supported by group norms and partly because the leaders who have articulated them typically hate to admit their mistakes (Mitchell, 1999, 2000).

Militant subgroups tend to become self-perpetuating because of *vested interests*. Group membership and participation in organized activities give some people status, others occupation and wealth, and still others a sense that life is meaningful. Such benefits are hard to surrender; hence, group members work hard to ensure that their group survives. If the raison d'être for a group is the conduct of contentious conflict, there are vested interests in the persistence of such conflict. This is another mechanism by which escalation tends to be self-perpetuating. The UB Strike Committee described in Chapter 6 is a case in point. This committee gave status and meaning to the lives of hundreds of students who would otherwise have been consigned to the routine of going to class and

---

[5] Coleman (2000) points out that collective rumination can be a method of *intergenerational* perpetuation of conflict.

preparing for tests. These students had a vested interest in the perpetuation of the Strike Committee and thus a vested interest in the continuation of the crisis. Once formed, the Strike Committee could not easily be disbanded, and it continued to challenge the university administration.

Similar events have occurred many times in history (Schumpeter, 1955, first published in 1919), and the danger is not necessarily far from home. In his farewell address to the United States, President Eisenhower warned about the development of a built-in lobby for international conflict centered in what he called the "military-industrial complex."

Vested interests extend as well to *leaders,* who are almost always motivated to maintain their leadership positions. If they have gained these positions because of their militancy or skill at waging conflict, they have a vested interest in the perpetuation of conflict. Hence, they have incentives for resisting conflict resolution and for starting new conflicts. This is another mechanism by which escalation tends to be self-perpetuating.

Vested interests may have been at work in the Japanese attack on Pearl Harbor in 1941. According to Russett (1967), the Japanese leaders knew this attack was very risky. Indeed, in advocating the attack, one of them commented, "Sometimes it is necessary to close one's eyes and jump from the temple wall." But the alternative to the attack was apparently worse in their eyes. These leaders were military men who had gained high government positions in the late 1930s as a result of the great importance to the Japanese of the war they were waging in China and Indochina. In 1941 the United States began to block the shipment of oil from what is now Indonesia, which made it difficult to continue the war effort. Had the war effort stopped, these generals and admirals would almost surely have been demoted. Hence, they were willing to risk the future of their country in order to perpetuate the war effort and maintain their positions.

THE PERSISTENCE OF COMMUNITY POLARIZATION

We have already seen that escalating conflicts tend to polarize the communities around them. Formerly neutral parties gravitate or are pulled toward one side or the other. Fewer and fewer community members are left sitting on the fence or standing on the sidelines. Severely polarized communities become fractured into two large camps, with positive relations among the people in each camp and negative relations between the camps.

There are several mechanisms that cause community polarization, once established, to be perpetuated. Polarization means the destruction of crosscutting organizations (trade unions, professional associations, etc.) that are so important in putting a damper on escalation. It also means the disappearance of neutral third parties who would otherwise urge moderation and mediate the controversy. In addition, people lose loyalty to the community as a whole, and hence, feel less responsible to be tolerant toward other community members (Coleman, 1957). As a result of these developments, the controversy tends to persist, maintaining the pressure on third parties to take sides.

In addition, community members who have joined one camp often have difficulty reestablishing their credentials with the other camp. They have become outsiders, forever distrusted because they have fraternized with the enemy. This means that polarization tends to persist even when the conflicts that gave rise to it have been resolved. Like Humpty Dumpty after his fall, it is hard to put polarized communities back together again.

OVERCOMMITMENT AND ENTRAPMENT

There is one other explanation for the persistence of escalation. This is that *commitments to contentious behavior* tend to be self-reinforcing. One reason for this is the pervasive tendency for Party to rationalize its own behavior, which was mentioned earlier. Another reason is a process of overcommitment that has been studied in research on *entrapment*, a dysfunctional but pervasive human phenomenon.

An Aside on the Dollar Auction

In order to understand better the dynamics of overcommitment to an escalating course of action, consider a simple parlor game, first proposed by Shubik (1971) and extensively researched by Teger (1980). This game, known as the dollar auction, is played as follows: Several people are invited to participate in the auction of a dollar bill by calling out bids until a high bid has been reached. The high bidder is then awarded the dollar bill, in exchange for paying the amount that he or she bid. Thus, if the winning (high) bid were 15 cents, the winner would be awarded 85 cents (1 dollar minus 15 cents). The catch in this game is that the *second-highest bidder is* also required to pay the auctioneer the amount of his or her bid but does not receive a dollar bill in return. So, if the bidding for the dollar stopped with a high bid of 35 cents and a next-highest bid of 25 cents, the winner would receive a total of 65 cents and the next-highest bidder would have to pay the auctioneer 25 cents.

People typically start this game by calling out a small amount of money. And why not? If the dollar bill can be won with a bid of 10, 20, or 30 cents, why not give it a try? Perhaps no one else will elect to play the game. Unfortunately, other people typically reason in much the same way, and the result is that several people begin to bid. Eventually the bidding approaches $1 (the objective value of the prize), and at this point two important things happen: the number of players typically decreases until only the two highest bidders remain in contention, and the motivation of each remaining bidder shifts from an initial concern about maximizing gain (doing as well for oneself as possible) to a concern with minimizing losses instead. As the bidding passes $1, the issue is no longer how much Party can win but how much it can keep from losing. Often the bidding goes much higher than $1.

Why does Party not quit at this point? Largely, it appears, because it is aware of how much time and money it has already spent and is reluctant to give up on this "investment." Moreover, Party continues to hold out hope that Other will stop bidding, lick its wounds, and depart from the scene—leaving victory to Party. "If I persist just a bit longer," Party reasons, "I can still snatch victory from the jaws of defeat." The problem is that if both Party and Other reason this way, neither is apt to quit and the conflict will continue to escalate.

As the conflict grows with each bidding increment, yet another transformation—one described in Chapter 5—takes place. Party's concern with maximizing winnings, which was first replaced by a concern with minimizing losses, is now supplanted by a determination to make certain that Other loses at least as much as Party. "I may go down in flames," Party reasons, "but in doing so I will take Other down with me." It is in this last stage of the dollar auction that concerns about looking foolish come to the fore. In other words, Party becomes increasingly preoccupied with threats to its image.

This illustration of Shubik's dollar auction game suggests that people in escalating conflicts may *overcommit* themselves in ways that appear quite irrational to most external observers. Shubik has reported, for example, that a dollar bill is often auctioned off for as much as $5 or $6.[6] Surely this is an illustration of commitment in the service of irrationality. How can this be explained? Why does Party sometimes commit itself and its resources above and beyond all reason? To develop a partial answer to this query, we must explore the topic of entrapment.

Characteristics of Entrapment

Entrapment is a process in which Party, pursuing a goal over a period of time, expends more of its time, energy, money, or other resources than seems justifiable by external standards. People can become entrapped in their interactions with the environment, for example, sinking ever more money into a failing old car. However, the situations of greatest interest in this book are *social* in nature, entailing a competitive relationship between

---

[6] In a variation on this game, in which a $100 bill was auctioned off before a large group of business people, one of our colleagues managed to sell the prize for $3,000!

two or more individuals or groups. The dollar auction game is a quintessential illustration of an entrapping interpersonal conflict. At an intergroup level, consider the example of two sides persisting in a strike, partly because each has suffered so much already that to give up would be to have suffered in vain. The longer each side has clung to an intransigent position, the more compelled it will probably feel to justify this position through continued intransigence.

Finally, at the level of international decision making, one can analyze the role and extended involvement of the United States in the Vietnam War as an illustration of entrapment. In his book *The Best and the Brightest,* Halberstam (1969) explains U.S. involvement in very much these terms. The "doves" argued time and again that the United States had embarked on a fool's journey (and an unethical one) and that we should withdraw our forces from Southeast Asia immediately before another American (or Vietnamese) life was lost. But this is exactly why we should remain in Vietnam, retorted the "hawks," exactly why we *should* persist. To withdraw now, they argued, would be to have sacrificed countless lives in vain, on an escapade that would be regarded as meaningless. And anyway, victory in Vietnam and the security of an anticommunist regime in Southeast Asia seemed just a battle or two away. A similar analysis is possible of the aftermath of Israel's 1982 invasion of Lebanon and the Soviet intervention in Afghanistan.

Combating Entrapment

In one form or another, both in the psychologist's laboratory and in the field, entrapment has been the object of investigation by a number of researchers (see Brockner & Rubin, 1985). These studies suggest a few strategies that can combat entrapment:

- *Setting limits.* When Party specifies a limit to its involvement before beginning a quest for a goal, Party is less likely to become entrapped. Moreover, when Party publicly commits itself to such a limit, by announcing it to others, it is least likely to become entrapped.
- *Chunking.* A particular problem arises when the resource expended in an entrapping situation is time—for example, when Party is placed "on hold" by an automatic switchboard or somebody in the wrong office for its inquiry. The problem is that there are no natural points of decision about whether to continue that line of investment. Party is passively involved in the expenditure and is at the mercy of decisions made elsewhere. Party is particularly vulnerable to entrapment in such situations.

    Entrapment can be avoided in such situations by encouraging Party to engage in periodic reappraisal of its commitment, a process called *chunking*. Findings by Brockner et al. (1979) suggest that even the minimal provision of opportunities for chunking can help. Participants in an entrapping task were stopped every three minutes by the experimenter, who inquired whether they wished to continue or quit. Merely considering this question led them to quit the task after waiting less than half as long as those who were not interrupted.

- *Making costs salient.* The stopping points introduced by Brockner et al. (1979) not only allowed Party to chunk its involvement but also reminded Party of the costs associated with continued participation. In the presence of such reminders, entrapment is likely to decrease. This point was demonstrated in a study by Brockner et al. (1981) in which participants were given a "payoff chart" that depicted their investment costs at each of a number of possible stopping points. Those who did not have access to this chart—for whom costs were not salient—became significantly more entrapped than their counterparts. Other findings indicate that this effect is particularly striking when cost-salience information is introduced *early* in an entrapping task, before the pressures toward overcommitment come into play (Brockner et al., 1982).

- *Avoiding concern about Party's image.* In the last stages of the dollar auction, Party seems to persist largely in order to make sure that Other is forced to lose at least as much as Party does. It is in this last phase that Party becomes excessively concerned with the image of toughness that it projects to Other and to any observing audience. As conflict continues to intensify between individuals or groups, Party experiences a sense of threat that any conciliatory or friendly gesture will be taken to imply weakness and invite future exploitation.[7] This fear of humiliation further pressures Party to persist in the entrapping situation. It follows that keeping in mind the dangers associated with this concern may help to avoid entrapment.

SUMMARY AND CONCLUSIONS

In this chapter, we have explained why heavy escalation so often persists or recurs when new issues arise. There are three parts to this explanation. The first is that the cycle of escalation, like any vicious circle, tends to be self-perpetuating.

The second part of the explanation is that there are many mechanisms that cause structural changes to persist, once they are formed. Some are

---

[7] Such image threats were discussed in Chapter 6. They are found in virtually all forms of escalating conflict.

psychological processes that reinforce hostile attitudes and perceptions. These include the self-fulfilling prophecy, rationalization of hostile behavior, autistic hostility, and three forms of selective information processing: self-serving evaluation of own and Other's behavior, selective gathering of information, and attributional distortion. Other mechanisms cause hostile goals to persist. The desire for revenge, for example, is kept alive by hatred and dysphoric rumination about past insults or deprivations.

All the mechanisms just mentioned encourage the persistence of escalation in intergroup as well as interpersonal conflict. In addition, hostile group norms tend to be perpetuated by social pressure. And militant subgroups and their leaders sometimes engineer the continuation of the conflict that has brought them to power, so that they can continue to dominate the wider group. They have "vested interests" in the continuation of that conflict.

Escalated conflicts also persist because communities once polarized are hard to reunite. Once crosscutting organizations are destroyed and potential mediators have taken sides, the political processes that guard against civil strife are gone, and the result is continued polarization.

The third part of the explanation concerns entrapment processes whereby individuals and groups become committed to self-destructive tactics. Commitments that were made with an initial modicum of restraint too often become traps that produce a needless waste of precious resources and even lives. Strategies to avoid entrapment include setting limits to continued involvement in a conflict, chunking time, making costs periodically salient, and avoiding concern about one's image of toughness.

In escalating conflict, it is clearly easier to squeeze the toothpaste out of the tube than to put it back in. Once started, heavy escalation tends to be self-reinforcing. Yet we know that conflicts do not continue to escalate forever. At some point (if the parties are still alive), the turmoil subsides and conflict begins to abate. Chapter 9 examines the transitional circumstances that make it possible for escalation to stop and for settlement of conflict to begin.

PART III

STALEMATE AND SETTLEMENT

9

Perceived Stalemate and De-Escalation

❖

Why Conflicts Stop Escalating ✦ Perceived Stalemate ✦ *Recognizing the Stalemate* ✦ *The Cuban Missile Crisis* ✦ How De-Escalation Begins ✦ *Optimism* ✦ *Stalemate and Negotiation in the Middle East* ✦ Getting Unstuck ✦ *Contact and Communication* ✦ *Cooperation on Other Issues: Superordinate Goals* ✦ *Unilateral Conciliatory Initiatives* ✦ *De-escalatory Spirals: The Constructive Use of Entrapment* ✦ Summary and Conclusions

*I*n the last four chapters we have told the story of how and why heavy contentious tactics are chosen and conflicts escalate. We have also discussed why escalation, once in place, tends to persist. At some point, however, despite the mechanisms that hold it in place, *escalated conflict always ends.* For if it is sadly the case that most good things eventually come to an end, it is happily true that most bad things come to an end as well. People in a heavily escalated exchange can do only so much damage to each other, and for only so long. Why and how escalated conflict ends and de-escalation begins is the subject of this chapter. In addition, an important transition often occurs, bridging the end of escalation with the earliest moves toward conflict settlement. The nature of this transition is also of interest here.

WHY CONFLICTS STOP ESCALATING

Imagine two children arguing about whose turn it is to use a shiny new bicycle. The argument continues back and forth as the conflict between the children keeps escalating. Finally they start pushing each other. Yet, at some point this process stops and is replaced by de-escalation, typically for one of five possible reasons.

First, one party succeeds in *overwhelming* the other and the other yields, as when one child wins the argument and takes the bicycle. As another example, recall the prison fight described in Chapter 6. While the prisoner who lost the fight was undoubtedly most unhappy about the outcome, the two men who beat him up clearly felt otherwise. The conflict stopped escalating because the latter had prevailed.[1]

Second, one party is able to take *unilateral advantage* of the other. Suppose that one of the two children (Party) simply ends the conflict by climbing onto the bike's leather seat and riding off into sunset. The conflict stops escalating—not because Other is overwhelmed but because Party has taken advantage of the situation.

Third, the two parties *avoid* further conflict, leaving the bicycle and turning to other activities.

Fourth, a powerful third party (or parties) enters the scene and *imposes a settlement*. For example, the mother of one of the children might play this role, acting as an arbitrator.

Finally—and we will explore this option in much more detail—the two parties stop fighting and *negotiate a settlement,* perhaps with the help of a third party acting as a mediator.[2] Thus, the children might discuss the conflict and agree to take turns using the bicycle, deciding who will ride it first by the toss of a coin.

PERCEIVED STALEMATE

Negotiation and mediation ordinarily grow out of *perceived stalemate,* a situation in which one (or better, both) of the parties perceives that it cannot make further progress in the conflict at an acceptable cost or risk—that further efforts to win through escalation are unworkable and/or unwise.[3]

---

[1] This is a very common outcome in severe conflicts. For example, Heraclides (1997) has found that 75% of recent civil wars ended with victory for one of the parties.

[2] Arbitration and mediation will be discussed in Chapter 11.

[3] The discussion in this and the next section on "How De-escalation Begins" is based on *ripeness theory,* a theory of the conditions under which severe conflicts move into negotiation and mediation. Zartman (1989, 2000), the originator of this theory, argues that conflicts are ripe when two conditions prevail: (1) the parties are experiencing a mutually hurting stalemate, particularly if augmented by a recent or impending catastrophe, and (2) both

The sense of stalemate is exacerbated if Party perceives that its advantage over Other is weakening or that Other's advantage is strengthening.

At a point of perceived stalemate, Party will usually not escalate the conflict further, although it may not yet be willing to take the actions that will eventually generate an agreement. The point of maximum conflict intensity has probably been reached. Stalemate is a high-water mark for the conflictual ark. The waters will probably rise no more, nor have they yet begun to subside in de-escalation.

Even in perceived stalemate Party will probably continue to employ contentious tactics in an effort to prevail. Party's behavior, for a while at least, may appear unchanged. But what begins to change is Party's *outlook*. Though Party might like to "knock Other's block clean off," such an outcome is now seen as unattainable or too dangerous. Perhaps Other is refusing to yield. Perhaps Party's resources are flagging. Perhaps Party's costs or risks are becoming unacceptable. Whatever the reason, Party reaches the grudging realization that it hurts more to continue the conflict than to settle it. Out of such a realization emerge the elements of conflict reduction or resolution, especially if Other comes to the same realization.

There are four major reasons why Party might conclude that it is in a stalemate: failure of contentious tactics, exhaustion of necessary resources, loss of social support, and unacceptable costs or risks.

Contentious tactics that were used with some success in the past may begin to fail because they have lost their bite. Perhaps Party has tried once too often to mount persuasive arguments, employ threats, commit itself to a rigid position; and Other no longer finds such moves believable or worth heeding. Another possibility is that, like two people who have lived together for many years, the adversaries have come to know each other's moves and gestures so well that it is no longer possible to seize the advantage. Each move has its properly orchestrated, well-learned countermove; thrust and parry fit neatly together.

Exhaustion of the resources necessary to continue the struggle is also related to the failure of contentious tactics to work as intended. Like a boxer, bloodied and weakened after many rounds of being pounded against the ropes, one or both disputants in an escalating conflict simply

---

parties see a way out of the conflict. Our version of this theory takes the viewpoint of one of the parties ("Party" in our terminology) rather than looking at the two parties together. Our concepts are similar to Zartman's, but we talk of "perceived stalemate" and "optimism," characteristics of individual parties rather than of the two parties as a whole. We reject the notion that there always must be a "mutually hurting stalemate," in part because we know of cases in which negotiation started because of perceived stalemate on one side and optimism on the other (see footnote 9). Another difference is that our term "stalemate" is broader than Zartman's. For us, a stalemate may be due to Party's perception that its campaign against Other is not succeeding and/or that this campaign is producing intolerable costs or risks. For Zartman, a stalemate is only the perception that campaigns are not succeeding.

runs out of steam. There is no lack of determination to defeat Other, nor is there lack of insight into the necessary moves. Party would still like nothing more than to knock Other out and snatch a last-minute victory. But it just isn't possible. The verbal and tactical blows that once landed with such force and effect now have little impact on the adversary. Would that those arms could be raised once more to deliver a coup de grace, but by now they are heavy with fatigue.

There are several sorts of resources that may be exhausted as Party enters a perceived stalemate. One, suggested by the prizefighter analogy, is *energy*—the physical and/or psychological stamina necessary to sustain continued struggle. Another important resource in many competitive struggles is *money*—the ability to sustain the continued financial costs incurred by investing in those tangibles used to wage competition. For example, in the dollar auction game (see Chapter 8), when bidders have no more funds to continue their struggle, the auction is over. When both combatants' supply lines are cut, the battle must come to an end. Finally, time in and of itself is often a limited resource which, once exhausted, forces the adversaries into stalemate.

Related to the exhaustion of resources is the possibility that Party is forced into stalemate because of diminishing social support. People in conflict often rely on the support of constituencies or backers in order to sustain a competitive struggle. Labor and management negotiators can persist in their bargaining only so long as they continue to have the endorsement—passive though it may be—of the organizations they represent. Revolutionaries commonly rely on support—supplies, recruits, safe havens, and the like—from allies outside the country they are trying to take over.

Allies typically have a broader set of concerns than do the disputants, leading them, at times, to press the disputants to end the conflict.[4] Even prizefighters are best thought of not as individuals but as representatives of financial and social interests; and whether to continue fighting is typically not the fighter's decision alone. Thus, escalating conflicts often end in stalemate because Party is no longer able to secure the support of necessary constituents or allies.

Finally, there are important occasions when stalemate becomes apparent because Party concludes that the costs or risks associated with continued struggle will be so great that further escalation must be avoided.

---

[4] Huntington (1996) has argued that in the most severely escalated conflicts, such as those found at "fault lines" between world civilizations, the parties may be so incapable of dealing with each other that allies on either side must work together to "contain or halt" the struggle. The 1979 mediated settlement of the civil war in what is now Zimbabwe was partly due to pressure from leaders of the countries that were housing the African insurgent armies (Stedman, 1991).

Perhaps constituents are complaining that wealth is being exhausted or protesting that lives are being lost. Possibly, new issues and people are about to become involved that will poison (or further poison) the broader relationship with Other. Opportunity costs may be at issue, as when the conflict requires money that is desperately needed for other projects. Or there may be fear of a future catastrophe (Zartman, 2000). As the hands of the clock march toward midnight, Party may feel uncomfortably close to a point of no return—a point where the relationship with Other will be totally lost, where some third party will take advantage of Party's exhaustion, or where weapons of such destructive capacity will be used that Party will be seriously injured or destroyed.

Recognizing the Stalemate

Though they are actually in a stalemate, parties often don't recognize that this is the case. The structural changes may be so profound—their hatred of the enemy or militant ideology may be so strong—that they enthusiastically continue what is actually a losing fight. Or they may be cognitively entrapped in the conflict—too close to the details to see the unpromising broader picture or committed to continue by prior statements or the need to justify prior costs.

In such circumstances, some sort of *shock*[5] may be needed to bring them to their senses—a striking event that dramatizes the hopelessness of their campaign or the costs and risks involved in pursuing it—a catastrophe or near catastrophe that mobilizes careful examination of what is actually happening. In international relations, shocks might include enemy penetration of key defense lines, sudden severe loss of life, or an abrupt decline in power or leader legitimacy (Druckman & Green, 1995; Mitchell, 2000).

Such a shock apparently led to the negotiations that ended the war over Nagorno-Karabakh between Armenia and Azerbaijan in 1994. Mooradian and Druckman (1999) have found that a sudden upward spike in battlefield casualties produced these negotiations.

Recognition of stalemate can also come with a *change of leadership* in a group or nation (Haass, 1990; Lieberfeld, 1999; Mitchell, 2000). Thus, changes in government have often led to new thinking about an existing conflict and search for a peaceful solution. The Cold War started to wind down when Gorbachev came to power in the Soviet Union. Negotiations leading to broadly representative elections began when De Klerk took

---

[5] The term "shock" comes from Goertz & Diehl (1995), who trace the end of most enduring international rivalries to large political shifts, such as wars and changes in international power distributions.

over as president of South Africa. And Israel started serious talks with the Palestinians when Rabin took the office of president and again when Barak took that office. There are several reasons why new leaders tend to engage in new thinking. They are often younger and more flexible than the outgoing regime, they are not so committed to past decisions and hence can engage in a broad policy review, and they are usually accorded leeway for change in their initial, "honeymoon" period in office.

The Cuban Missile Crisis

The most frightening episode in the Cold War, the Cuban missile crisis of 1962, produced a perception of stalemate on both sides. Several months prior to the crisis, the Soviet Union had begun to send shipments of medium-range missiles and nuclear warheads to the island of Cuba, with the clear and unmistakable intention of targeting these weapons, once assembled at the major urban centers of the eastern United States. The crisis itself began when incontrovertible photographic evidence of this activity was brought to the attention of President John F. Kennedy. The President responded by threatening to impose a naval blockade of all Soviet shipments to Cuba unless the Russians immediately stopped all further shipments and destroyed those weapons and sites already on the island. The response was Soviet silence. The stage was set for one of the most dramatic superpower confrontations in the history of either nation.

President Kennedy announced that the naval blockade would be put into effect on Wednesday, October 24. American cruisers and aircraft carriers were dispatched to the waters off Cuba. As 10 a.m. approached, two Soviet ships were detected, proceeding toward the 500-mile quarantine barrier. The two ships, the *Gagarin* and the *Komiles,* neared the boundary; a Soviet submarine had moved into position between them. The American carrier *Essex* was ordered to signal the submarine to surface and identify itself; if it refused, depth charges were to be used.

The President's brother, Robert F. Kennedy, who was at his side during these events, described them in some detail in his moving history, *Thirteen Days* (Kennedy, 1969):

> I think these few minutes were the time of gravest concern for the President. Was the world on the brink of holocaust? Was it our error? A mistake? Was there something further that should have been done? Or not done? His hand went up to his face and covered his mouth. He opened and closed his fist. His face seemed drawn, his eyes pained, almost gray. . . . We had come to the time of final decision. (pp. 69–70)

At 10:25 came the message that the Soviet ships had stopped dead in the water. The President immediately issued an order that no Soviet ships were to be stopped or intercepted, giving the ships ample opportunity to turn back. RFK concludes:

> Then we were back to the details. The meeting droned on. But everyone looked like a different person. For a moment the world had stood still, and now it was going around again. (p. 72)

The United States and the Soviet Union had ample opportunity and ample resources to continue waging their contentious struggle off the shores of Cuba in October 1962. The costs and risks of doing so, however, were perceived by each to be so great that continued struggle was not possible. The costs of continued crisis were high for both sides—in money, manpower, and distraction from other pressing issues. And of greatest importance, a nuclear catastrophe was quite possibly in the making. The result was a classic stalemate, in which each side had carried the escalation as far as it dared go. In the aftermath of this eyeball-to-eyeball confrontation, negotiations were set in motion that led to an agreement by which the United States promised not to invade Cuba, in exchange for a Soviet commitment to withdraw and/or destroy its missiles in Cuba.[6] In addition, the incident was such a shock to both sides that it ushered in a period of "détente" in which several other agreements were reached through negotiation.

HOW DE-ESCALATION BEGINS

Thus far we have described the reasons for perceived stalemate—that is, the reasons why Party might conclude that a conflict is intolerable and should be ended as soon as possible. But what happens next, once a stalemate is perceived?

At first, probably very little. Party has come to the grudging realization that it cannot prevail at acceptable cost and risk, yet it is also unwilling to cede victory to Other through yielding or withdrawal. Yielding even a jot would be a blow to Party's pride and would run the risk of signaling weakness to Other. Withdrawal, the other option, would be tantamount to capitulation; hence, it would also be unacceptable.

---

[6] In a study of relations between the United States and the (erstwhile) Soviet Union, Patchen (1991) found that the two countries have tended to take cooperative actions and to reciprocate Other's cooperative actions under two conditions: first, when they lacked confidence in their ability to win advantage in competition; and second, when they were concerned about the costs of competition. This finding supports our contention that these conditions encourage impatience with escalation.

What's left is problem solving. The question is how to get there. Party is stuck, and probably blames Other for its misfortune. But Party has also come to understand that it cannot get what it wants without Other's consent. It is clear that such consent will be forthcoming only if Party can advance a proposal that Other will find acceptable.

The most important consequence of perceived stalemate, then, is that Party is forced into a grudging acceptance of Other as an interdependent partner with whom some quid pro quo will have to be worked out. Other is not a friend with whom collaboration is a welcome opportunity but a despised enemy whose cooperation is nevertheless needed. (When asked about Great Britain's decision to form an alliance with the Soviet Union to defeat Nazi Germany, Winston Churchill responded, "To beat the Nazis I would form an alliance with the devil himself.") As Party takes the first tentative steps out of stalemate, it regards Other as the devil that is needed, the enemy who must be catered to and leaned on if the conflict is to be settled. This opens the door to de-escalation and to *negotiation*, which has been defined as "a discussion among two or more parties with the apparent aim of resolving a divergence of interest" (Pruitt & Carnevale, 1993, p. 2).[7]

Negotiation is a mild form of overt conflict, in which the same strategic choices are found as in any other conflict. The difference between negotiation and most other forms of conflict behavior is that negotiation makes it possible to settle or even resolve the conflict that gives rise to it.

At the risk of oversimplification, we can state that negotiation tends to assume one of two forms in the extreme: Either the parties compete eyeball to eyeball with each other, using verbal forms of contentious tactics in an effort to win. Or they work side by side with each other, to solve the problem jointly. Often, although not always, negotiation assumes the first form before moving to the second; that is, negotiation starts out as a contentious exchange and only subsequently evolves into a more collaborative arrangement. As the parties try to wriggle their way out of stalemate, they first use negotiation for competitive advantage and shift to problem solving only if contending fails to yield an agreement.

---

[7] A great deal has been written about negotiation over the last several decades, ranging from theoretical treatises (see Brett, 2001; Douglas, 1962; Gulliver, 1979; Kochan, 1980; Morley & Stephenson, 1977; Schelling, 1960; Stein, 1989; Walton & McKersie, 1965) to summaries of research (see Carnevale & Pruitt, 1992; Druckman, 2003; Faure, 1987; Hopmann, 1996; Kremenyuk, 2002; Pruitt, 1981; Rubin & Brown, 1975; Zartman, 1994) to textbooks (see Lewicki et al. 1998, 2000; Pruitt & Carnevale, 1993; Thompson, 2001) to various efforts to bridge the divide between theory and practice (see Bazerman & Neale, 1992; Breslin & Rubin, 1991; Fisher & Brown, 1988; Fisher et al., 1991; Goldberg et al., 1992; Hall, 1993; Lax & Sebenius, 1986; Neale & Bazerman, 1991; Raiffa, 1982; Salacuse, 1991; Sjostedt, 1993; Susskind et al., 1983; Ury, 1991; Zartman, 1994; Zartman & Berman, 1982). While this is not a book about negotiation per se, the topic is clearly pertinent to the de-escalation of conflict.

Optimism

For Party to become involved in negotiation requires not only a perception of stalemate-based interdependence, but also some *optimism* about the chances of success (Pruitt, 1997).[8] At first, this optimism may be based on *working trust*,[9] a belief that Other is likely to behave reasonably if given a chance. Without some assurance along these lines, Party will continue fighting rather than engage in a fruitless sequence of negotiating activities that might be misunderstood as a sign of weakness. Working trust may derive from a sense that Other also perceives a stalemate—that Other, like Party, sees little chance of winning and/or is apprehensive about the costs and risks of continued conflict. Or it may derive from a belief that Party's and/or Other's aspirations have declined to the point that they are within range of each other. (Aspirations tend to decline in a stalemate, because they cannot be achieved.) Working trust is an element of perceived common ground (PCG), a concept presented in Chapter 3.

For Party to *stay* in negotiation once it starts, optimism must eventually be based on a *perceived way out*, a belief that the parties are actually approaching a mutually acceptable agreement. In other words, there must be light at the end of the tunnel. This is another element of PCG.

Another component of optimism is a belief that one is dealing with valid representatives of the other side—people who can commit enough segments of the political spectrum on the other side that a negotiated agreement will stick. Without a valid representative, there is no point in entering negotiation.

We have said a lot about Party so far and very little about Other. But for negotiation to actually begin, *both* sides must be ready to abandon escalated conflict and try something different, and both must be optimistic to some degree. It is best if both of them perceive that they are in a stalemate—that their chances of winning are low and/or the costs and risks of trying to win are too high. But it is only necessary for one of them (the one we are calling "Party") to see things this way provided that Party lowers its aspirations to the point where Other becomes optimistic about finding an acceptable settlement. For example, the negotiations that led to a black majority government in South Africa began when the white government became so discouraged about success in their conflict with the blacks (and about the anti-apartheid pressures from the outside world), that they lowered their aspirations to the point where leaders of the African National Congress (representing most of the blacks) became optimistic about achieving their aims through negotiation. Only the government perceived a stalemate; the ANC thought (correctly) that it was winning. Fortunately for

---

[8] Stein (1989) speaks of the combination of perceived stalemate and optimism as a perception of threat coexisting with a perception of opportunity.

[9] The term "working trust" comes from Kelman (1997).

peace in South Africa, the ANC's aspirations were sufficiently limited at this time that they overlapped with those of the government.[10]

Stalemate and Negotiation in the Middle East

The importance of perceived stalemate and optimism for starting negotiation and keeping it going is perhaps nowhere better demonstrated than in the aftermath of the Middle East War of October 1973 (the "October War"). The war began with a stunningly effective surprise attack launched simultaneously by the Egyptians and the Syrians against Israel while most Israelis were observing their religion's holiest day, Yom Kippur. Both the Egyptians and the Syrians made striking advances through territory that had been in Israeli possession since the so-called Six-Day War of 1967—a war in which Israel had seized control of the Sinai Peninsula, the West Bank of the Jordan River, and the strategically important Golan Heights. The October War eventually turned in Israel's favor, but not before a period of defeat that gave the Israelis a bad scare.

In his analysis of this period, Zartman (1981) points out that the Israelis, Egyptians, and Syrians were stalemated in a number of ways at the war's end. For one thing, they had reached a moment of truth about the military situation between them. Israel had discovered that it could be defeated (at least temporarily) by a worthy adversary, while Egypt and Syria discovered that they could not eventually defeat the Israelis. Furthermore, an Israeli counterattack had completely encircled the Egyptian Third Army. At another level, the Israelis had territory (the Sinai) but not the recognition and legitimacy that they desired from their Arab neighbors. For their part, the Egyptians and the Syrians lacked the territory but had the advantage of growing numbers on their side, as well as the ability to withhold recognition of Israel as a legitimate sovereign state.

American Secretary of State Henry Kissinger moved immediately into high gear, serving for several months as a mediator, shuttling back and forth between Israel and its adversaries. His constant argument was that both sides were in stalemate—that neither side could hope to move further through force and that their relative equality of power made genuine trade-offs possible. He also chose easy issues to mediate first, thus fostering a sense of momentum in the negotiators. In these ways he kept alive the sense of stalemate and added to it an element of optimism—a belief on the part of the principals that a mutually acceptable agreement could be

---

[10] A related but somewhat different interpretation of these events is given by Lieberfeld (1999). Another case in which there was a one-sided perception of stalemate came toward the end of the Vietnam War, when the United States became discouraged with the conflict and agreed to withdraw in negotiations with the North Vietnamese. Only the U.S. perceived a stalemate; for the North Vietnamese this was an opportunity to get rid of the U.S. and thus eventually win the war.

reached if they would only stay the course with Henry. Zartman writes of Kissinger's skill in this regard as follows:

> Even as Kissinger was fostering the perception of stalemate, his real tactical skill came from an ability simultaneously to convince the parties that compromise was theoretically possible and that, wherever it lay, such compromise was preferable to the dire alternatives of unilateral action and inaction. (p. 152)

GETTING UNSTUCK

In Chapters 6 and 8, we had a lot to say about structural changes that take place during escalated conflict and keep the escalation going. These stand in the way of de-escalation and movement into negotiation, even when the situation is otherwise ripe for negotiation because of a sense of stalemate and optimism on both sides (Coleman, 1997, 2000). How can these structural changes be mitigated to the point where negotiation can go forward? Three approaches have been discussed in the literature: contact and communication, superordinate goals, and unilateral conciliatory initiatives. The first two can be initiated by one or both parties or by a third party who is trying to render assistance.[11] The third requires a more or less risky action by one of the parties.

Contact and Communication

Direct contact between antagonists and the communication that often goes with it can have a number of beneficial effects. First, contact and communication allow Party to explain actions and proposals that might otherwise elicit defensive reactions or retaliation. Second, they contribute to Party's understanding of Other's motives, sensitivities, and the like; this can enhance trust and allow Party to act in ways that will not upset Other. Third, contact and communication permit problem solving in which substantive and procedural issues can be resolved. Without such discussions, the search for a mutually acceptable formula must take the form of trial and error, which has many pitfalls. The surest way to achieve an integrative agreement is through discussion of needs and priorities. Fourth, they help lift the veil of dehumanization. Rather than seeing Other as evil and as one who enjoys inflicting suffering, Party begins to see Other as a fellow human being who also suffers from the conflict. This "humanization" fosters empathy toward Other, creating an opportunity to include Other in Party's own moral community. Finally, contact and communication contribute to interpersonal attraction, and hence to the

---

[11] There are other things third parties can do, but discussion of these will be reserved for Chapter 11.

development of positive bonds. Research (Drolet & Morris, 2000; Miller & Brewer, 1984; Zajonc, 1968) shows that contact encourages attraction more often than antagonism.

Despite their potential advantages, contact and communication should not be regarded as panaceas. In intense conflict, they tend to be useless or worse than useless (Rubin, 1980). Party will not use available communication channels when it distrusts Other or is too angry to consider any solution that is acceptable to Other (Deutsch, 1973). When Party uses communication channels, it is often to threaten or try to trick Other rather than to engage in problem solving (Worchel, 1979). Indeed, when severe escalation has taken place, intergroup contact strengthens identification with the ingroup and increases anxiety toward outgroup members (Greenland & Brown, 2000; Pettigrew, 1998). In such circumstances, communication can be exceedingly explosive, with angry, insulting interchanges.

This effect was observed in Sherif's experimental boys' camp mentioned in Chapter 2 (Sherif et al., 1961; Sherif & Sherif, 1969). The boys in the camps were separated into cabins and encouraged to frustrate one another, producing considerable antagonism and some fights. Thereafter, contact between the cabins, even though noncompetitive (for example, eating together in the same cafeteria), led to arguments and name calling, which served to exacerbate the controversy. Couples locked in distressed relationships often show the same effect (Gottman & Levenson, 1988; Noller & Fitzpatrick, 1990).

These points qualify the value of contact and communication but do not completely invalidate this approach to conflict management. They suggest, for example, that if Party is very angry with Other, a cooling-off period may be needed before communication is productive. Or a mediator may have to shuttle between the parties for a period of time, improving mutual images and laying the groundwork for agreement, before direct contact is of value. Or, in intergroup relations, it may be necessary to have extensive informal contact between moderates on both sides before formal negotiation begins.[12]

Cooperation on Other Issues: Superordinate Goals

After experimenting with a number of unsuccessful approaches to conflict resolution, including the provision of opportunities for contact and communication, Sherif and his colleagues hit on a method that succeeded

---

[12] Such contact, in the form of "Track 2" meetings between Russian and western scientists and other professionals, made it easier for leaders on both sides to wind down the Cold War in the late 1980s. The Oslo negotiations between Israel and the Palestinian Liberation Organization (PLO) in 1993 started with a series of informal meetings between Israeli professors and PLO officials before formal negotiation began (Pruitt et al., 1997).

in breaking down the antagonism between the two cabins of boys in their camps. This was to have the boys cooperate on issues other than those involved in the controversy. For example, the counselors arranged for a breakdown in the water supply to the camp. The boys had to work together to disassemble the water tower and carry it to a truck that would take it into town for repair. Performance of these tasks reversed the prior escalation, building bonds between the groups.

Sherif called this the method of *superordinate goals*, because it involves development of an objective that is common to both parties and beyond the capability of either alone. The most common superordinate goals result from the emergence of a common enemy. A Pushtun proverb says: "I against my brothers; my brothers and I against my cousins; my brother, my cousins, and I against the world." Such a development was seen in the United States during the Second World War, when the negative sentiments toward Russia rapidly shifted to positive feelings in the face of the common enemy, Nazi Germany. After that war was over, these sentiments turned sour, but they have revived again recently with recognition of a common enemy in the form of international terrorism.

Having and working on superordinate goals enhances bonds with Other (Johnson et al., 1984). This occurs in a number of ways. One is by the principle of psychological balance—my enemy's enemy is my friend (Aronson & Cope, 1968). A second is by reducing the salience of group boundaries; people who are working toward common goals develop a sense of shared identity. They are, in some sense, members of the same group and hence are less likely to be antagonistic toward one another (Bettencourt et al., 1992; Gaertner & Dovidio, 2000; Turner, 1981). A third is by increased knowledge about the other side, which reduces anxiety toward outgroup members (Islam & Hewstone, 1993). A fourth is by a reinforcement mechanism; as we work together, each of us rewards the other and produces a sense of gratitude and warmth in the other. Pursuing superordinate goals also means that Party sees itself as working on behalf of Other, a view that is likely to foster positive attitudes toward Other and cut through the concerns with image loss that are often characteristic of stalemate.

The existence of superordinate goals is a powerful contributor to stability under most conditions—but not all. If cooperation toward these goals is unsuccessful (for example, if the common enemy wins), unity may disintegrate and an argument ensue about who is to blame for the loss. This is particularly likely to happen if there was prior tension in the relationship, because previously established images tend to leave residues (Worchel et al., 1977; Worchel & Norvell, 1980).

How can superordinate goals be developed in conflict situations? Sometimes circumstances force them on the parties, as when two nations are attacked by a third. At other times, the parties may develop such goals in an effort to overcome their conflict, as when a married couple try to save their marriage by deciding to have a child.[13] It is also possible for third parties to impose superordinate goals, as when a boss arranges for two quarreling employees to work together on a Christmas party.

Because the principals in an escalated conflict are so antagonistic toward one another, it is often hard to get them to agree on common goals or to persuade them to cooperate. People who are engaged in a struggle may have difficulty agreeing on anything, even on superordinate goals to curb the struggle. Hence, like contact and communication, superordinate goals cannot be viewed as a cure-all. They can help, however, in the often painful process of moving from stalemate through de-escalation and into problem solving.

Unilateral Conciliatory Initiatives

The two procedures just discussed have their value, but they share the difficulty that both of them require some acquiescence or collaboration by Other. Contact and communication require that Other be willing to associate with and talk with Party. For Party to work with Other on a superordinate goal requires that Other also work with Party. The difficulty is that sometimes the relationship is too escalated for Other to be willing to have anything to do with Party.

When this is the case, Party can simply reach out and make cooperative moves on its own that require no acquiescence from Other. The aim of such unilateral conciliatory initiatives is to enhance Other's trust to the point where productive communication and cooperation can begin.

Unilateral conciliatory initiatives may be small in scope, designed to provide a safe and subtle test of Other's state of mind. If Other is also in stalemate and ready to move toward resolution, it may notice the initiative and respond in kind. However, the most interesting kind of initiatives are large and dramatic in nature, designed to crack through enemy images and other profound structural changes on the other side.

Osgood (1962, 1966) has outlined a strategy of dramatic conciliatory initiatives. This strategy, which is called "graduated and reciprocated initiatives in tension reduction" (GRIT), requires Party to take a series of striking actions aimed at eroding the distrust and other structural changes on the other side and starting a de-escalatory spiral of positive action and reaction.

A useful set of guidelines for these initiatives is as follows (Aggestam & Jonsson, 1997; Hopmann, 1996; Lindskold, 1978; Mitchell, 1999, 2000; Stein, 1996):

---

[13] This is seldom a good idea, because children can also put a strain on a relationship and can be the innocent losers if the tactic does not work, but it is a common "remedy" nevertheless (Rubin & Rubin, 1989).

- The initiatives should be clear-cut and unexpected, so as to get Other's attention, challenge its preconceptions, and thus encourage new thinking.
- They should be voluntary and irreversible and should involve some cost or risk to Party, so that they cannot be interpreted as a cheap trick.
- They should be announced ahead of time as an effort to reduce tensions, and Other should be invited to reciprocate.
- The series of initiatives should be continued for a while even if Other does not reciprocate, so that they look like a change in policy and so that Other has time to rethink its strategy.
- Other should be rewarded for cooperating, the level of reward being pegged to its level of cooperation.
- Party should be ready to retaliate if Other misinterprets or attempts to exploit these initiatives and engages in escalation.

One example of a unilateral conciliatory initiative was Egyptian President Anwar Sadat's dramatic 1977 flight to Jerusalem. Sadat said that his trip was designed to reduce tensions (that is, to improve Israeli trust in Egypt) so as to pave the way for negotiations. He apparently viewed the prior escalation and war between the two countries as mainly due to a conflict spiral in which the countries were alternately antagonizing each other. His initiatives followed the first three guidelines listed above. They were unexpected and irreversible. They were announced ahead of time as a bid for conflict resolution. And by making his trip, Sadat clearly suffered severe costs, in terms of alienation from the rest of the Arab world and from some of his own citizens (Stein, 1996).[14] Hence, it was hard to doubt the genuineness of his interest in peace. Indeed, his trip appears to have engendered considerable trust among Israelis (Kelman, 1985; Mitchell, 2000). The development of this trust did not guarantee solution to all problems, but it contributed to the initiation and success of the subsequent negotiation.

It is important to note that Sadat made his trip to Jerusalem after the 1973 war. If he had done so before that war, it is questionable whether Israel would have responded in a conciliatory way. Before the war, Egypt seemed militarily weak, so Israel did not see itself as in a stalemate. Israel was "top dog" in the Middle East and had little reason to seek a jointly acceptable solution to its Egyptian problem. Furthermore, Sadat's initiatives might well have been interpreted in Israel as a sign of weakness rather than as evidence of a change of heart. But after Egypt's attack, Israel was ready to rethink its strategy and could hardly misperceive Sadat as weak.

---

[14] Sadat was later assassinated for having made peace with Israel.

The point is that Sadat's conciliatory initiative was part of a broader "firm but conciliatory" strategy (discussed in Chapter 10). He first sent a message of firmness about defending Egypt's basic interests by going to war against Israel. Within the context of this earlier message, the later conciliatory message embodied in his trip to Jerusalem probably had a greater chance of working than if it had been sent alone.

Of course, in such a highly escalated relationship, conciliatory messages are often quite hard to get across because of the suspicions that have been generated by the escalation. Hence, it is usually necessary to employ a dramatic and concerted tension-reduction program that involves striking unilateral initiatives, such as Sadat's trip to Jerusalem.

A special form of unilateral conciliatory initiative is the *apology*, where Party conveys to Other its regret about some prior actions it has taken. A sincere "I am sorry" by Party often diminishes Other's desire for revenge (Kim & Smith, 1993), thus increasing Other's empathy toward Party (McCullough et al., 1997), and opening a door to forgiveness and reconciliation (Fisher, 2001). Most importantly, an apology can serve as a double line of sorts, a temporal divide separating events that have taken place in the past from those that are yet to come. An apology is a way of helping bygones to be bygones—of distinguishing a period of heavy escalation from a new, more generous problem-solving phase.

To be sure, an apology is no panacea. If improperly timed or meant insincerely, an apology can arouse suspicion on the part of Other. Also, when the harm is severe, an apology by itself, even if well-timed and sincere, may be insufficient to create a climate for problem solving (Yamamoto, 1999). Moreover, an apology is a public admission of responsibility for causing harm to Other (Ohbuchi et al., 1989; Tavuchis, 1991). For Party, bearing this public disgrace and the financial or legal liability that can accompany admission of responsibility may be more painful than remaining in the dispute. Nevertheless, this simple but powerful tool can and should be used more often to alter the climate of a conflictual relationship.

De-escalatory Spirals: The Constructive Use of Entrapment

Unilateral initiatives are successful when they result in a de-escalatory spiral, a sequence of alternating conciliatory actions by the two sides producing enough trust on both sides for negotiation to seem viable. In such a spiral, each action is a confidence-building move that encourages reciprocal action from the other side. De-escalatory spirals are the mirror image of conflict spirals, which play such an important role in the development of escalation (see Chapter 5).

One of the authors (Pruitt, 2000b) has described de-escalatory spirals as a kind of "courtship dance." He gives an example that appears to have occurred in the years preceding the negotiations that produced the 1998 Northern Ireland Peace Agreement. One of the parties was the Irish Republican Army (IRA) and its political wing, Sinn Fein, both predominantly Catholic organizations. The other was the British government. The head of Sinn Fein was (and still is) Gerry Adams; and the dance was apparently guided along by a third party, John Hume, head of the moderate (predominantly Catholic) Social Democratic and Labour Party. Amazingly, this de-escalatory spiral took place while military action continued. The stages in this spiral were as follows:

- In 1988, Sinn Fein sent signals that it was reexamining its policies, most notably by engaging in the Hume-Adams dialog (a well-publicized set of discussions between Adams and Hume that dealt with how to resolve the conflict).
- In 1989 and 1990, the British secretary of state for Northern Ireland, Peter Brooke, made conciliatory speeches in which he said that Britain had no selfish economic or strategic interests in Northern Ireland and would respond with "imaginative steps" if the IRA abandoned violence. Hume had urged him to make these statements, which challenged some of Sinn Fein's stereotypes about Britain. The violence continued, but the IRA did declare a three-day cease-fire at Christmas 1990.
- In 1992 Sinn Fein published a conciliatory statement, "Towards a lasting peace in Ireland," and the following September Hume persuaded Adams to state that Sinn Fein was "more willing than ever to explore new avenues toward a settlement."
- October 1993 produced the Downing Street Declaration by Britain and Ireland, in which Britain indicated that "new doors could open" if the IRA would renounce violence. Shortly after this declaration, Major indicated that he would talk with Sinn Fein if the IRA stopped its violence.
- Finally, in August 1994, the IRA declared a cease-fire and called for negotiations.

Several more years went by before the final negotiations commenced, but this de-escalatory spiral (along with some secret, behind-the-scenes talks) led the way to those meetings. This spiral took a long time to complete because there were many hostile incidents and much ill will at this time. It was successful because there was receptivity to negotiation on both sides due to perceptions of stalemate, motivating the parties to reciprocate each other's conciliatory initiatives (Pruitt, 2000b).

De-escalatory spirals sometimes involve positive entrapment, which is a mirror image of the pathological kind of entrapment discussed at the end of Chapter 8. Positive entrapment occurs when the conflicting parties become committed to a pattern of de-escalation they cannot escape. Momentum has been established in the prior phases, and the parties have come to feel that they have too much invested in the de-escalation sequence to give it up.

SUMMARY AND CONCLUSIONS

All escalated conflicts eventually end, either by victory for one side, mutual withdrawal, an arbitrated settlement, or a negotiated agreement. This chapter is devoted to the conditions and processes that produce the last of these outcomes—de-escalation and a negotiated settlement.

We present a version of ripeness theory that traces de-escalation and the beginning of negotiation to a combination of perceived stalemate and optimism about achieving a minimally acceptable solution. Perceived stalemate implies that Party sees that it is dependent on Other and cannot coerce Other to cooperate. Perceived stalemate can result from any or all of the following conditions: failure of contentious tactics, exhaustion of resources necessary to employ such tactics, loss of support from allies, and the development of unacceptable costs or risks. Optimism may start with working trust—a sense that Other is in the same boat as oneself and is also ready to seek settlement. But to stay engaged in negotiation, Party must eventually see light at the end of the tunnel—an acceptable alternative that can be achieved. In intergroup conflict, optimism also requires the belief that one is dealing with a valid spokesperson—a negotiator who can commit the other side to a binding agreement.

Conditions that should produce perceived stalemate and optimism do not always do so. There are two ways this can happen. One is that Party may be so shortsighted and entrapped in the struggle that it does not see things clearly. Clarity of vision may only come as a result of a shocking event or a change in group leadership. The other is that structural changes may have created such negative views of Other that Party is unwilling to make meaningful contact with Other and is totally lacking in trust. There are three ways of combating such negative views: contact and communication (this mainly works with mild conflict), the development of superordinate goals, and unilateral conciliatory initiatives (which include apology).

If there is a perceived stalemate on both sides, unilateral conciliatory initiatives often lead to a de-escalatory spiral—a series of increasingly reassuring actions by both parties. Such a spiral may create enough trust for negotiation to begin.

For negotiation to work, problem solving is almost always needed. This is the main focus of Chapter 10, which also discusses reconciliation and other components of lasting agreements.

10

Problem Solving and Reconciliation

❖

The theme of Chapter 9 was that escalating conflict often reaches a point of stalemate, where one or both parties find the further use of harsh contentious tactics either unworkable or unwise. To move to negotiation, two more changes are needed. Both parties must develop some optimism about finding a mutually acceptable agreement. And the forces that encourage negotiation must outweigh the structural changes that keep escalation going.

When negotiation begins, contending usually does not stop but takes a verbal form; for example, persuasive arguments instead of yelling or shooting. However, to reach an agreement, problem solving—defined as any effort to identify a formula that will satisfy both sides' aspirations—is usually also needed. Problem solving is by no means always the last step in a controversy. Many conflicts of a milder variety are resolved through early problem solving and only escalate a little or not at all.

While problem solving—which is the main topic of this chapter—is almost always essential for ending a harsh conflict, it is usually not enough. Attention must also be paid to compliance with the agreement and the future of the relationship between the parties—to creating conditions under which the agreement will stick and new conflicts will not escalate the way the old one did. Among other things, this often requires *reconciliation* efforts, aimed at building a new relationship between the parties. Reconciliation will be discussed at the end of the chapter.

PROBLEM SOLVING

At its best, problem solving involves a *joint* effort to find a mutually acceptable solution. The parties or their representatives talk freely to one another. They exchange information about their interests and priorities, work together to identify the true issues dividing them, brainstorm in search of alternatives that bridge their opposing interests, and collectively evaluate these alternatives from the viewpoint of their mutual welfare.

However, a full problem-solving discussion of this kind is not always practical or feasible because of the realities of divergent interests and because of structural changes. Party may fear that such openness will deny it an opportunity for competitive gain or will give Other such an opportunity. When these fears exist, individual problem solving is a practical alternative. Party—either an individual or a small partisan group—can privately perform all the functions just described: seeking insight into Other's interests, identifying the true issues, devising mutually beneficial alternatives, and evaluating these alternatives from a joint perspective. Another approach, described in Chapter 11, is for a mediator to do the problem solving.

Outcomes of Problem Solving

Problem solving is by no means always successful in dealing with conflict. But when it is successful, there are three possible outcomes. It can lead to *conflict management,* in which the parties work out ways of de-escalating and avoiding future escalation. Examples would be a cease-fire agreement or an agreement to establish a "hot-line" between the parties to talk over new issues as they arise. Conflict management involves a procedural rather than a substantive agreement. Alternatively, problem solving can produce a *settlement,* a substantive agreement dealing with enough of the issues that the parties are willing to give up their escalated struggle. The difficulty with settlement is that other issues remain that can cause the conflict to heat up again in the future. An example would be the agreement that ended the Cuban Missile Crisis—the United States promised not to invade Cuba in exchange for Soviet withdrawal of its missiles. America's underlying problem of having a communist outpost in the Western Hemisphere was not addressed by this settlement; hence, a subsequent Cuban crisis could easily have occurred (though fortunately it did not). If problem solving is really successful, it can lead to *conflict resolution,* an agreement in which most or all of the issues are cleared up.[1] Agreements in which the parties get most of what they are seeking are more likely to last than superficial agreements of the kind usually reached in settlements. An example would be the agreement that freed India from British rule and produced a working relationship that has withstood the test of time.[2]

Outcomes of problem solving can also be classified in terms of their *structure,* the way they are put together. Thus, successful problem solving can lead either to a compromise or an integrative solution.

Compromise   A compromise is an agreement reached when both parties concede to some middle ground along an obvious dimension. For examples, the parties to a wage dispute can split the difference between their proposals; Sales and Production can agree to a production schedule halfway between their respective positions; or a couple can resolve a dispute about whether to vacation in Maine or Florida by going to a beach in North Carolina.[3]

Compromises can sometimes be very good for both parties and sometimes very bad. Most commonly they provide both parties with a middling outcome—by no means as good as they had hoped for or as bad as they had feared. Where it can be achieved, an integrative solution is usually much better for both parties than a compromise. Yet many conflicts end in compromise. Among the reasons for this are aspirations that are not sufficiently high, time pressure that makes it hard to embark on a search for new options (Yukl et al., 1976), fear of prolonged conflict, and a societally endorsed fetish for "fairness" that often attracts unwarranted attention to the fifty-fifty division. In addition, compromises sometimes grow out of an unduly escalated episode. The parties have devoted so much energy to trying to beat each other, and so much attention is focused

---

[1] The distinction between settlement and resolution is not hard and fast but a matter of degree. They are opposite ends of a dimension of the extent to which an agreement serves the basic interests that have propelled the parties into the conflict. Resolutions are at the high end of this dimension; if basic interests can be resolved, the conflict will probably not resurface.

[2] It is often the case that conflict management—e.g., a cease-fire—precedes negotiation of a settlement or resolution, and some authors have argued that this is a necessary progression (Olonisakin, 2000). However, it is possible to negotiate *in secret* while heavily escalated conflict continues. This was the case in the secret Oslo negotiations, which produced a settlement between Israel and the PLO in 1992.

[3] The popular use of the term *compromise* is somewhat broader; it often means any agreement in which the parties abandon their initial demands. Following the lead of Follett (1940), we have adopted a narrower definition in order to distinguish simple compromises from integrative solutions.

on partisan options, that they cannot engage in creative efforts to devise new alternatives. Hence, when they finally see that they are in a hurting stalemate, they reach out for an obvious compromise.

Integrative Solutions   An integrative solution is one that reconciles (that is, integrates) the interests of Party and Other. Integrative solutions produce the highest joint outcomes of the three types of agreement. Consider, for example, the story of two sisters who are quarreling over an orange. The sisters could reach a compromise agreement to split the fruit in half—the first sister can squeeze her half for juice while the other uses the peel from her half to bake a cake. But both would clearly profit more from the integrative solution of giving the first sister all the juice and the second all the peel. If they are intent on compromise, the sisters will never find the best solution.

In this story, it is possible for a *fully* integrative solution to be reached, one that totally satisfies both parties' aspirations. However, most integrative solutions are not so successful. They *partially* reconcile the parties' interests, leaving them fairly content but not quite so happy as if they had achieved all they had hoped for.[4]

Integrative solutions sometimes entail known alternatives, but more often they involve the development of novel alternatives and require some creativity and imagination. For this reason, it is proper to say that they usually emerge from a process of creative thinking. Integrative solutions can be devised by Party and/or Other acting separately, by the two of them in joint session, or by a third party such as a mediator.

Situations that allow for the development of integrative solutions are said to be high in *integrative potential* (Walton & McKersie, 1965). Not all situations have such potential. For example, there is little integrative potential when a tourist dickers with a North African merchant about the price of a rug; Party's gain is almost surely Other's loss. But there is more integrative potential in most situations than is usually assumed. Hence, a skilled and sustained problem-solving effort is often richly rewarded.

Integrative solutions are often advantageous to the parties, both collectively and individually, so they are worth pursuing if at all possible. This is so for four main reasons:

1. If aspirations are high and there is resistance to yielding on both sides, it may be impossible to reach agreement unless a way can be found to join the two parties' interests.
2. Compromises (and mechanical agreements such as tossing a coin) can produce settlements. But full conflict resolution usually

---

[4] Integrative solutions are sometimes called "win-win solutions" (see Pruitt & Carnevale, 1993). However, we prefer the term "integrative" because, as noted here, such solutions are seldom perfect "wins" for both sides. They usually require some yielding from one or both parties.

requires the development of integrative solutions, in which both sides' major concerns are addressed. Hence, the parties will put more energy into the implementation of integrative solutions; and integrative solutions are less likely to come apart than the other two kinds of agreement (Thomas, 1976).

3. Because they are mutually rewarding, integrative solutions tend to strengthen the relationship between the parties. Strengthened relationships usually have inherent value and also facilitate the development of integrative solutions in subsequent situations.

4. Integrative solutions ordinarily contribute to the welfare of the broader community of which the two parties are members. For example, a firm usually benefits as a whole when its departments are able to reconcile their differences creatively (Pruitt & Carnevale, 1993).

The discovery of an integrative solution diminishes, and can even abolish, perceived divergence of interest. This point is demonstrated in Figure 2.2d, which shows a fairly severe perceived divergence of interest. The center alternative provides a possible compromise, but it comes nowhere near satisfying the two parties' aspirations (which are shown by the dashed lines). This divergence of interest disappears in Figure 2.2a as a result of developing an integrative solution (shown at the upper right). It follows that if an integrative solution is known at the outset of concern about an issue, conflict can be avoided. Had the sisters in our example thought immediately about exchanging peel for pulp, there would have been no conflict.

Types of Integrative Solutions

Clearly integrative solutions are important to achieve. So how do they emerge? What are the routes for moving from opposing demands (i.e., positions) to an alternative that reconciles the interests of Party and Other? We have identified five such routes, leading to five types of integrative solutions: expanding the pie, nonspecific compensation, logrolling, cost cutting, and bridging. In addition to its theoretical value, this typology should be useful as a checklist for any negotiator or mediator seeking a way to settle a conflict.[5]

---

[5] The reader interested in learning more about theoretical assumptions underlying the development of integrative solutions should read Chapter 5 of Lax & Sebenius' (1986) book, *The Manager as Negotiator,* and Chapter 6 of Hopmann's (1996) *The Negotiation Process and the Resolution of International Conflicts.* The reader interested in learning more about specific techniques for encouraging the development of integrative solutions in negotiation should read Fisher et al.'s (1991) *Getting to YES.*

To increase the theoretical and practical value of our presentation, we mention the kind of *information* needed in order to formulate each type of solution. The types of solutions are listed in order of the difficulty of getting that information, with the least difficult listed first. We also pose several *reframing questions* that can help to reformulate the issues and hence aid in the search for each type of solution. Reframing a controversy is a very important step in breaking out of the box produced by repetitive enunciation of demands. Hence it facilitates moving toward the discovery of integrative solutions. The most fundamental reframing question, from which all the others follow, is simply "How can both parties succeed?"

Our typology of integrative solutions is illustrated by a running example concerning a husband and wife (or any two people) who are trying to decide where to go on a two-week vacation. The husband wants to go to the mountains, the wife to the seashore. They have considered the compromise of spending one week in each location but are hoping for something better. What approach should they take?

Expanding the Pie   Some conflicts hinge on a resource shortage. Time, money, space, automobiles, handsome men, or what have you—all are in long demand but short supply. In such circumstances, integrative solutions can be devised by expanding the pie, which means increasing the available resources. For example, our couple might solve the problem by persuading their employers to give them two additional weeks of vacation so that they can spend two weeks in the mountains *and* two weeks at the seashore. Follett (1940) cites another example—two milk companies, vying to be first to unload cans on a creamery platform, resolved their controversy when somebody thought of widening the platform.

Expanding the pie is a useful formula when Party finds Other's proposals inherently acceptable but rejects them because they pose opportunity costs. For example, the husband rejects the seashore because it keeps him away from the mountains, and the wife rejects the mountains because they deny her the pleasures of the seashore. However, expanding the pie is by no means a universal remedy. If there are inherent costs, as opposed to opportunity costs, in Other's proposal (the husband cannot stand the seashore or the wife the mountains), broadening the pie may yield strikingly poor results. Other types of integrative solutions are better in such cases.

The information requirements for expanding the pie are very small. All that is required is knowledge of the parties' demands. This does not mean that such a solution is always easy to find. There may be no resource shortage, or it may be expensive to enlarge the pool of resources. Furthermore, it may not be apparent that there is a resource shortage. In an argument over who goes first on the loading platform, it may not be clear that the real issue is the size of the platform.

Several reframing questions can be useful in seeking a solution by expanding the pie. How can Party and Other both get what they are asking?

Does the conflict hinge on a resource shortage? How can the critical resource be expanded?

Nonspecific Compensation   In nonspecific compensation, Party gets what it wants and Other is repaid in some unrelated coin. Compensation is nonspecific when it does not remedy the precise costs incurred by Other. For example, the wife in our example might agree to go to the mountains—even though she finds them boring—if her husband agrees that some of the family resources can be spent on buying her a new car. Another example is a supervisor giving an employee a bonus for going without dinner in order to meet a deadline.

Compensation usually comes from the party whose demands are granted, because that party is "buying" concessions from the other party. But it can also originate with a third party or even with the party who is compensated. An example of the latter is an employee who pampers himself or herself by finding a nice office to work in while going without dinner.

Two kinds of information are useful for devising a solution via nonspecific compensation: (1) information about one or more realms of value to Other, for example, knowledge that Other values attention or is money-mad; and (2) information about how badly Other is hurt by making the concessions. The latter information is useful for devising adequate compensation. If only one of these kinds of information (or neither) is available, it may be possible to conduct an "auction" for Other's acquiescence, changing the sort of benefit offered or raising Party's offer in trial-and-error fashion until a formula is found to which Other can agree.

Reframing questions can help locate a means of compensation. For example, what does Other value that Party can supply? How valuable is this to Other? How much is Other hurt by conceding to Party?

Though it is often useful, nonspecific compensation has its limitations. Burton (1990) has argued that it is usually not possible to compensate people for their failure to satisfy basic human needs. In other words, they usually cannot be paid in some other coin to forgo food, security, group identity, and the like. Or if they accept such an agreement, it is likely to be unstable, coming apart as the need resurfaces. Other limitations are due to normative constraints. For example, it is not proper to pay a government employee for food stamps.[6]

---

[6] Foa & Foa (1975) have developed a general theory about the kinds of compensation that are considered appropriate as repayment for certain kinds of concessions. They classify resources on two dimensions: concreteness (tangibility) and particularism (the extent to which the value of the resource depends on the identity of the person delivering it). Status and love are abstract, particularistic resources; goods and money are concrete, nonparticularistic resources. These authors have shown, in a series of studies, that a form of compensation appears more appropriate the closer it is in this dimensional space to the resource received. Thus goods can properly be exchanged for money and status for love. But money cannot properly be exchanged for love.

Logrolling   In a solution by logrolling, each party concedes on issues that are of low priority to itself and high priority to the other party. In this way, each gets that part of its demands that it deems most important. Like the other types of solutions, logrolling is not a universal route to integrative solutions. It is possible only when several issues are under consideration and the parties have different priorities among these issues. Suppose that in addition to disagreeing about where to go on vacation, the wife in our example prefers a first-class hotel and the husband wants to go to a tourist home. If accommodations are most important to the wife and location is most important to the husband, they can reach a fairly integrative solution by agreeing to go to a first-class hotel in the mountains.

Another example is a hypothetical case of bargaining between labor and management in which labor initially demands a 20 percent increase in overtime rate and 20 more minutes of rest breaks, and management indicates unwillingness to provide either concession. If the overtime rate is especially important to labor and if long rest breaks are particularly abhorrent to management, a reasonably integrative solution can be achieved if labor drops its demands for more rest breaks in exchange for management giving in on the overtime rate. This sort of solution is better for both parties than a compromise on the two issues, such as a 10 percent increase in overtime rate and 10 more minutes of rest time.

Logrolling can be viewed as a variant of nonspecific compensation in which the parties stay within the set of issues under discussion rather than reaching out for new issues, and each party gives in on issues of importance to the other. Both logrolling and nonspecific compensation rely for their effectiveness on what Lax and Sebenius (1986) describe as "the trading of differences."[7]

To develop solutions by logrolling, it is useful to have information about the two parties' priorities among the issues under discussion so that concessions can be matched up. Information about priorities is not always easy to get. One reason for this is that people often try to conceal their priorities for fear that they will be forced to concede on issues of lesser importance to themselves without receiving compensation. Another reason is that people often erroneously project their own priorities onto others, assuming that what they want is what others also want.

---

[7] Lax & Sebenius (1986) offer the following quaint example: "If a vegetarian with some meat bargains with a carnivore who owns some vegetables, it is precisely the *difference* in their known preferences that can facilitate reaching an agreement" (p. 92). Jack Sprat (who could eat no fat) and his wife (who could eat no lean) worked out a similar arrangement. These authors identify six kinds of differences that can be exploited in conflict in order to help create (negotiated) agreements. These are differences of relative value (as in the preceding examples), expectation, capacity, risk-taking propensity, and time preference. For more detailed analysis of these forms of difference, see pp. 90–105 of Lax & Sebenius (1986).

Solutions by logrolling can also be developed by a process of trial and error: Party offers a series of possible packages, keeping its own aspirations as high as possible, until an alternative is found that is acceptable to Other (Kelley & Schenitzki, 1972).

Several reframing questions can be useful for developing solutions by logrolling: Which issues are of higher priority and which of lower priority to Party? Which issues are of higher priority and which of lower priority to Other? Are some of Party's high-priority issues of lower priority to Other, and vice versa?

Cost Cutting   In solutions by cost cutting, Party gets what it wants and Other's costs are reduced or eliminated. The result is high joint benefit, not because Party has changed its position but because Other suffers less. For instance, suppose that the husband in our example dislikes the beach because of the hustle and bustle. He may be willing to go there on vacation if his costs are cut by renting a house with a quiet inner courtyard where he can read while his wife goes out among the crowds.[8]

Cost cutting often takes the form of *specific* compensation, in which the party who concedes receives something in return that satisfies the precise values frustrated. For example, if the wife's main objection to the mountains is the absence of seafood, it may be possible to reach agreement by locating a mountain hotel that serves seafood. Specific compensation differs from nonspecific compensation in that it deals with the precise costs incurred rather than providing repayment in an unrelated coin. The costs are actually canceled out rather than being overbalanced by benefits achieved in some other realm.

Information about the nature of Other's costs is, of course, helpful for developing solutions by cost cutting. This is a deeper kind of information than knowledge of Other's priorities. It involves knowing something about the interests—the values and needs—underlying Other's overt position.

Reframing questions can help in developing solutions by cost cutting: What costs are posed for Other by Party's proposal? How can these costs be mitigated or eliminated?

Bridging   In bridging, neither party achieves its initial demands, but a new option is devised that satisfies the most important interests underlying

---

[8] A variation in which costs are cut on *both* sides is offered by Lax & Sebenius (1986) in their discussion of economies of scale: Two health care institutions are interested in setting up a new clinic in an underserved area. Instead of each organization building its own clinic, they might agree to establish one facility, thereby sharing the various expenses incurred while making their services available to a larger clientele. Thus, instead of expanding the pie, this proposal calls for reducing the cost to both parties of baking a pie of fixed size.

those demands. For example, suppose the husband in our vacation example is mainly interested in fishing, and the wife wants mainly to swim. These high-priority interests might be bridged by finding an inland resort with a lake that is close to woods and streams. Follett (1940) gives another example of two women reading in a library room. One wants to open the window for ventilation, the other to keep it closed in order not to catch cold. The ultimate solution involves opening a window in the next room, thereby letting in the fresh air while avoiding a draft.

Bridging typically stems from a reframing of the issue(s) on the basis of analysis of underlying interests. For example, a critical turning point in our vacation example is likely to come when the initial formulation "Shall we go to the mountains or the seashore?" is replaced by "Where can we find opportunities for fishing and swimming?" This new formulation becomes the basis for a search model (Simon, 1957) that is employed in an effort to find a new alternative.

It is rare that a solution can be found that bridges all interests of Party and Other, as the window in the next room of the library does. More often, higher-priority interests are served while lower-priority interests are discarded. For example, the wife who agrees to go to an inland lake may have to forego the lesser value of smelling the sea air, whereas the husband may have to give up his predilection for spectacular mountain vistas.

It follows that people who seek to develop bridging solutions must usually have information about the nature of the two parties' interests and about their priorities among these interests. Information about priorities among interests is different from information about priorities among demands (which is useful for developing solutions by logrolling). Demands are the proposals the parties are making—the positions they are taking—in the negotiation, while interests are the hidden concerns that underlie these demands.

To achieve an optimal solution by bridging, the information just described should be used as follows: In an initial phase, one's search model should include all of the interests on both sides. But if this does not generate a mutually acceptable alternative, some of the lower priority interests should be discarded from the model and the search begun anew. This cycle should be repeated until an agreement is reached. The result will not be an ideal solution, but it is likely to be one that is mutually acceptable. Dropping low-priority values in the development of bridging solutions is analogous to dropping low-priority demands in the search for a solution by logrolling. But the latter is in the realm of concrete proposals, while the former is in the realm of the interests underlying these proposals.

A number of reframing questions can be raised in searching for a solution by bridging: What are the two parties' basic interests? What are the priorities among these interests? How can both sets of high-priority interests be achieved?

The Analysis of Underlying Interests

To devise an integrative solution involving cost cutting or bridging, we usually need to know something about the interests underlying one party's position (in the case of cost cutting) or both parties' positions (in the case of bridging).

The most obvious way to get this information about other parties' interests is to persuade them to talk about those interests. This is helped along by *active listening*, "paying attention to what the other is saying, asking questions when the other's meaning is unclear, and periodically checking on one's understanding by rephrasing the other's position" (Pruitt & Carnevale, 1993, p. 42). However, there are two problems with this method. One is that people do not always understand the precise nature of the interest underlying their preferences. Their position in a controversy is often a matter of what "feels" best. They feel good about their own proposal or uneasy about the other's proposal without knowing precisely why. For example, the wife may feel comfortable at the seashore and uncomfortable in the woods but not be sure why she feels this way. Hence, she may not be able to talk clearly about these interests.

The other problem is fear of information loss. Party may be unwilling to reveal its interests for fear that Other will use this information to personal advantage—for example, for constructing threats. This problem arises when distrust exists. An example is unwillingness to tell one's spouse that one is greatly in need of affection for fear that the spouse will later withdraw affection whenever he or she wants a concession.

Fortunately, there are other approaches to gathering information about interests besides getting people to talk about them directly. These include role reversal or empathizing—Party trying to put itself in Other's shoes. Some people are better at empathizing than others, and they have been shown to achieve more integrative agreements (Neale & Bazerman, 1983). Another approach is "listening with the third ear" (Reik, 1952)—that is, being attentive to the points Other emphasizes, the places where it becomes emotional, the issues it neglects to mention, and its behavior in other situations (Fisher et al., 1991). It is also possible to ask third parties about Other's needs and values.

Interests Underlying Interests   Learning about the interests that *immediately* underlie a party's proposals is often not enough. It will often be necessary to seek the interests underlying these interests, or the interests underlying the interests underlying these interests, and so on. The point is that interests are usually organized into hierarchical trees, with more basic interests underpinning more superficial ones. If one moves far enough down one party's tree, it is often possible to locate an interest that can be easily bridged with an interest on the other side.

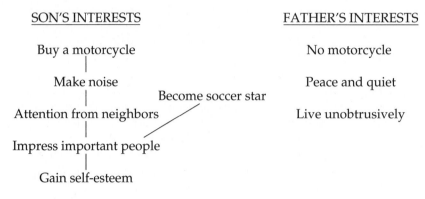

FIGURE 10.1

Son's interest tree in a controversy with his father.

An example of an interest tree appears on the left of Figure 10.1. It is that of a boy trying to persuade his father to let him buy a motorcycle. At the right are listed those of the father's interests that conflict with the son's. At the top of the tree is the boy's initial position (buy a motorcycle), which is hopelessly opposed to his father's position (no motorcycle). Analysis of the boy's proposal yields a first-level underlying interest: to make noise in the neighborhood. But this is opposed to his dad's interest in maintaining peace and quiet. Further analysis of the boy's position reveals a second-level interest underlying the first level: to gain attention from the neighbors. But again this conflicts with one of his father's interests, to live unobtrusively. The controversy is resolved only when someone (the father, the boy, the boy's mother, or someone else) discovers an even more basic interest underlying the boy's desire for a motorcycle: the desire to impress important people. This discovery is significant because there are other ways of impressing important people that do not contradict the father's interests—for example, the bridging solution of going out for the high school soccer team. At the bottom of the boy's preference tree is a fourth-level interest, self-esteem. But it is unnecessary to go down this far, because the controversy can be resolved at the third level.[9]

In the example just given, it is fairly easy to discern the boy's underlying needs and values because his demands are logically derived from them.

---

[9] By putting self-esteem at the bottom of the boy's interest tree, we are agreeing with Burton (1990) and Rothman (1997) that basic human needs—for such things as security, recognition, justice, dignity, having a separate identity, control over own environment, and self-esteem—underlie many conflicts and account for the strong feelings and rigidities that often accompany them. However, we do not agree with these authors about the need to draw a sharp distinction between interest-based conflicts and need-based conflicts. For us, interests always underlie conflicts, and basic human needs are often situated at the bottom of interest trees.

ONE PARTY CARES MORE ABOUT	THE OTHER PARTY CARES MORE ABOUT
Substance	Form, appearance
Economic considerations	Political considerations
Internal considerations	External considerations
Symbolic considerations	Practical considerations
Immediate future	More distant future
Ad hoc results	The relationship
Hardware	Ideology
Progress	Respect for tradition
Precedent	This case
Prestige, reputation	Results
Political points	Group welfare

FIGURE 10.2

Polar opposites that are not necessarily in conflict (from Fisher, Ury, & Patton, 1991, p. 74).

But such is not always the case. Demands are sometimes *displaced* from an underlying need rather than logically derived from it, requiring a good deal more digging. For example, a complaint about Other's behavior may not be the real issue but only a legitimate or safe proxy for another more pressing concern. Thus a husband who complains that his wife is always late from work, which delays his dinner, may actually be expressing a concern that she is no longer affectionate. His complaints about late dinner may seem more legitimate, safer to verbalize, less embarrassing, or easier to talk about than his complaints about lost love. Or he may not be clear in his own mind about what really underlies his complaints.

Same Issue—Different Meaning   In analyzing the interests underlying divergent positions, one often finds that the issue under consideration has a different meaning for the two parties. Though there appears to be disagreement, there is no fundamental opposition in what they are really asking. Figure 10.2 shows some dimensions that leave room for bridging.

One controversy was resolved when a mediator discovered that one party was seeking substance while the other was seeking appearance (Golan, 1976). A cease-fire in the 1973 October War found the Egyptian Third Army surrounded by Israeli forces. A dispute arose about the control of the only road available for bringing food and medicine to this army, and the two parties appeared to be at loggerheads. After careful analysis, the mediator (Henry Kissinger) concluded that Israel wanted *actual* control of the road, whereas Egypt mainly wanted the *appearance* that Israel did not control it (in order to avoid embarrassment back home). A bridging solution was found that involved having three United Nations checkpoints on the road (to give the impression of international control) but retaining Israeli sovereignty over the road and the right to inspect trucks at the first check point to be sure that they did not contain arms.

Another conflict was resolved when it was discovered that one party had *immediate* concerns while the other's concerns were *more distant.* This situation involved a strike by public transit workers in Buffalo. The mayor of the city, who was asked to mediate the dispute, found that the bus company's refusal to pay stemmed from budget problems, whereas the workers' main concern was their salary in future years. Hence, the mediator recommended that the workers get half of what they were asking immediately and the other half a year later, after the company had a chance to petition the city for an increase in the fare. This was another bridging solution.

Beliefs, Narratives, and Metaphors   The demands a party makes and the goals and values underlying these demands are often based on beliefs or assumptions about the way the world is structured. Thus, for the son to seek a motorcycle as a way to impress important people, he must believe that his neighbors are important people and that making noise is a way to impress them.

Developing a common set of beliefs or assumptions—one that is agreed to by both sides—is often the key to successful problem solving, because it allows each side to understand and even to empathize with the other's position. Hence, the father might be more willing to allow his son to own a motorcycle if he also believed that riding it would contribute to the boy's self-esteem, especially if he believed that it was the best or the only way to satisfy that basic need. Developing a common vocabulary is a first step toward developing a common set of beliefs.

The goals and values that produce a conflict, and the emotions attached to that conflict, often rest on the parties' *narratives* about the conflict and related events (Cobb, 2003). Each side has its own narrative and, when conflict is severe, the two parties often interpret the same events in radically different ways. Thus, Israelis explain their military campaigns against Palestinians by talking about the Holocaust and the many times they have been attacked by the Arabs, who seem to be challenging their right to exist as a nation. Palestinians explain their assaults against Israel by talking about Israel's steady encroachment on their territory and freedoms.

Understanding the other side's narrative is an essential step toward grasping the interests and beliefs that give rise to conflict and that must be remedied for the conflict to be solved. And *showing* an understanding of the other side's narrative is a way of encouraging trust by the other side. Thus, Egyptian President Anwar Sadat, in his successful 1977 conciliatory trip to Jerusalem, visited a monument to the Holocaust, thus showing that he appreciated an important part of the Jewish narrative.

A further step toward conflict resolution occurs if the parties can come to share a common narrative about the history of their conflict and related events (Rothman, 1997). Thus German acceptance of responsibility for starting the Second World War and for many of the atrocities in that war has probably contributed to the recent push toward Western European unification. However, a common narrative is hard to achieve when conflicts are severe.[10]

Beliefs about a conflict and how it should be handled are also based on the *metaphors* that are used for understanding that conflict. A metaphor is a label given to something that likens it to something else. Some metaphors intensify a conflict and make it harder to solve. Consider the troubles in Northern Ireland. For a long time, the Irish Republican Army viewed British activities there as a form of "colonialism" and the British government viewed IRA activities as "criminality." These intensely negative metaphors made it difficult to resolve the conflict. Fortunately, these metaphors were eroded as the peace process moved ahead.

Using the wrong metaphor can impede solution of a knotty problem. Thus saying that we are involved in a "war on terrorism" can focus attention on military methods and divert attention from solving the human problems that give rise to terrorism. A more neutral and hence fruitful label might be the "campaign against terrorism" or the "drive against terrorism."

Adopting a common metaphor or slogan to describe their task can encourage negotiators to engage in effective joint problem solving. For example, conflict resolution was made easier in a multilateral negotiation about how to use a forest when the disputing parties agreed that they were trying to achieve "sustainable development" of a "healthy forest" (Blechman et al., 2000).

Metaphors differ from culture to culture, and success in negotiation is partly a function of how well the parties understand one another's metaphors and how they are used. Thus Gelfand and McCusker (2001) point out that Americans tend to view negotiation as a "sport" while Japanese view it as a "household gathering." This produces different perceptions and goals on the two sides, which can stand in the way of progress in intercultural talks if they are not understood.

How to Go about Problem Solving

It clearly makes sense to search for integrative solutions in most conflicts. How should Party go about this search—how should it be organized? This is the question of creative problem solving.

---

[10] Sluzki (2003) has argued that at every step along the way to conflict resolution and reconciliation, both parties must change their narratives. Often this entails a transformation from a narrative of victimization to one of evolution and empowerment.

Steps in Creative Problem Solving   The following sequence of steps can contribute to Party's search for creative solutions to apparent conflict with Other:

Step 1: Ask Whether There Really Is a Divergence of Interest. Conflict was defined earlier as perceived divergence of interest—a belief that the parties' current aspirations are incompatible. Such a perception may well be illusory, due to a misunderstanding about the circumstances, or a misconstruction of Other's proposals or interests.[11] If the parties can grasp this point, the conflict will go away and problem solving will be unnecessary. Hence, asking whether there is a real divergence of interest is the logical first step.

Illusory conflict can arise in at least three ways. Party may have a false impression about Other's intentions or aspirations. For example, a carpenter who came to look at a job in the home of one of the authors (DGP) said that the estimate would cost $50. When asked why he expected a fee, he indicated that he feared homeowners would file for an insurance payment on the basis of his estimate, then do the repairs themselves. When assured that this homeowner was all thumbs with tools, he withdrew the request for a fee. Second, Party may mistakenly believe that Other's intended actions will create costs that they actually will not create. For example, parents may oppose a teenage party because of the anticipated noise until they learn that the proposed party will take place while they are away. Third, Party may view Other's intentions as arbitrary or illegitimate when they really are not. For example, a university department chair thought she was in conflict with the dean of continuing education over the division of some student fees. At the "showdown" meeting between these two administrators, the dean argued that continuing education should get the larger share because more of its budget depended on "soft money." Once this argument had been presented, the dean's claims seemed nonarbitrary, and there was no longer a conflict in the eyes of the chair.

Step 2: Analyze Party's Own Interests and Beliefs. Set Reasonably High Aspirations, and Be Ready to Stick to Them. If Party concludes that a conflict really exists, the next step is to examine carefully its own interests—Party's basic goals and values. This avoids the danger of going off half-cocked and getting involved in controversy over nonessential issues. The methods for analyzing interests described earlier can be useful in this enterprise. Having done so, Party must set reasonably high aspirations regarding these interests and be ready to stick to them. In short, Party must be both ambitious and stubborn about its basic interests.

We acknowledge that by endorsing ambition and stubbornness we are saying that protracted conflict is often necessary for the development of

---

[11] Thompson (1990b) and Thompson & Hastie (1990) have demonstrated that negotiators often fall into illusory conflict, failing to see that the two sides are actually in agreement on some or all issues.

truly integrative solutions (Filley, 1975). Party must maintain high aspirations, fully cognizant of the fact that they may not be compatible with
Other's aspirations. However, we hasten to add that we are not endorsing
bullheadedness. Aspirations should start and stay high, but not so high as
to outrun any reasonable integrative potential. If they remain too high,
time will be lost, the conflict may become heavily competitive, and Other
may begin to see the conflict as hopeless and withdraw (see Step 4).

**Step 3: Analyze Other's Interests and Seek a Way to Reconcile Both
Parties' Aspirations.** Having set high aspirations, Party should seek a
way to reconcile these aspirations with those held by Other. In other
words, Party should engage in a search for information about Other's
perspectives and for integrative solutions. The various reframing questions discussed in one of the prior sections should be posed, and one or
more search models should be employed in an effort to achieve the goals
that both parties find most important.

It is not clear that any one of the five kinds of integrative solutions is
better or easier to achieve than the others. Hence, we do not recommend
starting the search with any particular type of solution in mind. The right
kind of solution depends in part on the kind of information available. If
Party cannot fathom the interests underlying Other's demands, cost cutting and bridging are not possible, and Party must be content with the
other three approaches. Party should always pursue several kinds of solutions at once—for example, to seek a way to expand the pie at the same
time that it seeks a logrolling solution.

Sometimes there is too little information about Other's situation to
permit a thoughtful approach to the development of integrative solution.
For example, Other may reject Party's proposals but refuse to give reasons
or make a counterproposal. When this happens, a policy of trial and error
must be adopted (Kelley & Schenitzki, 1972; Pruitt & Carnevale, 1982), in
which Party proposes a sequence of alternatives that satisfy its aspirations
in the hope of finding one that appeals to Other as well.

Step 4: Lower Aspirations and Search Some More. If agreement is
not reached in a reasonable period of time at step 3, a choice should be
made between two further options. Party can reduce its aspirations somewhat—that is, concede on low-priority issues or discard low-priority
interests—and try again. Alternatively, if Party's search model includes
Other's aspirations as well as its own, Party can lower its conception of
Other's aspirations and then, if a solution is found, try to persuade Other
that such a reduction is desirable.

Step 4 should be repeated until an agreement is reached or withdrawal becomes inevitable.

Being Firm but Conciliatory   The policy described in steps 2, 3, and 4 of
the sequence just given can be viewed as *firm but conciliatory.* Party should
be firm about its basic interests—yielding only when it is clear that they
cannot be attained—but also conciliatory toward Other in the sense of

seeking out and being responsive to Other's basic interests.[12] An important aspect of being conciliatory is for Party to be flexible about how its interests are achieved, in order to be open to new ideas about how to reconcile its interests with Other's. Hence, this policy can also be described as involving *firm flexibility;* Party should be firm with regard to ends, but flexible with regard to the means used to reach these ends. A quotation from Fisher et al. (1991) captures the essence of firm flexibility: "It may not be wise to commit yourself to your position, but it is wise to commit yourself to your interests. This is the place . . . to spend your aggressive energies" (p. 54).[13]

A firm but conciliatory strategy is often employed with success in child rearing. Wise parents are strict about ethical standards and such minimal goals as cleanliness, safety, and parental peace of mind. They urge their children to live within the framework of these values and discipline a child who moves outside of them. Yet the same parents are concerned about their children's welfare, so they are flexible about the means by which their values are achieved, allowing and even helping their children to accomplish the children's own goals within the framework of the parents' values. For example, a father may be firm with his son about straightening up his room yet be flexible about when and how this work will be done. The result of such an approach is likely to be conformity to parental values, high joint benefit, and a good relationship between parent and child.

The firm but conciliatory approach is closely related to Tjosvold's notion of "constructive controversy," which involves airing of differences in the context of cooperative goals (Tjosvold et al., 2000). Tjosvold's research in organizations shows that when Party presents a position that is opposed to that of Other, it causes Other to become curious and seek information about what underlies this view. This, in turn, promotes successful problem solving. Chinese, who are from a collectivist society, are more

---

[12] The firm but conciliatory approach is reflected in Zartman's (1995) advice to governments that face an internal rebellion from some of their citizens. He recommends that they adopt a "two-handed policy," "engaging in dialogue to find common ground for both sides' reasonable demands, while combating the extremes" (p. 336).

[13] Van de Vliert (1997) calls firm flexibility a "conglomerated conflict behavior," because it is a mixture of cooperative and competitive elements. Hopmann (1996) provides two criticisms of firm flexibility: "On the one hand, in negotiations where there are fundamental conflicts of interest, rigidity about the goals might block progress altogether, no matter how flexible one is about means. On the other hand, too much tactical flexibility may be perceived by the other as a sign of weakness the other party may exploit to its own benefit" (p. 92). Hopmann's first criticism is answered by step 4 in the creative problem-solving sequence, which recommends lowering aspirations if agreement is not reached in a reasonable period of time. His second criticism is answered later in this chapter, where it is asserted that it may be necessary to employ contentious tactics in order to underscore firmness. Such an assertion should go a long way toward counteracting a perception of weakness by Other.

reluctant to air opposing viewpoints than are westerners, but Tjosvold finds that doing so promotes the development of integrative agreements in China just as it does in the West.

Structuring the Agenda   The firm but conciliatory approach and the step model to which it is related are useful for dealing with either a single issue or a small group of related issues. But when many issues are being discussed in a joint problem-solving session, an agenda must be developed specifying the order in which the issues are to be taken up. Three guidelines for constructing such an agenda can be stated.

First, it often makes sense to put easier issues earlier in an agenda. This is because the success of problem solving is to some extent cumulative, in that earlier achievement establishes the impression that later achievement is possible—that there is integrative potential. This is not a hard-and-fast rule. Sometimes there is an overriding issue on which most other issues depend or which is poisoning the relationship between the parties and making it difficult for them to talk effectively. If so, that issue should be considered a "boulder in the road" that must be settled first and removed from the agenda (Weiss, 2002).

If solutions involving logrolling are to emerge from a problem-solving discussion, it is necessary to consider several issues at the same time, so that concessions on one issue can be traded for concessions on another. This implies the second guideline, that it is often desirable to expand the agenda to include seemingly extraneous matters. In doing so, problem solvers must be careful not to slip into the error of insisting that all issues that have been put on the table must be resolved before agreement can be reached. We are advocating discussing a number of issues, not trying to resolve them all.

The third guideline is useful when the agenda contains so many items that logrolling opportunities may be missed because the issues on which it is possible to trade concessions are considered at different times. To avoid settling for a less attractive solution in such a situation, it may be possible at the beginning of problem solving to adopt the ground rule that no element of the agreement can be finally approved until all issues have been thoroughly discussed. This allows earlier issues to be reconsidered in light of later ones.

Searching for a Formula   When complex issues are under consideration, a twofold approach is often essential. The early stage of problem solving must be devoted to devising an overarching formula—a brief statement of common objectives that can serve as a road map to the eventual agreement. Only then is it possible to devise an efficient agenda for working out the details of the agreement (Zartman, 1977). If a formula is not developed, the proceedings are likely to get so mired in details that momentum is lost and the parties withdraw or resort to a contentious approach.

An example of such a formula is the basic agreement in the 1978 Camp David talks between Israel and Egypt, which followed up Sadat's dramatic trip to Jerusalem. In essence, Israel agreed to withdraw from the Sinai Peninsula and begin talks about Palestinian autonomy in exchange for a peace treaty with Egypt. This formula became the basis for many years of further negotiation.

Breaking Linkages   Totally integrative solutions, in which both parties get all they were seeking, occasionally occur; but such agreements are quite rare. It is usually necessary for one or both parties to make selective concessions in search of a partially integrative solution. They must give up certain demands, diminish certain aspirations, or compromise certain values, while firmly adhering to others.

Demands, goals, aspirations, and values often come in bundles—that is, they are psychologically linked to other demands, goals, aspirations, and values. Hence, in order to make a concession, a process of unlinking must take place, in which some items in a bundle are psychologically separated from others. Fisher (1964) calls this process "fractionation" and Hopmann (1996) calls it "disaggregation." The 1962 Cuban missile crisis appeared, at first glance, to be comprised of a single issue: the relative toughness or weakness of the United States and the Soviet Union. Over the course of the thirteen days of the conflict, however, this monolithic, zero-sum issue was fractionated by the disputants themselves into a number of sub-issues (timing of missile removal, American compensation for this removal, and so on) that could be negotiated and that led eventually to a peaceful conclusion of the crisis.

Another example concerns the married couple who disagree about where to go on vacation. If they cannot find a solution like those discussed earlier, unlinking may be helpful. Most couples assume that they must take a vacation together; that is, they link the concept of vacation to that of togetherness. Separating these concepts may yield the most integrative solution possible for some couples. It is not always necessary to go on vacation together.

Covert Problem Solving

Problem-solving behavior makes a lot of sense in many situations. But what if Other has adopted a contentious approach and is unwilling to engage in problem solving? Might Party's problem-solving efforts be misinterpreted or exploited?

The answer is yes. As mentioned in Chapter 3, engaging in problem solving poses three risks if Other is not ready for it. All problem-solving behavior poses the risk of *image loss*—that is, a perception that Party is weak or irresolute, and hence, willing to make extensive concessions. This perception can actually undermine problem solving by encouraging Other to adopt contentious behavior in an effort to persuade Party to make those concessions. There is also some risk of *position loss* if Party makes tentative suggestions of possible agreements. Position loss is a perception by Other that Party has conceded from a previous position. A third risk is *information loss,* which can occur if Party talks about its interests or reveals information about its fallback position. The danger is that Other may be able to use this information to fashion threats or to demand further concessions.

One solution to the problem of image loss, position loss, and information loss is to employ *covert problem solving.* It is possible to conceive of a continuum of problem-solving tactics, ranging from the highly overt to the highly covert. At the overt end are such moves as openly engaging in a discussion of possible alternatives, conceding on one issue in the hope of receiving a reciprocal concession on another, and proposing a compromise or integrative solution. At the covert (hidden) end are four basic kinds of tactics: back-channel contacts, track two diplomacy, communication through intermediaries, and efforts to send signals to Other. Such tactics allow Party to explore possible solutions or to move toward overt problem solving while allowing Party to disavow these efforts if they do not work (Mitchell, 2000). If Party discovers through such exploration that Other is ready to accept a solution that is also acceptable to Party or to join in a problem-solving process, Party can then become more overt—confident that there is no need to worry about image loss, position loss, or information loss.

Another value of covert problem solving is its compatibility with contentious behavior. If Party wants to explore the feasibility of problem solving or of certain problem solutions while maintaining an overtly contentious stance, covert problem solving is the answer. The point is that there are psychological contradictions between overt problem solving and highly contentious behavior. The attitudes required for these two kinds of performance are different. Covert problem solving is easier to reconcile with contentious behavior because it involves less commitment to cooperation. It is also less jarring for constituents if they are dedicated to a belligerent campaign. It is hard for Party to rally its forces around the battle cry that Other is partly right. Hence, leaders are often overtly contentious while engaging in covert problem solving—out of sight of their constituents.

Covert problem solving is commonly found after a period of escalation when both parties have come to perceive a stalemate. Each is groping separately for a new approach to the conflict, but neither is fully clear about the other's frame of mind. Is Other ready for problem solving? If we make conciliatory moves, will Other reciprocate or simply exploit our initiatives and turn them to competitive advantage? By employing covert initiatives, Party can test Other's interest in problem solving without taking undue risks.

If Other passes the test, Party can then turn with confidence to more overt forms of problem solving.

If covert approaches were not available, stalemates would often be insoluble despite both parties' desire for problem solving, because Party would not have a low-risk way of checking out Other's readiness to co-operate.

Let us now examine four types of covert approaches in greater detail.

Back-Channel Contacts   Back-channel contacts consist of informal problem solving discussions behind the scenes. Such discussions usually involve a small number of people and often take place in relaxed and neutral settings, such as over a shared meal. Back-channel contacts commonly occur during negotiation while seemingly rigid, contentious posturing is taking place on the official level. Reports of such contacts are found in accounts of negotiation in the international (Alger, 1961), industrial (Douglas, 1962), and domestic commercial (Pruitt, 1971) arenas. Some negotiations are entirely back-channel; for example, the Oslo negotiations in 1993 that produced the agreement establishing the Palestinian Authority (Pruitt et al., 1997). Back-channel contacts provide a more flexible arena for the development of integrative solutions than is usually available at the negotiating table.

Back-channel contacts are also found outside the context of formal negotiation. For example, Egypt's deputy foreign minister and Israel's foreign minister met secretly in Morocco to lay the groundwork for Egyptian President Anwar Sadat's historic trip to Jerusalem in 1977 (Stein, 1996).

Back-channel contacts reduce the three risks mentioned earlier. Position loss is seldom a problem, because both parties ordinarily understand that ideas mentioned in a private discussion are not official positions unless or until they are formally labeled as such. Image loss and information loss cannot be completely averted, but they can be minimized by arranging for the participants to speak for themselves as individuals rather than for their organizations. This reduces the likelihood that their problem solving activities will be seen as a sign that their constituents are ready to capitulate, or that information about the needs and values of their constituents will be derived from what the informal representatives say. Additional insurance against these latter losses can be achieved by assigning to back-channel meetings lower-status members of the organizations (such as technical experts) who are capable of problem solving but cannot be assumed to speak definitively for their superiors. These devices make it easier for top decision makers to disavow what has been said in a back channel if there is no progress in that channel.

There are trade-offs in assigning low-level personnel to such meetings and allowing participants to speak for themselves. Image loss and information loss are indeed minimized, but there is also a danger that these people will be less capable of engaging in effective problem solving because they are not fully acquainted with their organization's perspective or are not fully believed when they speak about this matter. This danger can be minimized by a two-step progression in which informal problem-solving discussions are followed by more formal meetings where actual commitments can be made. The informal discussions make their contribution by increasing Party's assurance that Other is genuinely interested in problem solving, and by identifying possible directions in which the final agreement can go. The formal discussions put the finishing touches, and the official stamp of approval, on the agreement.

Back-channel meetings also have the virtue of being *secret* and hence out of the public eye. This overcomes the group norms against communicating with the other side that are sometimes found in severely escalated conflict. In addition, the people at these meetings can reveal information and take positions without worrying about the reactions of allies, third parties, and constituents. This allows a degree of flexibility that may not be possible in more open contexts.

There is, however, a downside to secret meetings. If they produce an actual agreement, the people excluded from them may become "spoilers" and undermine that agreement (Kriesberg, 1998). Hence, after secret exploration of possible agreements, potential spoilers should be brought into the negotiation process if at all possible.

Track Two Diplomacy   Back-channel meetings sometimes involve track two diplomacy—unofficial contacts by private citizens or nongovernmental organizations (Diamond & McDonald, 1996; Montville, 1987). An example would be the Pugwash meetings between scientists from the Western and Soviet blocs, which took place during the Cold War and contributed to the development of arms control. Track two meetings allow even greater flexibility than back-channel meetings between officials, as there is very little danger of image, position, and information loss. In addition, the people involved often have a different perspective from government officials and hence may develop ideas that would not come up in official diplomacy. Such meetings also have the advantage of combating the negative stereotypes that so often develop in escalated conflict (Jeong, 2000) and creating a corps of people on each side who understand the goals and narratives on the other side. A recent study has shown that American diplomats are increasingly accepting track two diplomacy as an adjunct to the formal "track one" diplomacy that they practice (Chataway, 1998).

Use of Intermediaries   When the risks seem too great for back-channel meetings, or when it is impossible for the parties to make direct contact, third parties can sometimes be used as intermediaries for problem solving. An American newsman, John Scali, carried messages back and forth between the governments of the United States and the Soviet Union during the Cuban missile crisis (Young, 1968).

Intermediaries provide greater protection against image loss and information loss than is found in back-channel meetings, because it is less clear whether they represent the thinking of the people who sent them. If they seem soft, Party cannot be sure that Other is ready to make deep concessions. If they reveal information about underlying interests, Party cannot be sure that this information is accurate, so it is not useful for constructing threats. Yet intermediaries are often able to find enough common ground and provide enough assurance of Other's commitment to problem solving to make it seem worthwhile to launch more direct contacts. Intermediaries can also develop new ideas, and thus help to produce common ground; and they can coordinate de-escalatory spirals of the kind discussed at the end of Chapter 9.

Conversations through intermediaries avoid confrontation between disputants and hence potential friction in their relationship. This is why indirect channels are frequently used to resolve conflict in collectivist cultures, a point made in Chapter 3.[14]

Sending Conciliatory Signals   Conciliatory signals (also called tacit communication or sign language) are hints of a willingness to make a particular concession or to take some other cooperative action. Consider Peters' (1952) account of an exchange between negotiators for labor and management, after a mediator had just suggested a compromise raise of 9 cents per hour:

> Frazier and Turner looked each other in the eye. Somewhere a communication established itself without a word between them. The question in each other's eye was, "If I move to 9 cents will you move to 9 cents?" Frazier said, "Well, we are willing to give it some consideration for the sake of averting a strike." Turner nodded his acquiescence. The tension was gone as he buzzed his secretary to come in and take down a memorandum of agreement. (p. 18)

Both the glances and the tentative statement by Frazier can be regarded as signals. The latter signal was less ambiguous than the former, presumably because the glances convinced Frazier that the risks were small enough so that he could afford to gamble on a tentative endorsement of the mediator's suggestions. Ping-Pong-like sequences such as this, advancing to greater and greater clarity, are very common in conversations by signaling and are closely related to the de-escalatory spirals discussed at the end of Chapter 9.

An effective signal must be both noticeable and disavowable (Mitchell, 2000). It must be noticeable or it will have no effect. It must be

---

[14] We will have more to say about intermediaries in Chapter 11.

disavowable so that image loss and position loss are minimized in the event that Other is not ready to accept the proposal implied by the signal. Otherwise Party's negotiation position may be weakened.

Conciliatory signals are useful for sending up trial balloons about proposed compromises or integrative solutions. They are also useful for proposing that joint problem solving begin while minimizing image loss if Other is not interested. However, unlike back-channel contacts and the activities of intermediaries, signals can seldom contribute directly to the development of new ideas for integrative solutions, because they are not useful for expressing complex ideas.

STRATEGIES FOR PERSUADING OTHER TO ENGAGE IN PROBLEM SOLVING

When Party is ready for problem solving (whether because of being in a perceived stalemate or because of feeling a genuine interest in Other's welfare), it is helpful if Other is also ready for problem solving. This is so for two reasons. First, Party can now employ more overt forms of problem-solving tactics, confident that Other will not take advantage of them. Such tactics are usually more effective. Second, joint problem solving—wherein the two parties exchange information about their values and perceptions and work together in search of a jointly acceptable solution—is usually more efficient than individual problem solving. If the two parties can talk things over, they can develop a search model that will represent a true melding of their separate interests.

As mentioned earlier, if Party is uncertain about Other's readiness for problem solving, it often adopts covert moves to explore this readiness. However, this is not the only possible approach. Party can sometimes take the initiative and try to *convert* Other to problem solving.

A key to success in the latter enterprise is for Party to adopt *overtly* a firm but conciliatory stance (Komorita & Esser, 1975; McGillicuddy et al., 1984). Earlier we argued that a firm but conciliatory stance helps generate creative solutions. What we are arguing now is that such a stance, *if clearly telegraphed to Other*, encourages Other to follow Party into problem solving.

Our reasoning is as follows: The firm part of this strategy is needed in order to (a) persuade Other that contentious tactics are infeasible, because Party is unalterably committed to achieving its basic interests, and (b) to prevent Other from misinterpreting the conciliatory part of Party's message as a sign of weakness. The conciliatory part of this strategy is needed in order to convince Other that there is integrative potential in the situation—that Party can be trusted to help find a mutually acceptable solution and will not revert to contentious behavior if Other decides to initiate problem solving. There is a bumper sticker that says "Courtesy is catching." Good problem solving, we believe, is catching, too.

An example of an overtly firm but conciliatory stance can be seen in President John F. Kennedy's statements and actions during the 1961 Berlin crisis, an episode in the Cold War. The Soviet Union, under Premier Nikita Khrushchev, had been trying to end American occupation of West Berlin—and hence to end the rapid flight of skilled personnel from East Germany—by threatening to sign a separate peace treaty with East Germany and buzzing American planes in the Berlin Corridor. Recognizing that some concessions had to be made, Kennedy "decided to be firm on essentials but negotiate on non-essentials" (Snyder & Diesing, 1977, p. 566). In a speech delivered on July 25, he announced three fundamental principles that ensured the integrity and continued American occupation of West Berlin. The firmness of these principles was underscored by a pledge to defend them by force and a concomitant military buildup. Kennedy also indicated flexibility and a concern about Russian sensitivities by calling for negotiations to remove "actual irritants" to the Soviet Union and its allies.

Two results were achieved. One was the building of the Berlin Wall. At the time, this action was seen in the West as a contentious move by the Soviet Union. But in retrospect, it can be viewed as an outcome of a kind of joint problem solving, because it was the culmination of a sequence of public statements on both sides hinting at the desirability of building a wall (Pruitt & Holland, 1972). It solved both parties' problems, stopping the population loss from East Germany without disturbing American rights in West Berlin. The second result was eventual negotiations, which made these American rights explicit in writing.

Specific guidelines for demonstrating that one has adopted the two sides of the firm but conciliatory stance are explored in the next several subsections.

Signaling Firmness

Our analysis suggests a variety of ways in which Party can signal firm commitment to its basic interests. One is to make a vigorous verbal defense of these interests. A second is to be unwilling to make unilateral concessions (Komorita & Esser, 1975). A third is to arrange for Party's constituents to make tough statements and to make it clear to Other that Party is accountable to these constituents (Wall, 1977). A fourth is to develop a moderate amount of threat capacity (Lindskold & Bennett, 1973), sufficient to impress Other with Party's firmness, but not so formidable as to provoke Other into adopting fear-based countermeasures.

It may also be necessary to employ contentious tactics in order to underscore firmness. This can be particularly important when Party has recently yielded ground. Otherwise, Other may interpret Party's flexibility as a sign of weakness, leading Other to maintain or raise its aspirations and redouble its dedication to a contentious approach. Again, Kennedy's performance is a good example. His pledge to use force if necessary to defend Western rights in Berlin and the concomitant American military buildup served this function. Contentious tactics are also sometimes needed in conjunction with problem-solving overtures, in order to motivate Other to take enough of an interest in Party's welfare to engage in problem solving.

In recommending the use of contentious tactics, we are mindful of their many problems. Using these tactics can undermine problem solving by encouraging both the user and the target to become more rigid in their positions. These tactics also tend to alienate the target, and hence, to encourage the development of conflict spirals. In short, contentious tactics have the capacity of both contributing to and detracting from the development of mutually acceptable solutions. How can Party obtain the advantages of these tactics while avoiding the pitfalls? There are several answers to this question:

- Use contentious tactics to defend basic interests rather than particular solutions to the conflict. Thus, Kennedy defended the American presence in Berlin without prejudging particular arrangements.
- Send signals of flexibility and of concern about Other's interests in conjunction with contentious displays. Kennedy did this by offering to negotiate about "actual irritants." Such maneuvers are designed to make the integrative potential appear great enough to Other that problem solving seems warranted.
- Insulate contentious behavior from conciliatory behavior so that neither part of the strategy undermines the other. The most common form of insulation is the "bad cop/good cop" routine, in which contentious behavior is assigned to one team member (the bad cop) and problem-solving behavior to another (the good cop). In the context of the bad cop's threats, the good cop's offer of cooperation is more likely to be reciprocated by the target. In the context of the good cop's blandishments, the bad cop's escalation is less likely to produce reciprocal escalation by the target. An example is the collection agent who indicates to a laggard creditor that his or her principal will sue unless the two of them can reach a mutually acceptable agreement.
- Employ deterrent rather than compellent threats. Compellent threats require Other to adopt a specific option. Deterrent threats rule out an action or solution favored by Other but do not comment on the adequacy of other options, allowing Other to choose among them. In short, deterrent threats involve saying no to Other without demanding that Other say yes.

Signaling Conciliatory Intentions

Party can signal concern about Other's outcomes and flexibility about the shape of the final agreement in a number of ways:

- Openly express concern about Other's welfare and "acknowledge its interests as part of the problem" (Fisher et al., 1991, p. 51).
- Indicate a willingness to change its proposals if a way can be found to bridge the interests of Party and Other.
- Demonstrate problem-solving capacity—for example by assembling an expert negotiating team so that it is obvious to Other that Party has the capacity to develop useful new ideas.
- Maintain open communication channels to show Other that it is ready for cooperation.
- Reward Other for taking any cooperative initiatives (Deutsch, 1973).
- Reexamine any elements of its supposed interests that are clearly unacceptable to Other to be sure that they are essential to Party's welfare. If these turn out to be low in priority to Party, it may be possible to drop them. If they turn out to be high in priority, it may be possible for Party to discover interests underlying these interests that are not incompatible with Other's stance.

The Debate between the Hawks and the Doves

Most communities (small groups, organizations, and nations) contain subgroups of hawks and doves who take opposing positions with respect to external relations. The hawks favor a tough, contentious defense of collective interests; the doves favor negotiation and problem solving with the outgroup in question. Our analysis of the importance of being firm but conciliatory suggests that both factions are needed to conduct external relations sanely: doves to work out agreements and hawks to avoid giving away the store. An experiment on negotiation supports this conclusion. Jacobson (1981) showed that more integrative agreements were reached when the teams on both sides contained both hawks and doves than when they consisted only of hawks or only of doves. His interpretation was that the mixed teams employed a firm but conciliatory approach. The hawks insisted on achieving high benefits for their team and the doves worked hard to find a formula that would satisfy the hawks on both sides.

Groups in conflict usually try to conceal the hawk-dove debate in an effort to present a united front to the adversary. However, our analysis suggests that this may not be such a good idea, because revealing such a division sends a firm but conciliatory message to Other. The presence of hawks sends a message of firmness and determination, while the presence of doves sends a message of readiness for conciliation. This combination should encourage Other to cooperate. This effect should be even stronger if one can demonstrate that these two factions are about equal in political strength. If so, contentious behavior from the outgroup will backfire by leading to the ascendancy of the hawks, whereas cooperative behavior will be rewarded by encouraging political triumph by the doves. This effect is closely related to that produced by the bad cop/good cop routine.

BEYOND THE AGREEMENT

This chapter has gone into great detail about how to create agreements that settle arguments and stop fights. Unfortunately, in many cases, these agreements tend to be fragile and prone to collapse unless additional steps are taken. As Rothstein (1999) has pointed out, these agreements often cause temporary euphoria and raise unrealistic expectations for continued cessation of conflict. In the midst of these celebratory periods, both sides may neglect or undervalue additional work that must be done to avoid breakdown of the agreement or the development of new escalated conflict. At a bare minimum, two additional things are needed: building lasting agreements and repairing the relationship.

Building Lasting Agreements

As mentioned earlier, more integrative agreements are likely to be more lasting, because the parties have fewer unmet needs at the end of negotiation. Such agreements come closer to a true resolution of the conflict. Procedures for achieving and monitoring compliance can also be built into an agreement, as when a United Nations peacekeeping force is stationed on a boundary to monitor troop movements.

For an agreement between groups or nations to succeed, it may also be necessary to control potential *spoilers*—people or groups on one or both sides who seek to overturn the agreement. Hamas, a radical Palestinian group, is an example of a spoiler. Their terrorist activities after 1993 have been aimed, in part, at overturning the Oslo agreements that sought to initiate a peace process between Palestinians and Israelis. Spoilers have been active on the Israeli side as well.

Stedman (2000) suggests three approaches to controlling potential spoilers: (1) meeting potential spoilers' demands, if these demands are limited; (2) marginalizing the spoilers among potential supporters and thus bringing normative pressures to bear on them; and (3) coercing potential spoilers by denying them resources, monitoring their activities, and punishing them if they act against the agreement. In addition, third parties that help produce an agreement often need to maintain their involvement thereafter, "to ensure that the process does not become derailed" (Hampson, 1996, pp. 11–12).

Repairing the Relationship: Reconciliation

Structural changes resulting from harsh struggle are often difficult to reverse, even when the conflict that produced them has been settled. The net result of these structural changes is a rupture in the relationship between the parties. And their relationship is often so damaged that an agreement to end the conflict is likely to be short-lived at best, particularly when the parties must continue interacting after it is reached. Either the old conflict will resurface or the distrust and other structural changes will make it easy for a new conflict to emerge.

It follows that what is needed in a post-settlement phase is repair of the damaged relationship—undoing the structural changes produced by the prior escalation. In severely escalated conflict, it is usually not sufficient to undo only one kind of structural changes—hostile attitudes, feelings, or goals, negative perceptions—because the others will cause it to be reasserted (Pruitt & Olczak, 1995). Rather what is needed is broad-gauged repair of the entire faulty relationship. The process of relationship repair is commonly called *reconciliation,* a topic that has received much attention from theorists in the last few years.

Although the specific ingredients of reconciliation differ among researchers (see Deutsch, 2000b; Kriesberg, 2001; Rigby, 2001; Shriver, 2001; Yamamoto, 1999), there seems a consensus on two points: (1) effective, sustainable reconciliation has to deal with the painful past and at the same time devise a shared future; and (2) it should contain at minimum the following set of ingredients, as named by Lederach (1997): truth, forgiveness, justice, and peace.[15] Below we examine each of these ingredients.

Truth   Steps toward reconciliation begin with facts about the past. One or, as is usually the case, both parties have suffered—there are victims on one or both sides. The truth about this past must be unearthed, making it visible to all parties—victims, victimizers, and third parties (Lederach, 1997).

After conflict, both parties are often motivated to try to bury the painful past. Victims hate to revisit the past because it forces them to relive their pain and humiliation, while to victimizers (and some bystanders), confronting the past makes them feel shame and guilt. However, as Archbishop Desmond Tutu has said, "Without memory there

---

[15] Lederach uses the term "mercy" rather than "forgiveness."

can be no healing" (cited in Hawk, 2001, p. 307). Thus, uncovering truth, however painful, is a first step in the reconciliation process.

The important role of truth in the process of reconciliation is nowhere better articulated than in the goals of the South African Truth and Reconciliation Commission (TRC).[16] In 1994, there was a peaceful transition from an oppressive apartheid system, in which whites dominated blacks, to a democratic system. South Africa, like many other societies experiencing a dramatic political shift, confronted the problem of how to deal with the perpetrators of past injustices. Historical precedents focused on either full amnesty or full prosecution, but neither of these was suitable for a society that was badly in need of reconciliation. The result was a social invention, the TRC, which aimed at healing South African society by forgiving perpetrators who admitted their wrongdoing. Although judgment on the ultimate effectiveness of the TRC has to await the passage of time, the TRC was certainly one of the boldest and most innovative social and political experiments of the 20th century.

The goals of the TRC were "to establish the truth about the past, grant amnesty where appropriate, and establish measures for reparation, with the ultimate aim of rehabilitating and restoring the human dignity of victims of violations of human rights" (Friedman, 2000, p. 400). As its name signifies, the Commission recognized the prime importance of recovering the hidden truth about past injustices as a first move toward reconciliation. As a result, it devoted considerable effort and resources to gathering facts about injustices. In doing so, the Commission encouraged not only victims to come forward with stories of their suffering but also perpetrators to acknowledge their wrongdoing.

One reason why truth helps promote reconciliation is that it provides an opportunity for victims to publicly recount their suffering. This, by itself, can foster considerable healing (Shriver, 2001; Staub, 2001). A man jailed and blinded by the police, who had a chance to describe his suffering to members of the TRC, sums up the therapeutic value of revealing the truth: ". . . I feel what has been making me sick all the time is the fact that I couldn't tell my story. But now . . . it feels like I got my sight back by coming here and telling you the story" (cited in Shriver, 2001, pp. 27–28). When unable to tell their story, many victims of injustice are trapped in the awful past, suffering from a kind of posttraumatic stress disorder (McFarlane, 2000).

Another reason is that the truth leads to revising inaccurate or distorted accounts about the past. Memories and accounts are malleable in ways that suit our motives and interests (Loftus, 1979). Victims tend to overplay their suffering, while perpetrators tend to downplay their role

---

[16] See Rigby (2001) for a detailed description of the TRC and similar commissions used by other societies.

in creating suffering (Baumeister et al., 1990). This produces tension between victims and perpetrators, which is often passed on to future generations. Thus victims recount stories of their suffering—via novels, songs, and history books—with the hope that their descendants will avenge their suffering.[17] And perpetrators pass on embellished or rationalized versions of what they have done.

Consider the current relationship between Japan and Korea. Japan conquered Korea before the Second World War, and many Koreans suffered under the heavy Japanese domination. Though these former enemies were able to co-host the 2002 World Cup, many thorny issues remain to be resolved before they will achieve full reconciliation. One issue that still evokes passionate enmity in Koreans is Japan's reluctance to revise its history textbooks, which fail to acknowledge Japan's past brutality and aggression against Koreans and other Asians. This example shows how inaccurate memories and accounts can perpetuate the cleavage between victims and victimizers, posing obstacles to reconciliation. The process of correcting the published historical accounts of a conflict is now considered a crucial element of reconciliation (Montville, 1993).

Digging up the forgotten past can be counterproductive if it stirs up dormant antagonism. But if past suffering is remembered by the victims, full reconciliation has to begin with the truth. Ideally, the process of uncovering this truth should involve a joint analysis of the past by the parties involved in the conflict, with victimizers fully acknowledging their role in creating suffering (Fisher, 2001; Montville, 1993).

Forgiveness   Forgiveness plays such a crucial role in reconciliation that these two concepts are often used interchangeably. Impressed by the transforming ability of forgiveness, Simmel (1955) once noted that forgiveness possesses magical power that "rationally is not fully comprehensible" (p. 118).

All definitions of "forgiveness" have one feature in common: Letting go of the desire for vengeance.[18] We mentioned the power and persistence

---

[17] Volkan (1997) calls memories of victimization in prior generations "chosen traumas." When chosen traumas exist, prior conflicts have a tendency to reassert themselves.

[18] Among the definitions of "forgiveness" are the following: "Giving up rage, the desire for vengeance, and a grudge toward those who have inflicted grievous harm on you, your loved ones, or the groups with whom you identify. It also implies willingness to accept the other into one's moral community so that he or she is entitled to care and justice" (Deutsch, 2000b, pp. 58–59). "A willingness to abandon one's right to resentment, condemnation, and subtle revenge toward an offender who acts unjustly, while fostering the undeserved qualities of compassion, generosity, and even love toward him/her" (Enright & Human Development Study Group, 1996, p. 108). "The set of motivational changes whereby one becomes decreasingly motivated to retaliate against an offending partner, decreasingly motivated to maintain estrangement from the offender, and increasingly motivated by conciliation and goodwill toward the offender despite the offender's hurtful actions" (McCullough et al., 1997, pp. 321–322). "An act that joins moral truth, forbearance, empathy, and commitment to repair a fractured human relation" (Shriver, 1995, p. 9).

of vengeful desires in Chapters 6 and 8. Forgiveness is one of the few ways to overcome these desires. Forgiveness does not mean forgetting or condoning injustice. Rather, it is a conscious decision not to act upon the urge of vengeance. It frees both parties from the bondage of vengeance and separates the painful past from a hopeful future.

Forgiveness is sometimes an *intra*personal process, a unilateral initiative that places no requirement on the offender. The victim forgives the victimizer unconditionally, regardless of whether the latter shows remorse, wants to be forgiven, or is even aware of committing an injustice. This type of forgiveness certainly promotes victim healing, as the victim is free from the unrelenting demand of vengeful desires (Scobie & Scobie, 1998; Worthington, 2001), and it can also break a conflict spiral.

Yet, unconditional forgiveness poses three possible problems. One is that it may not help restore the relationship between the victim and the victimizer. A wife may forgive her husband for his betrayal but does not want to be married to him any longer. According to Jacoby (1983), unconditional forgiveness is "simply a state of mind—a condition that may be emotionally or morally meaningful to the one who forgives but has no significance as a social bond, as a medium for restoring a civilized relationship between the injured and the injurer" (p. 347). A second problem is that unconditional forgiveness, if communicated, is easily misunderstood as a statement of moral superiority over the victimizer: "I'm at higher moral ground than you are, and I'll not stoop to your level. So, I'll forgive you." This message communicates arrogance rather than respect (Murphy & Hampton, 1988) and may provoke further harm from the offender. Finally, unconditional forgiveness may be perceived as a sign of weakness, also inviting further harm. Frost (1991, p. 123) provides an example of this danger. Thomas Borge, the then Sandinista Interior Minister, was jailed and tortured by members of the Nicaraguan National Guard. His wife was raped and murdered by them. After the 1979 Sandinista Revolution, Borge paid a visit to a jail where those guardsmen were kept, recognizing two of them. He apparently told them: "Don't you know me? . . . I am Borge whom you tortured—and whose wife your colleagues killed . . . Now you are going to discover the full weight of this Revolution . . . I forgive you. . . . Go on. Out through the door. You are free" (cited in Montville, 1993, p. 120). Borge's unconditional forgiveness backfired on him. Most guardsmen who were released as a result of his generous gesture later banded together to fight against the Sandinista Regime.

Forgiveness can also be an *inter*personal process, a "transaction between two parties" (Augsburger, 1992, p. 283). As such, the victim forgives *in exchange for* genuine remorse and repentance by the offender. Such a transaction symbolically erases the identities of victim and perpetrator, providing an opportunity for each to "rehumanize" the other (Shriver, 2001).

Empirical work suggests that such a transaction is the main way to achieve forgiveness. The transgressor's apology or expression of remorse often promotes forgiveness, while their absence seldom does so (McCullough et al., 1997; Ohbuchi, et al., 1989).

The virtues of forgiveness are repeatedly taught and emphasized in many religions and in most contemporary cultures. Despite this, the reality is that forgiveness is difficult to come by. The movie, *The War of the Roses*, illustrates how hard it is to let go of vengeful desire in interpersonal relations. It is about a couple (the husband played by Michael Douglas, the wife by Kathleen Turner) whose once love-filled marriage gives way to an ever-escalating cycle of revenge and counter-revenge. In the final scene of the movie, their violent struggle results in both of them dangling from a huge chandelier. Soon, the chandelier crashes to the hard floor, and the couple find themselves lying among smashed pieces of glass. Critically injured, the husband musters his last strength and reaches out to touch his wife—as if offering apology and asking for forgiveness. In response, the wife, also critically injured and barely able to move, raises her hand—but only to push away her husband's hand. The desire for vengeance prevails.

If forgiveness is difficult to achieve at the interpersonal level, imagine how hard it is to achieve between groups. In fact, some authors (Hawk, 2001) have questioned whether group forgiveness is even possible. If forgiveness exclusively belongs to the injured, only the injured can forgive—not their friends and relatives.

While acknowledging the challenge of achieving collective forgiveness, Shriver (1995) argues that it can be attained when political leaders on one or both sides voice contrition. Consider an exchange that took place in 1972 between Leonid Brezhnev, then Soviet leader, and Helmut Schmidt, then the leader of West Germany. During an informal meeting at the home of a mutual friend, Brezhnev spoke of the German soldiers' brutality against Russians during the Second World War. Schmidt responded by revealing his own experiences as a young soldier who participated in the invasion of Russia and expressed his deep guilt over what had happened during the invasion. Although Brezhnev did not offer forgiveness to Schmidt, there was a hint of it. Schmidt writes: "Probably it was this exchange of bitter war memories that significantly contributed to the mutual respect which has characterized our relationship between 1972 and up to his death" (cited in Montville, 1993, p. 117).

Justice   Justice is about "making things right, creating equal opportunity, rectifying the wrong, and restitution" (Lederach, 1997, p. 28). "I wait only for justice," says Nyirabeza, the Rwandan Tutsi who survived the 1994 horrific killing spree done by Hutus but who lost ten members of her family. The killer was her former neighbor who used to share food and drink with her. Now, he is back to the village, living freely without being punished for his crime. That only deepens her pain over her murdered children and grandchildren (Gourevitch, 1997).

Reconciliation needs a balance between forgiveness and justice. Without justice, apology and forgiveness are hollow.[19] Without forgiveness, a demand for justice is harsh. Both extremes are likely to derail the reconciliation process.

Shriver (2001) distinguishes two types of justice for victims: retributive justice and restorative justice. The former involves meting out appropriate punishment to the perpetrator. The latter involves reparation, the repair of damage done to the victim. Of these, restorative justice is more likely to lead to reconciliation, because retributive justice often provokes resentment and may start a conflict spiral. In addition to contributing directly to reconciliation, acts of reparation communicate the perpetrator's sincere contrition, thereby promoting forgiveness.[20] Restorative justice also helps to rehumanize both victim and perpetrator in the other party's eyes, reversing one of the most important structural changes that accompanies escalation (Fisher, 2001; Montville, 2001; Shriver, 2001). Hence, restorative justice is a way to reconnect both sides with the cord of humanity.

Peace   Full reconciliation needs a two-pronged approach—one putting to rest the painful past and the other devising a more promising future. The three components of reconciliation discussed so far—truth, forgiveness, and justice—focus on the past. The final component—peace—focuses on the future.

Sustainable reconciliation requires "positive" peace rather than "negative" peace. Negative peace is only the halting of violence. Positive peace means promoting harmony, unity, cooperation, and security among all parties affected by a conflict (Borris & Diehl, 1998; Deutsch, 2000b; Galtung, 1996). Positive peace is encouraged by "the promotion of crosscutting ties; institutionalized procedures for resolving (future) conflicts; and the creation of shared identities and vested interests in advancing (those shared identities)" (Kriesberg, 1998, p. 204).[21]

SUMMARY AND CONCLUSIONS

Problem solving—which is any effort to identify a formula that will satisfy both parties' aspirations—works best if it is a joint undertaking; but it can be done by one of the parties or a third party. Three kinds of agreement can emerge from problem solving: conflict management, settlement, or resolution. Conflict management involves a procedural agreement that

---

[19] Thus Archbishop Desmond Tutu says: "If you steal my pen and say 'I'm sorry' without returning the pen, your apology means nothing" (Shriver, 1995, p. 224).

[20] See Yamamoto (1999) for examples of acts of intergroup reparation.

[21] See Alger (1999) and Lund (2001) for various "tools" needed for building negative and positive peace.

produces de-escalation and/or guards against future escalation. Settlements are substantive agreements that stop the fighting but are often too superficial to endure. Resolution involves solving the basic problems on both sides and, hence, is likely to be long lasting.

Problem solving sometimes leads to a simple compromise—both parties concede to some middle ground along an obvious dimension. But it is often not possible to reach agreement this way, and true conflict resolution usually requires development of an integrative agreement that reconciles the parties' most basic interests. Integrative agreements can take five forms: expanding the pie, nonspecific compensation, logrolling, cost cutting, and bridging.

Cost cutting and bridging require an analysis of one or both parties' underlying interests—the goals, values, and assumptions that have produced the demands they are making. This often requires following interest trees down to their roots. It may also involve locating subtle differences between the parties in the meaning of the issues, for example, concern about substance vs. form or the immediate vs. more distant future. Examining the parties' cause-and-effect beliefs and their narratives and metaphors can also be fruitful.

After checking to be sure that there is really a divergence of interest, good problem solving requires being firm but conciliatory, firm about one's basic interests but also concerned about Other's interests and flexible about the precise agreement reached. A firm but conciliatory stance, if clearly communicated to Other, can encourage Other to turn toward problem solving.

When there are many complex issues, care must be taken to construct an agenda that will maintain optimism and bring together items that can be traded off. Negotiation of complex matters often involves two stages, development of an overall formula followed by discussion of the details associated with each element of the formula. If there is one issue on which many others depend—a "boulder in the road"—it must be settled first as part of the framework. Otherwise it makes sense to start with easier issues, so as to establish momentum. In thinking about the issues, it is important to look for unnecessary linkages between them.

If overt problem–solving efforts are counterproductive, it may be possible for the parties to communicate covertly by means of back-channel contacts, track two diplomacy, sending messages through intermediaries, or exchanges of signals. These must be done to assure compliance to an agreement and avoid the development of new escalatory conflict. More integrative agreements are more likely to last, as are agreements that detail the steps needed for compliance and those that monitor compliance. Procedures for controlling potential spoilers are sometimes needed.

It may also be necessary to reconcile the disputants—to repair their relationship. This is especially the case if severe escalation has taken place. Theorists argue that there are four requirements for reconciliation: truth, forgiveness, justice, and peace. Truth requires setting the record straight with regard to past injustices. Forgiveness, at its best, is part of a transaction between two parties, in which the victim forgives in exchange for genuine remorse and repentance by the perpetrator. Justice comes in many forms, of which restorative justice is most compatible with reconciliation. Peace means establishing the conditions for future harmony, unity, cooperation, and security between the parties.

In this chapter we have demonstrated the importance of problem solving and reconciliation as techniques for resolving conflict. It is not always possible for the parties to a conflict to take these approaches. Escalation may have made them too rigid and suspicious of one another to embark on such a course, or they may have little faith in the integrative potential of their situation. In such circumstances, it is usually necessary to involve third parties in the controversy, a topic to which we now turn.

11

The Intervention of Third Parties

❖

What is a Third Party? ✦ *Third Party Roles and Settings* ✦ Advantages and Disadvantages of Third Party Involvement ✦ How and Why Do Third Parties Enter a Conflict? ✦ *Agreeing to the Entry of a Third Party* ✦ *Imposed Third Parties* ✦ *Third Party Motivation* ✦ Mediation ✦ *Modification of Physical and Social Structure* ✦ *Modification of Issue and Alternative Structure* ✦ *Increasing Disputant Motivation to Reach Agreement* ✦ *The Effectiveness of Mediation* ✦ Other Forms of Third Party Intervention ✦ *Intermediation* ✦ *Arbitration* ✦ *Training* ✦ *Relationship Therapy* ✦ *Changing Social Structures and Systems* ✦ *Peacekeeping, Peace Enforcement, and Peace Building* ✦ *Designing Conflict Management Systems* ✦ Choice among Intervention Methods ✦ Summary and Conclusions

In the course of this book, we have seen that people in the throes of escalation become heavily invested in waging conflict. Positions are far apart, and they tend toward rigidity because of hostility and fear that any conciliatory gesture will be misconstrued as a sign of weakness. Communication may be cut off or so strained that the parties cannot negotiate effectively. Moreover, even in moderately escalated conflicts, the parties may lack the objectivity, trust and/or creativity necessary to work their way out of the pit they have jointly engineered—not because they don't want to, but because they don't know how. Thus, for a variety of reasons, disputants are sometimes either unable or unwilling to move toward agreement of their own accord.

Under these circumstances, third parties often become involved with the aim of moving the conflict toward settlement or resolution.[1] They may enter the situation either at the behest of one or more of the disputants,[2] on their own initiative, or by community or institutional arrangement.

In this chapter, we examine more closely the important role played by third parties.[3] We begin by considering what is meant by a third party and the advantages and disadvantages of third party inclusion in a conflict. Next we examine how and when third parties enter a conflict. Then we take a closer look at the kinds of things that mediators, the most common type of third party, can do to help settle disputes and at the effectiveness of mediation. Next we examine several other types of third party intervention—including those aimed at reconciliation—and the conditions under which each type of intervention is appropriate. We close the chapter with a discussion of guidelines for choosing among the many intervention methods that are now available.

WHAT IS A THIRD PARTY?

Stated most simply, the kind of third party we are talking about is the one that is external to a dispute between two or more people and that tries to help them end their conflict. Intervention by a third party may be classified broadly into two types: contractual and emergent (Kressel & Pruitt, 1989; Pruitt & Carnevale, 1993). Contractual intervention is performed by a conflict management specialist (e.g., a professional mediator or judge) who follows pre-existing formal procedures and has no personal interest in the conflict or its resolution. Emergent intervention—the more common type—is performed by a nonspecialist who typically has an ongoing relationship with the disputants and often has a stake in the outcome of the dispute. The procedures used in emergent mediation tend to be informal, in the sense of not following a preordained schedule (Botes, 2003). A parent's intervention in a quarrel between two siblings, a manager's mediation of a disagreement between two workers, a nation's intervention in a land dispute between two of its neighbors—all are examples of emergent intervention.

---

[1] Third parties do not always seek to end the conflict. Sometimes, they move the conflict in the opposite direction by urging one or both parties to escalate ("You shouldn't take his insults lying down") or to fight on.

[2] There are a variety of other reasons why Party might contact a third party, including seeking advice or sympathy, and hoping the third party will denounce or pressure Other (Averill, 1983; Keating et al., 1994).

[3] Reviews of the theoretical and research literature on third party functions may be found in Bercovitch (1984; 2002a,b), Bercovitch & Rubin (1992), Crocker et al. (1999), Fisher (1997), Goldberg et al. (1985), Kolb (1983, 1994), Kressel & Pruitt (1989), Pruitt & Carnevale (1993), Rubin (1980,1981), Smith (1987), Touval & Zartman (1985), Wall & Lynn (1993), Wall et al. (2001), and Zartman & Rasmussen (1997).

Third Party Roles and Settings

Third parties have probably been in business since the dawn of humanity. Their various roles are well documented in such sources as the Bible, the *Iliad,* and the *Odyssey.*

Some types of third parties are more directive than others, pushing their views more vigorously and decisively onto the disputants. *Judges* and *conventional arbitrators* are at the directive end of this dimension, being empowered to make a binding decision in order to settle a dispute. *Mediators, intermediaries,* and *advisory arbitrators* are toward the nondirective end. They have the right to suggest new approaches and possible agreements, but they leave it up to the disputants to reach agreement. Judges differ from arbitrators in that they operate in courts under an elaborate set of rules and legal precedents, while arbitrators can hear cases anywhere and have more leeway in how they structure hearings. After hearing both sides of a case, conventional arbitrators make binding decisions while advisory arbitrators issue recommended settlements, which the disputants are free to follow or not as they please. The role of a mediator is to aid the parties with their negotiation, and this aid takes different forms depending on the mediator's diagnosis of what is blocking agreement. Intermediaries act like mediators except that they shuttle between the parties rather than talking to them in a joint session.

Other kinds of third parties that will also be discussed in this chapter include *peacekeepers, relationship therapists,* and *conflict management trainers.* The form of third party intervention that has received the most attention—in research, theory, and practice—is mediation. For that reason, mediation will command much of our attention.

Third party intervention can take place in any realm where conflict is found. Thus we see all of these types of interventions at the international level, between factions in civil wars, and in labor-management disputes. Contractual mediation and arbitration were previously found only in labor-management relations; but in recent years, these procedures have moved into many new arenas, under the general name of *alternative dispute resolution* (ADR).[4] Settings where ADR has become common include community conflict (between neighbors, landlords and tenants, former lovers, etc.); disputes within schools; the siting of large projects that impact the environment, such as dams and oil wells; and government rule making (Spector, 1999).

ADR has even ventured into areas that were formerly only settled by judges, including divorce and child custody, small claims, and business contract disputes (Wall & Rude, 1989, 1991). ADR is cheaper and often

---

[4] For discussions of ADR, see Costantino & Merchant (1996), Duffy et al. (1991), Kressel & Pruitt (1989), and Pruitt (2000a).

more successful than earlier procedures, including courtroom adjudication. Another big advantage of using ADR rather than the courts is that there is less recourse to rigid legal principles. As a result, the disputant's interests and needs are more likely to be served (Rubenstein, 2003) and more integrative solutions obtained, increasing the parties' level of satisfaction and reducing conflict between the parties.[5] Because of these advantages, increasing numbers of cases are being diverted into the ADR venue. For example, many contracts now being written include a provision for mediation or arbitration if a dispute arises.

ADVANTAGES AND DISADVANTAGES OF THIRD PARTY INVOLVEMENT

The mere presence of a third party, in either contractual or emergent intervention, is likely to profoundly change the interactions between disputants. Under most circumstances, such change will be beneficial. The destructive path of the escalating conflict is diverted, at least momentarily, because the third party is there. But third party intervention can also prove problematic. Involvement in a conflict where the disputants are making effective progress toward settlement may have the costly effect of breaking the momentum toward agreement. Indeed, research shows that third party intervention, particularly if it is active and forceful, is counterproductive when the disputants are able to move toward settlement by themselves (Hiltrop, 1985, 1989; Lim & Carnevale, 1990; Zubek et al., 1992). For example, a mediator's active intervention in divorce mediation has been found to be harmful when couples are already engaging in constructive conversation (Donohue, 1989).

A more general point is that *third party intervention is not a panacea.* Rather, it is like a strong medicine that may have undesirable side effects, and that should therefore be employed with caution and some reluctance.

---

[5] An example of this is a case that was mediated in a hearing observed by one of the authors (DGP). A not-so-bright, older employee of a tire replacement company had threatened to kill his boss, an offense that could have led to a jail term. The judge who heard the case realized that the incident resulted from a solvable conflict and diverted it to a community mediation center. In the hearing, it was revealed that the boss had fired the worker after many years of employment, on the grounds that he was slowing down in replacing tires. It came out that the employee had no other way to feed and house himself. At this point, the boss agreed to keep him on. It is not altogether clear why he reached this decision, but it may have been because he got tired of the conflict with this employee, because of the adverse publicity this conflict was bringing him, or because the guilt he would feel for putting a long-standing employee out on the street was not worth the small financial gain that would result from firing him. The employee readily agreed to withdraw his threat. The diversion to ADR in this case can be said to have tempered justice with mercy.

The best, most effective third parties become involved only when needed and are so successful at helping the principals find a settlement and develop a good working relationship with each other that their intervention is no longer necessary.

HOW AND WHY DO THIRD PARTIES ENTER A CONFLICT?

Agreeing to the Entry of a Third Party

Third parties sometimes enter a conflict because the disputants invite them. For example, labor and management will often agree to get an arbitrator's ruling on a dispute about disciplining a difficult worker.[6] At other times, third parties take the initiative, but the disputants agree to their participation.

What leads parties to agree to the entry of a third party into their dispute? Four conditions come to mind. One is that the parties are motivated to escape the conflict. In the words of Chapter 9, both are experiencing a stalemate in which their current conflict tactics are not working or are too costly or risky. A second condition, also mentioned in Chapter 9, is that the parties have some optimism about resolving their conflict peacefully—they are not too far apart in their positions, they see each other as not too unreasonable, and/or the third party has a sound reputation. A third condition is that cultural norms encourage the parties to seek out third-party intervention. These norms are more prevalent in collectivist cultures such as China than in individualist cultures such as America (Gire & Carment, 1993; Tinsley, 1998).

A fourth and critical condition is that they despair of solving the conflict on their own. Most individualists have autonomy needs that make them unreceptive to third party intervention under conditions of mild conflict. But when conflict is intense, these autonomy needs may be swamped by an even greater sense of stalemate and a need to escape the conflict, which encourages disputants to work with third parties.

Imposed Third Parties

Third party intervention is not always a consensual matter. Third parties sometimes impose themselves on reluctant disputants. For example, mothers often intervene in disputes between their children. Third parties

---

[6] The job of such an arbitrator will usually be to interpret the contract between these two groups as it applies to this particular case.

are also sometimes imposed by the surrounding community, which appoints people to help settle conflicts between disputants in their midst. In the United States, the law often imposes third parties, and many states have passed mandatory mediation statutes (Winston, 1996). The motivation for imposing third parties is usually self-protection. The conflict is annoying or threatening to the third party or the surrounding community that sends the third party.

Consider the Public Employee Relations Board in the State of New York. This board provides a sequence of procedures for dealing with impasse in negotiations in police and firefighter disputes. A mediator is first sent to help the parties in their search for a mutually acceptable agreement. If mediation is unsuccessful, a fact finder is dispatched to look into the issues and render an advisory judgment.[7] If fact finding does not produce agreement, the controversy must go before an arbitrator, who renders a binding judgment. Protection for the community is clearly the governing motive here. Consider what would happen if the police and firefighters went on strike in your community!

Third parties, or the communities that send them, have to be powerful to impose their services on reluctant disputants.

Third Party Motivation

What motivates third parties to become involved in a conflict? This question is not hard to answer for people who have a job as a third party, for example judges and professional mediators. But what about the emergent type, who step in voluntarily? Why do they get involved in a task that is typically costly in time and annoyance and may even be dangerous?

There are three main answers to this question (Bercovitch, 2002b; Touval & Zartman, 1985; Wall et al., 2001). One is that conflict may endanger their own welfare or that of fellow group members or people they like (which may include one or both disputants). Thus mothers step into fights between their children because they are troubled by the disturbance and fear for their children's safety. A second answer is that cultural norms often exist to encourage third parties—particularly those with high status—to intervene in a dispute. Such norms are particularly strong in collectivist cultures. Thus, managers in Chinese and Korean companies follow the cultural norm that a person with higher status should intervene in disputes among subordinates (Jia, 2002; Tinsley & Brett, 2001). The final answer is that third parties are sometimes trying to pay debts of

---

[7] The fact finder is acting as an advisory arbitrator in this case. The job of other fact finders is to assemble information about a dispute. For more about fact finding (also called "enquiry"), see Jeong (2000).

friendship or to curry favor with one or both disputants or with those elements of the community that want to see the conflict resolved (Touval & Zartman, 1985).

MEDIATION

Mediation is third party assistance with negotiation. Its goal is to help the conflicting parties reach a voluntary agreement.[8] Since agreements are ordinarily reached through yielding and problem solving, mediators must spend a lot of time urging disputants to lower their aspirations and encouraging or engaging in problem solving. Mediators have ways of dealing with most of the obstacles that can block disputants from reaching agreements on their own. In this section, we develop the view that there are three basic kinds of things a mediator can do to intervene effectively: modify the physical and social structure of the dispute, alter the issue structure of the dispute, and motivate the parties to move toward settlement.

Modification of Physical and Social Structure

A mediator who wishes to move the disputants closer to settlement can modify the physical and/or social structure of the conflict in many ways. The possibilities for such modification include manipulating the openness and neutrality of the site in which the talks take place, imposing secrecy on the talks, and structuring contact and communication between the principals.

Mediators who confine themselves to these activities are said to engage in *good offices*. When conflict is mild, good offices are all that is needed.

Site Neutrality   Systematically varying site neutrality is a useful tactic. It is often advantageous for negotiation to take place at a neutral site—one that is not on the home turf of either disputant. This helps the third

---

[8] Some recent authors (Bush & Folger, 1994; Lederach, 1995) view the goal of reaching an agreement as too narrow, arguing that mediators should also aim to "transform" the conflict with which they are dealing. Thus Bush and Folger urge mediators to help the disputants improve their relationship, gaining greater self-understanding and improved conflict management skills, and reaching a fuller understanding and appreciation of each other. Research supports this advice, showing that the long-term success of interpersonal agreements often hinges on the quality of the subsequent relationship between the parties (Pruitt, 1995). However, Phillips (2001) has cautioned that disputants may not always be interested in improving the quality of their relationship and may be unwilling to work with a mediator who pushes such an agenda. She urges instead that mediators adapt their goals to the needs and wishes of the disputants.

party control the access of observers to the negotiations and also prevents either side from gaining a tactical advantage by virtue of site location. Research supports the importance of site neutrality: international mediations that take place in neutral sites have higher success rates than those that take place in the territory of one of the disputants (Bercovitch, 2002a,b). However, when one party is much weaker than the other, the effective third party may do well to offset this power difference by deliberately staging discussions on the home turf of the less powerful party.

Site Openness   An effective mediator may be able to generate movement toward agreement by systematically varying the openness of the site in which discussions between the principals take place. An open site is one that can be readily observed and influenced by a variety of audiences, including constituents and the media. A closed site is characterized by privacy, that is, limited access on the part of external observers to the discussions that take place.

An effective mediator would do well to recommend that all early discussions between the disputants take place under closed-site conditions. This is partly because site openness allows outsider interference and encourages disputant rigidity. In the presence of an observing audience, including the media, disputants are likely to take far more seriously the image of strength or weakness that they project. As a result, premature site openness is apt to encourage the adoption of tough and intransigent bargaining positions, which make it difficult to reach agreement. Closed sites also encourage informal interpersonal interaction, which can help build positive images of the other party and encourage joint problem solving.

Paradoxically, site openness makes sense at a later time, when settlement has been, or is about to be, reached. This is because the presence of external observers is likely to commit the parties to their agreement in a way that does not permit reversal.

During the 1978 Camp David negotiations between Israel and Egypt (described in Chapter 1), U.S. President Carter apparently incorporated into the discussions virtually all aspects of the preceding analysis. Throughout the thirteen days of negotiations, Carter went out of his way to shield Prime Minister Begin of Israel and Egyptian President Sadat from public view. Virtually nothing was made known to the public other than the fact that Begin was watching particular television programs at night while Sadat was enjoying his stay in a particular cabin in the woods. Only at the conclusion of the meetings, when an agreement had been reached in principle, did the parties surface. At the very end of the negotiations, they appeared on the lawn of the White House, where they signed multiple documents in full view of a world of onlookers.

Site Secrecy   If privacy provides some protection from outside interference, secrecy provides even more. Indeed negotiating or mediating in a secret is essential when there are extremists back home, on one or both sides, who will block the talks if they learn about them. Leaders reason that if an agreement is reached, the other side will have made enough concessions to quiet the extremists; and if an agreement is not reached, the leaders can disavow the talks—deny that they took place or claim that they were unauthorized—thus cutting the ground from under suspicious extremists. Secrecy also makes it possible to initiate and continue talks in the face of hostile moves by one or both parties.

An example of secrecy is the 1993 Oslo talks, which led to establishment of the Palestinian Authority. The meetings were held in out-of-the-way spots in Norway under the auspices of Norwegian facilitators. The delegates, from Israel and the PLO headquarters in Tunis, traveled to Norway by circuitous routes so as not to alert news people. Secrecy was essential because super-hawks abounded in Israel and the PLO, who viewed meetings with the other side's representatives as acts of treason. Non-secret negotiations between Israel and non-PLO Palestinians were going on at about the same time in Washington, but the Palestinians broke them off when Israel deported 415 Hamas activists in December 1992. By contrast, the secret Oslo talks "began and continued during this period without incident" (Pruitt, 1997, p. 246).

There is one disadvantage to secrecy. If they produce an actual agreement, the people excluded from them, on one or both sides, may become "spoilers" and undermine that agreement (Kriesberg, 1998). Something like this appears to have happened in Israel after the Oslo talks, when there was a great deal of harsh criticism of the Oslo agreement culminating in the assassination of Israeli Prime Minister Yitzhak Rabin by a right-wing extremist. A solution to this problem, in some cases, is to bring potential spoilers into the negotiation or ratification process after secret exploration of possible agreements.

Contact and Communication   At first blush, it might appear that a mediator should always encourage direct contact between the disputants. What better way for parties to work through a conflict than by openly airing their differences? However, as mentioned in Chapter 9, research does not fully support this advice. Direct contact helps only when hostility is low or the parties are highly motivated to reach agreement, and quite the opposite is likely to happen when conflict is intense or heavily escalated. There, direct contact may lead to angry, insulting interchanges, which make an already bad situation even worse (Rubin, 1980). Under such circumstances, a mediator would be well advised to *prevent* direct contact between the principals until a point is reached where it appears that such contact will improve the situation rather than exacerbate it.

When direct contact is ill advised, a mediator can meet with the two parties separately, shuttling between them and thus controlling their communication with each other. Such meetings, which are called *caucusing*, are a favorite mediator tactic when hostility runs high and disputants will not engage in joint problem solving (Welton et al., 1992). Through caucusing, the mediator can obtain insight into Party's underlying interests and concerns in ways that are not possible when Other is present. Joint problem solving between the mediator and each disputant often occurs in caucus sessions (Welton et al., 1988, 1992). "Disputants tend to be less angry and defensive and hence more flexible and creative in caucus sessions than in joint sessions" (Pruitt, 1995, p. 319).

Mediators can also encourage agreement by improving the parties' images of each other and facilitating their communication (Kriesberg, 1998). Thus at Oslo, the Norwegian third parties arranged for common needs and recreation, with the aim of helping the delegates to become friendly with each other and to appreciate each other as human beings rather than as representatives of a hated outgroup. They explained each party's perspective to the other, making it easier for the parties to generate integrative agreements. At points when the talks were in danger of breaking down, they met privately with each side to explain the other side's behavior and encourage faith in the final product. They also passed messages between the delegations when the talks were not in session (Pruitt, 1997).

Modification of Issue and Alternative Structure

People in the throes of escalating conflict often lose sight of the issues with which they began their struggle. They experience zero-sum thinking and an associated lack of creativity that deprives them of the opportunity to work their way out of the hole they have dug for themselves. An effective mediator can be helpful in this regard, assisting the disputants in the identification of issues and alternatives, reframing the issues in more productive terms, helping them to sequence issues in ways that lead toward agreement, and creating new alternatives that did not occur to the disputants themselves.

Issue Identification, Reframing, and Sequencing   Research indicates that one of the most useful things a mediator can do is help the principals identify the several issues in dispute (Carnevale et al., 1989; Hiltrop, 1989). Because escalating conflict is often characterized by distorted perceptions of the other party and the issues in question, accurate information about what each party is seeking should move the disputants closer to agreement. One useful tactic is to probe each party's interest tree—as shown in Figure 10.1—in search of underlying interests that can be reconciled with those on the other side.

Unfortunately, there are also some dangers in issue identification. If the disputants differ substantially on basic values or hold decidedly uncomplimentary views of one another, the mediator must be very careful *not* to allow certain issues to come to the fore—lest the result be an unproductive explosion. Unearthing issues that are rooted in opposing values tends to harden the disputants' position and foster hostile behavior.

Another important mediator function is to reframe the issues so that they reflect both parties' interests and thus encourage problem solving. Mediators can employ the reframing questions that lead to the five types of integrative solutions mentioned in Chapter 10 (expanding the pie, etc.). As they reframe the issues, mediators should challenge the parties to think up new ideas that are suggested by each new frame.

Mediators can also explore for subtly divergent meanings to the issues such as those shown in Figure 10.2 (substance vs. appearance, etc.). They can break linkages between issues that should be discussed separately, for example, by separating discussion of the substance of an agreement and the means for its implementation. They can control the agenda and hence the order in which issues are discussed, packaging together items that can be traded off in a logrolling agreement (Hopmann, 1996). They can distinguish between broader issues that must be settled first to create an overarching formula and details that can be resolved later once the formula has been agreed upon. They can identify issues that are likely to block agreement and explore whether these issues can be put off to a subsequent negotiation. They can move issues of principle that are likely to block agreement off the table entirely, in favor of more concrete issues that have a chance of settlement.

Sometimes mediators are able to identify areas in which the parties have identical interests allowing them to introduce superordinate goals that help the disputants transcend the existing conflict. As mentioned in Chapter 9, superordinate goals have the capacity to transform a competitive struggle into a cooperative opportunity (Sherif et al., 1961; Sherif & Sherif, 1969). The peoples of the Middle East, for example, although they have been at each other's throats for years and are clearly in the throes of an intense competitive struggle, share several concerns that are potentially superordinate in nature. These include a harsh climate, drought, shared economic concerns, and a number of common enemies. At some point, a skillful mediator may be able to help them bridge at least a portion of their ongoing conflict by getting them to work on common objectives that offer possibilities for mutual cooperation.

Mediators usually have control of the agenda, the sequence in which issues will be discussed. Some guidelines for structuring agendas were presented in Chapter 10.

Creating New Alternatives   It is usually best if the disputants think up their own solutions to the conflict at hand. They are the experts on their own circumstances, and they will usually work harder to implement solutions they have devised than those devised by the mediator. Hence, the mediator should challenge them to do some creative thinking on their own. However, if they are firmly committed to their initial positions or too emotional to think creatively, the mediator may have to develop solutions for them. Mediators have the advantage of standing in the middle and hence tend to be less biased, to engage in less perceptual distortion, and to be more flexible and inventive.

Some mediators prefer to provide a proposal at the outset, using what is called the "single text" (or "one text") procedure. First they interview the disputants so as to grasp their goals and the interests underlying them. Then they present—for critique—a new proposal that bridges both sides' interests. They revise this proposal, on the basis of disputant reactions, and present it again. This cycle continues until agreement has been reached or they have run out of possible changes and must ask the disputants to make a yes or no decision. According to Fisher et al. (1991), U.S. President Carter used this procedure successfully at the Camp David talks between Israel and Egypt.

Mediators sometimes take a proposal generated by one of the parties in caucus and present it *as their own creation.* This may seem strange, but it has two important functions. One is to counteract *reactive devaluation,* the process by which negotiators typically discount the value of any proposal generated by the other side (Ross & Stillinger, 1991). Reactive devaluation occurs because negotiators tend to take a zero-sum perspective, assuming that what is good for the other side must be bad for them. The other function is to help the parties avoid image loss—the challenge to their image of toughness that is likely to result from accepting a proposal made by the other side.

By claiming authorship for proposals, mediators can deflect the responsibility for making concessions from the shoulders of the disputants onto their own shoulders. A concession that each side was unwilling to grant before, lest it be seen as a chink in the armor that invites exploitation in the future, can now be made with the understanding that the mediator has suggested it (Pruitt & Johnson, 1970). Party can now say to Other, and to its constituents, that it has not been forced to concede but has done so in the spirit of being a fair-minded individual who is working with the mediator to move toward a reasonable settlement.

Circumventing Commitments   One function of new alternatives is to circumvent commitments that are blocking progress toward settling the conflict. As we saw in Chapter 8, people in conflict may find themselves committed to a course of action that privately makes no sense but from which they feel unable to escape. A skillful mediator may be able to help them escape from such entrapment by introducing a formula that allows them to circumvent their commitment. There are three ways in which this can be done. One is by dividing a concept into two or more subconcepts that can coexist. For example, when the state of Texas was ready to join the Union, it was committed to retaining a navy—a commitment that was incompatible with statehood. This was circumvented by dividing the concept of navy into two subconcepts, naval personnel and naval vessels. Texas was allowed to have all the naval personnel it wanted, but no ships!

A second way of circumventing a commitment is by relabeling an object or event so that it no longer falls within the scope of the commitment. Instead of demanding that the Israelis meet with the PLO, the United States, in devising the 1991 Madrid Conference, encouraged preliminary discussions by Israel with an entity identified simply as "Palestinians." This allowed the Israelis a face-saving way to meet with spokespersons for a group that had not yet recognized the right of Israel to exist as a sovereign nation.

Finally, a mediator can help the disputants circumvent commitments through an "agreement to disagree." The United States and the People's Republic of China appear to have agreed to disagree about the status of Taiwan, thereby allowing the two nations to develop cooperation on a number of other issues. Agreeing to disagree permits the disputants to circumvent prior commitments to a competitive struggle by compartmentalizing those areas of disagreement in such a way that the remaining areas are available for work and discourse.

Increasing Disputant Motivation to Reach Agreement

A mediator's effectiveness hinges on its ability to move the disputants out of stalemate, in the direction of concession making and problem solving. A mediator can sometimes goad the disputants into such movement, but it is far better if the disputants themselves are motivated to seek a peaceful solution to their conflict. Only then will an agreement be engineered that is apt to last. How can a mediator induce the disputants want to move toward settlement? The answer entails five basic tactics: encouraging perceived stalemate, encouraging optimism, encouraging yielding, defusing emotions, and imposing time limits.

Encouraging Perceived Stalemate   In Chapter 9, we said that in highly escalated conflicts, disputants usually must perceive that they are in a stalemate before they will accept mediation. Party accepts mediation because the contentious tactics it is using are not moving toward victory at acceptable cost or risk. Powerful third parties—those who control Party's outcomes—can sometimes engineer a stalemate, making it impossible or highly costly for Party to continue hostilities. For instance, at the end of the 1973 Middle East War, when Israel had the Egyptian 3rd Army surrounded, U.S. Secretary of State Henry Kissinger forbade Israel to attack that army—making it quite risky for Israel to do so since the United States was Israel's major outside supporter. The result was a stalemate between Israel and Egypt, which led to mediated talks that culminated in a peace treaty. Similarly, parents often intervene in their children's fights, stopping their yelling or hitting and thus propelling them into an effort to find a solution.

Most mediators do not have the kind of power wielded by the U.S. Secretary of State or many parents. Hence, they are reduced to trying to persuade the parties that they are in a stalemate—that they do not hold a winning hand in the conflict and should therefore be ready to make concessions to the other side. Such arguments will be successful if the mediator can muster enough evidence to support its point.

Encouraging Optimism   Optimism is another element of the motivation to begin talks and pursue them vigorously. Mediators are often well situated to encourage optimism by building trust and by promoting the belief that there is common ground between the parties.

For disputants to be motivated to engage in problem solving, they must have some modicum of trust in each other; otherwise they will be too fearful of image loss, position loss, and information loss to proceed. For example, the level of trust that one spouse has for the other has been found to be a strong predictor of joint problem solving (Indvik & Fitzpatrick, 1982).

There are several things mediators can do to enhance Party's trust in Other. They can talk positively about Other in caucus sessions and present evidence of Other's good intentions. They can point out areas of overlapping interests while downplaying areas of disagreement and conflict. They can encourage Other to take unilateral conciliatory initiatives, no matter how small, in an effort to create tangible evidence of a willingness to give something up and to build commitment to a conciliatory process. If and when such concessions are made, they can advise Party to reciprocate with a return concession and thus reward the concession maker.[9]

It is also possible for mediators to minimize the need for trust. They can coordinate concession making so that it occurs simultaneously and is not dependent on faith that Other will reciprocate. They can also offer to guarantee or supervise compliance with the final agreement.

Trust in the mediator can substitute for trust in the adversary up to a point (Coleman, 1997). In addition, when disputants are from very different backgrounds (e.g., teacher vs. student, Chinese vs. Arab), trust in the mediator may be encouraged by *co–mediation*. Co–mediation involves having two mediators whose backgrounds match those of the disputants and who work together as a team. In addition to encouraging trust, co–mediation allows better understanding of the disputants and more effective interpretation of each disputant to the other.

Trust is useful up to a point, but motivation to continue negotiation or mediation ultimately depends on a belief that there is common ground—that agreement is forthcoming. There is nothing more desperate or hopeless than the sense that Party is working to no avail and that its best, most conciliatory efforts have little chance of bearing the fruit of

---

[9] This was the role taken by John Hume in pushing along the Northern Ireland de-escalatory spiral described at the end of Chapter 9.

agreement. A mediator can create the sense that agreement is possible by initiating and sustaining momentum in the negotiations. One way to do so is by engineering a series of small agreements linked to one another in chainlike fashion.

Encouraging Yielding   Mediators often argue, during caucus sessions, that Party's aspirations are too high and should be lowered. They may assert that Other will never accept Party's proposal, and hence that there is no point in continuing to advance it. Or they may point out that the situation is deteriorating and Party must concede before it is too late.

Powerful mediators can go further than this and elicit concessions by the use of threats and promises, rewards and penalties (Touval & Zartman, 1985). Such tactics are called *mediation with muscle* (Straus, 1981).[10] Mediators often have access to the domain of public sentiment and can unleash the "mad dogs of the media" by presenting information about the ongoing discussion in ways that apply pressure for settlement. Thus, a mediator can reward a party for conceding by lavishing public praise, or punish intransigence by judicious public criticism (Wall, 1979). Mediators worth their salt know the power of a timely press release.

Alternatively, powerful mediations can encourage other third parties—for example, allies of one or both disputants—to put pressure on disputants to make concessions. This was done in the British mediation of independence for Zimbabwe (Stedman, 1991). Crocker et al. (1999) have likened the assembly of groups of third parties to "herding cats."

Wealthy mediators can sometimes wrap up a negotiation by offering to compensate one or both parties for making concessions. A good example is the role the United States played as mediator between Egypt and Israel in the Camp David talks. The United States promised continued military and economic assistance in exchange for flexibility in these talks. Increasing the size of the pie in this way transformed a zero-sum game into one in which both sides could do well.

There is, however, a danger in offering or hinting at compensation by the mediator. The infusion of third party resources may encourage a sort of blackmail. In this regard, Harris and Carnevale (1990) have found that when disputants realize that a mediator can compensate them for their concession making, they make fewer concessions and send more contentious messages in order to elicit this compensation. The mediator comes to be seen as wanting agreement so badly that it can be bullied into providing increased assistance.

Defusing Emotions   Escalating struggles typically generate heavy emotions such as anger, resentment, and frustration. Such emotions can make

---

[10] Research shows that mediators in collectivist cultures employ these tactics more heavily than those in individualist cultures because their cultures empower them to do so (Abu-Nimer, 1996).

a positive contribution to negotiation, by motivating the parties to work hard on their problem and helping to clarify which issues are of greatest priority. However, emotions often get in the way of settlement by producing rigid adherence to fixed positions and heavy contentious behavior.

Emotions sometimes reflect deep-seated concerns that cannot be easily brushed away. In such cases, while discouraging heavy emotional *display*, mediators need to help Party to *identify* emotions in itself and in Other and to deal with them sympathetically and realistically rather than in a punitive fashion. Helping Party understand Other's high-running emotions often helps to cool off those emotions (Bies, 1989; Weiner et al., 1987).

At other times, emotions constitute only "hot steam," the venting of which permits the principals to work more effectively toward a settlement of their differences (Russell & Drees, 1989). While disputants are venting their emotions, the mediator can listen carefully and empathically (while being careful not to endorse the disputants' indictments of their adversaries). Such active listening alone can help cool off the parties' high-running emotions. Consider the account of a female student at Bryant High School in Astoria, New York, who participated in the school's mediation program (Davis, 1986):

> I came into a mediation session as a disputant with four girls on the other side. I thought, "Who needs this? What am I doing here?" I just wanted to punch these girls out. I figured that the mediator would tell me what I was going to have to do. But she didn't. Instead she drew me out, listened to me. It felt so good to let it all out: then I wasn't angry anymore. (p. 289)

A final, important way in which a mediator can help the disputants come to grips with their angry feelings is through the timely infusion of humor. Humor can help to create a good mood in the midst of angry displays. In doing so, it may place the disputants in a state of mind that makes them more amenable to reaching agreement. As mentioned in Chapter 3, a good mood fosters genuine concern for Other, which can reduce retaliatory behavior (Baron, 1984,1990; Baron & Ball, 1974), encourage concession making (O'Quin & Aronoff, 1981), and facilitate creative problem solving (Carnevale & Isen, 1986; Hollingshead & Carnevale, 1990). Humor also contributes to a willingness to trust the mediator (Kressel, 1972). Many professional mediators are keenly aware of the effectiveness of humor in defusing a hostile climate and moving toward settlement (Kressel & Pruitt, 1989).

Imposing Deadlines   A third party can sometimes get the principals moving by unilaterally suggesting or imposing deadlines. When faced with such time limits, the disputants are forced to come to grips with the costs that will result if agreement is not reached in time. This makes them more likely to move toward settlement. As an example of the effectiveness of time limits, consider the deadline imposed by President Carter on Begin and Sadat toward the end of the Camp David talks. Carter indicated that he would have to abandon his mediation and turn to other pressing activities in Washington if they were unable to reach agreement by a certain date. Agreement was reached shortly thereafter.

Mediators must be careful not to move too early in a negotiation. Principals need time to reduce their aspirations or to engage in the creative thinking necessary to develop an integrative solution (Carnevale & Lawler, 1986; Yukl et al., 1976). Thus, the best advice for third parties is to wait to impose a deadline until a solution has been devised or is just around the corner. The effect of such a judiciously timed deadline is to inspire the parties to finish the process rather than waiting endlessly for the other side to make the next move. Carter adhered to this principle at Camp David, announcing a deadline only after the negotiators had made considerable progress toward agreement.

The Effectiveness of Mediation

Research on community mediation has found considerable evidence of success (Kressel & Pruitt, 1989). Disputant satisfaction is generally quite high, agreement is commonly reached, and compliance rates are impressive. In one study, mediated settlements of small claims were more likely to be paid than those awarded by judges (McEwen & Maiman, 1989). The authors suggested three reasons for this unexpected finding: mediated settlements required that less money be paid, installment payments were more frequently arranged in mediated settlements, and mediated settlements were voluntary whereas adjudicated settlements were coerced.

Various studies have shown that mediation is more likely to be successful when escalation is moderate rather than high, the parties are motivated to reach agreement, resources are abundant, issues of principle are not involved, the parties are of roughly equal power, and there is an absence of severe internal discord within the parties (Kressel & Pruitt, 1989).[11] None of this is surprising, since these are the same conditions that make unmediated negotiation more successful. The difference between the two procedures is only that mediation—while no "magic bullet"—is more effective under these conditions than unmediated negotiation.

Research has pinpointed certain kinds of mediator behavior and characteristics that are especially likely to produce success. Facilitating communication and interpreting the other party's positions got high marks in two studies (Hiltrop, 1989; Pearson & Thoennes, 1982). Clarifying the issues and proposing an agenda were important in several others (see Kressel & Pruitt, 1989). However, when conflict is intense, directive strategies

---

[11] Internal discord makes it hard for leaders to make the concessions needed to reach agreement. This is because such concessions are easily challenged by political opponents, who hope to increase their support by claiming that the leaders are giving away the store.

that put pressure on the disputants are usually needed in addition to facilitative strategies (Donohue, 1989; Hiltrop, 1989). Research on international mediation (Bercovitch, 2002a,b) has shown that high status mediators and those who share an identity with the disputants are more likely to succeed than low status mediators who are viewed as outsiders. Also international mediators who are invited to intervene by both disputants are more successful than those who are invited by only one party or who intrude themselves into a dispute. These findings may well hold up in domestic mediation as well.

Mediator Bias   A mediator who is seen as fair and impartial is more likely to be successful than one who is not. When disputants believe that a mediator is biased against them, they are likely to be less receptive to mediation (Welton & Pruitt, 1987) and less likely to comply with a mediated agreement (Pruitt et al., 1993). However, impartiality is by no means an absolute requirement for effectiveness—and fortunately so, because impartiality in a third party is virtually impossible to obtain.

As Fisher (1981) points out, people in conflict often expect a third party to be some sort of "eunuch from Mars." Such pure, dispassionate, and disinterested individuals rarely exist. Indeed, in emergent mediation, third parties are almost always closer to one side than the other. This partiality may even help reach agreement if they are closer to the party who must make bigger concessions to reach agreement (Faure, 1989; Kressel, 1972). Since disputants usually have as their main concern the mediator's ability to get them what they want, they may well be receptive to a biased third party who can "deliver the other side" (Touval & Zartman, 1989). Hopmann (1996) gives an example of this.

> U.S. Secretary of State Henry Kissinger was found to be an acceptable mediator between Israel and both Egypt and Syria after the 1973 war in the Middle East, even though he was widely perceived to be very pro-Israeli. But this fact alone made it possible for him to extract concessions from Israel that no one else could have obtained. And he could do so without ever running the risk that Israel would believe that he would sell out their most fundamental interests. (p. 226)

In addition, it is not unusual for mediators to take sides in order to offset a power disparity. Before the disputants can be motivated to work toward settlement, they may need to feel that they are relatively equal in power. This causes both of them to view the situation as a stalemate and encourages them to employ problem-solving tactics, including collaboration with the third party. Knowing this, a mediator who is confronted with a situation of power disparity often sides with the less powerful disputant. By suggesting that discussions take place on the home turf of the weaker party, or even by favoring the interests and positions of that party, a mediator may be able to create more nearly ideal conditions for joint problem solving.

OTHER FORMS OF THIRD PARTY INTERVENTION

Mediation may be the most common kind of third party activity. But there are many other approaches, and the list is growing. Here we will deal with several of the most common kinds of third party activity.

Intermediation

Intermediaries (also called "go-betweens") are third parties who confine themselves to shuttling back and forth between the disputants. They are like mediators in that they help disputants to find their own agreement rather than imposing a judgment. But theirs is a life of virtually perpetual caucusing.[12]

Intermediaries are needed when the parties to a conflict are reluctant or unable to talk with each other or are kept apart by social constraints. Thus, Kissinger acted as an intermediary between Egypt and Israel in the early stages of conflict resolution after the 1973 war, flying back and forth between Cairo and Tel Aviv. Both sides were motivated to resolve their conflict, but they were unwilling to meet each other. So they talked through Kissinger.

Conversations through intermediaries also avoid confrontation between disputants and hence potential friction in their relationship. Gelfand et al. (2001) have found that in cultures that emphasize interpersonal harmony, such as that of Japan, indirect channels are frequently used to resolve conflict.

When conflicting parties have very poor relations with each other, chains of two intermediaries are sometimes found. Thus, the formal negotiations that produced the Northern Ireland Peace Agreement in 1998 were made possible by years of informal communications through a communication chain that stretched from Gerry Adams of Sinn Fein (the political wing of the predominantly Catholic Irish Republican Army in Northern Ireland) through John Hume of the SDLP (a moderate Catholic party in Northern Ireland), through members of the Irish government, and thence to members of the British Government (Pruitt, 2000b). Toward the end of the Vietnam War, a chain went from the United States government through officials in Great Britain, through officials in Eastern Europe, and finally to the government of North Vietnam (Kraslow & Loory, 1968).

Such chains work because the relations between the parties at each point in the chain are stronger than the relations between the parties at

---

[12] One function of intermediaries was mentioned in Chapter 10: assistance with covert problem solving.

either end. They have more of a fellow feeling, know each other better, and are more inclined to help each other. Adams could deal effectively with Hume because they were both Northern Ireland Catholics; Hume could deal effectively with the Irish prime minister because they were both moderate Irish, The Irish prime minister could deal effectively with the British prime minister because they were leaders of countries that were friendly with each other. But Adams could not have dealt effectively with the British Prime Minister, even if it had been politically feasible, because they were on such different wave lengths. Chains of three intermediaries are possible in theory, though the authors have not yet found one.

Not all intermediaries are third parties. In negotiations between organizations (including nations), chains of intermediaries are usually found *within* each of the parties. These chains link up with each other when the negotiators on either side talk with each other. For example, in a typical negotiation between a teachers' union and a school board, the teachers talk with their union president, who talks with the union negotiator, who talks with the school board negotiator, who talks with the president of the school board, who talks with school board members (Pruitt & Carnevale, 1993). All of the parties between the teachers and the school board members are intermediaries, whose job is to reconcile the differences between their counterparts on either side of them. (Thus the job of the school board negotiator is to reconcile the claims and perspectives of the president of the school board with those of the union negotiator.) The first author (Pruitt, 1994) has developed a theory about chains of this kind. One postulate of this theory is that the quality of the agreements reached in negotiations between two organizations depends on the overall quality of the relationships between counterparts along the chain that links these organizations.[13]

Arbitration

In arbitration, the third party must be acceptable to both disputants. A hearing is held, in which the parties present their arguments and the evidence underlying them. The arbitrator then renders a judgment on the issues in the case. In conventional arbitration, this judgment is binding on

---

[13] We distinguish intermediaries from mediators because they can be located within as well as between conflicting parties and because they often communicate with each other in chains. Colosi (1983) and Kriesberg (1991) use the term "quasi-mediators" to refer to intermediaries who are within conflicting parties, such as the negotiators on either side. But there is no need for an extra term, because it can be argued that there is little difference in function between intermediaries who are within conflicting parties and those who operate between parties. Both kinds of intermediaries seek to reconcile the discrepancies between the parties on either side of them in the chain.

the parties; in advisory arbitration, it is optional and they must negotiate about whether to accept it.

Arbitration is most often used when a set of rules already exists and the issue is how to interpret them. Thus, in industrial relations, arbitration is ordinarily used to decide on disputes that arise after a contract has been negotiated; for example, controversies about whether the contract allows firing or suspension of a particular employee. Mediation is much more common when it comes to negotiating the contract itself.

An exception to the latter point can be seen in disputes involving public employees whose services save people's lives and property, such as police and firefighters. Strikes by such employees can be devastating to a community. Hence, if mediation fails to resolve a dispute about a new contract, many states (like New York in the example above) impose conventional arbitration. The advantage of doing so is that the arbitrator's decision is binding, so that no strike can legitimately take place.[14] Furthermore, the anticipation of arbitration—with its implication that control will be wrested from the hands of the disputants—is capable of goading the disputants into working out their own agreements.

Conventional Arbitration   Conventional (binding) arbitration has two advantages over negotiation and mediation. One is that a decision is always made. It is not certain that the parties will abide by an arbitrator's decision, but they usually do so because they have agreed to the arbitration and the result is tantamount to a contract between them. The other advantage is that arbitration usually goes faster—a hearing is held and the arbitrator renders a judgment; no need to wait for the parties to make up their minds. A major disadvantage of arbitration is that it seldom produces an integrative agreement because arbitrators usually don't understand the parties' interests and tend to rely on simple formulas, such as splitting the difference.

Advisory Arbitration   Advisory arbitration might seem like a strange procedure—why hire a third party merely to give an opinion? However, this procedure has its value because it provides a judgment about what is fair and hence a focal point for further discussion. After the arbitrator provides a ruling, the parties must resume their negotiation. Since neither of them is likely to concede beyond the arbitrator's ruling, that ruling will often loom large as the only possible solution, thus precipitating an agreement

---

[14] Strikes by police officers and firefighters are ordinarily illegal. The same is often the case for strikes by professors and teachers in public schools. We will leave it up to the reader to decide whether these professionals provide services of sufficient importance that strikes by them will be devastating to the public welfare.

(Pruitt, 1981). Agreement is particularly likely if the next step after arbitration is a courtroom hearing, because the advisory judgment, if made by a competent authority, is likely to be seen as close to the way a judge will rule. Why endure the trouble and expense of going to trial if one already knows what the judge will decide?[15]

Mediation/Arbitration (Med/Arb)   In this combination of mediation and arbitration, binding arbitration is imposed if the disputants fail to reach agreement through mediation. There are two forms of med/arb: med/arb (same), in which the same person serves as mediator and arbitrator, and med/arb (diff), in which the mediator and the arbitrator are different people. Med/arb has three advantages over mediation alone (Pruitt et al., 1989). One is that the disputants may be motivated to reach agreement during mediation because of fear that they will lose control over the final outcomes if mediation fails and the conflict is settled through arbitration. A second advantage is that a final settlement is always reached. A third advantage, which applies only to med/arb (same), is that it enhances the mediator's status, making the disputants more attentive to that individual's recommendations.

The New York State procedure for dealing with police and firefighter disputes described earlier is a form of med/arb, and med/arb is often used in community mediation. Med/arb is also employed in many non-industrial societies for dealing with controversies that might otherwise polarize and destroy a village, family, or clan. As described by Gulliver (1979) and Merry (1989), certain high-ranking individuals in these societies gain a reputation as third parties. When conflict arises, community members summon one of these individuals, who talks with the disputants alone or in a larger group setting. If the disputants are willing to settle, the result is a mediated agreement. If not, the third party, often working with the rest of the community, imposes a settlement in the interest of community harmony.

There is some evidence that med/arb is more effective than mediation alone (Kochan & Jick, 1978; McGillicuddy et al., 1987). In a field experiment conducted at a community mediation center, McGillicuddy assigned dispute cases to three conditions: mediation, med/arb (same), and med/arb (diff). Med/arb (same) produced the highest level of problem-solving behavior, med/arb (diff) the next highest level, and mediation the least problem solving.

Med/arb also has its share of disadvantages. It may decrease the disputants' satisfaction and commitment, since they may feel they have been

---

[15] In a closely related procedure, the *minitrial*, disputants have a chance to see what might happen if their conflict went to trial.

forced into settlement by the threat of arbitration hanging over their head (Ury et al., 1988). Another disadvantage is that the mediator in med/arb (same), by having the power to impose a settlement, may become so forceful during the mediation session that he or she is, in reality, arbitrating the case from the outset. This denies the disputants the right to settle their own case if they can and thus to find a more integrative solution than the arbitrator is likely to produce.

Training

Training in conflict management and resolution is becoming increasingly popular today. It is sometimes a component of a broader third party effort such as mediation or relationship therapy and sometimes a stand-alone. One can attend a workshop on conflict management, take a master's degree in this field, or even a Ph.D.[16]

Training always involves the development of skills, which can include some or all of the following (Diamond, 1997; Novaco, 1975; Raider et al., 2000):

- *Analyzing conflict.* Identifying the conditions that produce conflict, clarifying own and Other's interests, detecting conflict spirals and structural changes.
- *Communicating effectively.* Active listening, putting oneself in Other's shoes, speaking clearly, providing feedback to the speaker.
- *Negotiating and problem solving.* Creating a collaborative climate, prioritizing and reframing the issues, developing creative solutions, moving to agreement.
- *Coping with anger and other emotions.* Monitoring one's own emotions, thinking one's way through emotional episodes, detecting and coping with Other's emotions.
- *Taking action.* Creating conflict management systems, managing and evaluating programs.

One part of skill development involves conceptual learning of the kind offered in this book. Another part involves hands-on use of this knowledge—analyzing cases and role playing in simulated conflict situations.

Training in how to negotiate is particularly prominent in the United States today. Most management schools offer this training in their MBA

---

[16] The Institute for Conflict Analysis and Resolution (ICAR) at George Mason University has offered a master's degree in this field for many years and has recently moved to a Ph.D. One of the authors (DGP) is a visiting scholar at this institute.

programs, using textbooks such as those by Lewicki et al. (1998, 2000) and Thompson (2001). Raider (1995) reports that almost half of the middle-sized and large U.S. firms offer such training to their employees.

Training in conflict management and resolution is also found in a large number of U.S. high schools and some elementary schools (Raider, 1995; Van Slyck & Stern, 1991). Many of the schools that give such training also offer peer mediation services to their students. Students who have received special training are available to help solve conflicts between other students. Among the pioneers in school-based programs are Johnson and Johnson (1991), who have developed training materials and fielded a successful peer mediation program with elementary school students (Johnson et al., 1995).

Trainers are often called to communities and countries that are experiencing conflict, and they work with the actual participants in the conflict or others who wish to restore peace. Skill training is usually followed by analysis of that particular conflict and efforts to develop solutions to it (Broome, 1997; Fisher, 1997). Indeed Lederach (2000) has argued that skill training is by no means as important as helping participants think about their conflict and develop a strategy for dealing with it that reflects their culture and local situation. Thus a trainer might help participants to identify networks of local people who could reach out to both sides in a conflict to help them resolve their differences. The re-entry problem always looms large in such programs—how to sustain the conflict management effort once the training program is over.

Relationship Therapy

Third party procedures have been developed for repairing the bad relationships, produced by structural changes, that often accompany severe conflict. Relationship repair often takes place before the building of substantive agreements that resolve particular issues. The improved relationship allows effective negotiation or mediation to take place. As mentioned in Chapter 10, it is also important to repair relationships after an agreement has been reached in order to assure long-term success of that agreement. There are techniques for dealing with both interpersonal and intergroup relationships.

Interpersonal Therapy   Marital therapy is the oldest tradition of relationship therapy (Baucom & Epstein, 1990). In earlier times, marital therapists acted like mediators, trying to help husband and wife to develop contracts that bound them to behavior that would improve their relationships. It was discovered that these contracts seldom outlived the period of therapy (Jacobson & Follette, 1985); hence, the field shifted to a training perspective.

Modern marital therapists try to help husband and wife solve their own problems, teaching them joint problem-solving skills and helping them grasp and overcome the persistent patterns of interaction that are creating tension in their relationship (Johnson & Greenberg, 1985). Similar treatments are also available for persistent parent-child conflicts (Van Slyck et al., 1992) and conflicts between co-workers (Walton, 1969).

As a recent development, there are an increasing number of therapies and educational intervention programs designed for promoting forgiveness and reconciliation. For example, one therapeutic approach (Gordon et al., 2000) helps couples forgive their spouse's betrayal. Therapists first assist couples to assess the full impact of the betrayal and then help them to develop ways of dealing with their negative emotions. These therapists also aid couples in exploring various contributors to the betrayal and in developing empathy toward each other. Finally, they help couples evaluate the possibility of reconciliation. Such efforts are compatible with the steps in reconciliation discussed in Chapter 10. Empirical work thus far supports the overall efficacy of these therapeutic and educational interventions (Worthington et al., 2000).

Intergroup Therapy: Interactive Conflict Resolution Workshops   Third party methods have also been developed for repairing faulty intergroup relationships (see Burton, 1969; Cheldelin & Lyons, 2003; Fisher, 1997; Kelman, 1992). They are variously called interactive conflict resolution, consultation, and problem-solving workshops. These methods were originally designed for dealing with international conflict and intranational ethnic conflict, but they are applicable to all kinds of intergroup conflict. They have been used with the following parties among others: Indians and Pakistanis, Greek and Turkish Cypriots, Israelis and Palestinians, Catholics and Protestants in Northern Ireland.

Interactive conflict resolution involves workshops that last several days and are usually run by scholar-practitioners. These are attended by opinion leaders and mid-level decision makers from both sides of a conflict, who Lederach (1997) argues are usually the key to long-term conflict resolution. The main aims of these workshops are to teach the parties about conflict in general, to help them understand the particular conflict they are experiencing, and to encourage them to see conflict as a problem to be solved rather than as a battle to be won. Considerable emphasis is placed on gaining insight into the other side's grievances and the narrative underlying these grievances, and seeing the other side as reasonable people grappling with a problem. The latter helps to counteract the structural changes that usually accompany escalation and that produce negative attitudes and stereotyped perceptions. Secondary aims are to develop ties between the parties and plan projects for addressing their conflict. As with conflict management training, there is a re-entry problem, which is ordinarily discussed toward the end of the workshop. A new development in this field is the continuing workshop, in which the participants come back together again and again (Rouhana & Kelman, 1994).

Evaluation studies have shown that these workshops improve attitudes toward the other side, increase complexity of thinking about the conflict, and facilitate communication with people on the other side (Fisher, 1997). It is hard to assess the impact of these workshops on conflict outcomes. However, it stands to reason that they can contribute to the resolution of severe conflict, by producing a corps of knowledgeable people on each side who can spring into action when a stalemate develops and facilitate productive negotiation (Pruitt, 1997). Indeed, there is reason to believe that this was the effect of the Dartmouth conferences that brought Soviet and American professionals together during much of the Cold War. Some of the veterans of these conferences became advisors to Soviet Premier Mikhail Gorbachev in the late 1980s when the Cold War was winding down (Fisher, 1997).

Changing Social Structures and Systems

Relationship therapy, both interpersonal and intergroup, can be effective as long as the relationship is the problem. However, conflict is often rooted in *social structures or systems*—legal, political, social, economic—that create divergence of interest and distorted relationships (Rubenstein, 1999). Hence, relationship therapy may need to be accompanied by other intervention efforts designed to transform faulty systems.

Dugan (2001) argues that the ultimate source of a conflict may lie at any one of the following three levels: the issues themselves (issues-based conflicts), the relationship between the parties (relational conflicts), and the broader social systems (structural conflicts). It is often the case that issue-based conflicts are embedded, or "nested" as Dugan says, in relational conflicts, which in turn are embedded in structural conflicts. Consider a dispute between two brothers over inheritance from their parents. At first glance, this conflict may seem limited to specific issues—who gets what. But when the dispute is further probed, it may turn out that an ongoing sour relationship between the two brothers also contributes to their conflict. They may fight over a piece of old furniture, not because they really want it, but because they can use this issue to prove a point or vent their anger. Further probing may reveal that the ultimate source of conflict lies in a flawed social system in which the first-born son automatically inherits all the property of his parents. This norm may seem exceedingly unfair from the younger brother's perspective.

Analyzing the nature of embedment found in a conflict is important. Treating a given conflict as simply an issues-based or a relationship-based conflict, when it actually arises from structural injustice, is like "applying a Band-Aid to a cancer" (Dugan, 2001, p. 367). The structural problem must be addressed as well.

Peacekeeping, Peace Enforcement, and Peace Building

Peacekeeping is the use of lightly armed troops to manage conflict in a war zone.[17] Most peacekeeping has been done by the United Nations, drawing on the military forces of its members. Peacekeepers ordinarily enter a region with the consent of the major disputants, remain neutral in all disputes, and keep their use of force to a minimum.

The role of peacekeepers has expanded considerably over the last few decades (Jeong, 2000). Traditional peacekeeping occurred after a cease-fire had been negotiated and involved occupying a buffer zone between opposing forces, supervising troop withdrawals, and enforcing the cease-fire. Such operations have been carried out in Cyprus, the Sinai, and south Lebanon. But since the late 1980s, with the advent of much internal war, the role has grown to include some or all of the following: protection or delivery of humanitarian aid, prisoner release, mine clearance, escorting refugees to the border, restoring facilities (bridges, electricity), election supervision, disarming factions, and maintaining law and order (Diehl et al., 1998). Such services have been provided in Bosnia, Cambodia, and Somalia, where peacekeepers have usually worked closely with local authorities and other aid workers.

As they go out day after day to provide these services, peacekeepers inevitably become involved in negotiation and mediation with members of the local community (Wall et al., 2002; Druckman et al., 1999). For example, about 70 percent of peacekeepers interviewed by Wall reported efforts at mediation in Bosnia, where they had come to monitor the truce between Serbs, Croats, and Muslims. Examples of conflicts mediated include civilians blocking a utility building to protest excess charges (mediated by a lieutenant colonel), Croats firing upon Muslims (mediated by a major), Serbs not allowed to travel though a Muslim town to get to a cemetery (mediated by a sergeant).[18]

Outside armed forces have also become involved in some conflicts as combatants, seeking to protect victims and right wrongs. Examples include the Gulf War, in which United Nations troops (under the leadership of the United States) fought to liberate Kuwait after its invasion by Iraq and the NATO defense of Kosovo against Serbian attack. Such campaigns

---

[17] For literature on peacekeeping, see Fetherston (1994), Gordon & Toase (2001), Olonisakin (2000), Woodhouse & Ramsbotham (2000).
[18] Private communication from James A. Wall.

are usually called *peace enforcement* rather than peacekeeping. The line between peacekeeping and peace enforcement is somewhat hazy, as peacekeepers sometimes become involved in campaigns against local militias, as occurred in Somalia.

Peace building is another major activity in politically unstable and war torn regions.[19] It consists of efforts to reconcile the disputing parties[20] and rebuild the political, administrative, and economic segments of a society in such a way as to diminish the chances of further escalated conflict. Without peace building, peacekeeping and peace enforcement are likely to have little long-term impact. Hence the United Nations usually sends political officers along with peacekeepers, and nongovernmental organizations (NGOs) are often involved. And the United States and its allies became engaged in peace building in Afghanistan at the end of the Afghan War. (The Afghan War can be viewed as a peace enforcement campaign designed to root out Al Qaeda, a terrorist organization with headquarters in that country.)

Among the tasks of peace builders are setting up a government, creating an independent judiciary, reforming business practices, building dispute resolution facilities, providing seed money for new business, and organizing civil society. High on the list of many of these groups is the development of crosscutting institutions that provide a link between disputing factions. Repairing faulty social systems that hurt relationships and produce conflict should also be part of peace building.

Designing Conflict Management Systems

Most of the third party roles described so far involve officiating at hearings and workshops. But third parties are by no means confined to these settings. A newly evolved role for third parties involves designing conflict management systems—for communities, mines, factories, and the like—that are available to help people settle their conflicts effectively and efficiently whenever they arise.

Ury, Brett, and Goldberg (1988), the major innovators in this new field, emphasize the importance of developing procedures that spring into action when conflict arises and allow the parties to reconcile their underlying interests. They argue that an interests-oriented (i.e., a problem-solving) approach to resolving conflict is usually preferable to an approach that is rights-oriented (determining who is right, e.g., courtroom procedures) or

---

[19] For literature on peace building, see Leatherman et al. (1999), Lederach (1997), Reychler (1999), Sampson & Lederach (2000).

[20] Some possible steps for reconciling previously warring parties were discussed in Chapter 10.

power-oriented (determining who is more powerful, e.g., strikes). An interests-oriented approach tends to produce more satisfying, lasting outcomes that contribute to the development of better working relationships. Better relationships, in turn, are likely to prevent the recurrence of the dispute.[21]

Ury et al. (1988) offer the following basic guidelines for designing interests-oriented dispute resolution systems:

- Specify ahead of time which community members will be the negotiators and mediators, what timetable will be followed, and what procedures will be used if negotiation and mediation fail.
- Build in "loop-backs" to negotiation that encourage disputants to move away from issues of who is right or power contests to an interests-oriented approach. For example, a procedure that can help to avoid rights contests is advisory arbitration, in which a third party provides an opinion about how the dispute would probably be settled in court. This information should narrow the differences between disputants regarding the likely outcome of a rights contest, thereby encouraging them to adopt a more interests-oriented approach. One procedure that can help avoid power contests is the *cooling-off period*—a requirement that disputants take no action for a period of time.
- Teach the disputants negotiation skills, motivate them to use low-cost procedures, and provide them with necessary resources such as easy access to third parties who can encourage interests-based negotiation. Teach potential third parties mediation skills.
- Provide low-cost rights-oriented and power-oriented procedures that disputants can fall back on in case an interests-oriented approach fails. There are a variety of such procedures—including med/arb, voting, and courtroom trials—that restrict the use of costly, destructive tactics in power contests.
- Arrange procedures in such a way that disputants start with low-cost procedures and turn to high-cost procedures only if the low-cost procedures fail to resolve disputes.[22]

---

[21] These authors acknowledge that an interests-oriented approach may not be sufficient when (1) the interests are totally opposed, (2) the disputants have very different perceptions of who is right or who is more powerful, or (3) settlement through adjudication is necessary to resolve a matter of public policy. In cases such as these, a dispute resolution system should also contain low-cost procedures that determine who is right and who is more powerful.

[22] Other authors add to this the importance of establishing early warning systems for detecting escalating conflict early enough to head it off. For an insightful treatment of this issue and of the tools available to detect the development of international conflict, see Leatherman et al. (1999).

Costantino and Merchant (1996), who are experts on systems design for organizations, have provided three critiques of the Ury et al. design just presented: (1) Such systems should be developed by the disputants with assistance by outside experts not by the experts themselves. (2) Such systems should stress conflict prevention as well as conflict resolution. By this they mean that organizations should ensure that there is broad participation in decision making so that unpopular policies are eliminated before they produce escalated conflict. This can be accomplished by providing training in communication and consensus-building skills, team building, and holding conferences among employees to develop broadly endorsed directions for the organization. (3) Such systems should get at the root of repetitive types of conflicts rather than simply trying to solve them once they arise. There are often larger systemic issues that need to be resolved. The authors provide a step-by-step procedure for third parties to help organizations develop new conflict management systems.

CHOICE AMONG INTERVENTION METHODS

Given the vast array of procedures just enumerated, how can a third party decide what approach to take? Two answers have been given to this question. One, presented by Sander and Goldberg (1994), concerns what form of third party intervention to recommend for conflicts that arise on the domestic scene. They suggest the following guidelines for a choice between mediation, arbitration, and courtroom adjudication. If the goals of the disputants are to minimize costs, resolve the issue quickly, or maintain/improve their relationship, they should be steered into mediation. If their goals are vindication, to achieve a precedent, or to end the conflict definitely, they should be steered into arbitration or adjudication. Between the latter two procedures, arbitration provides much more privacy and somewhat more speed and economy than adjudication.

Fisher and Keashly (1990) have developed another kind of answer to this question out of their experience with international and internal (ethnopolitical) conflict. This distinguishes four levels of escalation in the relationship between the parties (pp. 236–237):

- Discussion, in which "perceptions are still accurate, commitment to the relationship strong, and belief in possible joint gain predominant."
- Polarization, in which "trust and respect are threatened, and distorted perceptions and simplified stereotypes emerge."
- Segregation, in which "competition and hostility are the basic themes and the conflict is . . . perceived as threatening basic needs."
- Destruction, in which "the primary intent of the parties is to destroy or at least subjugate each other through the use of violence."

The essence of the theory can be summarized in two propositions: (a) higher levels of escalation require more forceful third party procedures; and (b) if a forceful procedure is successful, the level of escalation will decline and the third party can move downward to a less forceful procedure.

More precisely, the theory holds that at the lowest, or discussion, level of escalation the third party should act as a mediator, facilitating communication and being careful to apply no more pressure than is needed to produce agreement. At the polarization level, where the parties' relationship is beginning to fray, the third party needs to start with relationship therapy to reverse this dynamic. [23] Then it may be possible to move into mediation. At the segregation level, the third party needs to employ incentives in order to discourage the parties from hostile actions toward each other. This implies mediation with muscle or arbitration. If the third party is able to control the hostility and achieve a partial settlement in this way, relationship therapy and eventually ordinary mediation may be possible. Finally, at the destruction level, the third party must first employ peacekeeping, which involves the use of weapons to prevent the parties from destroying each other. Once this goal is accomplished, it may be possible to move to the less extreme levels of intervention.

Level of escalation is probably not the only consideration in choosing a form of third party intervention. Even in the most severe of conflicts, if both sides become motivated to escape the conflict, it may be possible for the third party to employ less forceful tactics. Thus, in the 1993 Oslo talks, the Norwegians could confine their services to good offices—the mildest form of mediation—because a severe stalemate had developed in the thinking of PLO and Israeli leaders. The conflict between these parties was severely escalated, but their motivation to solve it was also quite strong.

SUMMARY AND CONCLUSIONS

In this concluding chapter, we have examined various third party roles, the things that a third party can do to intervene in conflict. Third parties are called in or intrude themselves when disputants seem unable to resolve their conflict—negotiation is not working or not taking place. A distinction needs to be made between contractual and emergent intervention. Contractual intervention is done by conflict management specialists, while emergent intervention involves parties from the disputants' milieu that become involved because the conflict threatens their interests or those of the broader community. When given a choice, disputants are more likely to welcome third party involvement when they perceive that they are in a stalemate and are optimistic about the outcome of this involvement.

---

[23] Fisher and Keashly only mention the intergroup variety of relationship therapy, but their theory can easily be extended to the interpersonal level of therapy.

Mediation—third party assistance with negotiation—is the most common type of third party service. It involves three classes of tactics: (1) Structuring physical and social structure, which includes manipulating site neutrality and openness, encouraging secrecy when hostilities are ongoing or there are extremists on one or both sides, and separating the parties if they are unable to talk rationally or their discussion is circling. (2) Modifying issue and alternative structure. This is the most important task of the mediator. It involves identifying the real issues under discussion, reframing them productively, and sequencing them optimally. The parties need to be challenged to think up solutions that satisfy both sets of interests, with the mediator suggesting new ideas if they are unable to do so. (3) Stimulating disputant motivation to reach agreement. Part of this involves encouraging the parties to see that they are in a stalemate and to be optimistic about the outcome of the mediation. There is a tendency for the parties to delay final concessions, waiting for the other party to move. To prevent this, mediators usually set deadlines and urge the parties to concede.

Mediation is often effective where negotiation has failed, but both techniques can be defeated if there have been severe structural changes, issues of principle are involved, one or both parties have little motivation to settle, or there is internal discord within one or both parties. Neutral mediators are usually more effective; but neutrality is not an absolute requirement. One reason for this is that in emergent mediation, there often is no neutral party available. Furthermore, one of the parties may prefer to have a mediator who has ties with the other side, so as to put effective pressure on that side.

An important rule for third party success is to stay out of controversies that are being effectively handled by the disputants. A related principle is to intervene more vigorously the less capable the parties are of settling their controversy.

Third party intervention is a growth industry. Every year, it seems that there are more types of third party roles. We discuss ten distinct methods altogether. Five of them—mediation, intermediation, arbitration, peacekeeping, and peace enforcement—aim to stabilize the current situation by stopping the fighting or producing an agreement. The other five—conflict management training, interpersonal therapy, interactive conflict resolution workshops, peace building, and the design of conflict management systems—have longer term goals. Their goal is to leave positive residues—in the form of new understandings, new skills, or new community structures and institutions—that will help the parties solve their own conflicts and avoid future escalation. That is the direction of growth in this field.

We close the chapter with a discussion of choice among the many types of third party strategies. Theorists have argued that the proper choice depends on the disputants' goals, the level of escalation they have reached, and their level of motivation to escape the conflict.

It is fitting that our book conclude right about here, in the transition from theory to practice, between the sometimes rarefied world of research and the often messy problems that arise when the parties to real and pressing social conflicts require assistance if settlement is to be achieved. But we cannot resist one last story . . .

Anthropologist William Ury likes to tell the apocryphal tale of an old gentleman who, anticipating the day of his death, announced that his estate would be divided among his three sons as follows: one-half to the oldest, one-third to the middle son, and one-ninth to the youngest. The old gentleman eventually died, and his estate consisted of seventeen camels. The three sons attempted to divide up the estate according to their father's wishes but quickly found that they couldn't—at least not without doing violence to the camels. They argued and argued, to no avail.

Around this time, a village elder rode up on her own dusty camel, dismounted, and asked what the problem seemed to be. After listening to the three brothers, she offered to make her own camel available if that might help. And it did. With the addition of an eighteenth camel, the problem suddenly seemed soluble. The oldest son took his nine camels (one-half of eighteen), the middle son pried loose six more (one-third of eighteen), and the youngest son extracted two camels (one-ninth of eighteen). Nine plus six plus two equals seventeen. Almost before the three brothers knew what had happened, the old wise woman climbed back onto her own camel and rode off into the setting desert sun.

We have told this story for two reasons: first, to illustrate, yet again, what creative third parties can do; and second, so that we could convey to you, the reader, our sincere hope that—in the form of a new idea—you have found an eighteenth camel (or two) in the pages of this book.

References

———— ❖ ————

"A just verdict" (2002, January 12). *The Boston Globe*, p. A14.

ABU-NIMER, M. (1996). Conflict resolution approaches: Western and Middle East-ern lessons and possibilities. *American Journal of Economics and Sociology, 55*, 35–52.

ACKERMAN, P., & KRUEGLER, C. (1994). *Strategic nonviolent conflict*. Westport, CT: Praeger.

ADAMS, J. S. (1965). Inequity in social exchange. In L. Berkowitz (Ed.), *Advances in experimental social psychology* (Vol. 2, pp. 267–299). New York: Academic Press.

AGGESTAM, K., & JONSSON, C. (1997). (Un)ending conflict: Challenges in post-war bargaining. *Millennium: Journal of International Studies, 26*, 771–793.

ALGER, C. F. (1961). Non-resolution consequences of the United Nations and their effect on international conflict. *Journal of Conflict Resolution, 5*, 128–145.

ALGER, C. F. (1999). The expanding tool chest for peacebuilders. In H. Jeong (Ed.), *The new agenda for peace research* (pp. 13–42). Brookfield, VT: Ashgate.

ALLRED, K. G. (1999). Anger and retaliation: Toward an understanding of impas-sioned conflict in organizations. In R. J. Bies, R. J. Lewicki, & B. H. Sheppard (Eds.), *Research on negotiations in organizations* (Vol. 7). Greenwich, CT: JAI Press.

ALLRED, K. G. (2000). Anger and retaliation in conflict: The role of attribution. In M. Deutsch & P. T. Coleman (Eds.), *The handbook of conflict resolution: Theory and practice* (pp. 236–255). San Francisco: Jossey-Bass.

AMATO, P. R., & BOOTH, A. (2001). The legacy of parents' marital discord: Conse-quences for children's marital quality. *Journal of Personality and Social Psychol-ogy, 81*, 627–638.

AMERICAN PSYCHIATRIC ASSOCIATION (2000). *Desk reference to the diagnostic criteria from DSM-IV-TR*. Washington: Author.

ANDERSON, E. (1999). *Code of the street: Decency, violence, and the moral life of the inner city*. New York: W. W. Norton.

ANDREWS, B., & BREWIN, C. R. (1990). Attributions of blame for marital violence: A study of antecedents and consequences. *Journal of Marriage and the Family, 52*, 757–767.

ARCHER, D., & GARTNER, R. (1984). *Violence and crime in cross-national perspective*. New Haven, CT: Yale University Press.

ARONSON, E. (2000). *Nobody left to hate: Teaching compassion after Columbine*. New York: W.H. Freeman.

ARONSON, E., & COPE, V. (1968). My enemy's enemy is my friend. *Journal of Personality and Social Psychology, 8,* 8–12.

AUGSBURGER, D. W. (1992). *Conflict mediation across cultures: Pathways and patterns.* Louisville, KY: Westminster/John Knox.

AVERILL, J. R. (1982). *Anger and aggression.* New York: Springer-Verlag.

AVERILL, J. R. (1983). Studies on anger and aggression: Implications for theories of emotion. *American Psychologist, 38,* 1145–1160.

AVRUCH, K. (1998). *Culture and conflict resolution.* Washington D.C.: United States Institute of Peace Press.

AXELROD, R. (1984). *The evolution of cooperation.* New York: Basic Books.

AZAR, E. E. (1990). *The management of protracted social conflict: Theory and cases.* Hampshire, England: Dartmouth.

BACK, K. W. (1951). Influence through social communication. *Journal of Abnormal and Social Psychology, 46,* 9–23.

BANDURA, A. (1990). Selective activation and disengagement of moral control. *Journal of Social Issues, 46,* 27–46.

BARON, R. A. (1978). Aggression-inhibiting influence of sexual humor. *Journal of Personality and Social Psychology, 36,* 189–197.

BARON, R. A. (1984). Reducing organizational conflict: An incompatible response approach. *Journal of Applied Psychology, 69,* 272–279.

BARON, R. A. (1990). Environmentally induced positive affect: Its impact on self-efficacy, task performance, negotiation, and conflict. *Journal of Applied Social Psychology, 20,* 368–384.

BARON, R. A., & BALL, R. L. (1974). The aggression-inhibiting influence of non-hostile humor. *Journal of Experimental Social Psychology, 10,* 23–33.

BARON, R. A., & BELL, P. A. (1977). Sexual arousal and aggression by males: Effects of type of erotic stimuli and prior provocation. *Journal of Personality and Social Psychology, 35,* 79–87.

BARON, R. A., & KEPNER, C. R. (1970). Model's behavior and attraction toward the model as determinants of adult aggressive behavior. *Journal of Personality and Social Psychology, 14,* 335–344.

BAR-TAL, D. (2000). *Shared beliefs in a society : Social psychological analysis.* Thousand Oaks, CA: Sage.

BATSON, C. D. (1998). Altruism and prosocial behavior. In D. T. Gilbert, S. T. Fiske, & G. Lindzey (Eds.), *The handbook of social psychology* (4th ed., Vol. 2, pp. 282–316). Boston: McGraw-Hill.

BAUCOM, D. H., & EPSTEIN, N. (1990). *Cognitive-behavioral marital therapy.* New York: Brunner/Mazel.

BAUMEISTER, R. F., BRATSLAVSKY, E., MURAVEN, M., & TICE, D. M. (1999). Ego depletion: Is the active self a limited resource? In R. F. Baumeister (Ed.), *The self in social psychology* (pp. 317–336). Philadelphia, PA: Psychology Press.

BAUMEISTER, R. F., SMART, L., & BODEN, J. M. (1996). Relation of threatened egotism to violence and aggression: The dark side of high self-esteem. *Psychological Review, 103,* 5–33.

BAUMEISTER, R. F., STILLWELL, A., WOTMAN, S. R. (1990). Victim and perpetrator accounts of interpersonal conflict: Autobiographical narratives about anger. *Journal of Personality and Social Psychology, 59,* 994–1005.

BAZERMAN, M. H., & NEALE, M. A. (1992). *Negotiating rationally.* New York: Free Press.

BELL, P. A., & BARON, R. A. (1976). Aggression and heat: The mediating role of negative affect. *Journal of Applied Social Psychology, 6*, 18–30.

BEM, D. J. (1972). Self-perception theory. In L. Berkowitz (Ed.), *Advances in experimental social psychology* (Vol. 6, pp. 1–62). New York: Academic Press.

BENTON, A. A., & DRUCKMAN, D. (1974). Constituent's bargaining orientation and intergroup negotiations. *Journal of Applied Social Psychology, 4*, 141–150.

BEN-YOAV, O., & PRUITT, D. G. (1984a). Resistance to yielding and the expectation of cooperative future interaction in negotiation. *Journal of Experimental Social Psychology, 20*, 323–353.

BEN-YOAV, O., & PRUITT, D. G. (1984b). Accountability to constituents: A two-edged sword. *Organizational Behavior and Human Performance, 34*, 282–295.

BEN-ZE'EV, A. (2000). *The subtlety of emotions.* Cambridge, MA: MIT Press.

BERCOVITCH, J. (1984). *Social conflicts and third parties: Strategies of conflict resolution.* Boulder, CO: Westview.

BERCOVITCH, J. (2002a). Putting mediation in context. In J. Bercovitch (Ed.), *Studies in international mediation: Essays in honor of Jeffrey Z. Rubin.* London & New York: Palgrave/Macmillan.

BERCOVITCH, J. (2002b). *Theory and practice of international mediation.* Unpublished manuscript.

BERCOVITCH, J., & RUBIN, J. Z. (1992). *Mediation in international relations: Multiple approaches to conflict management.* London: Macmillan.

BERKOWITZ, L. (1993). *Aggression: Its causes, consequences, and control.* New York: McGraw-Hill.

BERKOWITZ, L., COCHRAN, S. T., & EMBREE, M. C. (1981). Physical pain and the goal of aversively stimulated aggression. *Journal of Personality and Social Psychology, 40*, 687–700.

BERSCHEID, E. (1983). Emotion. In H. H. Kelley, E. Berscheid, A. Christensen, et al. (Eds.), *Close relationships* (pp. 110–168). New York: Freeman.

BETTENCOURT, B. A., BREWER, M. B., CROAK, M. R., & MILLER, N. (1992). Cooperation and the reduction of intergroup bias: The role of reward structure and social orientation. *Journal of Experimental Social Psychology, 28*, 301–319.

BIES, R. J. (1989). Managing conflict before it happens: The role of accounts. In M. A. Rahim (Ed.), *Managing conflict: An interdisciplinary approach* (pp. 83–91). New York: Praeger.

BIES, R. J., TRIPP, T. M., & KRAMER, R. M. (1997). At the breaking point: Cognitive and social dynamics of revenge in organizations. In R. Giacalone & J. Greenberg (Eds.), *Antisocial behavior in organizations* (pp. 18–36). Thousand Oaks, CA: Sage.

BIXENSTINE, V. E., & GAEBELEIN, J. W. (1971). Strategies of "real" opponents in eliciting cooperative choice in a prisoner's dilemma game. *Journal of Conflict Resolution, 15*, 157–166.

BLACKMAN, C. (1997). *Negotiating China: Case studies and strategies.* St Leonards, Australia: Allen & Unwin.

BLAKE, R. R., & MOUTON, J. S. (1962). Overevaluation of own group's product in intergroup competition. *Journal of Abnormal and Social Psychology, 64*, 237–238.

BLAKE, R. R., & MOUTON, J. S. (1964). *The managerial grid.* Houston, TX: Gulf.

BLECHMAN, F., CROCKER, J., DOCHERTY, J., & GARAN, S. (2000). *Finding meaning in a complex of environmental policy dialogue: Research into worldviews on the Northern Forest Lands Council dialogue: 1990–94* (Working Paper No. 14). Fairfax, VA: Institute for Conflict Analysis and Resolution, George Mason University.

BLOOMFIELD, L. P. (1997). Why wars end: A research note. *Millennium: Journal of International Studies, 26,* 709–726.

BLUMENTHAL, M. D., KAHN, R. L., ANDREWS, F. M., & HEAD, K. B. (1972). *Justifying violence: Attitudes of American men.* Ann Arbor, MI: Institute for Social Research.

BOND, M. H., & WANG, S. H. (1983). China: Aggressive behavior and the problem of maintaining order and harmony. In A. P. Goldstein & M. H. Segall (Eds.), *Aggression in global perspective* (pp. 58–74). New York: Pergamon.

BONOMA, T. V., & TEDESCHI, J. T. (1973). Some effects of source behavior on target's compliance to threats. *Behavioral Science, 18,* 34–41.

BORRIS, E., & DIEHL, P. E. (1998). Forgiveness, reconciliation, and the contribution of international peacekeeping. In H. J. Langholtz (Ed.), *The psychology of peacekeeping* (pp. 207–222). Westport, CT: Praeger.

BOTES, J. (2003). Informal roles. In S. Cheldelin, D. Druckman, & L. Fast (Eds.), *Conflict: From analysis to resolution.* London: Continuum.

BOWERS, J. W., & OCHS, D. J. (1971). *The rhetoric of agitation and control.* Reading, MA: Addison-Wesley.

BOXALL, B. (2002, March 29). Violence leaves Merced County at a loss. *The Los Angeles Times.* Retrieved March 29, 2002, from http://www.latimes.com.

BRADBURY, T. N., & FINCHAM, F. D. (1990). Attributions in marriage: Review and critique. *Psychological Bulletin, 107,* 3–33.

BRADBURY, T. N., & FINCHAM, F. D. (1992). Attributions and behavior in marital interaction. *Journal of Personality and Social Psychology, 63,* 613–628.

BRAITHWAITE, J. (1989). *Crime, shame and reintegration.* Cambridge, England: Cambridge University Press.

BREEN, M. (1998). *The Koreans: Who they are, what they want, where their future lies.* New York: St. Martin's Press.

BREHM, S. S. (1992). *Intimate relationships* (2nd ed.). New York: McGraw-Hill.

BREHM, S. S., & KASSIN, S. M. (1993). *Social psychology* (2nd ed.). Boston: Houghton Mifflin.

BRESLIN, J. W., & RUBIN, J. Z. (Eds.). (1991). *Negotiation theory and practice.* Boston: Program on Negotiation Books at Harvard Law School.

BRETT, J. M. (2001). *Negotiating globally: How to negotiate deals, resolve disputes, and make decisions across cultural boundaries.* San Francisco: Jossey-Bass.

BREWER, M. B. (1979). Ingroup bias in the minimal intergroup situation: A cognitive motivational analysis. *Psychological Bulletin, 86,* 307–324.

BREWER, M. B., & BROWN , R. J. (1998). Intergroup relations. In D. T. Gilbert, S. T. Fiske, & G. Lindzey (Eds.), *The handbook of social psychology* (4th ed., Vol. 2, pp. 554–594). Boston: McGraw-Hill.

BREWER, M. B., & KRAMER, R. M. (1986). Choice behavior in social dilemmas: Effects of social identity, group size, and decision framing. *Journal of Personality and Social Psychology, 50,* 543–549.

BROCKNER, J., & RUBIN, J. Z. (1985). *The social psychology of conflict escalation and entrapment.* New York: Springer-Verlag.

BROCKNER, J., RUBIN, J. Z., & LANG, E. (1981). Face-saving and entrapment. *Journal of Experimental Social Psychology, 17,* 68–79.

BROCKNER, J., RUBIN, J. Z., FINE, J., HAMILTON, T. P., THOMAS, B., & TURETSKY, B. (1982). Factors affecting entrapment in escalating conflicts: The importance of timing. *Journal of Research in Personality, 16,* 247–266.

BROCKNER, J., SHAW, M. C., & RUBIN, J. Z. (1979). Factors affecting withdrawal from an escalating conflict: Quitting before it's too late. *Journal of Experimental Social Psychology, 15,* 492–503.

BRONFENBRENNER, U. (1961). The mirror-image in Soviet-American relations. *Journal of Social Issues, 17,* 45–56.

BROOME, B. J. (1997). Designing a collective approach to peace: Interactive design and problem-solving workshops with Greek-Cypriot and Turkish-Cypriot communities in Cyprus. *International Negotiation, 2,* 381–407.

BROWN, B. R. (1968). The effects of need to maintain face on interpersonal bargaining. *Journal of Experimental Social Psychology, 4,* 107–122.

BRYANT, J., & ZILLMANN, D. (1979). Effect of intensification of annoyance through unrelated residual excitation on substantially delayed hostile behavior. *Journal of Experimental Social Psychology, 15,* 470–480.

BULMAN, R. J., & WORTMAN, C. B. (1977). Attributions of blame and coping in the "real world": Severe accident victims react to their lot. *Journal of Personality and Social Psychology, 35,* 351–363.

BURTON, J. W. (1962). *Peace theory.* New York: Knopf.

BURTON, J. W. (1969). *Conflict and communication.* New York: Macmillan.

BURTON, J. W. (1987). *Resolving deep-rooted conflict: A handbook.* Lanham, MD: University Press of America.

BURTON, J. W. (Ed.). (1990). *Conflict: Human needs theory.* London: Macmillan.

BUSH, R. A. B., & FOLGER, J. P. (1994). *The promise of mediation: Responding to conflict through empowerment and recognition.* San Francisco: Jossey-Bass.

BUSHMAN, B. J. (2002). Does venting anger feed or extinguish the flame? Catharsis, rumination, distraction, anger and aggressive responding. *Personality and Social Psychology Bulletin, 28,* 724–731.

BUSS, D. M. (1999). *Evolutionary psychology: The new science of the mind.* Boston: Allyn & Bacon.

BYRNE, D. (1971). *The attraction paradigm.* New York: Academic Press.

CAMPBELL, D. T. (1965). Ethnocentric and other altruistic motives. In D. Levine (Ed.), *Nebraska Symposium on Motivation* (pp. 283–311). Lincoln, NE: University of Nebraska Press.

CARLSON, M., & MILLER, N. (1987). Explanation of the relation between negative mood and helping. *Psychological Bulletin, 102,* 92–108.

CARNEVALE, P. J., & ISEN, A. M. (1986). The influence of positive affect and visual access on the discovery of integrative solutions in bilateral negotiation. *Organizational Behavior and Human Decision Processes, 37,* 1–13.

CARNEVALE, P. J., & LAWLER, E. J. (1986). Time pressure and the development of integrative agreements in bilateral negotiation. *Journal of Conflict Resolution, 30,* 636–659.

CARNEVALE, P. J., LIM, R. G., & MCLAUGHLIN, M. E. (1989). Contingent mediator behavior and its effectiveness. In K.. Kressel, D. G. Pruitt, & Associates, *Mediation research* (pp. 213–240). San Francisco: Jossey-Bass.

CARNEVALE, P. J., & PRUITT, D. G. (1992). Negotiation and mediation. *Annual Review of Psychology, 43,* 531–582.

CARNEY, A. (1994). Lack of care in Rwanda. *British Journal of Psychiatry, 165,* 556.

CARVER, C. S., & GLASS, D. C. (1978). Coronary-prone behavior pattern and interpersonal aggression. *Journal of Personality and Social Psychology, 36,* 361–366.

CHAIKEN, S. L., GRUENFELD, D. H., & JUDD, C. M. (2000). Persuasion in negotiations and conflict situations. In M. Deutsch & P. T. Coleman (Eds.), *The handbook of conflict resolution: Theory and practice* (pp. 144–165). San Francisco: Jossey-Bass.

CHATAWAY, C. J. (1998). Track II diplomacy: From a track I perspective. *Negotiation Journal, 14,* 269–287.

CHELDELIN, S., & LYONS, T. (2003). Facilitation and consultation. In S. Cheldelin, D. Druckman, & L. Fast (Eds.), *Conflict: From analysis to resolution.* London: Continuum.

CHEN, G. (2002). The impact of harmony on Chinese conflict management. In G. Chen, & R. Ma (Eds.), *Chinese conflict management and resolution* (pp. 3–17). Westport, CT: Ablex.

CHRISTIAN-HERMAN, J. L., O'LEARY, K. D., & AVERY-LEAF, S. (2001). The impact of severe negative events in marriage on depression. *Journal of Social and Clinical Psychology, 20,* 24–40.

CIALDINI, R. B. (2001). *Influence: Science and practice.* Needham Heights, MA: Allyn & Bacon.

CIALDINI, R. B., & KENRICK, D. T. (1976). Altruism as hedonism: A social development perspective on the relationship of negative mood state and helping. *Journal of Personality and Social Psychology, 34,* 907–914.

CLARK, M. S., & MILLS, J. (1979). Interpersonal attraction in exchange and communal relationships. *Journal of Personality and Social Psychology, 37,* 12–24.

COBB, S. (2003). Fostering coexistence within identity-based conflicts: Towards a narrative approach. In A. Chayes & M. L. Minow (Eds.), *Imagine coexistence.* San Francisco: Jossey-Bass.

COHEN, A. K. (1955). *Delinquent boys: The culture of the gang.* Glencoe, IL: Free Press.

COHEN, R. (1991). *Negotiating across cultures: Communication obstacles in international diplomacy.* Washington, DC: United States Institute of Peace Press.

COLEMAN, J. S. (1957). *Community conflict.* New York: Free Press.

COLEMAN, P. T. (1997). Redefining ripeness: A social-psychological perspective. *Journal of Peace Psychology, 3,* 81–103.

COLEMAN, P. T. (2000). Intractable conflict. In M. Deutsch & P. T. Coleman (Eds.), *The handbook of conflict resolution: Theory and practice* (pp. 428–450). San Francisco: Jossey-Bass.

COLOSI, T. (1983). Negotiation in the public and private sectors: A core model. *American Behavioral Scientist, 27,* 229–253.

COOPER, J. (2001). Motivating cognitive change: The self-standards model of dissonance. In J. P. Forgas, K. D. Williams, & L. Wheeler (Eds.), *The social mind: Cognitive and motivational aspects of interpersonal behavior* (pp. 72–91). New York: Cambridge University Press.

COOPER, J., & FAZIO, R. H. (1979). The formation and persistence of attitudes that support intergroup conflict. In W. G. Austin & S. Worchel (Eds.), *The Social Psychology of Intergroup Relations* (pp. 149–159). Monterey, CA: Brooks/Cole.

COSER, L. A. (1956). *The functions of social conflict.* New York: Free Press.

COSTANTINO, C. A., & MERCHANT, C. S. (1996). *Designing conflict management systems: A guide to creating productive and healthy organizations.* San Francisco: Jossey-Bass.

CROCKER, C. A., HAMPSON, F. O., & AALL, P. (Eds.). (1999). *Herding cats: Multiparty mediation in a complex world.* Washington D.C.: United States Institute of Peace.

CROCKER, J., THOMPSON, L., MCGRAW, K. M., & INGERMAN, C. (1987). Downward comparison, prejudice, and evaluations of others: Effects of self-esteem and threat. *Journal of Personality and Social Psychology, 52,* 907–916.

DA GLORIA, J., & DE RIDDER, R. (1979). Sex differences in aggression: Are current notions misleading? *European Journal of Social Psychology, 9,* 49–66.

DAHRENDORF, R. (1959). *Class and class conflict in industrial society.* Stanford, CA: Stanford University Press.

DALY, M., & WILSON, M. (1998). The evolutionary social psychology of family violence. In C. Crawford & D. L. Krebs (Eds.), *Handbook of evolutionary psychology: Ideas, issues, and applications.* Mahwah, NJ: Erlbaum.

DANIEL, M. (2002, January 4). Hockey death trial opens with two views. *The Boston Globe,* p. B1.

DAVIES, J. C. (1962). Toward a theory of revolution. *Sociological Review, 27,* 5–19.

DAVIS, A. M. (1986). Dispute resolution at an early age. *Negotiation Journal, 2,* 287–297.

DE DREU, C. K. W., NAUTA, A., & VAN DE VLIERT, E. (1995). Self-serving evaluation of conflict behavior and escalation of the dispute. *Journal of Applied Social Psychology, 25,* 2049–2066.

DE DREU, C. K. W., WEINGART, L. R., & KWON, S. (2000). Influence of social motives on integrative negotiation: A meta-analytic review and test of two theories. *Journal of Personality and Social Psychology, 78,* 889–905.

DEDMAN, B. (2000, October 16). Shooters usually tell friends what they are planning. *The Chicago Sun-times.* Retrieved March 12, 2002, from http://www.suntimes.com/shoot/evan16.htm.

DENGERINK, H. A. (1976). Personality variables as mediators of attack-instigated aggression. In R. G. Geen & E. C. O'Neal (Eds.), *Perspectives on aggression* (pp. 61–98). New York: Academic Press.

D'ESTREE, T. P. (2003). Dynamics. In S. Cheldelin, D. Druckman, & L. Fast (Eds.), *Conflict: From analysis to resolution.* London: Continuum.

DEUTSCH, M. (1958). Trust and suspicion. *Journal of Conflict Resolution, 2,* 265–279.

DEUTSCH, M. (1973). *The resolution of conflict: Constructive and destructive processes.* New Haven, CT: Yale University Press.

DEUTSCH, M. (1991). Subjective features of conflict resolution: Psychological, social, and cultural influences. In R. Vayrynen (Ed.), *New directions in conflict theory* (pp. 26–56). London: Sage.

DEUTSCH, M. (2000a). Cooperation and competition. In M. Deutsch & P. T. Coleman (Eds.), *The handbook of conflict resolution: Theory and practice* (pp. 21–40). San Francisco: Jossey-Bass.

DEUTSCH, M. (2000b). Justice and conflict. In M. Deutsch & P. T. Coleman (Eds.), *The handbook of conflict resolution: Theory and practice* (pp. 41–64). San Francisco: Jossey-Bass.

DEUTSCH, M., & COLLINS, M. (1951). *Interracial housing: A psychological evaluation of a social experiment.* Minneapolis: University of Minnesota Press.

DEUTSCH, M., & KRAUSS, R. M. (1960). The effect of threat upon interpersonal bargaining. *Journal of Abnormal and Social Psychology, 61,* 181–189.

DIAMOND, L. (1997). Training in conflict-habituated systems: Lessons from Cyprus. *International Negotiation, 2,* 353–380.

DIAMOND, L., & MCDONALD, J. W. (1996). *Multi-track diplomacy: A systems approach to peace* (3rd ed.). Kumarian Press.

DIEHL, P. F., DRUCKMAN, D., & WALL, J. A. (1998). International peacekeeping and conflict resolution: A taxonomic analysis with implications. *Journal of Conflict Resolution, 42*, 33–55.

DION, K. L. (1973). Cohesiveness as a determinant of ingroup-outgroup bias. *Journal of Personality and Social Psychology, 28*, 163–171.

DION, K. L. (1979). Intergroup conflict and intragroup cohesiveness. In W. G. Austin & S. Worchel (Eds.), *The social psychology of intergroup relations* (pp. 211–224). Belmont, CA: Wadsworth.

DONOHUE, W. A. (1989). Communicative competence in mediators. In K. Kressel, D. G. Pruitt, & Associates (Eds.), *Mediation research* (pp. 322–343). San Francisco: Jossey-Bass.

DOUGLAS, A. (1962). *Industrial peacemaking*. New York: Columbia University Press.

DRIGOTAS, S. M., & RUSBULT, C. E. (1992). Shall I stay or should I go? A dependence model of breakups. *Journal of Personality and Social Psychology, 62*, 62–87.

DROLET, A. L., & MORRIS, M. W. (2000). Rapport in conflict resolution: Accounting for how face-to-face contact fosters mutual cooperation in mixed-motive conflicts. *Journal of Experimental Social Psychology, 36*, 26–50.

DRUCKMAN, D. (1994). Determinants of compromising behavior in negotiation: A metaanalysis. *Journal of Conflict Resolution, 38*, 507–556.

DRUCKMAN, D. (2003). Situations. In S. Cheldelin, D. Druckman, & L. Fast (Eds.), *Conflict: From analysis to resolution*. London: Continuum.

DRUCKMAN, D., BROOME, B. J., & KORPER, S. H. (1988). Value differences and conflict resolution: Facilitation or delinking? *Journal of Conflict Resolution, 32*, 489–510.

DRUCKMAN, D., & GREEN, J. (1995). Playing two games: Internal negotiations in the Philippines. In I. W. Zartman (Ed.), *Elusive peace: Negotiating an end to civil wars* (pp. 299–331). Washington D.C.: The Brookings Institution.

DRUCKMAN, D., WALL, J. A., & DIEHL, D. F. (1999). Conflict resolution roles in international peacekeeping missions. In H-W. Jeong (Ed.), *The new agenda for peace research*. Aldershot, England & Brookfield, VT: Ashgate.

DUFFY, K. G., GROSCH, J. W., & OLCZAK, P. V. (Eds.). (1991). *Community mediation: A handbook for practitioners and researchers*. New York: Guilford.

DUGAN, M. A. (2001). Imaging the future: A tool for conflict resolution. In L. Reychler & T. Paffenholz (Eds.), *Peacebuilding: A field guide* (pp. 365–372). Boulder, CO: Lynne Rienner.

DUTTON, D. G. (1999). Traumatic origins of intimate rage. *Aggression and Violent Behavior, 4*, 431–447.

DYCK, R. J., & RULE, B. G. (1978). Effect on retaliation of causal attributions concerning attack. *Journal of Personality and Social Psychology, 36*, 521–529.

EAGLY, A. H., & STEFFEN, V. J. (1986). Gender and aggressive behavior: A meta-analytic review of the social psychological literature. *Psychological Bulletin, 100*, 309–330.

EASTMAN, K. K. (1994). In the eyes of the beholder: An attributional approach to ingratiation and organizational citizenship behavior. *Academy of Management Journal, 37*, 1379–1391.

ELSTER, J. (1990). Norms of revenge. *Ethics, 100*, 862–885.

ELSTER, J. (1999). *Alchemies of the mind: Rationality and the emotions*. Cambridge, England: Cambridge University Press.

ENRIGHT, R. D., & HUMAN DEVELOPMENT STUDY GROUP (1996). Counseling within the forgiveness triad: On forgiving, receiving forgiveness, and self-forgiveness. *Counseling and Values, 40,* 107–122.

ERIKSON, E. (1969). *Gandhi's truth.* New York: Norton.

ERWIN, P. (2001). *Attitudes and persuasion.* Hove, England: Psychology Press.

ETZIONI, A. (2001). *The monochrome society.* Princeton, NJ: Princeton University Press.

EVANS, C. (2001). *Great feuds in history: Ten of the liveliest disputes ever.* New York: John Wiley & Sons.

FALBO, T. (1977). Multidimensional scaling of power strategies. *Journal of Personality and Social Psychology, 35,* 537–547.

FALBO, T., & PEPLAU, L. A. (1980). Power strategies in intimate relationships. *Journal of Personality and Social Psychology, 38,* 618–628.

FALEY, T. E., & TEDESCHI, J. T. (1971). Status and reactions to threats. *Journal of Personality and Social Psychology, 17,* 192–199.

FANG, T. (1999). *Chinese business negotiating style.* Thousand Oaks, CA: Sage.

FAUBER, R. L., FOREHAND, R., THOMAS, A. M., & WIERSON, M. (1990). A mediational model of the impact of marital conflict on adolescent adjustment in intact and divorced families: The role of disrupted parenting. *Child Development, 61,* 1112–1123.

FAURE, G. O. (1987). Les théories de la négociations. In P. Messerlin & F. Vellas (Eds.), *Conflits et négociations dans le commerce international: l'Uruguay Round.* Paris: Economica.

FAURE, G. O. (1989). The mediator as a third negotiator. In F. Mautner-Markhof (Ed.), *Processes of international negotiations.* Boulder, CO: Westview Press.

FAURE, G. O., & RUBIN, J. Z. (1993). *Culture and negotiation.* Newbury Park, CA: Sage.

FELLMAN, G. (1998). *Rambo and the Dalai Lama: The compulsion to win and its threat to human survival.* Albany, NY: State University of New York Press.

FELSON, R. B. (1982). Impression management and the escalation of aggression and violence. *Social Psychology Quarterly, 45,* 245–254.

FERGUSON, T. J., & RULE, B. G. (1983). An attributional perspective on anger and aggression. In R. G. Geen & E. Donnerstein (Eds.), *Aggression: Theoretical and empirical reviews* (Vol. 1, pp. 41–74). New York: Academic Press.

FESTINGER, L. (1950). Informal social communication. *Psychological Review, 57,* 271–292.

FESTINGER, L. (1957). *A theory of cognitive dissonance.* Stanford, CA: Stanford University Press.

FESTINGER, L., SCHACHTER, S., & BACK, K. (1950). *Social pressures in informal groups: A study of human factors in housing.* New York: Harper & Row.

FETHERSTON, A. B. (1994). *Toward a theory of United Nations peacekeeping.* New York: St. Martin's.

FILLEY, A. C. (1975). *Interpersonal conflict resolution.* Glenview, IL: Scott, Foresman.

FINKEL, E. J., & CAMPBELL, W. K. (2001). Self-control and accommodation in close relationships: An interdependence analysis. *Journal of Personality and Social Psychology, 81,* 263–277.

FINKEL, N. J. (2001). *Not fair! The typology of commonsense of unfairness.* Washington D. C.: American Psychological Association.

FISHER, R. (1964). Fractionating conflict. In R. Fisher (Ed.), *International conflict and behavioral science: The Craigville papers.* New York: Basic Books.

FISHER, R. (1981). Playing the wrong game. In J. Z. Rubin (Ed.), *Dynamics of third-party intervention: Kissinger in the Middle East* (pp. 95–121). New York: Praeger.

FISHER, R., & BROWN, S. (1988). *Getting together: Building a relationship that gets to YES*. Boston: Houghton Mifflin.

FISHER, R., URY, W. L., & PATTON, B. (1991). *Getting to YES: Negotiating agreement without giving in* (2nd ed.). Boston: Houghton Mifflin.

FISHER, R. J. (1990). *The social psychology of intergroup and international conflict resolution*. New York: Springer-Verlag.

FISHER, R. J. (1997). *Interactive conflict resolution*. Syracuse, NY: Syracuse University Press.

FISHER, R. J. (2000). Intergroup conflict. In M. Deutsch & P. T. Coleman (Eds.), *The handbook of conflict resolution: Theory and practice* (pp. 166–184). San Francisco: Jossey-Bass.

FISHER, R. J. (2001). Social-psychological processes in interactive conflict analysis and reconciliation. In M. Abu-Nimer (Ed.), *Reconciliation, justice, and coexistence: Theory and practice* (pp. 25–45). Lanham, MD: Lexington Books.

FISHER, R. J., & KEASHLY, L. (1990). A contingency approach to third party intervention. In R. J. Fisher (Ed.), *The social psychology of intergroup and international conflict resolution* (pp. 234–238). New York: Springer-Verlag.

FISKE, S. T., & TAYLOR, S. E. (1991). *Social Cognition* (2nd ed.). New York: McGraw-Hill.

FITNESS, J. (2001). Betrayal, rejection, revenge, and forgiveness: An interpersonal script approach. In M. R. Leary (Ed.), *Interpersonal rejection* (pp. 73–103). New York: Oxford University Press.

FOA, U. G., & FOA, E. B. (1975). *Resource theory of social exchange*. Morristown, NJ: General Learning Press.

FOLGER, R., & SKARLICKI, D. P. (1998). A popcorn metaphor for employee aggression. In R. W. Griffin, A. O'Leary-Kelly, & J. Collins (Eds.), *Monographs in organizational behavior and industrial relations: Vol. 23. Dysfunctional behavior in organizations: Part A. Violent and deviant behavior* (pp. 43–81). Greenwich, CT: JAI.

FOLLETT, M. P. (1940). Constructive conflict. In H. C. Metcalf & L. Urwick (Eds.), *Dynamic administration: The collected papers of Mary Parker Follett* (pp. 30–49). New York: Harper.

FRANK, J. (1982). *Sanity and survival* (rev. ed.). New York: Vintage Books.

FREEDMAN, J. L., WALLINGTON, S. A., & BLESS, E. (1967). Compliance without pressure: The effects of guilt. *Journal of Personality and Social Psychology, 7*, 117–124.

FREEDMAN, S. C. (1981). Threats, promises, and coalitions: A study of compliance and retaliation in a simulated organizational setting. *Journal of Applied Social Psychology, 11*, 114–136.

FRENCH, J. R. P., & RAVEN, B. H. (1959). The bases of social power. In D. Cartwright (Ed.), *Studies in Social Power* (pp. 150–167). Ann Arbor, MI: Institute for Social Research.

FRIEDMAN, M. (2000). The Truth and Reconciliation Commission in South Africa as an attempt to heal a traumatized society. In A. Y. Shalev, R. Yehuda, & A. C. McFarlane (Eds.), *International handbook of human response to trauma* (pp. 399–411). New York: Kluwer Academic/ Prenum.

FRIEDMAN, T. (1995). *From Beirut to Jerusalem*. New York: Anchor Books.

FRIJDA, N. H. (1993). The lex talionis: On vengeance. In S. H. M. Van Goozen, N. E. Van de Poll, & J. A. Sergeant (Eds.), *Emotions: Essays on emotion theory* (pp. 263–289). Hillsdale, NJ: Erlbaum.

FROST, B. (1991). *The politics of peace*. London: Darton, Longman and Todd.

FRY, W. R., FIRESTONE, I. J., & WILLIAMS, D. L. (1983). Negotiation process and outcome of stranger dyads and dating couples: Do lovers lose? *Basic and Applied Social Psychology, 4,* 1–16.

FUKUYAMA, F. (1995). *Trust: The social virtues and the creation of prosperity*. New York: Free Press.

GAERTNER, S. L., & DOVIDIO, J. F. (2000). *Reducing intergroup bias: The common ingroup identity model*. Philadelphia, PA: Psychology Press.

GALTUNG, J. (1996). *Peace by peaceful means: Peace and conflict, development and civilization*. London: Sage.

GANDHI, M. K. (1949). *For pacifists*. Ahmedabad, India: Navajivan Publishing House.

GANDHI, M. K. (1967). *Non-violent resistance*. New York: Schoken.

GEEN, R. G. (1975). The meaning of observed violence: Real vs. fictional violence and consequent effects on aggression. *Journal of Research in Personality, 12,* 15–29.

GEEN, R. G. (1978). Effects of attack and uncontrollable noise on aggression. *Journal of Research in Personality, 12,* 15–29.

GEEN, R. G. (1990). *Human aggression*. Pacific Grove, CA: Brooks/Cole.

GEEN, R. G., & STONNER, D. (1973). Context effects in observed violence. *Journal of Personality and Social Psychology, 25,* 145–150.

GELFAND, M. J., & CHRISTAKOPOULOU, S. (1999). Culture and negotiator cognition: Judgment accuracy and negotiation processes in individualistic and collectivistic cultures. *Organizational Behavior and Human Decision Making, 79,* 248–269.

GELFAND, M. J., & MCCUSKER, C. (2001). Metaphor and the cultural construction of negotiation: A paradigm for theory and research. In M. Gannon & K. I. Newman (Eds.), *Handbook of cross-cultural management* (pp. 292–314). New York: Blackwell.

GELFAND, M. J., NISHII, L. H., HOLCOMBE, K. M., DYER, N., OHBUCHI, K., & FUKUMO, M. (2001). Cultural influences on cognitive representations of conflict: Interpretations of conflict episodes in the United States and Japan. *Journal of Applied Psychology, 86,* 1059–1074.

GILLIGAN, J. (1996). *Violence: Our deadly epidemic and its causes*. New York: Putnam.

GIRE, J. T., & CARMENT, D. W. (1993). Dealing with disputes: The influence of individualism-collectivism. *Journal of Social Psychology, 133,* 81–95.

GLASL, F. (1982). The process of conflict escalation and roles of third parties. In G. B. J. Bomers & R. B. Peterson (Eds.), *Conflict management and industrial relations* (pp. 119–140). Boston: Kluwer-Nijhoff.

GLASS, D. C. (1964). Changes in liking as a means of reducing cognitive discrepancies between self-esteem and aggression. *Journal of Personality, 32,* 491–549.

GLUCKMAN, M. (1955). *Custom and conflict in Africa*. Glencoe, IL: Free Press.

GOERTZ, G., & DIEHL, P. F. (1995). The initiation and termination of enduring rivalries: The impact of political shocks. *American Journal of Political Science, 39,* 30–52.

GOLAN, M. (1976). *The secret conversations of Henry Kissinger*. New York: Quadrangle.

GOLDBERG, S. B., GREEN, E. D., & SANDER, F. E. A. (1985). *Dispute resolution.* Boston: Little Brown.

GOLDBERG, S. B., SANDER, F. E. A., & ROGERS, N. H. (1992). *Dispute resolution: Negotiation, mediation, and other processes* (2nd ed.). Boston: Little, Brown.

GOLDING, W. (1954). *Lord of the flies.* New York: Perigee.

GORDON, D. S., & TOASE, F. H. (2001). *Aspects of peacekeeping.* London: Frank Cass.

GORDON, K. C., BAUCOM, D. H., & BERRY, J. W. (2000). The use of forgiveness in marital therapy. In M. E. McCullough, K. I. Pargament, & C. E. Theoresen (Eds.), *Forgiveness: Theory, research, and practice* (pp. 203–227). New York: Guilford.

GORDON, R. A. (1996). Impact of ingratiation on judgments and evaluations: A meta-analytic investigation. *Journal of Personality and Social Psychology, 71,* 54–70.

GOTTMAN, J. M. (2001). Meta-Emotion: Children's emotional intelligence and buffering children from marital conflict. In C. D. Ryff & B. H. Singer (Eds.), *Emotion, social relationships, and health* (pp. 23–40). New York: Oxford University Press.

GOTTMAN, J. M., & LEVENSON, R. L. (1988). The social psycho-physiology of marriage. In P. Noller & M. A. Fitzpatrick (Eds.), *Perspectives on marital interaction* (pp. 182–200). Clevendon, England: Multilingual Matters.

GOUREVITCH, P. (1997, January 20). The return. *The New Yorker,* pp. 44–48, 52–54.

GOUREVITCH, P. (1998). *We wish to inform you that tomorrow we will be killed with our families: Stories from Rwanda.* New York: Farrar, Straus and Giroux.

GRAHAM, M. (2000, April). Regulation by shaming [Electronic version]. *The Atlantic Monthly.* Retrieved August 22, 2002, from http://www.theatlantic.com/issues/2000/04/graham.htm.

GREENBERG, J. (1996). *The quest for justice on the job: Essays and experiences.* Thousand Oaks, CA: Sage.

GREENLAND, K., & BROWN, R. (2000). Categorization and intergroup anxiety in intergroup contact. In D. Capozza & R. Brown (Eds.), *Social identity processes: Trends in theory and research* (pp. 167–183). Thousand Oaks, CA: Sage.

GRUDER, C. L. (1971). Relationship with opponent and partner in mixed-motive bargaining. *Journal of Conflict Resolution, 15,* 403–416.

GULLIVER, P. H. (1979). *Disputes and negotiations: A cross-cultural perspective.* New York: Academic Press.

GURR, T. R. (1970). *Why men rebel.* Princeton, NJ: Princeton University Press.

GURR, T. R. (1996). Minorities, nationalists, and ethnopolitical conflict. In C. Crocker & F. Hampson (Eds.), *Managing global chaos: Sources of and responses to international conflict* (pp. 53–78). Washington D.C.: United States Institute of Peace Press.

HAASS, R. (1990). *Conflicts unending: The US and regional disputes.* New Haven, CT: Yale University Press.

HALBERSTAM, D. (1969). *The best and the brightest.* New York: Random House.

HALL, E. T. (1976). *Beyond culture.* Garden City, NY: Doubleday.

HALL, L. (1993). *Negotiation: Strategies for mutual gain.* Newbury Park, CA: Sage.

HAMILTON, D. L., & BISHOP, G. D. (1976). Attitudinal and behavioral effects of initial integration of white suburban neighborhoods. *Journal of Social Issues, 32,* 47–67.

HAMPSON, F. O. (1996). Why orphaned peace settlements are more prone to failure. In C. Crocker & F. Hampson (Eds.), *Managing global chaos: Sources of and responses to international conflict* (pp. 533–550). Washington D. C.: United States Institute of Peace Press.

HAMPSON, F. O. (1997). Third-party roles in the termination of intercommunal conflict. *Millennium: Journal of International Studies, 26,* 727–750.

HARFORD, T., & SOLOMON, L. (1967). "Reformed sinner" and "lapsed saint" strategies in the prisoner's dilemma game. *Journal of Conflict Resolution, 11,* 104–109.

HARRELL-COOK, G., FERRIS, G. R., & DULEBOHN, J. H. (1999). Political behaviors as moderators of the perceptions of organizational politics—work outcomes relationships. *Journal of Organizational Behavior, 20,* 1093–1105.

HARRIS, K. L., & CARNEVALE, P. J. (1990). Chilling and hastening: The influence of third-party power and interests on negotiation. *Organizational Behavior and Human Decision Processes, 47,* 138–160.

HASTORF, A. H., & CANTRIL, C. (1954). They saw a game: A case study. *Journal of Abnormal and Social Psychology, 49,* 129–134.

HAWK, G. W. (2001). Transcending transgression: Forgiveness and reconciliation. In W. W. Wilmot & J. L. Hocker (Eds.), *Interpersonal conflict* (6th ed.)(pp. 293–317). New York: McGraw-Hill.

HAWTHORNE, N. (1850/1962). The Scarlet Letter. In S. Bradley, R. C. Beatty, & E. H. Long (Eds.), *The Scarlet Letter: An annotated text* (pp. 5–186). New York: Norton.

HAYDEN, T., & MISCHEL, W. (1976). Maintaining trait consistency in the resolution of behavioral inconsistency: The wolf in sheep's clothing? *Journal of Personality, 44,* 109–132.

HEALY, P. (2002, January 5). Doctors hope peace will heal psychological scars. *The Boston Globe,* p. A1.

HEIDE, J. B., & MINER, A. S. (1992). The shadow of the future: Effects of anticipated interaction and frequency of contact on buyer-seller cooperation. *Academy of Management Journal, 35,* 265–291.

HEIDER, F. (1958). *The psychology of interpersonal relations.* New York: Wiley.

HEILMAN, M. E. (1974). Threats and promises: Reputational considerations and transfer of credibility. *Journal of Experimental Social Psychology, 10,* 310–324.

HERACLIDES, A. (1997). The ending of unending conflicts: Separatist wars. *Millennium: Journal of International Studies, 26,* 679–707.

HERO, D. (2002, July 28). Axis of evil ramifications: Bush's tactics could bring Iran and Iraq together. *The Washington Post,* p. B4.

HILTROP, J. M. (1985). Mediator behavior and the settlement of collective bargaining disputes in Britain. *Journal of Social Issues, 41,* 83–99.

HILTROP, J. M. (1989). Factors associated with successful labor mediation. In K. Kressel, D. G. Pruitt, & Associates, *Mediation research* (pp. 241–262). San Francisco: Jossey-Bass.

HILTY, J. A, & CARNEVALE, P. J. (1993). Black-hat/white-hat strategy in bilateral negotiation. *Organizational Behavior and Human Decision Processes, 55,* 444–469.

HINTON, W. (1966). *Fanshen: A documentary of revolution in a Chinese village.* New York: Random House.

HOCKSTADER, L. (2001, December 5). Jerusalem bombers: Little in common but a mission. *The Washington Post,* p. A23.

HOFSTEDE, G. (1980). *Culture's consequences: International differences in work-related values.* Beverly Hills, CA: Sage.

HOGG, M. A. (1995). Social identity theory. In A. S. R. Manstead & M. Hewstone (Eds.), *The Blackwell encyclopedia of social psychology* (pp. 555–560). Oxford, England: Blackwell.

HOLLANDER, E. P. (1978). *Leadership dynamics: A practical guide to effective relationships.* New York: Free Press.

HOLLINGSHEAD, A. B., & CARNEVALE, P. J. (1990). Positive affect and decision frame in integrative bargaining: A reversal of the frame effect. *Proceedings of the Fiftieth Annual Conference of the Academy of Management* (pp. 385–389), San Francisco.

HOLSTI, O. (1967). Cognitive dynamics and images of the enemy: Dulles and Russia. In D. Finlay, O. Holsti, & R. Fagen (Eds.), *Enemies in politics* (pp. 26–27). Chicago: Rand McNally.

HOLTZWORTH-MUNROE, A., & JACOBSON, N. S. (1985). Causal attributions of married couples: When do they search for causes? What do they conclude when they do? *Journal of Personality and Social Psychology, 48,* 1398–1412.

HOPMANN, P. T. (1996). *The negotiation process and the resolution of international conflicts.* Columbia, SC: University of South Carolina Press.

HORAI, J., & TEDESCHI, J. T. (1969). Effects of credibility and magnitude of punishment on compliance to threats. *Journal of Personality and Social Psychology, 12,* 164–169.

HORNSTEIN, H. A. (1976). *Cruelty and kindness: A new look at aggression and altruism.* Englewood Cliffs, NJ: Prentice-Hall.

HOROWITZ, D. L. (2001). *The deadly ethnic riot.* Berkeley, CA: University of California Press.

HOVLAND, C. I., & SEARS, R. R. (1940). Minor studies of aggression. VI: Correlation of lynchings with economic indices. *Journal of Psychology, 9,* 301–310.

HUBER, E. L., PRUITT, D. G., & WELTON, G. L. (1986). *The effect of prior negotiation experience on the process and outcome of later negotiation.* Poster presented at the annual meeting of the Eastern Psychological Association, New York.

HUGHES, J. (2002, March 27). Murder suspect harassed couple for years after suit. *The Lexington-Herald Leader,* pp. A3, A11.

HUNTINGTON, S. P. (1996). *The clash of civilizations and the remaking of world order.* New York: Touchstone.

HYNAN, D. J., & GRUSH, J. E. (1986). Effects of impulsivity, depression, provocation, and time on aggressive behavior. *Journal of Research in Personality, 20,* 158–171.

INDVIK, J., & FITZPATRICK, M. A. (1982). "If you could read my mind, love . . .," understanding and misunderstanding in the marital dyad. *Family Relations, 31,* 43–51.

ISEN, A. M., & LEVIN, P. F. (1972). Effect of feeling good on helping: Cookies and kindness. *Journal of Personality and Social Psychology, 21,* 384–388.

ISENBERG, D. J. (1986). Group polarization: A critical review and meta-analysis. *Journal of Personality and Social Psychology, 50,* 1141–1151.

ISLAM, M. R., & HEWSTONE, M. (1993). Dimensions of contact as predictors of intergroup anxiety, perceived out-group variability, and out-group attitude: An integrative model. *Personality and Social Psychology Bulletin, 19,* 700–710.

JACOBSON, D. (1981). Intraparty dissensus and interparty conflict resolution. *Journal of Conflict Resolution, 25,* 471–494.

JACOBSON, N. S., & FOLLETTE, W. C. (1985). Clinical-significance of improvement resulting from 2 behavioral marital-therapy components. *Behavior Therapy, 16,* 249–262.

JACOBY, S. (1983). *Wild justice: The evolution of revenge.* New York: Harper & Row.

JAFFE, Y., & YINON, Y. (1983). Collective aggression: The group-individual paradigm in the study of collective antisocial behavior. In H. H. Blumberg, A. P.

Hare, V. Kent, & M. Davies (Eds.), *Small groups and social interaction* (Vol. 1, pp. 267–275). New York: Wiley.

JANIS, I. L. (1972). *Victims of groupthink: A psychological study of foreign-policy decisions and fiascos.* Boston: Houghton Mifflin.

JEONG, H-W. (2000). *Peace and conflict studies: An introduction.* Aldershot, England & Brookfield, VT: Ashgate.

JERVIS, R. (1976). *Perception and misperception in international politics.* Princeton, NJ: Princeton University Press.

JIA, W. (2002). Chinese mediation and its cultural foundation. In G. Chen & R. Ma (Eds.), *Chinese conflict management and resolution* (pp. 289–295). Westport, CT: Ablex.

JOHNSON, D. W., & JOHNSON, R. T. (1991). *Teaching children to be peacemakers.* Edina, MN: Interaction Book Company.

JOHNSON, D. W., JOHNSON, R. T., DUDLEY, B., & MAGNUSON, D. (1995). Training elementary school students to manage conflict. *Journal of Social Psychology, 135,* 673–686.

JOHNSON, D. W., JOHNSON, R. T., & MARUYAMA, G. (1984). Goal interdependence and interpersonal attraction in heterogeneous classrooms: A meta-analysis. In N. Miller & M. B. Brewer (Eds.), *Groups in contact: The psychology of desegregation* (pp. 187–212). New York: Academic Press.

JOHNSON, S. M., & GREENBERG, L. C. (1985). Differential effects of experiential and problem-solving interventions in resolving marital conflict. *Journal of Consulting and Clinical Psychology, 53,* 175–184.

JONES, E. E. (1990). *Interpersonal perception.* New York: Freeman.

JONES, E. E., & GORDON, E. M. (1972). Timing of self-disclosure and its effects on personal attraction. *Journal of Personality and Social Psychology, 24,* 358–365.

JONES, E. E., & WORTMAN, C. (1973). *Ingratiation: An attributional approach.* Morristown, NJ: General Learning Press.

JOURILES, E. N., BOURG, W. J., & FARRIS, A. M. (1991). Marital adjustment and child conduct problems: A comparison of the correlation across subsamples. *Journal of Consulting and Clinical Psychology, 59,* 354–357.

JOWITT, K. (2001). Ethnicity: Nice, nasty, and nihilistic. In D. Chirot & M. E. P. Seligman (Eds.), *Ethnopolitical warfare: Causes, consequences, and possible solutions* (pp. 27–36). Washington, DC: American Psychological Association.

JUSSIM, L., & ECCLES, J. (1995). Naturally occurring interpersonal expectancies. *Review of Personality and Social Psychology, 15,* 74–108.

KAHN, H. (1960). *On thermonuclear war.* Princeton, NJ: Princeton University Press.

KAUFMAN, S. J. (2001). *Modern hatreds.* Ithaca, NY: Cornell University Press.

KAZDIN, A. E. (1975). *Behavior modification in applied settings.* Homewood, IL: Dorsey.

KEATING, M. E., PRUITT, D. G., EBERLE, R. A., & MIKOLIC, J. M. (1994). Strategic choice in everyday disputes. *International Journal of Conflict Management, 5,* 143–157.

KELLEY, H. H. (1966). A classroom study of the dilemmas in interpersonal negotiations. In K. Archibald (Ed.), *Strategic interaction and conflict: Original papers and discussion* (pp. 49–73). Berkeley, CA: Institute of International Studies.

KELLEY, H. H., BECKMAN, L. L., & FISCHER, C. S. (1967). Negotiating the division of reward under incomplete information. *Journal of Experimental Social Psychology, 3,* 361–398.

KELLEY, H. H., & SCHENITZKI, D. P. (1972). Bargaining. In C. G. McClintock (Ed.), *Experimental social psychology* (pp. 298–337). New York: Holt.

KELLEY, H. H., & STAHELSKI, A. J. (1970). Social interaction basis of cooperators' and competitors' beliefs about others. *Journal of Personality and Social Psychology, 16,* 66–91.

KELMAN, H. C. (1985). Overcoming the psychological barrier: An analysis of the Egyptian-Israeli peace process. *Negotiation Journal, 1,* 213–234.

KELMAN, H. C. (1992). Informal mediation by the scholar/practitioner. In J. Bercovitch & J. Z. Rubin (Eds.), *Mediation in international relations* (pp. 64–96). New York: St. Martin's.

KELMAN, H. C. (1997). Some determinants of the Oslo breakthrough. *International Negotiation, 2,* 183–194.

KELMAN, H. C., & HAMILTON, V. L. (1989). *Crimes of obedience: Toward a social psychology of authority and responsibility.* New Haven, CT: Yale University Press.

KENNEDY, R. F. (1969). *Thirteen days: A memoir of the Cuban missile crisis.* New York: Norton.

KIECOLT-GLASER, J. K., GLASER, R., CACIOPPO, J. T., MACCALLUM, R. C., et al. (1997). Marital conflict in older adults: Endocrinological and immunological correlates. *Psychosomatic Medicine, 59,* 339–349.

KILMANN, R. H., & THOMAS, K. W. (1977). Developing a forced-choice measure of conflict handling behavior: The "Mode" instrument. *Educational and Psychological Measurement, 37,* 309–325.

KIM, S. H. (2002). *The causes and consequences of vengeful motives.* Unpublished manuscript. University of Kentucky.

KIM, S. H., & SMITH, R. H. (1993). Revenge and conflict escalation. *Negotiation Journal, 9,* 37–43.

KIM, S. H., SMITH, R. H., & BRIGHAM, N. L. (1998). Effects of power imbalance and the presence of third parties on reactions to harm: Upward and downward revenge. *Personality and Social Psychology Bulletin, 24,* 353–361.

KIM, S. H., & WEBSTER, J. M. (2001). Getting competitors to cooperate: A comparison of three reciprocal strategies. *Representative Research in Social Psychology, 25,* 9–19.

KING, M. L. (1963). *Why we can't wait.* New York: Harper & Row.

KLIMOSKI, R. J. (1972). The effects of intragroup forces on intergroup conflict resolution. *Organizational Behavior and Human Performance, 8,* 363–383.

KLINE, M., JOHNSON, J. R., & TSCHANN, J. M. (1991). The long shadow of marital conflict: A model of children's postdivorce adjustment. *Journal of Marriage and the Family, 53,* 297–309.

KOCHAN, T. A. (1980). *Collective bargaining and industrial relations.* Homewood, IL: Irwin.

KOCHAN, T. A., & JICK, T. (1978). The public sector mediation process: A theory and empirical examination. *Journal of Conflict Resolution, 22,* 209–240.

KOGAN, N., LAMM, H., & TROMMSDORFF, G. (1972). Negotiation constraints in the risk-taking domain: Effects of being observed by partners of higher or lower status. *Journal of Personality and Social Psychology, 23,* 143–156.

KOLB, D. M. (1983). *The mediators.* Cambridge, MA: MIT Press.

KOLB, D. M. (1994). *When talk works: Profiles of working mediators.* San Francisco: Jossey-Bass.

KOMORITA, S. S., & ESSER, J. K. (1975). Frequency of reciprocated concessions in bargaining. *Journal of Personality and Social Psychology, 32,* 699–705.

KOMORITA, S. S., & LAPWORTH, C. W. (1982). Cooperative choice among individuals vs. groups in an n-person dilemma situation. *Journal of Personality and Social Psychology, 42,* 487–496.

KONECNI, V. J. (1975). The mediation of aggressive behavior: Arousal level vs. anger and cognitive labeling. *Journal of Personality and Social Psychology 32,* 706–712.

KONOSKE, P., STAPLE, S., & GRAF, R. G. (1979). Compliant reactions to guilt: Self-esteem or self-punishment. *Journal of Social Psychology, 108,* 207–211.

KRAMER, R. M., & BREWER, M. B. (1984). Effects of group identity on resource use in a simulated commons dilemma. *Journal of Personality and Social Psychology, 46,* 1044–1057.

KRASLOW, D., & LOORY, S. H. (1968). *The secret search for peace in Vietnam.* New York: Vintage Books.

KREMENYUK, V. A. (Ed.). (2002). *International negotiation: Analysis, approaches, issues* (2nd ed.). San Francisco: Jossey-Bass.

KRESSEL, K. (1972). *Labor mediation: An exploratory survey.* Albany, NY: Association of Labor Mediation Agencies.

KRESSEL, K., & PRUITT, D. G. (1989). Conclusion: A research perspective on the mediation of social conflict. In K. Kressel, D. G. Pruitt, & Associates, *Mediation research* (pp. 394–435). San Francisco: Jossey-Bass.

KRIESBERG, L. (1982). *Social conflicts* (2nd ed.). Englewood Cliffs, NJ: Prentice-Hall.

KRIESBERG, L. (1991). Formal and quasi-mediators in international disputes: An exploratory analysis. *Journal of Peace Research, 28,* 19–27.

KRIESBERG, L. (1998). *Constructive conflicts: From escalation to resolution.* Lanham, MD: Rowman & Littlefield.

KRIESBERG, L. (2001). Changing forms of coexistence. In M. Abu-Nimer (Ed.), *Reconciliation, justice, and coexistence* (pp. 47–64). Lanham, MD: Lexington Books.

KUSCHEL, R. (1988). *Vengeance is their reply: Blood feuds and homicides on Bellona Island*—Part I and Part II. Denmark: Dansk Psykologisk Forlag.

LANE, C. (1992, December 28). Mob rule. *The New Republic,* pp. 22–23.

LAQUER, W. (1999). *The new terrorism: Fanaticism and the arms of mass destruction.* New York: Oxford University Press.

LAWRENCE, P. R., & LORSCH, J. W. (1967). *Organizational and environment.* Cambridge, MA: Harvard University Press.

LAX, D. A., & SEBENIUS, J. K. (1986). *The manager as negotiator: Bargaining for cooperation and competitive gain.* New York: Free Press.

LAZARUS, R. S. (1991). *Emotion and adaptation.* New York: Oxford University Press.

LEATHERMAN, J., DE MARS, W., GAFFNEY, P. D., & VAYRYNEN, R. (1999). *Breaking cycles of violence: Conflict prevention in intrastate crises.* W. Hartford, CT: Kumarian Press.

LEBOW, R. N., JERVIS, R., & STEIN, J. G. (1984). *Psychology and deterrence.* Baltimore, MD: Johns Hopkins University Press.

LEDERACH, J. P. (1995). *Preparing for peace: Conflict transformation across cultures.* Syracuse, NY: Syracuse University Press.

LEDERACH, J. P. (1997). *Building peace: Sustainable reconciliation in divided societies.* Washington D.C.: US Institute of Peace Press.

LEDERACH, J. P. (2000). Journey from resolution to transformative building. In C. Sampson & J. P. Lederach (Eds.), *From the ground up: Mennonite contributions to international peacebuilding.* New York: Oxford University Press.

LEUNG, K. (1988). Some determinants of conflict avoidance. *Journal of Cross-Cultural Psychology, 19,* 125–136.

LEUNG, K., & BOND, M. H. (1984). The impact of cultural collectivism on reward allocation. *Journal of Personality and Social Psychology, 4,* 793–804.

LEWICKI, R. J., SAUNDERS, D. M., & MINTON, J. W. (Eds.). (1998). *Negotiation: Readings, cases, and exercises* (3rd ed.). Chicago: Irwin/McGraw-Hill.

LEWICKI, R. J., SAUNDERS, D. M., & MINTON, J. W. (2000) *Essentials of Negotiation* (2nd ed.). Chicago: Irwin/McGraw-Hill.

LIEBERFELD, D. (1999). *Talking with the enemy: Negotiation and threat perception in South Africa and Israel/Palestine.* Westport, CT: Praeger.

LIFTON, R. J. (1999). *Destroying the world to save it: Aum Shinrikyo, apocalyptic violence, and the new global terrorism.* New York: Holt.

LIKERT, R. (1961). *New patterns of management.* New York: McGraw-Hill.

LIM, R. G., & CARNEVALE, P. J. (1990). Contingencies in the mediation of disputes. *Journal of Personality and Social Psychology, 58,* 259–272.

LIND, E. A., & TYLER, T. R. (1988). *The social psychology of procedural justice.* New York: Plenum.

LINDSKOLD, S. (1978). Trust development, the GRIT proposal, and the effects of conciliatory acts on conflict and cooperation. *Psychological Bulletin, 85,* 772–793.

LINDSKOLD, S., & BENNETT, R. (1973). Attributing trust and conciliatory intent from coercive power capability. *Journal of Personality and Social Psychology, 28,* 180–186.

LINDSKOLD, S., & TEDESCHI, J. T. (1971). Reward power and attraction in interpersonal conflict. *Psychonomic Science, 22,* 211–213.

LOFTUS, E. F. (1979). *Eyewitness testimony.* Cambridge, MA: Harvard University Press.

LONGLEY, J., & PRUITT, D. G. (1980). A critique of Janis's theory of groupthink. In L. Wheeler (Ed.), *Review of personality and social psychology* (Vol. 1, pp. 74–93). Beverly Hills, CA: Sage.

LOOMIS, J. L. (1959). Communication, the development of trust, and cooperative behavior. *Human Relations, 12,* 305–315.

LUND, M. (2001). A toolbox for responding to conflicts and building peace. In L. Reychler & T. Paffenholz (Eds.), *Peacebuilding: A field guide* (pp. 16–20). Boulder, CO: Lynne Rienner.

LYONS, T. (2002). The role of postsettlement elections. In S. J. Stedman, D. Rothchild, & E. M. Cousens (Eds.), *The implementation of peace agreements.* Boulder, CO: Lynne Rienner.

MALLICK, S. K., & MCCANDLESS, B. R. (1966). A study of catharsis of aggression. *Journal of Personality and Social Psychology, 4,* 591–596.

MARCUS, N. A., PEDERSEN, W. C., CARLSON, M., & MILLER, N. (2000). Displaced aggression is alive and well: A meta-analytic review. *Journal of Personality and Social Psychology, 78,* 670–689.

MARKUS, H., & KITAYAMA, S. (1991). Culture and self: Implications for cognition, emotion and motivation. *Psychological Review, 98,* 224–253.

MARONGIU, P., & NEWMAN, G. (1987). *Vengeance: The fight against injustice.* Totowa, NJ: Rowman & Littlefield.

McCLINTOCK, C. G. (1988). Evolution, systems of interdependence, and social values. *Behavioral Science, 33,* 59–76.

McCORD, J. (1986). Instigation and insulation: How families affect antisocial aggression. In D. Olweus, J. Block, & M. Radke-Yarrow (Eds.), *Development of antisocial and prosocial behavior: Research, theories, and issues* (pp. 343–357). Orlando, FL: Academic Press.

McCULLOUGH, M. E., BELLAH, C. G., KILPATRICK, S. D., & JOHNSON, J. L. (2001). Vengefulness: Relationships with forgiveness, rumination, well-being, and the Big Five. *Personality and Social Psychology Bulletin, 27,* 601–610.

McCULLOUGH, M. E., WORTHINGTON, E. L. JR., & RACHAL, K. C. (1997). Interpersonal forgiving in close relationships. *Journal of Personality and Social Psychology, 73,* 321–336.

McEWEN, C. A., & MAIMAN, R. J. (1989). Mediation in small claims court: Consensual processes and outcomes. In K. Kressel & D. G. Pruitt (Eds.), *Mediation research* (pp. 53–67). San Francisco: Jossey-Bass.

McEWEN, C. A., & MILBURN, T. W. (1993). Explaining a paradox of mediation. *Negotiation Journal, 9,* 23–36.

McFARLANE, A. C. (2000). On the social denial of trauma and the problem of knowing the past. In A. Y. Shalev, R. Yehuda, & A. C. McFarlane (Eds.), *International handbook of human response to trauma* (pp. 11–25). New York: Kluwer Academic/Plenum.

McGILLICUDDY, N. B., PRUITT, D. G., & SYNA, H. (1984). Perceptions of firmness and strength in negotiation. *Personality and Social Psychology Bulletin, 10,* 402–409.

McGILLICUDDY, N. B., WELTON, G. L., & PRUITT, D. G. (1987). Third party intervention: A field experiment comparing three different models. *Journal of Personality and Social Psychology, 53,* 104–112.

MEARSHEIMER, J. J. (2001). *The tragedy of great power politics.* New York: Norton.

MERRY, S. E. (1989). Mediation in nonindustrial societies. In K. Kressel, D. G. Pruitt, & Associates, *Mediation research* (pp. 68–90). San Francisco: Jossey-Bass.

MICHENER, H. A., VASKE, J. J., SCHLEIFER, S. L., PLAZEWSKI, J. G., & CHAPMAN, L. J. (1975). Factors affecting concession rate and threat usage in bilateral conflict. *Sociometry, 38,* 62–80.

MIKOLIC, J. M., PARKER, J. C., & PRUITT, D. G. (1997). Escalation in response to persistent annoyance: Groups vs. individuals and gender effects. *Journal of Personality and Social Psychology, 72,* 151–163.

MILBURN, T. W., & WATMAN, K. H. (1981). *On the nature of threat: A social psychological analysis.* New York: Praeger.

MILGRAM, S. (1992). *The individual in a social world: Essays and experiments* (2nd ed.). New York: McGraw-Hill.

MILLER, D. T. (2001). Disrespect and the experience of injustice. *Annual Review of Psychology, 52,* 527–553.

MILLER, N., & BREWER, M. B. (Eds.). (1984). *Groups in contact: The psychology of desegregation.* New York: Academic Press.

MITCHELL, C. (1999). The anatomy of de-escalation. In H-W. Jeong (Ed.), *Conflict resolution: Dynamics, process and structure* (pp. 37–58). Aldershot, England & Brookfield, VT: Ashgate.

MITCHELL, C. (2000). *Gestures of conciliation: Factors contributing to successful olive branches.* London: Macmillan.

MOGY, R. B., & PRUITT, D. G. (1974). Effects of a threatener's enforcement costs on threat credibility and compliance. *Journal of Personality and Social Psychology, 29,* 173–180.

MONTVILLE, J. V. (1987). The arrow and the olive branch: The case for track two diplomacy. In J. W. McDonald & D. B. Bendahmane (Eds.), *Conflict resolution: Track two diplomacy* (pp. 5–20). Washington D.C.: Foreign Service Institute, Department of State.

MONTVILLE, J. V. (1993). The healing function in political conflict resolution. In D. J. D. Sandole & H. van der Merwe (Eds.), *Conflict resolution theory and practice: Integration and application* (pp. 112–127). New York: Manchester University Press.

MONTVILLE, J. V. (2001). Justice and the burdens of history. In M. Abu-Nimer (Ed.), *Reconciliation, justice, and coexistence: Theory and practice* (pp. 129–143). Lanham, MD: Lexington Books.

MOORADIAN, M., & DRUCKMAN, D. (1999). Hurting stalemate or mediation? The conflict over Nagorno- Karabakh, 1990–95. *Journal of Peace Research, 36,* 709–727.

MORLEY, I. E., & STEPHENSON, G. M. (1977). *The social psychology of bargaining.* London: Allen and Unwin.

MORRILL, C., & THOMAS, C. K. (1992). Organizational conflict management as disputing process: The problem of social escalation. *Human Communication Research, 18,* 400–428.

MORRIS, M. W., & GELFAND, M. J. (in press). Cultural differences and cognitive dynamics: Expanding the cognitive perspective on negotiation. In M. J. Gelfand & J. M. Brett (Eds.). *Culture and negotiation: Integrative approaches to theory and research.*

MORRIS, M. W., LARRICK, R. P., & SU, S. K. (1999). Misperceiving negotiation counterparts: When situationally determined bargaining behaviors are attributed to personality traits. *Journal of Personality and Social Psychology, 77,* 52–67.

MOSCOVICI, S., & ZAVALLONI, M. (1969). The group as a polarizer of attitudes. *Journal of Personality and Social Psychology, 12,* 125–135.

MURPHY, J. G., & HAMPTON, J. (1988). *Forgiveness and mercy.* New York: Cambridge University Press.

MURRAY, S. L., & HOLMES, J. G. (1997). A leap of faith? Positive illusions in romantic relationships. *Personality and Social Psychology Bulletin, 23,* 586–604.

MYLROIE, L. (2000). *Study of revenge: Saddam Hussein's unfinished war against America.* Washington, DC: AEI Press.

NAIMARK, N. M. (2001). *Fires of hatred: Ethnic cleansing in twentieth-century Europe.* Cambridge, MA: Harvard University Press.

NANSEL, T. R., OVERPECK, M., PILLA, R. S., RUAN, W. J., SIMONS-MORTON, B., & SCHEIDT, P. (2001). Bullying behaviors among US youth: Prevalence and association with psychosocial adjustment. *Journal of the American Medical Association, 285,* 2094–2100.

NEALE, M. A. (1984). The effect of negotiation and arbitration cost salience on bargaining behavior: The role of arbitrator and constituency in negotiator judgment. *Organizational Behavior and Human Performance, 34,* 97–111.

NEALE, M. A., & BAZERMAN, M. H. (1983). The role of perspective-taking ability in negotiating under different forms of arbitration. *Industrial and Labor Relations Review, 36,* 378–388.

NEALE, M. A., & BAZERMAN, M. H. (1985). The effects of framing and negotiator overconfidence on bargaining behaviors and outcomes. *Academy of Management Journal, 28,* 34–39.

NEALE, M. A., & BAZERMAN, M. H. (1991). *Negotiator cognition and rationality.* New York: Free Press: New York.

NEUBERG, S. L. (1989). The goal of forming accurate impressions during social interactions: Attenuating the impact of negative expectancies. *Journal of Personality and Social Psychology, 56,* 374–386.

NEUFFER, E. (2001). *The key to my neighbor's house: Seeking justice in Bosnia and Rwanda.* New York: Picador.

NEW YORK STATE SPECIAL COMMISSION ON ATTICA (1972). *Attica: The official report of the New York State Special Commission on Attica.* New York: Bantam Books.

NEWCOMB, T. M. (1947). Autistic hostility and social reality. *Human Relations, 1,* 69–86.

NISBETT, R. E., & COHEN, D. (1996). *Culture of honor: The psychology of violence in the South.* Boulder, CO: Westview.

NOLLER, P., & FITZPATRICK, M. A. (1990). Marital communication in the eighties. *Journal of Marriage and the Family, 52,* 832–843.

NORTH, R. C., BRODY, R. A., & HOLSTI, O. R. (1964). Some empirical data on the conflict spiral. *Peace Research Society (International) Papers, 1,* 1–14.

NOVACO, R. W. (1975). *Anger control.* Lexington, MA: Lexington Books.

O'FARRELL, T. J., & MURPHY, C. M. (2002). Behavioral couples therapy for alcoholism and drug abuse: Encountering the problem of domestic violence. In C. Wekerle & A. Wall (Eds.), *The violence and addiction equation: Theoretical and clinical issues in substance abuse and relationship violence* (pp. 293–303). New York: Brunner-Routledge.

OHBUCHI, K., KAMEDA, M., & AGARIE, N. (1989). Apology as aggression control: Its role in mediating appraisal of and response to harm. *Journal of Personality and Social Psychology, 56,* 219–227.

OHBUCHI, K-I. (1995). *Mitigation of interpersonal conflicts: Politeness and time pressure.* Unpublished.

OHBUCHI, K-I., FUKUSHIMA, O., & TEDESCHI, J. T. (1999). Cultural values in conflict management: Goal orientation, goal attainment, and tactical decision. *Journal of Cross-Cultural Psychology, 30,* 51–71.

OHBUCHI, K-I., & TAKAHASHI, Y. (1994). Cultural styles of conflict management in Japanese and Americans: Passivity, covertness, and effectiveness of strategies. *Journal of Applied Social Psychology, 24,* 1345–1366.

OHBUCHI, K-I., & TEDESCHI, J. T. (1997). Multiple goals and tactical behaviors in social conflicts. *Journal of Applied Social Psychology, 103,* 5–33.

OLONISAKIN, F. (2000). *Reinventing peacekeeping in Africa.* The Hague: Kluwer Law International.

OLSON, J. M., ROESE, N. J., & ZANNA, M. P. (1996). Expectancies. In E. T. Higgins & A. W. Kruglanski (Eds.), *Social Psychology: Handbook of Basic Principles* (pp. 211–238). New York: Guilford.

OPOTOW, S. (2000). Aggression and violence. In M. Deutsch & P. T. Coleman (Eds.), *The handbook of conflict resolution: Theory and practice* (pp. 403–427). San Francisco: Jossey-Bass.

O'QUIN, K., & ARONOFF, J. (1981). Humor as a technique of social influence. *Social Psychology Quarterly, 44,* 349–357.

ORVIS, B. R., KELLEY, H. H., & BUTLER, D. (1976). Attributional conflict in young couples. In H. H. Harvey, W. J. Ickes, & R. F. Kidd (Eds.), *New directions in attribution research* (Vol. 1, pp. 353–386). Hillsdale, NJ: Erlbaum.

ORWELL, G. (1968). Looking back on the Spanish War. In S. Orwell & I. Angus (Eds.), *The collected essays, journalism and letters of George Orwell: Vol. 2. My country right or left, 1940–1943* (pp. 249–267). New York: Harcourt, Brace & World.

OSGOOD, C. E. (1962). *An alternative to war or surrender.* Urbana; University of Illinois Press.

OSGOOD, C. E. (1966). *Perspective in foreign policy* (2nd ed.). Palo Alto, CA: Pacific Books.

OSKAMP, S. (1965). Attitudes toward U. S. and Russian actions: A double standard. *Psychological Reports, 16,* 43–46.

PARISH, W. L., & WHYTE, M. K. (1978). *Village and family in contemporary China.* Chicago: University of Chicago Press.

PATCHEN, M. (1991). Conflict and cooperation in American-Soviet relations: What have we learned from quantitative research? *International Interactions, 17,* 127–143.

PEARSON, J., & THOENNES, N. (1982). Mediation and divorce: The benefits outweigh the costs. *The Family Advocate, 4,* 26–32.

PEIRCE, R. S., PRUITT, D. G., & CZAJA, S. J. (1993). Complainant-respondent differences in procedural choice. *International Journal of Conflict Management, 4,* 199–222.

PETERS, E. (1952). *Conciliation in action.* New London, CT: National Foremen's Institute.

PETERSON, D. R. (1983). Conflict. In H. H. Kelley, E. Berscheid, A. Christensen, J. H. Harvey, T. L. Huston, G. Levinger, E. McClintock, L. A. Peplau, & D. R. Peterson (Eds.), *Close relationships* (pp. 360–396). New York: Freeman.

PETTIGREW, T. F. (1998). Intergroup contact theory. *Annual Review of Psychology, 49,* 65–85.

PETTY, R. E., & CACIOPPO, J. T. (1996). *Attitudes and persuasion: Classic and contemporary approaches.* Boulder, CO: Westview.

PFENNIG, D. W., & SHERMAN, P. W. (1995). Kin recognition. *Scientific American, 272,* 98–103.

PHILLIPS, B. A. (2001). *The mediation field guide.* San Francisco: Jossey-Bass.

PINKLEY, R. L. (1990). Dimensions of conflict frame: Disputant interpretations of conflict. *Journal of Applied Psychology, 75,* 117–126.

POTTER, S. (1948). *The theory and practice of gamesmanship: The art of winning games without actually cheating.* New York: Holt.

PRUITT, D. G. (1965). Definition of the situation as a determinant of international action. In H. C. Kelman (Ed.), *International behavior: A social-psychological analysis* (pp. 391–432). New York: Holt, Rinehart and Winston.

PRUITT, D. G. (1967). Reward structure and cooperation: The decomposed prisoner's dilemma game. *Journal of Personality and Social Psychology, 7,* 21–27.

PRUITT, D. G. (1969). Stability and sudden change in interpersonal and international affairs. *Journal of Conflict Resolution, 13,* 18–38.

PRUITT, D. G. (1970). Motivational processes in the decomposed prisoner's dilemma game. *Journal of Personality and Social Psychology, 14,* 227–238.

PRUITT, D. G. (1971). Indirect communication and the search for agreement in negotiation. *Journal of Applied Social Psychology, 1,* 205–239.

PRUITT, D. G. (1981). *Negotiation behavior.* New York: Academic Press.

PRUITT, D. G. (1994). Negotiation between organizations: A branching chain model. *Negotiation Journal, 10,* 217–230.

PRUITT, D. G. (1995). Process and outcome in community mediation. *Negotiation Journal, 11,* 365–377.

PRUITT, D. G. (1997). Ripeness theory and the Oslo talks. *International Negotiation, 2,* 237–250.

PRUITT, D. G. (2000a). Alternative dispute resolution. In A. E. Kazdin (Ed.), *Encyclopedia of psychology* (Vol. 1, pp. 124–125). Washington, DC: American Psychological Association.

PRUITT, D. G. (2000b). The tactics of third-party intervention. *Orbis: A Journal of World Affairs, 44,* 245–254.

PRUITT, D. G., BERCOVITCH, J., & ZARTMAN, I. W. (1997). A brief history of the Oslo talks. *International Negotiation, 2,* 177–182.

PRUITT, D. G., & CARNEVALE, P. J. (1982). The development of integrative agreements in social conflict. In V. J. Derlega & J. Grzelak (Eds.), *Living with other people* (pp. 151–181). New York: Academic Press.

PRUITT, D. G., & CARNEVALE, P. J. (1993). *Negotiation in social conflict.* Buckingham, England: Open University Press & Pacific Grove, CA: Brooks/Cole.

PRUITT, D. G., CARNEVALE, P. J., FORCEY, B., & VAN SLYCK, M. (1986). Gender effects in negotiation: Constituent surveillance and contentious behavior. *Journal of Experimental Social Psychology, 22,* 264–275.

PRUITT, D. G., & DREWS, J. L. (1969). The effect of time pressure, time elapsed, and the opponent's concession rate on behavior in negotiation. *Journal of Experimental Social Psychology, 5,* 43–60.

PRUITT, D. G., & GAHAGAN, J. P. (1974). Campus crisis: The search for power. In J. T. Tedeschi (Ed.), *Perspectives on social power* (pp. 349–392). Chicago: Aldine.

PRUITT, D. G., & HOLLAND, J. (1972). *Settlement in the Berlin Crisis, 1958–62.* Buffalo, NY: Council on International Studies, State University of New York at Buffalo.

PRUITT, D. G., & JOHNSON, D. F. (1970). Mediation as an aid to face saving in negotiation. *Journal of Personality and Social Psychology, 14,* 239–246.

PRUITT, D. G., McGILLICUDDY, N. B., WELTON, G. L., & FRY, W. R. (1989). Process of mediation in dispute settlement centers. In K. Kressel, D. G. Pruitt, & Associates, *Mediation research* (pp. 368–393). San Francisco: Jossey-Bass.

PRUITT, D. G., & OLCZAK, P. V. (1995). Beyond hope: Approaches to resolving seemingly intractable conflict. In B. B. Bunker, J. Z. Rubin, & Associates, *Conflict, cooperation and justice: Essays provoked by the work of Morton Deutsch* (pp. 59–92). San Francisco: Jossey-Bass.

PRUITT, D. G., PEIRCE, R. S., McGILLICUDDY, N. B., WELTON, G. L., & CASTRIANNO, L. M. (1993). Long-term success in mediation. *Law and Human Behavior, 17,* 313–330.

PRUITT, D. G., & SNYDER, R. C. (Eds.). (1969). *Theory and research on the causes of war.* Englewood Cliffs, NJ: Prentice-Hall.

RABBIE, J. M., & LODEWIJKX, H. F. M. (1995). Aggressive reactions to social injustice by individuals and groups as a function of social norms, gender, and anonymity. *Social Justice Research, 8,* 7–40.

RAHIM, M. A. (1983). A measure of styles of handling interpersonal conflict. *Academy of Management Journal, 26,* 368–376.

RAHIM, M. A. (1986). Referent role and styles of handling interpersonal conflict. *Journal of Social Psychology, 126*, 79–86.

RAHIM, M. A., & MAGNER, N. R. (1995). Confirmatory factor analysis of the styles of handling interpersonal conflict: First-order factor model and its invariance across groups. *Journal of Applied Psychology, 80*, 122–132.

RAIDER, E. (1995). Conflict resolution training in schools: Translating theory into applied skills. In B. B. Bunker, J. Z. Rubin, & Associates (Eds.), *Conflict, cooperation, and justice: Essays inspired by the work of Morton Deutsch* (pp. 93–121). San Francisco: Jossey-Bass.

RAIDER, E., COLEMAN, S., & GERSON, J. (2000). Teaching conflict resolution skills in a workshop. In M. Deutsch & P. T. Coleman (Eds.), *The handbook of conflict resolution: Theory and practice* (pp. 499–521). San Francisco: Jossey-Bass.

RAIFFA, H. (1982). *The art and science of negotiation.* Cambridge, MA: Harvard University Press.

RANSFORD, H. E. (1968). Isolation, powerlessness and violence: A study of attitudes and participation in the Watts riot. *American Journal of Sociology, 73*, 581–591.

RAPOPORT, A., & CHAMMAH, A. (1965). *Prisoner's dilemma: A study in conflict and cooperation.* Ann Arbor, MI: University of Michigan Press.

RAVEN, B. H., & RUBIN, J. Z. (1983). *Social psychology* (2nd ed.). New York: Wiley.

REGAN, D. T. (1971). Effects of a favor and liking on compliance. *Journal of Experimental Social Psychology, 7*, 627–639.

REGAN, D. T., STRAUS, E., & FAZIO, R. H. (1974). Liking and the attribution process. *Journal of Experimental Social Psychology, 10*, 385–397.

REIK, T. (1952). *Listening with the third ear: The inner experience of a psychoanalyst.* New York: Farrar, Straus.

REYCHLER, L. (1999). *Democratic peace-building and conflict prevention.* Leuven, Belgium: Leuven University Press.

RICE, O. (1982). *The Hatfields and McCoys.* Lexington, KY: University of Kentucky Press.

RICHARDSON, L. F. (1967). *Arms and insecurity.* Chicago: Quadrangle.

RIDLEY, M. (1996). *The origins of virtue: Human instincts and the evolution of cooperation.* New York: Viking.

RIGBY, A. (2001). *Justice and reconciliation: After the violence.* Boulder, CO: Lynne Rienner.

ROGERS, R. W., & PRENTICE-DUNN, S. (1981). Deindividuation and anger-mediated aggression: Unmasking regressive racism. *Journal of Personality and Social Psychology, 41*, 63–73.

ROSENTHAL, R., & JACOBSON, L. F. (1968). *Pygmalion in the classroom.* New York: Holt, Rinehart and Winston.

ROSS, L., & STILLINGER, C. (1991). Barriers to conflict resolution. *Negotiation Journal, 8*, 389–404.

ROTHMAN, J. (1997). *Resolving identity-based conflict in nations, organizations, and communities.* San Francisco: Jossey-Bass.

ROTHSTEIN, R. L. (1999). Fragile peace and its aftermath. In R. L. Rothstein (Ed.), *After the peace: Resistance and reconciliation* (pp. 223–253). Boulder, CO: Lynne Rienner.

ROTTON, J., & FREY, J. (1985). Air pollution, weather, and violent crime: Concomitant time-series analysis of archival data. *Journal of Personality and Social Psychology, 49*, 1207–1220.

ROUHANA, N. N., & KELMAN, H. C. (1994). Promoting joint thinking in international conflicts: An Israeli-Palestinian continuing workshop. *Journal of Social Issues, 50,* 157–178.

RUBENSTEIN, R. E. (1987). *Alchemists of revolution: Terrorism in the modern world.* New York: Basic Books.

RUBENSTEIN, R. E. (1999). Conflict resolution and the structural sources of conflict. In H-W. Jeong (Ed.), *Conflict resolution: Dynamics, process and structure* (pp. 173–195). Aldershot, England & Brookfield, VT: Ashgate.

RUBENSTEIN, R. E. (2003). Sources. In S. Cheldelin, D. Druckman, & L. Fast (Eds.), *Conflict: From analysis to resolution.* London: Continuum.

RUBIN, J. Z. (1980). Experimental research on third-party intervention in conflict: Toward some generalizations. *Psychological Bulletin, 87,* 379–391.

RUBIN, J. Z. (1981). *Dynamics of third-party intervention: Kissinger in the Middle East.* New York: Praeger.

RUBIN, J. Z., & BROWN B. R. (1975). *The social psychology of bargaining and negotiation.* New York: Academic Press.

RUBIN, J. Z., & LEWICKI, R. J. (1973). A three-factor experimental analysis of promises and threats. *Journal of Applied Social Psychology, 3,* 240–257.

RUBIN, J. Z., PRUITT, D. G., & KIM, S. H. (1994). *Social conflict: Escalation, stalemate, and settlement* (2nd ed.). New York: McGraw-Hill.

RUBIN, J. Z., & RUBIN, C. (1989). *When families fight: How to handle conflict with those you love.* New York: Ballantine.

RUBIN, J. Z., STEINBERG, B. D., & GERREIN, J. R. (1974). How to obtain the right of way: An experimental analysis of behavior at intersections. *Perceptual and Motor Skills, 39,* 1263–1274.

RUNCIMAN, W. G. (1966). *Relative deprivation and social justice.* Berkeley, CA: University of California Press.

RUSBULT, C. E., VERETTE, J., WHITNEY, G. A., SLOVIK, L. F., & LIPKUS, G. A. (1991). Accommodation processes in close relationships: Theory and preliminary empirical evidence. *Journal of Personality and Social Psychology, 60,* 53–78.

RUSSELL, C. S., & DREES, C. M. (1989). What's the rush? A negotiated slowdown. In J. F. Crosby (Ed.), *When one wants out and the other doesn't: Doing therapy with polarized couples* (pp. 93–117). New York: Brunner/Mazel.

RUSSETT, B. M. (1967). Pearl Harbor: Deterrence theory and decision theory. *Journal of Peace Research, 2,* 89–106.

RYEN, A. H., & KAHN, A. (1975). The effects of intergroup orientation on group attitudes and proxemic behavior: A test of two models. *Journal of Personality and Social Psychology, 31,* 302–310.

SALACUSE, J. W. (1991). *Making global deals: Negotiating in the international marketplace.* Boston: Houghton Mifflin.

SALOVEY, P., MAYER, J. D., & ROSENHAN, D. L. (1991). Mood and helping: Mood as a motivator of helping and helping as a regulator of mood. In M. S. Clark (Ed.), *Review of personality and social psychology: Vol. 12. Prosocial behavior* (pp. 215–237). Newbury Park, CA: Sage.

SAMPSON, C., & LEDERACH, J. P. (Eds.). (2000). *From the ground up: Mennonite contributions to international peacebuilding.* New York: Oxford University Press.

SANDER, F. E. A., & GOLDBERG, S. B. (1994). Fitting the forum to the fuss: A user-friendly guide to selecting and ADR procedure. *Negotiation Journal, 10,* 49–68.

SANDOLE, D. J. D. (2002). Virulent ethnocentrism: A major challenge for transformational conflict resolution and peacebuilding in the post-Cold War era. *Global Review of Ethnopolitics, 1*, 4–27.

SCHACHTER, S. (1951). Deviation, rejection, and communication. *Journal of Abnormal and Social Psychology, 46*, 190–207.

SCHEFF, T. J. (1994). *Bloody revenge: Emotions, nationalism, and war.* Boulder, CO: Westview.

SCHELLING, T. C. (1960). *The strategy of conflict.* Cambridge, MA: Harvard University Press.

SCHELLING, T. C. (1966). *Arms and influence.* New Haven, CT: Yale University Press.

SCHLENKER, B. R., BONOMA, T. V., TEDESCHI, J. T., & PIVNICK, W. P. (1970). Compliance to threats as a function of the wording of the threat and the exploitativeness of the threatener. *Sociometry, 33*, 394–408.

SCHLENKER, B. R., HELM, B., & TEDESCHI, J. T. (1973). The effects of personality and situational variables on behavioral trust. *Journal of Personality and Social Psychology, 25*, 419–427.

SCHOORMAN, F. D., BAZERMAN, M. H., & ATKIN, R. S. (1981). Interlocking directorates: A strategy for reducing environmental uncertainty. *Academy of Management Review, 6*, 243–251.

SCHOPLER, J., & INSKO, C. A. (1992). The discontinuity effect in interpersonal and intergroup relations: Generality and mediation. In W. Stroebe & M. Hewstone (Eds.), *European Review of Social Psychology* (Vol. 3, pp. 121–51). Chichester, England: Wiley.

SCHUMPETER, J. (1955). *The sociology of imperialism.* New York: Meridian.

SCHWARTZ, S. H., & STRUCH, N. (1989). Values, stereotypes, and intergroup antagonism. In D. Bar-Tal, C. R. Grauman, A. W. Kruglanski, & W. Stroebe (Eds.), *Stereotypes and prejudice: Changing conceptions* (pp. 151–167). New York: Springer-Verlag.

SCHWEITZER, M. E., & DeCHURCH, L. A. (2001). Linking frames in negotiations: Gains, losses and conflict frame adoption. *International Journal of Conflict Management, 12*, 100–113.

SCOBIE, E. D., & SCOBIE, G. E. W. (1998). Damaging events: The perceived need for forgiveness. *Journal of the Theory of Social Behaviour, 28*, 0021–8308.

SHALEV, A. Y., YEHUDA, R., & McFARLANE, A. C. (Eds.). (2000). *International handbook of human response to trauma.* New York: Kluwer Academic/Plenum.

SHARP, G. (1970). *Exploring nonviolent alternatives.* Boston: Porter Sargent.

SHAVER, K. G. (1985). *The attribution of blame: Causality, responsibility, and blameworthiness.* New York: Springer-Verlag.

SHERIF, M., HARVEY, O. J., WHITE, B. J., HOOD, W. R., & SHERIF, C. W. (1961). *Intergroup cooperation and competition: The Robbers Cave experiment.* Norman, OK: University Book Exchange.

SHERIF, M., & SHERIF, C. W. (1969). *Social psychology.* New York: Harper & Row.

SHRIVER, D. W. (1995). *An ethic for enemies: Forgiveness in politics.* New York: Oxford University Press.

SHRIVER, D. W. (2001). Where and when in political life is justice served by forgiveness? In N. Biggar (Ed.), *Burying the past: Making peace and doing justice after civil conflict* (pp. 23–39). Washington, DC: Georgetown University Press.

SHUBIK, M. (1971). The dollar auction game: A paradox in noncooperative behavior and escalation. *Journal of Conflict Resolution, 15*, 109–111.

SILLARS, A. L. (1981). Attributions and interpersonal conflict resolution. In J. H. Harvey, W. J. Ickes, & R. F. Kidd (Eds.), *New directions in attribution research* (Vol. 3, pp. 279–305). Hillsdale, NJ: Erlbaum.

SILLARS, A., ROBERTS, L. J., LEONARD, K. E., & DUN, T. (2000). Cognition during marital conflict: The relationship of thought and talk. *Journal of Social and Personal Relationships. 17,* 479–502.

SIMMEL, G. (1955). *Conflict and the web of group-affiliations.* New York: The Free Press.

SIMON, H. A. (1957). *Models of man: Social and rational.* New York: Wiley.

SJOSTEDT, G. (1993). *International environmental negotiation.* Newbury Park, CA: Sage.

SLUZKI, C. E. (2003). The process toward reconciliation. In A. Chayes & M. L. Minow (Eds.), *Imagine coexistence.* San Francisco: Jossey-Bass.

SMITH, A. H. (1900/1972). *Chinese characteristics.* London: Oliphant, Anderson, and Ferrier.

SMITH, D. L ., PRUITT, D. G., & CARNEVALE, P. J. (1982). Matching and mismatching: The effect of own limit, other's toughness, and time pressure on concession rate in negotiation. *Journal of Personality and Social Psychology, 42,* 876–883.

SMITH, E. R., & MACKIE, D. M. (2000). *Social psychology* (2nd ed.). Philadelphia, PA: Psychology Press.

SMITH, R. H., WEBSTER, J. M., PARROTT, W. G., & EYRE, H. L. (2002). The role of public exposure of moral and nonmoral shame and guilt. *Journal of Personality and Social Psychology, 83,* 138–159.

SMITH, W. P. (1987). Conflict and negotiation: Trends and emerging issues. *Journal of Applied Social Psychology, 17,* 641–677.

SMITH, W. P., & ANDERSON, A. J. (1975). Threats, communication, and bargaining. *Journal of Personality and Social Psychology, 32,* 76–82.

SNYDER, G. H., & DIESING, P. (1977). *Conflict among nations.* Princeton, NJ: Princeton University Press.

SNYDER, M., & SWANN, W. B., JR. (1978). Behavioral confirmation in social interaction: From social perception to social reality. *Journal of Experimental Social Psychology, 14,* 148–162.

SOLOMON, L. (1960). The influence of some types of power relationships and game strategies upon the development of interpersonal trust. *Journal of Abnormal and Social Psychology, 61,* 223–230.

SPECTOR, B. L. (1999). *Negotiated rulemaking: A participative approach to consensus-building for regulatory development and implementation* (Technical Note No. 10). Washington D.C. : USAID Implementing Policy Change Project.

STAUB, E. (2001). Ethnopolitical and other group violence: Origins and prevention. In D. Chirot & M. E. P Seligman (Eds.), *Ethnopolitical warfare: Causes, consequences, and possible solutions* (pp. 289–304). Washington, DC: American Psychological Association.

STEDMAN, S. J. (1991). *Peacemaking in civil wars: International mediation in Zimbabwe, 1974–1980.* Boulder, CO: Lynne Rienner.

STEDMAN, S. J. (2000). Spoiler problems in peace processes. In P. C. Stern & D. Druckman (Eds.). *Conflict resolution after the Cold War* (pp. 178–224). Washington D. C.: National Academy Press.

STEELE, C. M. (1988). The psychology of self-affirmation: Sustaining the integrity of the self. In L. Berkowitz (Ed.), *Advances in experimental social psychology* (Vol.21, pp. 261–302). Hillsdale, NJ: Erlbaum.

STEELE, C. M., & JOSEPHS, R. A. (1990). Alcohol myopia: Its prized and dangerous effects. *American Psychologist, 45,* 921–933.

STEERS, R. M. (1999). *Made in Korea: Chung Ju Yung and the rise of Hyundai.* New York: Routledge.

STEGER, M. B., & LIND, N. S. (1999). *Violence and its alternatives.* New York: Palgrave/McMillan.

STEIN, J. G. (1989). Getting to the table: The triggers, stages, functions, and consequences of prenegotiation. In J. G. Stein (Ed.), *Getting to the table: The processes of international prenegotiation* (pp. 239–268). Baltimore, MD: Johns Hopkins University Press.

STEIN, J. G. (1996). Image, identity, and conflict resolution. In C. Crocker & F. Hampson (Eds.), *Managing global chaos: Sources of and responses to international conflict* (pp. 93–112). Washington D.C.: United States Institute of Peace Press.

STENGEL, R. (2000). *You're too kind: A brief history of flattery.* New York: Simon & Schuster.

STERNBERG, R. J., & DOBSON, D. M. (1987). Resolving interpersonal conflicts: An analysis of stylistic consistency. *Journal of Personality and Social Psychology, 52,* 794–812.

STERNBERG, R. J., & SORIANO, L. J. (1984). Styles of conflict resolution. *Journal of Personality and Social Psychology, 47,* 115–126.

STRAUS, D. B. (1981). Kissinger and management of complexity: An attempt that failed. In J. Z. Rubin (Ed.), *Dynamics of third party intervention: Kissinger in the Middle East* (pp. 253–270). New York: Praeger.

STRUCH, N., & SCHWARTZ, S. H. (1989). Intergroup aggression: Its predictors and distinctness from in-group bias. *Journal of Personality and Social Psychology, 56,* 364–373.

SUMNER, W. G. (1906). *Folkways.* Boston: Ginn.

SUSSKIND, L., BACOW, L., & WHEELER, M. (1983). *Resolving environmental regulatory disputes.* Rochester, VT: Schenkman.

SWANN, W. B., JR. (1987). Identity negotiation: Where two roads meet. *Journal of Personality and Social Psychology, 53,* 1038–1051.

TAJFEL, H. (1970). Experiments in intergroup discrimination. *Scientific American, 223,* 96–102.

TAJFEL, H., & TURNER, J. C. (1979). An integrative theory of intergroup conflict. In W. G. Austin & S. Worchel (Eds.), *The social psychology of intergroup relations* (pp. 33–47). Monterey, CA: Brooks/Cole.

TAJFEL, H., & TURNER, J. C. (1986). The social identity theory of intergroup behavior. In S. Worchel & W. G. Austin (Eds.), *Psychology of intergroup relations,* (pp. 7–24). Chicago: Nelson-Hall.

TAVUCHIS, N. (1991). *Mea Culpa: A sociology of apology and reconciliation.* Stanford, CA: Stanford University Press.

TAYLOR, S. E. (1991). Asymmetrical effects of positive and negative events: The mobilization-minimization hypothesis. *Psychological Bulletin, 110,* 67–85.

TAYLOR, S. P., & LEONARD, K. E. (1983). Alcohol and human physical aggression. In R. G. Geen & E. Donnerstein (Eds.), *Aggression: Theoretical and empirical reviews,* Vol. 2: *Issues in research* (pp. 77–101). New York: Academic Press.

TEDESCHI, J. T., & BOND, M. H. (2001). Aversive behavior and aggression in cultural perspective. In R. M. Kowalski (Ed.), *Behaving badly: Aversive behaviors in interpersonal relationship* (pp. 257–293). Washington, DC: American Psychological Association.

TEDESCHI, J. T., SCHLENKER, B. R., & BONOMA, T. V. (1973). *Conflict, power and games*. Chicago: Aldine.

TEGER, A. I. (1980). *Too much invested to quit*. New York: Pergamon.

TETLOCK, P. E. (1983). Policymakers' images of international conflict. *Journal of Social Issues, 39,* 67–86.

THIBAUT, J. W., & KELLEY, H. H. (1959). *The social psychology of groups*. New York: Wiley.

THOMAS, K. (1976). Conflict and conflict management. In M. D. Dunnette (Ed.), *Handbook of industrial and organizational psychology* (pp. 889–935). Chicago: Rand McNally.

THOMPSON, L. L. (1990a). Negotiation behavior and outcomes: Empirical evidence and theoretical issues. *Psychological Bulletin, 108,* 515–532.

THOMPSON, L. L. (1990b). An examination of naive and experienced negotiators. *Journal of Personality and Social Psychology, 59,* 82–90.

THOMPSON, L. L. (2001). *The mind and heart of the negotiator* (2nd ed.). Upper Saddle River, NJ: Prentice–Hall.

THOMPSON, L. L., & HASTIE, R. (1990). Social perception in negotiation. *Organizational Behavior and Human Decision Processes, 47,* 98–123.

THOMPSON, L. L., & HREBEC, D. (1996). Lose-lose agreements in interdependent decision making. *Psychological Bulletin, 120,* 396–409.

THOMPSON, L. L., & NADLER, J. (2000). Judgmental biases in conflict resolution and how to overcome them. In M. Deutsch & P. T. Coleman (Eds.), *The handbook of conflict resolution: Theory and practice* (pp. 213–235). San Francisco, CA: Jossey-Bass.

TING-TOOMEY, S. (1994). Managing conflict in intimate intercultural relationships. In D. D. Cahn (Ed.), *Conflict in personal relationships* (pp. 47–77). Hillsdale, NJ: Lawrence Erlbaum.

TINSLEY, C. H. (1997). Understanding conflict in a Chinese cultural context. In B. Bies, R. Lewicki, & B. Sheppard (Eds.), *Research on negotiations in organizations* (Vol. 6, pp. 209–225). Beverly Hills, CA: Sage.

TINSLEY, C. H. (1998). Models of conflict resolution in Japanese, German, and American cultures. *Journal of Applied Psychology, 83,* 316–323.

TINSLEY, C. H. (2001). How negotiators get to yes: Predicting the constellation of strategies used across cultures to negotiate conflict. *Journal of Applied Psychology, 86,* 583–593.

TINSLEY, C. H., & BRETT, J. M. (2001). Managing workplace conflict in the United States and Hong Kong. *Organizational Behavior and Human Decision Making, 85,* 360–381.

TINSLEY, C. H., O'CONNOR, K., & SULLIVAN, B. (2001). "Tough" guys finish last: The perils of a distributive reputation. *Organizational Behavior and Human Decision Processes, 88,* 621–642.

TINSLEY, C. H., & PILLUTLA, M. M. (1998). The influence of culture on business negotiations in the U.S. and Hong Kong. *Journal of International Business Studies, 29,* 711–728.

TJOSVOLD, D. (1977). Commitment to justice in conflict between unequal persons. *Journal of Applied Social Psychology, 7,* 149–162.

TJOSVOLD, D., HUI, C., & LAW, K. S. (2001). Constructive conflict in China: Cooperative conflict as a bridge between East and West. *Journal of World Business, 36,* 166–183.

TJOSVOLD, D., LEUNG, K., & JOHNSON, D. W. (2000). Cooperative and competitive conflict in China. In M. Deutsch & P. T. Coleman (Eds.), *The handbook of conflict resolution: Theory and practice* (pp. 475–495). San Francisco: Jossey-Bass.

TJOSVOLD, D., & OKUN, M. A. (1976). *Corrupting effects of unequal power: Cognitive perspective-taking and cooperation.* Paper presented at the annual convention of the American Psychological Association, Washington, D.C.

TOCH, H. (1969). *Violent men: An inquiry into the psychology of violence.* Chicago: Aldine.

TOCH, H. (1970). The social psychology of violence. In E. I. Megargee & J. E. Hokanson (Eds.), *The dynamics of aggression* (pp. 160–169). New York: Harper & Row.

TOUVAL, S., & ZARTMAN, I. W. (1985). *International mediation in theory and practice.* Boulder, CO: Westview.

TOUVAL, S., & ZARTMAN, I. W. (1989). Mediation in international conflicts. In K. Kressel, D. G. Pruitt, & Associates, *Mediation research* (pp. 115–137). San Francisco: Jossey-Bass.

TRIANDIS, H. C. (1990). Theoretical concepts that are applicable to the analysis of ethnocentrism. In R. W. Brislin (Ed.), *Applied cross-cultural psychology* (pp. 34–55). Newbury Park: Sage.

TRIANDIS, H. C. (1994). *Culture and social behavior.* New York: McGraw-Hill.

TRIANDIS, H. C. (1995). *Individualism and collectivism.* Boulder, CO: Westview.

TRIANDIS, H. C. (2000). Culture and conflict. *International Journal of Psychology, 35,* 145–152.

TRIANDIS, H. C., CARNEVALE, P. J., GELFAND, M. J., et al. (2001). Culture, personality, and deception in negotiation: A multilevel analysis. *International Journal of Cross-Cultural Management, 1,* 73–90.

TSE, D. K., FRANCIS, J., & WALLS, J. (1994). Cultural differences in conducting intra- and inter-cultural negotiations: A Sino-Canadian comparison. *Journal of International Business Studies, 25,* 537–555.

TURNER, J. C. (1981). The experimental social psychology of intergroup behavior. In J. C. Turner & H. Giles (Eds.), *Intergroup behaviour* (pp. 66–101). Oxford, England: Basil Blackwell.

TURNER, J. C., HOGG M. A., OAKES, P. J., & SMITH, P. M. (1984). Failure and defeat as determinants of group cohesiveness. *British Journal of Social Psychology, 23,* 97–111.

TYLER, T. R. (1990). *Why people obey the law.* New Haven, CT: Yale University Press.

URY, W. L. (1991). *Getting past no: Negotiating with difficult people.* New York: Bantam.

URY, W. L., BRETT, J. M., & GOLDBERG, S. (1988). *Getting disputes resolved.* San Francisco: Jossey-Bass.

VAN DE VLIERT, E. (1990). Positive effects of conflict: A field assessment. *The International Journal of Conflict Management, 1,* 69–80.

VAN DE VLIERT, E. (1997). *Complex interpersonal conflict behaviour: Theoretical frontiers.* Hove, England: Psychology Press.

VAN DE VLIERT, E., & PREIN, H. C. M. (1989). The difference in the meaning of forcing in the conflict management of actors and observers. In M. A. Rahim (Ed.), *Managing conflict: An interdisciplinary approach* (pp. 51–63). New York: Praeger.

VAN DEN BROUCKE, S., VANDEREYCKEN, W., & NORRE, J. (1997). *Eating disorders and marital relationships.* London: Routledge.

VAN SLYCK, M., & STERN, M. (1991). Conflict resolution in educational settings: Assessing the impact of peer mediation programs. In K. G. Duffy, J. W. Grosch, & P. V. Olczak (Eds.), *Community mediation: A handbook for practitioners and researchers* (pp. 257–274). New York: Guilford.

VAN SLYCK, M., STERN, M., & NEWLAND, L. M. (1992). Parent-child mediation: An empirical assessment. *Mediation Quarterly, 10,* 75–87.

VANBESELAERE, N. (1991). The different effects of simple and crossed categorization: A result of the category differentiation process or of differential category salience? In W. Stroebe & M. Hewstone (Eds.), *European Review of Social Psychology* (Vol. 2, pp. 247–279). Chichester, England: Wiley.

VARSHNEY, A. (2002). *Ethnic Conflict and Civic Life: Hindus and Muslims in India.* New Haven, CT: Yale University Press.

VOLKAN, V. D. (1997). *Bloodlines: From ethnic pride to ethnic terrorism.* New York: Farrar, Straus and Giroux.

VOLKAN, V. D. (2001). Transgenerational transmissions and chosen traumas: An aspect of large-group identity. *Group Analysis, 34,* 79–97.

VONK, R. (1998). The slime effect: Suspicion and dislike of likeable behavior toward superiors. *Journal of Personality and Social Psychology, 74,* 849–864.

VONK, R. (1999). Differential evaluations of likeable and dislikeable behaviours enacted towards superiors and subordinates. *European Journal of Social Psychology, 29,* 139–146.

VOSSEKUIL, B., REDDY, M., FEIN, R., BORUM, R., & MODZELESKI, W. (2000). *Safe School Initiative: An interim report on the prevention of targeted violence in schools.* Washington, DC: U.S. Secret Service, National Threat Assessment Center.

WALL, J. A. (1975). Effects of constituent trust and representative bargaining orientation on intergroup bargaining. *Journal of Personality and Social Psychology, 31,* 1004–1012.

WALL, J. A. (1977). Intergroup bargaining: Effects of opposing constituent's stance, opposing representative's bargaining, and representative's locus of control. *Journal of Conflict Resolution, 21,* 459–474.

WALL, J. A. (1979). The effects of mediator rewards and suggestions upon negotiations. *Journal of Personality and Social Psychology, 37,* 1554–1560.

WALL, J. A., DRUCKMAN, D., & DIEHL, P. F. (2002). Mediation by international peacekeepers. In J. Bercovitch (Ed.), *Mediation in international relations* (2nd ed.). New York: St. Martin's.

WALL, J. A., & LYNN, A. (1993). Mediation; A current review. *Journal of Conflict Resolution, 37,* 160–194.

WALL, J. A., & RUDE, D. E. (1989). Judicial mediation of settlement negotiations. In K. Kressel, D. G. Pruitt, & Associates, *Mediation research* (pp. 190–212). San Francisco: Jossey-Bass.

WALL, J. A., & RUDE, D. E. (1991). The judge as mediator. *Journal of Applied Psychology, 76,* 54–59.

WALL, J. A., STARK, J. B., & STANDIFER, R. L. (2001). Mediation: A current review and theory development. *Journal of Conflict Resolution, 45,* 370–391.

WALSTER, E. H., WALSTER, G. W., & BERSCHEID, E. (1978). *Equity: Theory and research.* Boston: Allyn and Bacon.

WALTON, R. E. (1969). *Interpersonal peacemaking: Confrontations and third-party consultation.* Reading, MA: Addison-Wesley.

WALTON, R. E., & MCKERSIE, R. B. (1965). *A behavioral theory of labor negotiations: An analysis of a social interaction system.* New York: McGraw-Hill.

WEBSTER, N. (1983). *New Twentieth Century Dictionary* (2nd ed.). New York: Simon & Schuster.

WEINER, B., AMIRKHAN, J., FOLKES, V. S., & VERETTE, J. A. (1987). An attributional analysis of excuse giving: Studies of a naive theory of emotion. *Journal of Personality and Social Psychology, 52,* 316–324.

WEISS, J. N. (2002). *Mediator sequencing strategies in intractable communal conflicts.* Unpublished doctoral dissertation, George Mason University, Fairfax, Virginia.

WELTON, G. L., & PRUITT, D. G. (1987). The mediation process: The effects of mediator bias and disputant power. *Personality and Social Psychology Bulletin, 13,* 123–133.

WELTON, G. L., PRUITT, D. G., & McGILLICUDDY, N. B. (1988). The role of caucusing in community mediation. *Journal of Conflict Resolution, 32,* 181–202.

WELTON, G. L., PRUITT, D. G., McGILLICUDDY, N. B., IPPOLITO, C. A., & ZUBEK, J. M. (1992). Antecedents and characteristics of caucusing in community mediation. *International Journal of Conflict Management, 3,* 303–318.

WHEELER, L., & CAGGIULA, A. R. (1966). The contagion of aggression. *Journal of Experimental Social Psychology, 2,* 1–10.

WHITE, J. R. (1998). *Terrorism: An introduction* (2nd ed.). Belmont, CA: Wadsworth.

WHITE, R. K. (1984). *Fearful warriors: A psychological profile of U.S.-Soviet relations.* New York: Free Press.

WINSTON, D. S. (1996). Participation standards in mandatory mediation statutes: "You can lead a horse to water . . ." *Ohio State Journal on Dispute Resolution, 11,* 187–206.

WINTER, D. G. (1987). Enhancement of an enemy's power motivation as a dynamic of conflict escalation. *Journal of Personality and Social Psychology, 52,* 41–46.

WOLFGANG, M., & STROHM, R. B. (1956). The relationship between alcohol and criminal homicide. *Quarterly Journal of Studies on Alcohol, 17,* 411–425.

WOOD, J. V. (1989). Theory and research concerning social comparisons of personal attributes. *Psychological Bulletin, 106,* 231–248.

WOOD, M. M. (1934). *The stranger: A study in social relationships.* New York: Columbia University Press.

WOODHOUSE, T., & RAMSBOTHAM, O. (Eds.). (2000). *Peacekeeping and conflict resolution.* London: Frank Cass.

WORCHEL, S. (1979). Cooperation and the reduction of intergroup conflict: Some determining factors. In W. G. Austin & S. Worchel (Eds.), *The social psychology of intergroup relations* (pp. 262–273). Monterey, CA: Brooks/Cole.

WORCHEL, S., & ANDREOLI, V. A. (1978). Facilitation of social interaction through deindividuation of the target. *Journal of Personality and Social Psychology, 36,* 549–556.

WORCHEL, S., ANDREOLI, V. A., & FOLGER, R. (1977). Intergroup cooperation and intergroup attraction: The effect of previous interaction and outcome on combined effort. *Journal of Experimental Social Psychology, 13,* 131–140.

WORCHEL, S., & NORVELL, N. (1980). Effect of perceived environmental conditions during cooperation on intergroup attraction. *Journal of Personality and Social Psychology, 38,* 764–772.

WORTHINGTON, E. L., JR. (2001). *Five steps to forgiveness: The art and science of forgiving.* New York: Crown.

WORTHINGTON, E. L., JR., SANDAGE, S. J., & BERRY, J. W. (2000). Group interventions to promote forgiveness: What researchers and clinicians ought to know. In M. E. McCullough, K. I. Pargament, & C. E. Theoresen (Eds.), *Forgiveness: Theory, research, and practice* (pp. 228–253). New York: Guilford.

WORTMAN, C. B., & LINSENMEIER, J. A. W. (1977). Interpersonal attraction and techniques of ingratiation in organizational settings. In B. M. Staw & G. R. Salancik (Eds.), *New directions in organizational behavior* (pp. 133–178). Chicago: St. Clair Press.

YAMAGISHI, T. (1986). The provision of a sanctioning system as a public good. *Journal of Personality and Social Psychology, 51,* 110–116.

YAMAGISHI, T., & SATO, K. (1986). Motivational bases of the public goods problem. *Journal of Personality and Social Psychology, 50,* 67–73.

YAMAGISHI, T., & YAMAGISHI, M. (1994). Trust and commitment in the United States and Japan. *Motivation and Emotion, 18,* 129–166.

YAMAMOTO, E. K. (1999). *Interracial justice: Conflict and reconciliation in post-civil rights America.* New York: New York University Press.

YOUNG, O. R. (1968). *The politics of force.* Princeton, NJ: Princeton University Press.

YOUNGS, G. A., JR. (1986). Patterns of threat and punishment reciprocity in a conflict setting. *Journal of Personality and Social Psychology, 51,* 541–546.

YOVETICH, N. A., & RUSBULT, C. E. (1994). Accommodative behavior in close relationships: Exploring transformation of motivation. *Journal of Experimental Social Psychology, 30,* 138–164.

YUKL, G. A., MALONE, M. P., HAYSLIP, B., & PAMIN, T. A. (1976). The effects of time pressure and issue settlement order on integrative bargaining. *Sociometry, 39,* 277–281.

ZAJONC, R. B. (1968). Attitudinal effects of mere exposure. *Journal of Personality and Social Psychology. Monograph Supplement, 9* (2, Pt. 2).

ZAKARIA, F. (2001, October 15). Why do they hate us? The politics of rage. *Newsweek,* 22–40

ZARTMAN, I. W. (Ed.). (1977). *The negotiation process: Theories and applications.* Beverly Hills, CA: Sage.

ZARTMAN, I. W. (1981). Explaining disengagement. In J. Z. Rubin (Ed.), *Dynamics of third-party intervention* (pp. 148–167). New York: Praeger.

ZARTMAN, I. W. (1989). *Ripe for resolution: Conflict resolution in Africa* (2nd ed.). New York: Oxford.

ZARTMAN, I. W. (Ed.). (1994). *Multilateral negotiation.* San Francisco: Jossey-Bass.

ZARTMAN, I. W. (1995). Dynamics and constraints in negotiations in internal conflicts. In I. W. Zartman (Ed.), *Elusive peace: Negotiating an end to civil wars* (pp. 3–30). Washington D.C.: The Brookings Institution.

ZARTMAN, I. W. (2000). Ripeness: The hurting stalemate and beyond. In P. C. Stern & D. Druckman (Eds.), *Conflict resolution after the Cold War* (pp. 225–250). Washington D.C.: National Academy Press.

ZARTMAN, I. W., & BERMAN, M. R. (1982). *The practical negotiator.* New Haven, CT: Yale University Press.

ZARTMAN, I. W., & RASMUSSEN, J. L. (Eds.). (1997). *Peacemaking in international conflict: Methods and techniques.* Washington D.C.: United States Institute of Peace Press.

ZILLMANN, D. (1971). Excitation transfer in communication-mediated aggressive behavior. *Journal of Experimental Social Psychology, 7,* 419–434.

ZILLMANN, D. (1979). *Hostility and aggression.* Hillsdale, NJ: Erlbaum.

ZILLMANN, D., JOHNSON, R. C., & DAY, K. D. (1974). Attribution of apparent arousal and proficiency of recovery from sympathetic activation affecting activation transfer to aggressive behavior. *Journal of Experimental Social Psychology, 10,* 503–515.

ZIMBARDO, P. G. (1970). The human choice: Individuation, reason, and order versus deindividuation, impulse, and chaos. In W. J. Arnold & D. Levine (Eds.), *Nebraska Symposium on Motivation, 1969* (Vol. 17, pp. 237–307). Lincoln: University of Nebraska Press.

ZINNES, D. A., NORTH, R. C., & KOCH, H. E., JR. (1961). Capability, threat, and the outbreak of war. In J. N. Rosenau (Ed.), *International politics and foreign policy.* New York: Free Press.

ZUBEK, J. M., PRUITT, D. G., MCGILLICUDDY, N. B., PEIRCE, R. S., & SYNA, H. (1992). Short-term success in mediation: Its relationship to prior conditions and mediator and disputant behaviors. *Journal of Conflict Resolution, 36,* 546–572.

Glossary

❖

accountability A representative's responsibility to report and justify the outcome of his or her negotiations to powerful constituents.

aggression Intentionally hurting another person.

arbitration Nonjudicial third party decision making about a conflict. In conventional arbitration, the decision is binding; in advisory arbitration, it is only a recommendation.

arousal Activation of the autonomic nervous system.

aspirations What a party seeks or believes it must attain. Aspirations may take the form of goals that the party is striving for or standards that the party hopes to meet or exceed.

attitude Positive or negative feeling toward a person, group, or object.

attribution Interpretation of the cause or motivation for Other's actions.

attributional distortion Attributing Other's behavior that is consistent with one's expectations to Other's enduring characteristics, or attributing Other's behavior that is inconsistent with one's expectations to temporary environmental pressures on Other.

autistic hostility Antagonism that perpetuates itself by blocking further communication with Other.

avoiding A strategy that fails to deal with a conflict, either through inaction or withdrawing.

back-channel contacts Off-the-record meetings between disputing parties.

balance of power Distribution of resources such that all members of a community are deterred from attacking one another by a belief that they cannot succeed.

balance of terror Distribution of resources such that all members of a community are deterred from attacking one another by fear of retaliation.

blame Assignment of responsibility or fault for an unpleasant, frustrating, or painful experience.

bond Felt or perceived link between Party and Other. May be due to attraction, kinship, common group identity, perceived similarity, or the expectation of future dependence.

bridging A type of integrative solution in which a new alternative is devised that satisfies the most important interests underlying the parties' initial demands.

caucusing A mediation technique whereby the parties are physically separated and the mediator engages in a private conversation with each of them.

coercive commitment Communication indicating that Party will under no circumstances deviate from its present position.

cohesiveness   Group solidarity; overall attractiveness of a group to its members.

collectivism   Viewing oneself primarily as a group member rather than a separate individual and giving priority to the welfare of the group in contrast to one's own welfare. Collectivism may be a personal orientation or a cultural pattern. (See individualism.)

common group membership   The perception that Other is a member of a group to which Party also belongs.

community polarization   Recruitment of formerly neutral community members to one side or the other in a conflict. Neutral third parties become scarce during community polarization.

compromise   An obvious alternative that stands partway between the disputants' preferred positions.

conflict   Perceived divergence of interest; a belief that one's own aspirations are incompatible with Other's aspirations.

conflict group   A set of people who have a strong group identity and are mobilized to defend their group's interests against those of another group. (See mobilization.)

conflict management system   A set of trained individuals and their procedures that are ready to spring into action if a conflict threatens to escalate in their community.

conflict spiral model   Explanation of escalation as due to a vicious circle of contentious action and reaction.

conflict style   The way a person most commonly deals with conflict.

constituent   A party who is represented by another party in a conflict or negotiation.

contender-defender model   Explanation of escalation as due to one party's efforts to exploit or change another party and the other party's resistance to these efforts.

contending   A strategy in which Party tries to impose its preferred solution on Other. Also called "contentious behavior."

cost cutting   A type of integrative solution in which Party gets what it wants, while Other's costs are reduced or eliminated.

covert problem solving   Problem solving that takes place behind the scenes or in the form of signals.

credibility   Believability of a threat, promise, or coercive commitment.

crosscutting bonds   A type of community structure in which bonds are strong between groups. For example, if a community consists of workers and management, some workers are linked to some managers by kinship, common group membership, etc. (See overlapping bonds.)

culture   A set of shared and enduring meanings, values, and beliefs that distinguish national, ethnic, or other groups from each other and guide the behavior of group members.

cycle of escalation   A four-part, recurring sequence of events in which Party's escalated behavior produces (1) changes in Other or in the surrounding community, leading to (2) escalated behavior by Other, which produces (3) changes in Party or the surrounding community, leading to (4) more escalated behavior by Party.

de-escalation   Reduction in the intensity of conflict.

de-escalatory spiral   A benevolent spiral involving back-and-forth conciliatory actions on the part of Party and Other.

dehumanization Perception of Other as something less than human.

deindividuation Perception of Other as a member of a category rather than as an individual.

dependence Reliance on Other for one's outcomes.

disputant A party to a conflict.

distrust Perception of Other as not caring about, or being antagonistic to, one's interests.

dual concern model A theory stating that strategic choice is a function of the relative strength of self-concern and other-concern. It is a theory of both conflict style and the impact of conditions on behavior.

dysphoric rumination Brooding; obsessive thoughts about unpleasant prior incidents.

empathy Vicarious experience of Other's feelings and thoughts.

entrapment Persistence of unrewarding behavior in pursuit of a goal, often characterized by the belief that one has too much invested to quit.

escalation Used in two related senses: (1) a party's adoption of heavier tactics than it used before, or (2) an increase in the intensity of conflict as a whole.

expanding the pie A type of integrative solution in which a scarce resource is enlarged.

firm but conciliatory stance Strategy of standing firm on one's basic interests while also trying to be responsive to Other's basic interests.

firm flexibility Firmness with respect to ends, in conjunction with flexibility with respect to the means for achieving those ends.

formula A brief statement of the essential features of an agreement, which serves as a guide for later work on the fine details.

framing How Party conceptualizes alternatives between which it must choose. Positive framing implies a choice between several ways to gain; negative framing, a choice between several ways to lose.

fraternalistic deprivation A sense that one's own group has been deprived.

group A set of people who are capable of coordinated action—a small group, organization, community, or nation. Also called a "collective."

group identity A sense of "we-ness" among group members. The stronger a group's identity, the more concern group members feel for each other's welfare.

group polarization Strengthening of the dominant attitude or belief in a group as a result of group discussion.

heavy tactics Contentious tactics that impose great costs on Other.

identity An individual's or group's conception of itself, the latter being called "social identity." The need for a positive identity, especially a positive social identity, is usually quite strong; and denial of this need can be frustrating and conflict evoking. (Contrast with group identity.)

image loss Loss of status or credibility in the eyes of Other or of observers; often a perception that Party is weak.

image threat Threat to the way Party appears in the eyes of itself, Other, or observers.

inaction An avoidance tactic that involves doing nothing.

individualism Viewing oneself primarily as an individual rather than as a group member and giving priority to one's own welfare in contrast to that of the group. Individualism may be a personal orientation or a cultural pattern. (See collectivism.)

information loss   Discovery by Other of the nature of Party's interests or the location of Party's lower limit.

ingratiation   Trying to increase one's attractiveness to Other in order to exercise influence.

inhibition   Psychological forces that prevent one from taking a particular kind of action. Escalation is less likely when one or both parties are inhibited against aggression.

instability   Conditions under which conflict is likely to escalate.

integrative potential   Availability of a mutually beneficial solution to a conflict.

integrative solution   An alternative that reconciles the parties' basic interests; a mutually benefical option. Also called a "win-win solution."

interactive conflict resolution   Third-party led meetings involving a few people from each side of a conflict, designed to foster understanding of that conflict and, if possible, to develop strategies for dealing with it. Also called "problem-solving workshop."

interest tree   Hierarchical diagram showing a party's more basic interests at lower levels, and more superficial interests at higher levels.

interests   A party's feelings about what is basically desirable; its values and needs.

intermediary   Third party who provides a communication link between the parties. Chains of two intermediaries are sometimes found.

invidious comparison   Perception that Other receives more reward in comparison to its worth than does Party.

joint outcome space   Geometric representation of the perceived value to two parties of the available alternatives.

light tactics   Contentious tactics that impose relatively low cost on Other.

linkage   Association of demands, goals, aspirations, and values in a package that seems inviolable. Unbundling such a package is often necessary for the development of an integrative solution.

logrolling   A type of integrative solution in which each party concedes on issues that are of low priority to itself and high priority to the other party.

management of a conflict   Actions by disputants or third parties that reduce the likelihood that heavy contentious tactics will be used in a conflict.

mediation   A form of outside intervention in which a third party tries to help disputants reach a voluntary agreement.

mediation-arbitration (med-arb)   A hybrid of mediation and arbitration in which arbitration is imposed only if the parties fail to reach agreement through mediation.

mediator power   A mediator's capacity to reward or punish the parties.

meta-analysis   A statistical method for combining the results of a number of prior studies to test an hypothesis or set of hypotheses.

mobilization   The process by which a set of people develop a group identity and a goal of defending their group's interests against those of another group.

model   An abstract pattern of thought from which explanations or predictions of particular events can be derived.

momentum   Sense of forward motion in conflict resulting from prior success at achieving agreement.

negative reciprocity   Retaliation, for example, responding to Other's criticism with return criticism.

negotiation   A form of conflict behavior that seeks to resolve divergence of interest by means of a verbal exchange between the parties.

nonspecific compensation   A type of integrative solution in which Party gets what it wants and Other is repaid in an unrelated coin.

nonviolent resistance   A set of nonviolent tactics that can be used by low power individuals or groups to assert their rights against the powerful.

normative consensus   Agreement among group members about the norms of their group.

norms   Rules of behavior that a group imposes on its members.

opportunity costs   Benefits that would have been achieved if one had made a different decision.

optimism   Expectation of success in future negotiation with Other. The greater the sense of stalemate and optimism on both sides, the more likely are negotiation or mediation to start and persist.

other-concern   Importance placed on Other's outcomes. (See self-concern.)

overcommitment   Resolution to follow an unwise course of action.

overlapping bonds   A type of community structure in which bonds are weak or nonexistent between subgroups within the community. (See crosscutting bonds.)

party   A participant in conflict; a disputant. Parties can be individuals, groups, organizations, communities, or nations.

peace building   Third party efforts to rebuild institutions and relationships after a war so as to diminish the chances that the war will start again.

peace enforcement   Military actions by third parties designed to stop an invasion or war.

peacekeeping   Activities by lightly armed third party troops designed to manage conflict in a previous war zone.

perceived common ground (PCG)   The perceived likelihood of finding an alternative that satisfies both parties' aspirations.

perceived divergence of interest   A belief that the parties have incompatible aspirations.

perceived feasibility   The extent to which a strategy seems capable of achieving one's aspirations at a reasonable cost.

perceived stalemate   Circumstance in which a party becomes aware that it cannot make further progress in a conflict at an acceptable cost or risk.

perception   Belief about or view of a person, group, or object.

persuasive argumentation   Contentious tactics aimed at lowering Other's aspirations by means of logical appeals.

position loss   Other's perception that Party has conceded from an earlier position.

power   The capacity to persuade Other to yield.

priorities   Preferences among interests, such as a preference for wealth over social approval.

problem solving   A strategy that involves seeking a mutually satisfactory alternative.

promise   Verbal commitment to reward Other for complying with one's wishes.

psychological changes   Changes in individuals that result from escalation and produce more escalation.

reconciliation.   Process leading to the repair of an interpersonal or intergroup relationship that has been damaged by prior conflict.

reframing   Reconceptualizing—adopting a new view of—a conflict. Reframing often leads to the discovery of new integrative solutions.

relative deprivation   Failure to achieve one's aspirations.

resolution of a conflict   A substantive agreement dealing with most or all of the issues in a conflict. Resolution, in contrast to settlement, offers a permanent solution to the conflict.

runaway norms   Norms that get out of hand and commit a group to hostile behavior toward another group.

security dilemma   Situation in which distrust makes it rational for two or more parties to prepare for violent conflict against each other, yet the parties would be better off if none of them made those preparations.

selective information processing   Attending to, searching for, interpreting, retaining, or recalling information that supports a current belief or attitude.

self-concern   Importance placed on one's own outcomes. (See other-concern.)

self-fulfilling prophecy   A phenomenon that occurs when Party's expectations about Other cause Other to behave in ways that confirm these expectations.

settlement of a conflict   A substantive agreement dealing with enough of the issues that disputants are willing to give up their escalated struggle. Settlement, in contrast to resolution, may be only a temporary remedy to the conflict.

size of conflict   Apparent extent of the divergence of interest between two parties.

social identity theory   The theory that people think well of and favor their own group over other groups in order to enhance their self-esteem.

social structure   Enduring political, economic, social, or legal relationships between people that structure their interaction or attitudes toward each other.

stability   Conditions under which conflict is unlikely to escalate.

strategic choice   Choice among the four basic strategies for dealing with conflict.

strategy   A broad class of conflict behaviors. Four basic strategies are distinguished: contending, yielding, problem solving, and avoiding. (See tactic.)

structural change model   Explanation of escalation as due to persistent changes in individuals, groups, or communities.

superordinate goal   An objective that is shared by the parties and requires them to work together.

surveillance   Constituent monitoring of negotiation by their representatives.

tactic   A narrow class of conflict behaviors. Three of the basic strategies (contending, problem solving, and avoiding) have more than one tactic associated with them. (See strategy.)

third party   An external individual or group that tries to move a conflict toward management, settlement, or resolution.

threat   Verbal commitment to punish Other if it fails to comply with one's wishes.

tit-for-tat   A tactic for influencing Other by rewarding it for cooperation and punishing it for noncooperation.

track-two diplomacy   Unofficial meetings between private citizens or nongovernmental organizations on either side of an international conflict in an effort to settle or resolve that conflict.

transformations   Changes in the parties or the nature of the conflict that occur during escalation; e.g., light to heavy, small to large.

trust   Perception that Other is positively concerned about one's interests. (See working trust.)

unilateral conciliatory initiatives   Actions that are designed to enhance Other's trust and thus begin a process of tension reduction and de-escalation in a conflict.

vested interest   The motive to retain one's group membership leadership position because of the benefits that accrue from it.

violence   Behavior that is intended to physically injure another party or an object valued by that party.

withdrawing   An avoidance tactic that involves leaving the conflict, either physically or psychologically.

working trust   A belief that Other is interested in resolving a particular conflict and is willing to negotiate in good faith to achieve that end. It need not involve broader trust in Other. (See also trust.)

yielding   A strategy involving the lowering of aspirations.

zero-sum thinking   Belief that my gain is your loss, and vice versa. Also called "fixed-pie assumption."

Name Index

Subject Index

❖